DEVELOPING AND SUPPORTING ATHLETE WELLBEING

This pioneering book in elite athlete wellbeing brings together the narratives of athletes and wellbeing practitioners in high-performance sport with cutting-edge theorizing from world-leading academics to explore pertinent mental wellbeing matters that present for elite athletes both during and after their careers.

The journey of the elite athlete is considered from entering the high-performance system as a youth performer through to retirement, with contributions illuminating the ways in which mental wellbeing can be impacted – both negatively and positively – through common place experiences. Methods of creating holistic high-performance sports cultures along with common mental wellbeing influencers, such as parents, education, faith, injury and (de)selection are explored, as well as the ramifications of uncommon events on mental wellbeing, such as whistleblowing, legal disputes, psychological disorders and COVID-19. Drawing on this analysis, the book then proffers thought-provoking strategies for how the mental wellbeing of both athletes and staff can be understood, developed and supported, ultimately driving elite sport cultural transformation to put the person first and the athlete second.

Each chapter presents the wellbeing experience from the vantage of the athlete or the wellbeing practitioner, followed by an academic unpacking of the situation. This makes the book a must read for students and researchers working in sport coaching, sport psychology, applied sport science or sport management, as well as practitioners interested in facilitating a duty of care for high-performing athletes, and working in coaching, sport science support, athlete development programmes, NGB policy and administration or welfare services.

Natalie Campbell is a BPS-registered social psychologist and lifestyle management practitioner. She is also a senior lecturer at the University of Gloucestershire, UK.

Abbe Brady is an HCPC-registered sport psychologist and head of the Department of Psychology and Pedagogical Sciences at St Mary's University, UK.

Alison Tincknell-Smith is an International Athlete Commission Member and lecturer at the University of Bath, UK.

DEVELOPING AND SUPPORTING ATHLETE WELLBEING

Person First, Athlete Second

Edited by Natalie Campbell, Abbe Brady and Alison Tincknell-Smith

Routledge
Taylor & Francis Group

LONDON AND NEW YORK

First published 2022
by Routledge
2 Park Square, Milton Park, Abingdon, Oxon OX14 4RN

and by Routledge
605 Third Avenue, New York, NY 10158

Routledge is an imprint of the Taylor & Francis Group, an informa business

© 2022 selection and editorial matter, Natalie Campbell, Abbe Brady and Alison Tincknell-Smith; individual chapters, the contributors

The right of Natalie Campbell, Abbe Brady and Alison Tincknell-Smith to be identified as the authors of the editorial material, and of the authors for their individual chapters, has been asserted in accordance with sections 77 and 78 of the Copyright, Designs and Patents Act 1988.

All rights reserved. No part of this book may be reprinted or reproduced or utilised in any form or by any electronic, mechanical, or other means, now known or hereafter invented, including photocopying and recording, or in any information storage or retrieval system, without permission in writing from the publishers.

Trademark notice: Product or corporate names may be trademarks or registered trademarks, and are used only for identification and explanation without intent to infringe.

British Library Cataloguing-in-Publication Data
A catalogue record for this book is available from the British Library

Library of Congress Cataloging-in-Publication Data
Names: Campbell, Natalie (Social psychologist), editor. | Brady, Abbe, editor. | Tincknell-Smith, Alison, editor.
Title: Developing and supporting athlete wellbeing : person first, athlete second / edited by Natalie Campbell, Abbe Brady and Alison Tincknell-Smith.
Description: First Edition. | New York : Routledge, 2021. | Includes bibliographical references and index.
Identifiers: LCCN 2021014272 | ISBN 9780367254612 (Hardback) | ISBN 9780367254629 (Paperback) | ISBN 9780429287923 (eBook)
Subjects: LCSH: Sports—Psychological aspects. | Exercise—Psychological aspects. | Athletes—Mental health. | Coach-athlete relationships—Moral and ethical aspects. | Well-being.
Classification: LCC GV706.4 .D474 2021 | DDC 613.7/11—dc23
LC record available at https://lccn.loc.gov/2021014272

ISBN: 978-0-367-25461-2 (hbk)
ISBN: 978-0-367-25462-9 (pbk)
ISBN: 978-0-429-28792-3 (ebk)

DOI: 10.4324/9780429287923

Typeset in Bembo
by Apex CoVantage, LLC

Natalie Campbell: Over the last ten years, I have witnessed conversations regarding athlete mental health and wellbeing be ignored, trivialized and stigmatized. However, thanks to the braveness of elite athletes around the globe speaking out about their own struggles, the conversations are being heard, and most importantly, are shaping elite sport policy and practices moving forward. This book is dedicated to those athletes . . . and to my family for their constant support. A special thanks to Craig Hughes – student editing assistant extraordinaire!

Abbe Brady: To the athletes, parents, coaches, support staff, administrators, coach developers and researchers with whom I have shared a passion about achieving performance excellence alongside the person's holistic wellbeing as an athlete – thank you. This idea has not always been popular and because of the advocacy and efforts of so many, we are entering a new era where wellbeing is now a part of the conversation. Thank you to my partner Helen, our funny friends and families, and particularly my aunts Julia, Margaret and Pam, for their love, kindness and sense of humour.

Alison Tincknell-Smith: My heartfelt thanks to the athletes and practitioners who have shared their professional and personal experiences through this book. I continue to learn from you with every encounter, and I look forward to each opportunity to do so. Thank you also to the researchers who pursue further understanding of such important themes. Finally, thank you to Piers and Archer for always keeping me 'person first'.

CONTENTS

List of figures   x
List of tables   xi
List of contributors   xii
Preface   xv

1 **Introducing holistic wellbeing within the athlete journey**   1
 Abbe Brady

2 **The holistic wellbeing of elite youth performers: U MATTER**   18
 Tony Ghaye, Luke Allen and Neil Clark

3 **The role of parents and family in the wellbeing of athletes**   33
 Camilla J. Knight, Katie S. Uzzell and Catherine Shearer

4 **Dual careers and athlete wellbeing**   50
 Lindsay Woodford and Claire-Marie Roberts

5 **The role of coach leadership in promoting athlete wellbeing and performance**   62
 James Matthews and David Passmore

6 **Supporting athletes from different cultures and nationalities: the case of women's football**   76
 Claire-Marie Roberts and Katie Rood

7 The impact of selection and deselection on athlete
   wellbeing: Australian women's cycling   92
   *Jenny McMahon, Kerry R. McGannon
   and Chris Zehntner*

8 Supporting the wellbeing for athletes of faith   107
   *Charles H. Wilson, Jr., Christina M. Gipson
   and Natalie Campbell*

9 The ableism of athlete wellbeing support:
   additional needs of the paralympic athlete   122
   Natalie Campbell and Danielle Brown

10 The implementation of an integrated psychological
   support programme for injured athletes: 'stopping
   athletes from falling off the edge of the cliff'   137
   Misia Gervis

11 Developing caring cultures in football: a model
   for practice and change   150
   Colm Hickey and Colum Cronin

12 Supporting an athlete through legal action   166
   Seema Patel, Samantha Rippington and Pam Boteler

13 Wellbeing and whistleblowing: what happens?   181
   Pim Verschuuren and Silke Kassner

14 Supporting athlete careers and retirement from
   the vantage point of smaller national governing
   bodies   197
   Niels B. Feddersen and Laurence Halsted

15 Athlete welfare, stakeholder responsibility,
   and ethics of care in elite sport: an examination
   of para-sport organisation approaches in France   211
   Geoffery Z. Kohe, Laura G. Purdy, and Arnaud Litou

16 Fighting a system built to exclude queer(ing)
   bodies: an imperative for athlete wellbeing   225
   Sheree Bekker and Katlego K. Kolanyane-Kesupile

17 **The role of athletic identity foreclosure in the development of poor athlete mental health** 239
J. D. DeFreese and Jeni Shannon

18 **Supporting athlete wellbeing during a global pandemic: the case of COVID-19** 257
Natalie Campbell and Josh Rudd

Postscript 271
David Lavallee

Index *276*

FIGURES

1.1	An ecological systems approach for considerations of high-performance athlete wellbeing	5
10.1	A schematic of the RETURN programme	138
11.1	The Continual Change Model for Caring Cultures	159
19.1	An integrative model of Duty of Care in sport	274

TABLES

2.1	Forms, meanings and examples of mattering in the U MATTER project	26
7.1	Dimensions of humanisation and dehumanisation	98
14.1	Funding figures of NGBs that lost 100% of funding after the 2016 Summer Olympic Games	205
14.2	Overview of the most salient sports organisations in the United Kingdom	207
17.1	Therapeutic approaches for addressing poor mental health via athletic identity	252

CONTRIBUTORS

Luke Allen is a TASS Lifestyle Coach and U MATTER core team member, UK.

Sheree Bekker is an applied health researcher and an assistant professor (lecturer) in injury prevention in the Department for Health at the University of Bath, UK.

Pam Boteler is the president of the equality campaign platform WomenCAN International.

Danielle Brown is a former Team Great Britain Paralympic athlete in Para-Archery, UK.

Neil Clark is a doctoral student at Loughborough University and a research associate of Switch the Play, UK.

Colum Cronin is a senior lecturer in Physical Education and Sport Coaching at Liverpool John Moores University, UK.

J. D. DeFreese is a clinical assistant professor in University of North Carolina at Chapel Hill, USA.

Niels B. Feddersen is currently undertaking his PhD in organizational culture change in Olympic sports organizations in the United Kingdom at Liverpool John Moores University, UK.

Misia Gervis is a senior lecturer in Sport and Exercise Psychology at Brunel University London, UK.

Tony Ghaye is a professor in Sport Business at Loughborough University London, UK.

Christina M. Gipson is an assistant professor of Sport Management at Georgia Southern University, USA.

Laurence Halsted is a former Team Great Britain Olympic Fencer, UK.

Colm Hickey is a chargé de projet at the University of Lausanne, Switzerland.

Silke Kassner is a German International Athlete in Wild-Water Racing and the Athlete Representative and Member of the Advisory Board of German Anti-Doping Agency.

Camilla J. Knight is an associate professor in Sport and Exercise Science at Swansea University, UK.

Geoffery Z. Kohe is a lecturer in the School of Sport and Exercise Science at the University of Kent, UK.

Katlego K. Kolanyane-Kesupile is a communications specialist, development strategist, educator, cultural practitioner and human rights advocate.

David Lavallee is a professor of Duty of Care in Sport in the School of Applied Sciences at Abertay University, UK.

Arnaud Litou is a paralympic high-performance advisor at Agence Nationale du Sport, France.

James Matthews is a chartered psychologist and an assistant professor in the School of Public Health, Physiotherapy and Sports Science at University College Dublin, Republic of Ireland.

Kerry R. McGannon is a professor in Sport and Exercise Psychology at Laurentian University, Canada.

Jenny McMahon is a senior lecturer in Education and Curriculum at University of Tasmania, Australia.

David Passmore is a lecturer in Coaching Science and Education at Dublin City University, Republic of Ireland.

Seema Patel is a senior lecturer in Sports Law at Nottingham Trent University, UK.

Laura G. Purdy is a senior lecturer in the Department of Sport and Physical Activity at Edge Hill University, UK.

Samantha Rippington is a former Team Great Britain Olympian in Canoeing, UK.

Claire-Marie Roberts is a sport psychology consultant and a senior lecturer in Sport and Exercise Psychology at University of the West of England, UK.

Katie Rood is a professional football player, currently playing for Lewes Football Club Women in England and represents the New Zealand Women's National Football Team.

Josh Rudd is a performance lifestyle advisor with the English Institute of Sport, UK.

Jeni Shannon is a director of Mental Health and Performance Psychology at the University of North Carolina at Chapel Hill, USA.

Catherine Shearer is a senior sport psychologist and a strategic lead for System Building at Sport Wales, UK.

Katie S. Uzzell is a PhD student in Sport and Exercise Science at Swansea University, UK.

Pim Verschuuren is a doctoral student at the University of Lausanne, Switzerland.

Charles H. Wilson, Jr. is an associate professor of Coaching Education at Georgia Southern University, USA.

Lindsay Woodford is a senior lecturer in Sport and Exercise Psychology at University of the West of England, UK.

Chris Zehntner is a lecturer in Personal Development, Health and Physical Education at Southern Cross University, Australia.

PREFACE

Our inspiration

As the final words to this book are being written, the world of elite sport finds itself in a place it has never been. Over the past 18 months, a plethora of inspirational, stirring and devastating events around the globe have both shaken and shocked the high-performance sport environment. Newsworthy stories such as the controversy of the US Women's National Soccer Team losing their gender discrimination lawsuit against US Soccer, the provocation of athlete activism within the Black Lives Matter movement, exposed institutionalized abuse suffered by Japanese athletes, and the deaths (by suicide) of international athletes, such as US Cyclist Kelly Catlin, South Korean Triathlete Choi Suk-Hyeon and British judoka Craig Fallon are to consider but a few. Furthermore, 2020 encountered one of the largest global health emergencies with the spread of the coronavirus bringing elite (and recreational) sport worldwide to a complete standstill.

The need to understand the people at the centre at these sporting conditions – their health, their wellbeing, their voice – has, arguably, never been more important.

The aforementioned events unfolded as a contemporary landscape that serve to illuminate further the extant need for a book such as this. The inspiration for pursuing this text was drawn from a chance conversation; we (the editors) exchanging stories about some of the more serious breaches of athlete wellbeing we had experienced whilst working as practitioners within high-performance sport. It was beyond worrying to acknowledge that a number of the situations experienced some ten years ago could still be identified in modern performance settings. We began to reflect on our own (in)actions. Did we know the appropriate way to challenge the behaviours seen? How confident were we at voicing our concerns? What could we have done differently? Where are those athletes now?

Our collective thoughts shaped the topics presented in this book, and whilst the topics are not exhaustive by any means, they are the more salient considerations of what we felt affects the wellbeing of athletes the most, and critically what needs addressing within the industry.

The composition of each chapter of this book is purposeful. Traditionally, texts in this domain will present the academic content first, exploring the theoretical drive and then concluding with applications of such arguments to case studies or contextual examples. As the title of the book suggests, putting the 'person first' is the nexus of our academic and practitioner values, and so it seemed discernible that we should put the voice of the said person at the beginning of every chapter, not at the end. The voice of the athlete, or the practitioner working with the athlete, is given priority; it is their lived experience that provides the rich, contextual depth of both skill and struggle in all issues pertaining to wellbeing. We hope that through doing this we provide the athletic and practitioner populations with the assurance that we acknowledge their reality as an antecedent to theoretical development, and that we will continue to demonstrate advocacy of putting the 'person first' in everything we do.

How to read this book

This book aims to take the reader on a journey through the different contexts that affect wellbeing which a person might find themselves encountering as they move through a career in high-performance sport.

Chapters 1–5 explore topics from the beginning of the athlete journey. Chapter 1 provides the reader with an introduction to the editors' considerations of what wellbeing means to us and how we understand the concept to manifest within elite settings. Specifically, we seek to explore theoretical notions of wellbeing that sit outside of the traditional conversations in sport psychology. Chapter 2 discusses the importance of mattering and meaning making to youth athletes and explores how the system can best develop resilient, caring and engaged young people. Chapter 3 provides insight into how parents of elite youth athletes can both enhance and hinder wellbeing and performance, depending on their approaches to support. Chapter 4 explores how dual career programmes can both help and hinder athletes to combine their sport and academic aspirations. Chapter 5 introduces the concept of transformational leadership and explains how head coaches can build athlete wellbeing into elite sport organizational culture.

Chapters 6–11 present topics that might be considered typical experiences within the elite athlete career. Chapter 6 provides theoretical considerations of impact to athlete wellbeing when athletes train in cultures and nationalities different from their own. Chapter 7 provides insight in to how a gruelling selection and deselection process can negatively impact the wellbeing of an athlete. Chapter 8 discusses the complexities of mixing faith with elite sport and attempts to demonstrate the importance of spirituality to wellbeing – regardless of faith. Chapter 9 situates wellbeing support as an ableist service that fails to adequately address the specific wellbeing needs of para-athletes. Chapter 10 introduces a psychologically informed programme for supporting an athlete through injury in a way that enhances their state of wellbeing. Chapter 11 offers theoretical explorations of how elite sport systems can develop cultures of caring, which place athlete wellbeing at the centre of all work undertaken.

Chapters 12–18 provide the reader with examples of less common situations that an athlete might experience; specifically, experiences that would impact negatively on their wellbeing. Chapter 12 explores the challenges faced when an athlete wishes to challenge their sporting body with legal action. Chapter 13 details the choices and consequences of whistleblowing, and the knock-on effect this can have on the brave athletes who speak out. Chapter 14 unpacks the difficulties that can arise for athletes if a national governing body of sport is wholly reliant on government funding, especially if that funding is withdrawn. Chapter 15 outlines key concerns about the provision of athlete welfare and explores to what extent such welfare initiatives represent the social realities of athletes. Chapter 16 positions sports' organizational policy as a mechanism for (unintentional and intentional) organizational violence, leading to poor outcomes around wellbeing. Chapter 17 theorizes the relevance of athletic identity to the diagnosis, treatment and prognosis of poor athlete mental health, with the goal of bridging the gap between theory/research and practice. Chapter 18 explores the impact of the COVID-19 global pandemic on the Team Great Britain swimming, as told by the individual responsible for delivering a remote wellbeing service.

Beyond the final chapter

Upon receiving the postscript of this book, we were challenged by the author to confront a glaring contradiction that ran throughout our work and the work of our contributors. Despite our cogent efforts to push the message of 'person first', we unquestionably accepted that the individuals being discussed in each chapter were referred to as 'athletes, not people'. We had completely overlooked the need trailblaze our campaign by adopting a 'person first' language – the person who is a cyclist for Team USA; the person who is a swimmer for Team Australia. This nudge provided us an opportunity for deep reflectivity and reflexivity. How *do* we go about changing the industry lexicon to person first language? Is this even necessary? How would the people doing elite sport (the athletes) feel about this? The identifying label of 'an athlete', whether self-appointed or gifted, is sociologically construed, academically contentious and psychologically complex. For some, it is the best reason for their being alive; for others, it is the *only* reason for their being alive. And so, we ask our readers to consider, can we *really* encourage person first practice if the sports industry and academic disciplines perpetuate the language of athlete first?

It would be overly ambitious and potentially naive of the editorial team to assume that this book will promote and drive immediate change within high-performance sport. However, we are sincere in our attempts to elucidate examples of both exceptional and worrying practices in athlete wellbeing that are happening at this moment in time. With hope, this book invites a step change in person-centred behaviour with regard to a holistically deeper practitioner and academic reflection on how athlete wellbeing practices can be advocated and driven or (perhaps more importantly) questioned and disputed. Furthermore, we envisage this book serving as a bridge for theoretical influence into broader practical considerations of policy development, demonstrating the potential for greater dialogue between the two areas.

Without question, the conversations of athlete wellbeing are increasing in popularity and poignancy; the consideration of athlete mental health is slowly gaining visibility on the global sporting political agenda. And yet, despite seemingly outward efforts from multiple stakeholders – from national governments to international sporting bodies to independent regulators to bespoke services – incidents such as the ones identified at the beginning of this preface are still regular occurrences. Why, therefore, does it seem so problematic for the high-performance sport system to operate – in its completeness – with an enhanced duty of care? What tensions exist for an environment to promote compassion, empathy and humanness alongside competition, effort and achievement? This book aims to explore these questions and more by putting first the people who might have the answers.

1
INTRODUCING HOLISTIC WELLBEING WITHIN THE ATHLETE JOURNEY

Abbe Brady

Introduction

Over the past 70 years, wellbeing has become a term associated with increasing cultural capital worldwide among varied sectors of society, such as governments, economists and those in education, medicine and business. Wellbeing has increased cultural capital because there is growing recognition that wellbeing is valuable, not only because it feels good but also because wellbeing is central to achieving greater productivity, performance success, improved health, longevity, resilience, personal growth and quality of life (De Neve, Krekel, & Ward, 2018; Diener, Lucas, & Oishi, 2018; Fredrickson, 2000; Huppert & So, 2013; Keyes, 2002; Lyubomirsky, King, & Deiner, 2005; Ryff, Singer, & Love, 2004; The Global Happiness Council, 2018). Compared to those with low wellbeing, individuals with high wellbeing have better physical health, stronger immune systems, live longer, have fewer sleep problems, lower levels of burnout, greater self-control, better self-regulation and coping skills, are more prosocial, have more satisfying relationships and are more cooperative (ibid). Similarly, informed by the general literature and a small but growing body of knowledge about athlete wellbeing, those involved in performance sport are beginning to recognize the multilevel significance of wellbeing for athletes' health, development and performance as well as their lives beyond and after sport.

Attending to athlete wellbeing is a legal and ethical obligation associated with social responsibility and a duty of care to provide safeguarding against risk of harm. Additionally, because wellbeing confers personal benefits through health and thriving in life, it warrants significant attention in high-performance sport because these outcomes support sustainable health, developmental and performance objectives. Mirroring outcomes in business settings (De Neve et al., 2018), investing in athlete wellbeing could also have many organizational and economic benefits. Embracing contemporary ideas about wellbeing may raise questions for stakeholders about long-held beliefs and cultural practices deemed necessary for success. Those working in high performance (HP) sport will benefit from understanding why wellbeing is valuable and how to cultivate it to support an athlete during and after their career. Despite the inevitable ups and downs of an athletic career, success in HP sport should for the most part contribute to wellbeing both throughout an athlete's career and afterwards. However, contemporary narratives highlight how even those who have been very successful in HP sport do not necessarily experience the wellbeing they expected, resulting in them questioning the personal meaning of success (Bishop, 2020).

In this chapter, athlete wellbeing is presented as a complex and multidimensional concept best understood in context using a holistic lifespan approach. The term 'athlete' refers to sports performers across all sports. The term 'high performance (HP)' is used to refer to sport from the level of formal and substantive talent development through to professional and/or international competition. This chapter is organized in three parts. The first part considers being human in HP sport. This is important for appreciating how wellbeing may be deemed as relevant or not in a high-performance setting. The second part of the chapter addresses a wellbeing vocabulary by summarizing some key developments in our understanding of wellbeing, and the chapter concludes with considerations of holistic wellbeing over the lifespan.

Being human in high-performance sport

The economic, political and social value of international and domestic competition has continued to grow and, in the Olympics and Paralympics, more nations now compete than ever before (Westerbeek & Hahn, 2013). Underlying the expansion of HP sport has been its commodification, reflected in greater professionalization, globalization and a global medal market which have led to changes in the structures and ethos of HP sport (Walsh & Giulianotti, 2001; Barker-Ruchti, 2019). Though not necessarily perceptible to those outside of the industry, as Westerbeek and Hahn (2013) note, the development of HP sport has changed the scale and complexity of activities and the landscape of opportunities. As the HP sport industry has evolved so too has the nature of the demands on athletes. Contemporary HP sport is recognized as operating in a dynamic and sometimes highly volatile environment in which athletes, teams and staff are exposed to numerous pressures and demands associated with the primary goal of performance success (Sotiriadou & Bosscher, 2017).

Though there has been an increase in the provision of support services available to athletes, the benefits of these services to athletes' wellbeing may be offset by new challenges athletes are required to manage such as the contingent nature of support, the concomitant increase in demands associated with greater competition for places, increasing standards and expectations, and the omnipresent pressure to stay ahead of others. Thus, as the landscape of HP sport evolves, the athlete's experience changes and new challenges, enablers and threats to wellbeing emerge. Aside from considerations associated with evolving ideals about training, competition, health and lifestyle requirements, a career in contemporary HP sport requires an athlete to navigate a complex terrain of contracts, finances, micro-politics, personal brand management, social media and celebrity capital, often in the glare of the public eye. Learning to adapt to meet the demands of this precarious landscape with its many challenges and risks is a fundamental part of becoming an elite athlete (Barker-Ruchti, 2019). Only by acknowledging the realities of HP sport and athletes' lived experiences can we begin to understand the conditions which serve to enable or threaten athlete wellbeing in such contexts.

Linked to the professionalization and commodification of HP sport, organizations in the HP sport industry have adopted highly systematic approaches to the preparation of athletes and teams which resemble the general management, marketing and product development processes in other competitive industries looking to cultivate 'winning' products (Westerbeek & Hahn, 2013, p. 244). When performance production is the overriding focus, there is a danger that the person gets lost in the process (Ingham, Chase, & Butt, 2002), and we can fail to see the athlete as a person with human needs. Recognizing a person's humanness is essential for wellbeing and includes meeting human needs such as being recognized and valued as an individual, having a voice, agency and meaning in life, having a coherent personal journey and experiencing belongingness, inclusion and connection with others (e.g. Ryan & Deci, 2001; Todres, Galvin & Holloway, 2009). By contrast, when important qualities associated with being human are not considered, this is when people are at risk of being dehumanized and their wellbeing compromised. Considerable evidence exists which highlights how dehumanization is often a precursor to and feature of harmful behaviours, such as exclusion, humiliation and bullying (Christoff, 2014; Haslam & Stratemeyer, 2016). This is particularly pertinent in HP sport because it is a setting in which 'people's practices and experiences are often justified in the pursuit of excellence – and it is precisely in such settings that humanization may be most threatened and most possible' (Kavanagh & Brady, 2014, p. 26). Combined with the superhuman characterization of HP athletes, being like 'normal' people or 'just human' with associations of ordinariness or fallibility may reduce the palatability or seeming relevance of considering humanness among athletes and others in the HP sports industry. Whilst not framed as humanizing or dehumanizing behaviours per se, considerable research exists which shows how adopting humanizing behaviours are linked to greater athlete wellbeing and performance success (e.g. see Hodge, Henry, & Smith, 2014; Lavallee, 2019; Price, Morrison, & Arnold, 2010; Pink, Saunders, & Stynes, 2015). Thus, supporting athletes' humanness should not be viewed as contrary to performance excellence, but complementary, since personal excellence leads to performance excellence (Miller & Kerr, 2002) as exemplified by the idiom better people, make better players (e.g. New Zealand All Blacks in Hodge et al., 2014).

Understanding dehumanization at an organizational level has relevance for how HP settings operate. Whilst in some organizations dehumanizing strategies (e.g. systemization, mechanical rationality, objectification, rigidity and a lack of empathy) may be viewed as necessary to create the right culture, work ethic and direct efforts, Christoff (2014) notes, there is no evidence to support that such behaviours are effective and importantly, there are more ethical and sustainable alternatives. Whilst organizational or cultural systems and practices can be dehumanizing and people can act in ways that deny the essential humanness of others, people can also act in ways that dehumanize themselves. Research highlights how HP athletes actively engage in behaviours that have severe consequences for their health and particularly in the long term (Baker, Safai, & Fraser-Thomas, 2015; Miller & Hoffman, 2009; Theberge, 2008). Ideas and awareness about health and wellbeing reflect the performance culture and as Beamish and Ritchie (2006, p. 143) note, the longer one strives for excellence and the closer athletes get to elite success, 'the less and less easy it is to distinguish between health and pathology'. Athletes and those working in HP sport develop normalized views of health, which are context-based. An example of a cultural concept that reinforces traditional ideals of athlete behaviour with consequences for wellbeing is that of mental toughness. Whilst valorized in many HP settings as a desirable or even essential characteristic, mental toughness has been criticized for endorsing masculine values, justifying abusive treatment of athletes, and encouraging athletes to self-sacrifice, self-harm and perform when injured (see Kerr & Stirling, 2017).

Concern about the health and wellbeing of HP athletes is not new but a swell of evidence is now making these concerns more visible. HP sport was described by Wrisberg (1996) as having such hypnotic power that it discourages penetrating inquiry into its effects on the lives of participants. When a performance discourse dominates, people and their humanness may not be viewed as important and so a focus on wellbeing can be presented as being out of line with the culture and aims of HP sport (e.g. Brady & Maynard, 2010). Evidence that a support need exists which is not met within HP sport is apparent through the existence of private organizations and charities set up to meet the needs of athletes or ex-athletes struggling with issues, such as addictions, substance abuse, gambling, self-harm and mental health concerns (e.g. DociaSport, Switch the Play and The True Athlete Project). In a recent in-depth review of wellbeing in HP sport structures and systems in the Australian Institute of Sport (AIS), it was identified that the majority of elite athletes felt that the HP system favoured performance over people, valued physical health over mental wellbeing and 32% of athletes and 70% of support staff felt disposable (AIS, 2020). Linked to the increased specialization and diversification of roles is the potential absence of someone who can interpret the science, see the big picture, who knows the athlete well and who is therefore well placed to understand the athlete's wellbeing holistically. A concern is that whilst emerging specialized roles usually support athletes or coaches directly, their specialist lens may not allow them to identify the transdisciplinary or systemic factors which impact upon wellbeing. With evidence emerging that wellbeing is fundamental to health, developmental progress and performance outcomes, there is a risk that in environments dominated by a performance discourse, wellbeing may be viewed instrumentally as another performance variable and the role remit of another isolated specialist.

Wellbeing is a transdisciplinary concept that presents particular challenges for researchers, policymakers and practitioners because it cannot be captured by a single approach. At present, psychosocial approaches have been the dominant lens informing our understanding of athlete wellbeing (e.g. see Brady & Grenville-Cleave, 2018; Giles, Fletcher, Arnold, Ashfield, & Harrison, 2020) and a need exists for greater integration with sociocultural contributions to understand the wider contextual heuristics and processes involved. An ecological model approach adapted from Bronfenbrenner's work (1979) is useful for representing the multilayered and interconnecting systems that exert an influence on an athlete's experience and wellbeing (see Figure 1.1). Using such an approach is valuable because it recognizes that athlete wellbeing is not exclusively an individual matter but far more complex reflecting issues and priorities of other systems and stakeholders in HP sport. The requirement to look at the contribution of multiple systems in HP sport is demonstrated well in the recent publication Duty of Care in Sport Review in the UK (2017) which made recommendations

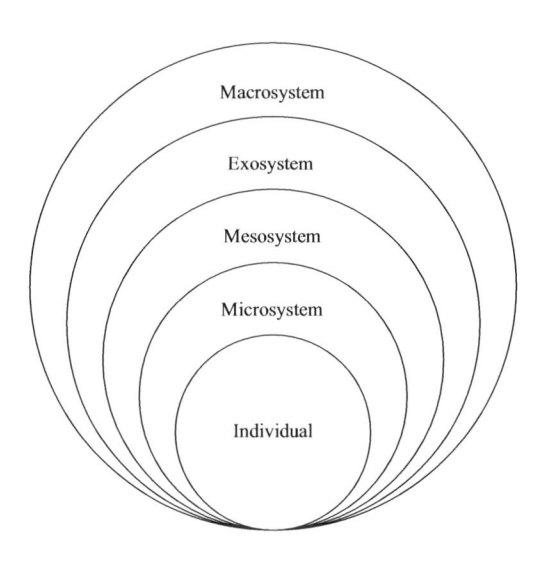

Macrosystem – broader national/global society e.g., national sporting culture, societal priorities, public expectations, media coverage, etc.

Exosystem – indirect environment e.g., International/national sport organization's structures, funding and policies, strategic priorities, legislative autonomy, branding and marketing, commercial partnerships and sponsors, fan base, high performance sport culture and mission, recruitment and training of senior HP personnel, etc.

Mesosystem – direct environment e.g., processes and requirements within or outside of the performance centre/club, culture and practices of support staff, medics, performance lifestyle advisors, player care managers, agents, etc.

Microsystem – immediate environment e.g., personal and interpersonal experiences and practices across domains of: home, team/squad, school/college, university, work, partner, family, coach, trainers, friends, teammates, etc.

Individual – the person e.g., their mental and physical health and wellbeing, their identity, beliefs and values, capacities and skills, their past experiences, present circumstances and hopes for the future, etc.

FIGURE 1.1 An ecological systems approach for considerations of high-performance athlete wellbeing

highlighting the need for considerable cultural and organizational engagement to support welfare and wellbeing of athletes in elite sport. As well as recognizing the structures and processes needed at each level of the ecosystem to support holistic wellbeing for athletes, adopting an ecological systems approach to athlete wellbeing requires us to ask questions about the reciprocal influences between the system levels, that is, how do structures and processes at one level constrain or assist activity at another level? The AIS (2020) undertook a multilevel internal review of how HP sport systems are perceived to support wellbeing of staff and athletes. Findings showed the problematic pervasiveness of a pre-professional mentality such as the attitude that wellbeing was a luxury. To achieve a fully realized wellbeing culture, the AIS proposed a number of sweeping changes in systems, communications and knowledge transfer as well as making wellbeing synonymous with HP sport to support excellent outcomes.

A wellbeing vocabulary

Associated with its everyday use, adoption by different disciplines and its applications in various spheres of life, wellbeing can mean quite different things to people. Our understanding of wellbeing will also differ according to the lenses we adopt to examine it. At its most basic wellbeing is a state of good (Veenhoven, 2007). A broadly accepted description of wellbeing which is applicable across disciplines and contexts is 'a positive and sustainable state that allows individuals, groups and nations to thrive and flourish. This means at the level of an individual, wellbeing refers to psychological, physical and social states that are distinctively positive' (Huppert, Baylis, & Keverne, 2004, p. 1331). Contemporary research confirms that many associations with wellbeing depend on the culture and values within the context in which people reside (Diener et al., 2018). Therefore, developing an understanding of positive psychological, physical and social states, thriving and flourishing and their interdependencies *in context* is an important task for those seeking to understand HP athlete wellbeing and its sustainability.

With considerable relevance for performance sport settings, a concern expressed about people with high wellbeing is that because they are satisfied with the status quo, they are not motivated to seek or accomplish new goals (Lyubomirsky et al., 2005). Notwithstanding the fact that sometimes specific dissatisfactions can also motivate people, based on the data in their extensive review, Lyubomirsky et al. (2005) state that those with high wellbeing are indeed more satisfied generally but that this does not prevent them from being achievement oriented and *happy people appear to be relatively more likely to seek approach goals* (p. 844). Furthermore, the characteristics found in those with high wellbeing, such as optimism, energy, productivity, likeability, good health and sociability are likely to assist them in the pursuit of new goals. Increasing evidence exists to show positive emotions and wellbeing are likely to play a much more significant role in successful sports performance than previously recognized (McCarthy, 2011; Ruiz & Rabozza, 2020).

A comprehensive understanding of wellbeing recognizes that it is complex and whilst important to know about because of its powerful effects, studying positive states in isolation presents just part of the picture of human experience. Not all positive states are desirable and not all negative states should be viewed as undesirable. Contemporary research in wellbeing now recognizes the dialectical nature of wellbeing and the dynamic harmony between positive and negative aspects of wellbeing and the need therefore to appreciate the complexity of wellbeing (Lomas, Waters, Williams, Oades, & Kern, 2020).

In the last decade, recent theoretical and measurement developments in wellbeing have occurred and among the most impactful has been the shift from looking at separate dimensions of wellbeing (e.g. social, physical, spiritual, psychological or subjective wellbeing – see Linton, Dieppe, & Medina-Lara, 2016) to more integrated and holistic accounts. Integrated models of wellbeing are valuable because they highlight the interrelatedness and reciprocity of different types of wellbeing. For example, we now know that psychological and social wellbeing have both direct and indirect impacts on physical and mental health (De Neve, Diener, Tay, & Xuereb, 2013; Su, Tay, & Diener, 2014) and directly reducing physiological and biological markers of stress, enhances psychological wellbeing which in turn is more likely to lead to the adoption of health promoting and other prosocial behaviours (De Neve et al., 2013). Based on their purpose and context, integrated models of wellbeing can vary considerably. Examples of different models of wellbeing (and their main constructs) include a generic model – PERMA (positive emotion, engagement, relationships, meaning and achievement; Seligman, 2018); a model used in public health initiatives – Five ways to wellbeing (connect, be active, taking notice, keep learning and give; Aked, Marks, Cordon, & Thompson, 2009); a model used in schools with adolescents – EPOCH (engagement, perseverance, optimism, connectedness and happiness; Kern, Benson, Steinberg, & Steinberg, 2016). The construct variance evident in integrated models of wellbeing reinforces the significance of wellbeing reflecting context-based priorities.

Lundqvist (2011) developed an integrated model of athlete wellbeing where each component of wellbeing (i.e. subjective, psychological and social wellbeing) was conceptualized at a global level and at a sport level. Using this model in elite sport, global wellbeing was found to act as a foundation for sport-specific wellbeing and offered a protective mechanism for wellbeing fluctuations in the sport domain (Lundqvist & Sandin, 2014). This finding reinforces the need to nurture the holistic development of sports performers. Using Lundqvist's model to examine wellbeing in para-athletes, Macdougall, O'Halloran, Sherry, and Shields (2016) added a physical health/wellbeing component at both global and sport domain levels of wellbeing. Such research supports the need to develop an understanding of how athlete wellbeing may differ across different cultures, contexts and populations, and we need to be careful to avoid adopting a 'one size fits all' approach.

One of the many challenges facing those who seek to understand athlete wellbeing is to understand the distinctions between nomenclature of wellbeing and the closely aligned concepts of flourishing, thriving, mental health and welfare. Mental health and wellbeing are closely related concepts, but they are not the same. As Galderisi, Heinz, Kastrup, Beezhold, and Sartorius (2015, p. 231) recognize, it is important to not assume that mental health is just about positive psychological states as 'people in good mental health are often sad, unwell, angry or unhappy, and this is part of a fully lived life for a human being'. Conversely, not all positive states are reflective of mental health such as gaining pleasure from intentionally inflicting harm or abusing others. Though frequently conflated, the distinction between wellbeing and mental health is important to understand. Similarly, welfare as *faring well* is similarly universally known, yet unique through individual interpretation and often used interchangeably with wellbeing. As Fleming (1952, p. 379) noted, welfare is an ethical concept which *relates to situations* and about fulfilling basic needs, such as security and safety (Greve, 2008). Whilst most of the research referring to athlete welfare is consistent with these ideas, that is, it focuses on safeguarding and protecting athletes, understanding types of maltreatment and abuse, developing policies and reporting procedures (e.g. Brackenridge & Rhind, 2014), more recent accounts adopt a broader account of athlete welfare to include mental health and wellbeing as a general state of good (e.g. Lang, 2021). Advocates of athlete welfare can be viewed as the cultural trailblazers who, by seeking change in sport policy and practice (often facing great resistance), paved the way for considerations of holistic athlete wellbeing.

Flourishing is broadly viewed as the gold standard of wellbeing (Seligman, 2011). Huppert and So (2013, p. 838) describe flourishing as 'the experience of life going well. It is the combination of feeling good and functioning effectively'. In a qualitative study of flourishing in athletes, Ashfield, McKenna, and Backhouse (2012) concluded that flourishing is a personalized and holistic experience of optimal wellbeing which may not always be dependent on athletic achievement. Flourishing is contrasted with the concept of languishing which refers to a state of low wellbeing and low functioning (i.e. reduced engagement, personal meaning or growth), and it is associated with poor emotional health (Keyes, 2002). In a study comparing those who were flourishing with those who were languishing, Wissing et al. (2019) found that whilst similar themes emerged about what was important and particularly relationships and relatedness (belonging), those who were flourishing were focused on contributing to others and a greater good, whereas those who were languishing had a self-focus on fulfilling their own needs and happiness. Thus, an exclusive focus on one's own wellbeing may not always be most productive, and encouraging athletes to contribute to others and worthwhile causes could be valuable ways of creating supportive relationships and environments whilst also enhancing athlete wellbeing.

At a general level thriving is presented as 'the state of positive functioning at its fullest range – mentally, physically, and socially' (Su et al., 2014, p. 256). In a population of elite athletes, Brown, Arnold, Reid, and Roberts (2018, p. 142) describe thriving in elite athletes as 'being optimistic, focused, and in control; having an active awareness of areas for improvement; possessing high-quality motivation; experiencing holistic development; displaying upward progression, and having a sense of belonging'. Importantly, Brown et al. (2018) distinguish between thriving and flourishing by identifying the requirement for developmental progress in performance terms for thriving among elite athletes. The goal of supporting athlete wellbeing in HP sport should be to achieve athlete thriving and flourishing.

Athlete wellbeing is particularly valuable when it is accessed via subjective methods capturing the individual's perception of personally salient experiences and circumstances in the sport setting and in life generally (rather than the objective view of outcomes or circumstances, e.g. medals achieved, events won, support provision, funding and time spent un/injured). Accessing subjective accounts of wellbeing can offer unique insights to the perceived conditions and personal imperatives of wellbeing from which we may start to appreciate whether the athlete is flourishing or perhaps languishing within the sport and/or in life more broadly. Individuals within the same sport may cite different sources and mechanisms by which they experience and understand their wellbeing. Understanding the diverse and highly personalized nature of wellbeing experience among athletes is important and so remaining open to using alternative lenses to view wellbeing in sport is vital (e.g. Mayoh & Jones, 2014). Wellbeing is a state that itself may influence an athlete's perceptions and values of wellbeing (Wissing et al., 2019) with consequences for the effectiveness of interventions and understanding individual variance in wellbeing. Thus, an intervention that works effectively with one athlete when they have high wellbeing may not be as effective when they have low wellbeing.

A helpful concept that acknowledges the importance of people's broader life circumstances for their wellbeing has been captured through the concept of quality of life (QoL). Whilst traditionally more commonly used by governments and organizations, QoL has begun to emerge in HP sport. QoL is the person's judgement of their general wellbeing based on their life circumstances, and it can provide a valuable frame for understanding wellbeing in context (Rapley, 2003). QoL may provide unique insights into an athletic population's experiences and expectations of what normal and deviant experiences look like and how these may be identified as precursors to wellbeing or ill-being within HP sport settings (Lundqvist, Träff, & Brady, 2020). Accessing context-based personal accounts of QoL offers an opportunity to develop an understanding of the distinctiveness of holistic wellbeing in a high-performance athlete population with its own ideals, norms and imperatives (ibid). As well as accessing subjective and personal accounts from athletes, as evidenced in this book, important insights can be gained from others, such as coaches, support staff and family, who work and reside with the athlete (e.g. see Lundqvist & Sandin, 2014; Giles et al., 2020). Such accounts will provide a fuller picture and provide the stakeholders (including athletes themselves) with an exceptional opportunity to establish a rich and contextualized evidence-base of both holistic individual and collective accounts of athlete wellbeing.

Holistic wellbeing over the lifespan

Linked to its multidimensionality, wellbeing is a holistic concept that develops in its expression over the life course according to a range of personal, interpersonal and social factors (Larkin, 2013). Typically an athlete's career starts in childhood, adolescence or early adulthood and can last anywhere from just a few years to decades. A lifespan approach to wellbeing is valuable because it acknowledges the cumulative impact of events, circumstances and effects experienced during the life course (Larkin, 2013), that is, what we expose young people to, can have long-term effects beyond that immediate experience.

Using a lifespan approach to understand how to support wellbeing is important because it asks questions beyond the immediacy of the present season or cycle and requires staff in sports organizations (NGBs/NSOs) to consider broader issues of wellbeing beyond sport-specific performance enhancement factors and interventions. Common features of high-performance cultures include the narrow and short-term thinking and decision-making associated with the pursuit of objective success which are problematic because they limit thinking about the athletic participant's wellbeing holistically and over the long term (Bishop, 2020).

The relative absence of enquiry into ex-athletes' lives and their wellbeing reflects the preoccupation with immediate performance objectives rather than paying attention to the longer-term consequences and experiences of elite/professional athletes whose careers have ended (Tracey & Elcombe, 2004). This raises questions about what can be done during the sport career to assist the realization of wellbeing and living well after sport. A whole person perspective recognizes the importance for development and wellbeing of investing in a range of areas in life beyond just sport, for example, family, friends, education/professional development and other meaningful pursuits, such as faith, music and social enterprises. Evidence from interventions in professional team sports shows that encouraging young professional athletes and their coaches to embrace meaningful interests and activities outside of their sport role has multiple benefits including direct and indirect benefits for performance (Jolley, McCready, Grenville-Cleave, & Brady, 2018; Pink et al., 2015; Price et al., 2010). However, this is not necessarily straightforward, since, not only might the high-performance culture demand exclusive investment in the sport, but also evidence shows that adolescent athletes' wellbeing can be heightened when they exclusively adopt an identity as an HP athlete before fully exploring their own needs, beliefs and values, because being an HP sportsperson helps them overcome the adolescent life stage dilemma of identity construction (Meeus, Iedema, Helsen, & Vollebergh, 1999). This is a good example of the need to appreciate that not all precursors of high wellbeing are necessarily desirable. It is, therefore, incumbent on those adults in the environment surrounding aspirant athletes, to provide the perspective required to ensure the young person develops holistically through sport and other domains of life.

The importance of different domains of life within the athlete's journey is recognized in Wylleman and Lavallee's (2004) developmental model of transitions in sport. This model highlights normative (expected) transitions across the lifespan which occur across the domains of athletic, individual, psychosocial and academic/vocational. This model of transitions is a valuable tool for supporting a whole person lifespan approach to wellbeing because it recognizes the connectivity of different domains in the person's athletic career development journey beyond that of the athletic domain. As well as the normative transitions across a range of life domains, athletes can also experience unexpected, involuntary events, for example, injury, deselection, loss of a family member, teammate or coach. Both expected and unexpected events have significant considerations for understanding and supporting athlete wellbeing, and new research is emerging around how personal growth may arise from specific adversities in elite sport (e.g. Howells, 2021).

People's priorities and identities develop across life domains and change over time as do their constructions of wellbeing. Capturing wellbeing across all domains at any one time would provide snapshots of holistic athlete wellbeing and tracking ongoing accounts of wellbeing over the life course would provide an insight into the dynamic and complex nature of wellbeing as well as appreciating its determinants and outcomes. Childhood, adolescent and adult wellbeing are distinct areas of knowledge, which place different emphases on various aspects of personal, social, psychological, spiritual and physical contributions to wellbeing (see Larkin, 2013). Hence, a comprehensive understanding of wellbeing in sport should recognize the varying determinants and outcomes of athlete wellbeing across the different domains of life and performance stages during and after a career in sport.

At present, knowledge about athlete wellbeing over the life course in HP sport is limited, and whilst biographical accounts could be viewed as sources of insight, there are many issues to consider associated with reliability and representativeness especially when commercially produced. Reliable insight about athlete wellbeing which is developed through rigorous research is mainly represented by studies examining discrete concepts and experiences as a snapshot at one point or life stage in the population investigated rather than life course research. Contextual factors, such as coach behaviour, coach wellbeing and motivational climate, have all been shown to impact upon an athlete's wellbeing (Berntsen, Ivarsson, & Kristiansen, 2019; Horn, 2019; Stebbings, Taylor, & Spray, 2015). Such findings highlight the importance of coaches appreciating their capacity to influence athlete wellbeing directly through their behaviours, the motivational climate cultivated and also via emotional contagion. The wellbeing contagion effect endorses the proposition that environments should support the wellbeing of all involved in

HP sport not just athletes. Thus, it is important to understand the wellbeing of others, such as coaches, squad/teams and support staff as important in its own right as well as because relationships with these people are particularly salient for influencing athlete wellbeing.

Developing accounts of wellbeing over the life course of an athletic career and also beyond it is important. As well as supporting the obligation to uphold a duty of care to protect athletes from undue harm, understanding wellbeing over the course of an athlete's career will support insight about sustainable development and performance enhancement. Emerging now through news reports, films, biographical or social media exposés of mainly ex-athletes are accounts of the acute and long-term impact on athletes of the extreme conditions and cultural practices normalized in some HP sport environments. Examples of these issues include cases of abuse, maltreatment and bullying which have undermined athletes' humanness and their health and wellbeing. In their text, Health and Elite Sport, Baker et al. (2015, p. 1) refer to the lack of critical evaluation about the health and wellbeing of HP athletes, despite our growing awareness of HP sport culture as that characterized by 'the unquestioned acceptance, production and reproduction of health compromising norms and practices', that is, a culture of risk. Acknowledging such challenges, an objective facing the high-performance athlete is to 'protect and stimulate his or her wellbeing in the highly demanding and performance-oriented elite context' (Lundqvist & Sandin, 2014, p. 245). Supporting athletes in developmentally appropriate ways to understand and adopt self-care strategies for their long-term health and wellbeing is an important objective in HP sport. Self-care can be viewed as an individual's deliberate engagement in activity intended to contribute to their health and wellbeing. Promoting self-care among coaches and support staff, which is important in its own right, may also enhance athlete wellbeing through a variety of mechanisms.

As recognized by contemporary researchers, there is presently a limited understanding about wellbeing in sport (Lundqvist & Sandin, 2014; Macdougall et al., 2016; Giles et al., 2020) so developing trustworthy knowledge is a priority. The majority of research in sport has been quantitative, deriving data from generic self-report measures with insufficient personal or contextual relevance, leading Lundqvist and Sandin (2014) to call for more athlete-generated accounts of wellbeing to capture the real-world complexities of personal and situated accounts of athletes' wellbeing. Without context-based accounts of HP athlete wellbeing and quality of life that capture the complexity and dynamic nature of human wellbeing in sport, there's a risk that we may misinterpret and pathologize a range of expected and normal behaviours and states (Lundqvist et al., 2020). Conversely, without context-based accounts of athlete wellbeing and quality of life, we may treat HP sport as an outlier not amenable to understanding using everyday concepts of health, which in turn, may justify the normalization of a range of harmful and inappropriate practices with significant long-term consequences for mental and physical heath for athletes and potentially others too. Without enquiry through rigorous research examining wellbeing and openness about findings, there is a risk that athletes and those who work with them in HP sport will not benefit from the insights that are presently driving significant change among governments, global businesses and contemporary approaches to health and education. The topic of wellbeing is not the latest fad or discrete intervention to supplement existing practices. Athlete wellbeing should be the starting point for designing sustainable systems and pathways in high performance to support those who invest a large part of their lives in the pursuit of performance success.

We have reached a tipping point in high-performance sport with a growing number of key national and international organizations now publishing landmark declarations and calls to action, at the heart of which is recognition of the importance of athlete wellbeing for personal development and success in sport and life. Examples include European Union Guidelines on Dual Careers of Athletes (2012); World Players Association, The World Player Development, Wellbeing, Transition and Retirement Standard (2017); International Olympic Committee Consensus Statement on Mental Health in Elite Athletes (Reardon et al., 2019); UK Government's Independent Duty of Care in Sport Review (2017); Sport New Zealand's Elite Athletes' Rights and Welfare Review (Cottrell, 2018); and the AIS High Performance Sport System: Wellbeing Review (2020). In publishing detailed policies, standards and position statements, these and other such organizations have signalled clear expectations about creating environments and practices that support athlete wellbeing (during and after a career in sport). Though these publications are expertly crafted and detailed, they each have their own focus and approach to wellbeing. Reading these documents could be a valuable starting place for those working in high-performance sport who want to understand why athlete wellbeing is a vital feature in the landscape of contemporary sport.

Advancing future knowledge about holistic athlete wellbeing requires us to acknowledge the complex and transdisciplinary nature of personal, interpersonal and cultural wellbeing in HP sport. This book provides a unique collection of firsthand accounts that highlight the significance of wellbeing throughout the athlete journey.

References

Aked, J., Marks, N., Cordon, C., & Thompson, S. (2009). *Five ways to wellbeing: A report presented to the Foresight project on communicating the evidence base for improving people's wellbeing*. London: New Economics Foundation.

Ashfield, A., McKenna, J., & Backhouse, S. (2012). The athlete's experience of flourishing. *Qualitative Methods in Psychology Bulletin, 14*, 4–12.

Australian Institute of Sport. (2020). *AIS High Performance Sport System: Duty of care & wellbeing review*. Retrieved from www.ais.gov.au/health-wellbeing/review

Baker, J., Safai, P., & Fraser-Thomas, J. (Eds.) (2015). *Health and elite sport: Is high performance sport a healthy pursuit?* Abingdon, Oxon: Routledge.

Barker-Ruchti, N. (Ed.) (2019). *Athlete learning in elite sport: A cultural framework*. Abingdon, Oxon: Routledge.

Beamish, R., & Ritchie, I. (2006). *Fastest, highest, strongest: A critique of high performance sport*. Abingdon, Oxon: Routledge.

Berntsen, H., Ivarsson, A., & Kristiansen, E. (2019). Need-supportiveness and athlete well-being: Coaches' competence-support at risk in the elite sport context throughout the season. *Current Issues in Sport Science (CISS)*, 4. https://doi.org/10.15203/CISS_2019.010

Bishop, C. (2020). *The long win: The search for a better way to succeed*. UK: Practical Inspiration Publishing.

Brackenridge, C., & Rhind, D. (Eds.) (2014). *Researching and enhancing athlete welfare*. London: Brunel University Press.

Brady, A., & Grenville-Cleave, B. (Eds.) (2018). *Positive psychology in sport and physical activity: An introduction*. Abingdon, Oxon: Routledge.

Brady, A., & Maynard, I. (2010). At an elite level the role of a sport psychologist is entirely about performance enhancement. *Sport and Exercise Psychology Review*, 6(1), 59–66.

Bronfenbrenner, U. (1979). *The ecology of human development: Experiments by nature and design*. Cambridge, MA: Harvard University Press.

Brown, D. J., Arnold, R., Reid, T., & Roberts, G. (2018). A qualitative exploration of thriving in elite sport. *Journal of Applied Sport Psychology*, 30(2), 129–149.

Christoff, K. (2014). Dehumanization in organizational settings: Some scientific and ethical considerations. *Frontiers in Human Neuroscience*, 8, 748–748.

Cottrell, S. (2018). *Elite athletes' rights and welfare*. Auckland: Sport New Zealand. Retrieved from https://sportnz.org.nz/media/3193/elite-athlete-right-and-welfare.pdf

De Neve, J. E., Diener, E., Tay, L., & Xuereb, C. (2013). The objective benefits of subjective well-being. In J. Helliwell, R. Layard, & J. Sachs (Eds.), *World happiness report 2013* (pp. 1–38). New York: UN Sustainable Development Solutions Network.

De Neve, J. E., Krekel, C., & Ward, G. (2018). Work and well-being: A global perspective. In J. D. Sachs, A. Bin Bashir, J-E. De Neve, M. Durand, E. Diener, J. F. Helliwell, R. Layard, & M. Seligman (Eds.), *Global happiness: Policy report* (pp. 74–128). New York: Sustainable Development Solutions Network. ISBN 978099 6851374

Diener, E., Lucas, R. E., & Oishi, S. (2018). Advances and open questions in the science of subjective well-being. *Collabra: Psychology*, 4(1), 15. https://doi.org/10.1525/collabra.115

European Union. (2012). *Guidelines on dual careers of athletes*. European Union, Brussels. Retrieved from https://ec.europa.eu/assets/eac/sport/library/documents/dual-career-guidelines-final_en.pdf

Fleming, M. (1952). A cardinal concept of welfare. *The Quarterly Journal of Economics*, 66(3), 366–384.

Fredrickson, B. L. (2000). Cultivating positive emotions to optimize health and well-being. *Prevention and Treatment*, 3 (1), 1–25. Retrieved December 5, 2007, from http://journals.apa.org/prevention

Galderisi, S., Heinz, A., Kastrup, M., Beezhold, J., & Sartorius, N. (2015). Toward a new definition of mental health. *World Psychiatry: Official Journal of the World Psychiatric Association (WPA)*, 14(2), 231–233.

Giles, S., Fletcher, D., Arnold, R., Ashfield, A., & Harrison, J. (2020). Measuring well-being in sport performers: Where are we now and how do we progress? *Sports Medicine (Auckland)*, 50(7), 1255–1270.

The Global Happiness Council. (2018). *Global happiness policy report 2018*. New York: UN Sustainable Development Solutions Network.

Greve, B. (2008). What is welfare? *Central European Journal of Public Policy*, 2(1), 50–73.

Haslam, N., & Stratemeyer, M. (2016). Recent research on dehumanization. *Current Opinion in Psychology, 11*, 25–29.

Hodge, K., Henry, G., & Smith, W. (2014). A case study of excellence in elite sport: Motivational climate in a world champion team. *The Sport Psychologist, 28*(1), 60–74.

Horn, T. S. (2019). Examining the impact of coaches' feedback patterns on the psychosocial well-being of youth sport athletes. *Kinesiology Review, 8*(3), 244–251.

Howells, K. (2021). Adversity- and growth-related experiences of elite sport performers. In R. Wadey, M. Day, & K. Howells (Eds.) *Growth following adversity in sport: A mechanism for positive change* (Chapter 11). New York: Routledge.

Huppert, F. A., Baylis, N., & Keverne, E. B. (2004). Introduction: Why do we need a science of well-being? *Philosophical Transactions of the Royal Society, Biological Sciences, 259*, 1331–1332.

Huppert, F. A., & So, T. T. (2013). Flourishing across Europe: Application of a new conceptual framework for defining well-being. *Social Indicators Research, 110*(3), 837–861.

Ingham, A. G., Chase, M. A., & Butt, J. (2002). From the performance principle to the developmental principle: Every kid a winner? *Quest, 54*(4), 308–331.

Jolley, D., McCready, C., Grenville-Cleave, B., & Brady, A. (2018). My Future Today: Reflecting on positive psychology in professional football academies. In A. Brady & B. Grenville-Cleave (Eds.), *Positive psychology in sport and physical activity: An introduction* (pp. 155–169). Abingdon, Oxon: Routledge.

Kavanagh, E., & Brady, A. (2014). Humanisation in high performance sport. In C. H. Brackenridge & D. Rhind (Eds.), *Athlete welfare: International perspectives*. London: Brunel University Press.

Kern, M. L., Benson, L., Steinberg, E. A., & Steinberg, L. (2016). The EPOCH measure of adolescent well-being. *Psychological Assessment, 28*(5), 586–597.

Kerr, G., & Stirling, A. (2017). Issues of maltreatment in high performance athlete development: Mental toughness as a threat to athlete welfare. In J. Baker, S. Cobley, J. Schorer, & N. Wattie (Eds.), *Routledge handbook of talent identification and development in sport* (1st ed., chapter 29). Abingdon, Oxon: Routledge. https://doi.org/10.4324/9781315668017

Keyes, C. L. M. (2002). The mental health continuum: From languishing to flourishing in life. *Journal of Health and Behavior Research, 43*, 207–222.

Lang, M. (2021). *Routledge handbook of athlete welfare*. Abingdon, Oxon: Routledge.

Larkin, M. (2013). *Health and well-being across the life course*. London: Sage.

Lavallee, D. (2019). Engagement in sport career transition planning enhances performance. *Journal of Loss & Trauma, 24*(1), 1–8.

Linton, M., Dieppe, P., & Medina-Lara, A. (2016). A review of 99 self-report measures for assessing well-being in adults: Exploring dimensions of well-being and developments over time. *BMJ Open, 6*, e010641. https://doi.org/10.1136/bmjopen-2015-010641

Lomas, T., Waters, L., Williams, P., Oades, L. G., & Kern, M. L. (2020). Third wave positive psychology: Broadening towards complexity. *The Journal of Positive Psychology*, 1–15.

Lundqvist, C. (2011). Well-being in competitive sports-the feel-good factor? A review of conceptual considerations of well-being. *International Review of Sport and Exercise Psychology, 4*(2), 109–127.

Lundqvist, C., & Sandin, F. (2014). Well-being in elite sport: Dimensions of hedonic and eudaimonic well-being among elite orienteers. *The Sport Psychologist, 28*(3), 245–254.

Lundqvist, C., Träff, M., & Brady, A. (2020). "Not everyone gets the opportunity to experience this": Swedish elite athletes' perceptions of quality of life. *International Journal of Sport Psychology, 51*(4).

Lyubomirsky, S., King, L., & Diener, E. (2005). The benefits of frequent positive affect: Does happiness lead to success? *Psychological Bulletin, 131*(6), 803–855.

Macdougall, H., O'Halloran, P., Sherry, E., & Shields, N. (2016). Needs and strengths of Australian para-athletes: Identifying their subjective psychological, social, and physical health and well-being. *The Sport Psychologist, 30*(1), 1–12.

Mayoh, J., & Jones, I. (2014). Making well-being an experiential possibility: The role of sport. *Qualitative Research in Sport, Exercise and Health, 7*(2), 235–252.

McCarthy, P. J. (2011). Positive emotion in sport performance: Current status and future directions. *International Review of Sport and Exercise Psychology, 4*(1), 50–69.

Meeus, W., Iedema, J., Helsen, M., & Vollebergh, W. (1999). Patterns of adolescent identity development: Review of literature and longitudinal analysis. *Developmental Review, 19*, 419–461.

Miller, K. E., & Hoffman, J. H. (2009). Mental well-being and sport-related identities in college students. *Sociology of Sport Journal, 26*, 335–356.

Miller, P. S., & Kerr, G. (2002). Conceptualizing excellence: Past, present and future. *Journal of Applied Sport Psychology, 14*, 140–153.

Pink, M., Saunders, J., & Stynes, J. (2015). Reconciling the maintenance of on-field success with off-field player development: A case study of a club culture within the Australian Football League. *Psychology of Sport and Exercise, 21*, 98–108.

Price, N., Morrison, N., & Arnold, S. (2010). *Life out of the limelight: Understanding the non-sporting pursuits of elite athletes.* Retrieved December 1, 2010, from www.ausport.gov.au/__data/assets/pdf_file/0003/383529/Life_out_of_the_Limelight,_Understanding_the_Non-Sporting_Pursuites_of_Elite_Athletes.pdf

Rapley, M. (2003). *Quality of life research: A critical introduction.* London: Sage.

Reardon, C. L., Hainline, B., Aron, C. M., Baron, D., Baum, A. L., Bindra, A., . . . & Engebretsen, L. (2019). Mental health in elite athletes: International Olympic Committee consensus statement. *British Journal of Sports Medicine, 53*, 667–699.

Ruiz, M. C., & Rabozza, C. (Eds.) (2020). *Feelings in sport: Theory, research, and practical implications for performance and well-being.* New York: Routledge.

Ryan, R. M., & Deci, E. L. (2001). On happiness and human potentials: A review of research on hedonic and eudaimonic well-being. *Annual Review of Psychology, 52*, 141–166.

Ryff, C. D., Singer, B. H., & Love, G. D. (2004). Positive health: Connecting well-being with biology. *Philosophical Transactions Royal Society, London B, 359*, 1383–1394.

Seligman, M. E. P. (2011). *Flourish: A new understanding of happiness and well-being – and How to achieve them.* London: Nicholas Brearley Publishing.

Seligman, M. E. P. (2018). PERMA and the building blocks of well-being. *The Journal of Positive Psychology, 13*(4), 333–335.

Sotiriadou, P., & Bosscher, V. (Eds.) (2017). *Managing high performance sport.* London: Routledge.

Stebbings, J., Taylor, I. M., & Spray, C. M. (2015). The relationship between psychological well- and ill-being, and perceived autonomy supportive and controlling interpersonal styles: A longitudinal study of sport coaches. *Psychology of Sport and Exercise, 19*, 42–49.

Su, R., Tay, L., & Diener, E. (2014). Comprehensive and brief inventory of thriving. *Applied Psychology: Health and Well-Being, 6*, 251–279.

Theberge, N. (2008). "Just a normal part of what I do": Elite athletes accounts of the relationship between health and sport. *Sociology of Sport Journal, 25*, 206–222.

Todres, L., Galvin, K.T., & Holloway, I. (2009). The humanization of healthcare: A value framework for qualitative research. *International Journal of Qualitative Studies on Health and Well-being, 4*(2), 68–77.

Tracey, J., & Elcombe, T. (2004). A lifetime of healthy meaningful movement: Have we forgotten all the athletes? *Quest, 56*, 241–260.

UK Government. (2017). *Duty of care in sport review*. Department for Digital, Culture, Media & Sport. Retrieved from www.gov.uk/government/publications/duty-of-care-in-sport-review

Veenhoven, R. (2007). Subjective measures of well-being. In M. McGillivray (Ed.), *Human Well-being: Issues, concepts and measurement* (pp. 214–239). New Hampshire: Palgrave Macmillan.

Walsh, A. J., & Giulianotti, R. (2001). This sporting mammon: A normative critique of the commodification of sport. *Journal of the Philosophy of Sport, 28*(1), 53–77.

Westerbeek, H., & Hahn, A. (2013). The Influence of commercialization and globalization on high performance sport. In P. Sotiriadou & V. Bosscher (Eds.), *Managing high performance sport*. London: Routledge.

Wissing, M. P., Schutte, L., Liversage, C., Entwisle, B., Gericke, M., & Keyes, C. (2019). Important goals, meanings, and relationships in flourishing and languishing states: Towards patterns of well-being. *Applied Research Quality Life, 16*, 573–609. https://doi.org/10.1007/s11482-019-09771-8

World Players Association. (2017). *World player development, wellbeing, transition and retirement standard, Paris 2017*. Nyon, Switzerland. Retrieved from www.uniglobalunion.org/sites/default/files/imce/paris_world_player_development_standard_7_sep_17.pdf

Wrisberg, C. (1996). Quality of life in male and female athletes. *Quest, 48*(3), 392–408.

Wylleman, P., & Lavallee, D. (2004). A developmental perspective on transitions faced by athletes. In M. Weiss (Ed.), *Developmental sport and exercise psychology: A lifespan perspective* (pp. 507–527). Morgantown, WV: FIT.

2
THE HOLISTIC WELLBEING OF ELITE YOUTH PERFORMERS

U MATTER

Tony Ghaye, Luke Allen and Neil Clark

Introduction

This chapter is a first of its kind where the psychological processes of mattering are being applied to sport. The chapter is generally positioned within the 'space' of athlete wellbeing. It is brought to life with an analysis of the lived experiences of one young female cricketer who has been part of the Global Human Rights and Wellbeing project called U MATTER. The core questions that give this chapter meaning and purpose are, 'In what ways do you feel you matter to others and they to you?' The complementary question is, 'And how would you feel if you didn't matter at all?' Leggy-Eggy's story speaks vividly to these two questions. We derive three core feelings from Leggy-Eggy's story that helped her to feel she truly mattered, namely, feeling noticed, appreciated and connected (attuned) with others. The chapter concludes with an illumination of the acronym M.A.G.I.C. as a practical way to ignite conversations-that-matter between all those in an athletes' relational 'system'. These are not just any kind of conversation but also life-giving ones that serve to open up new possibilities and elevate greatness in young athletes.

In 2020, Deloitte captured aspects of the bigger picture to which this chapter relates, in their report called, 'Mental health and employers: Refreshing the case for investment' (Hampson & Jacob, 2020). Some of the headlines were that:

- The burden of poor mental health at work affects young people disproportionately, and there has been an increase in the prevalence of mental health problems among this age group.
- A rise in 'presenteeism' with people attending work whilst ill and, therefore, not performing to their full ability.

- In the last three years a rise in 'leaveism', where employees are unable to disconnect from work due to the increased use of technology, contributing to burnout. This is often referred to as the 'always on' phenomenon.
- An increase in people working under short-term contracts, in freelance work or without sufficient employer support, is creating uncertainty about their financial future and with little concern for their mental health and wellbeing needs.

The broader 'space' within which the work reported in this chapter is situated is that of youth athlete wellness. In this space, we find research published in 2019 called, 'The Sport and Physical Activity Workforce Mental Health (SPAWMH) Survey'. It was a nationwide study of mental health in the sport and physical activity workforce (i.e. grassroots/community sport, high-performance sport, activity/lifestyle/recreation and education) in the United Kingdom. It contained a big message about youths in sport. The project was led by researchers at Edge Hill University in association with DOCIA sport and supported by the Sport and Recreation Alliance. The report examined the responses of over 1,200 people aged 16+ in over 50 roles across more than 50 sports. In general, they found that anxiety (74%) and depression (56%) were most often reported, with panic disorders, self-harm, post-traumatic stress disorder (PTSD) and obsessive-compulsive disorder (OCD) also most commonly reported concerns for men and women. Men also reported conditions such as substance use disorders and in women anorexia and bulimia. With regard to youth sport (16–24 years), 31% males and 37% females reported that they were experiencing some kind of mental illness.

U MATTER – the project

This chapter is related to an ongoing international and multi-sport project called 'U MATTER'. It is the first of its kind to be undertaken in sport and sports' business. The aims of the project are to understand, illuminate and determine the impact that other people (e.g. coaches) have on athletes and athletes' need to be valued by significant others in their lives. In general, mattering is central to our sense of identity and self-worth. More specifically, the athlete who feels they matter is secure in the knowledge that she/he has meaningful and positive connections with other people. They feel noticed and cared for by others. They recognise others are invested in them. Given this, they are likely to be more engaged, more motivated to be the best they can be and more resilient. The antithesis of mattering, (not mattering), comes with feelings that no one really cares about you, with feelings of being insignificant, unappreciated, undervalued, marginalised and even invisible.

The project is being developed within interactionist and relational frames that are cognizant of contextual experiences (e.g. particular sports, by particular athletes, at particular performance levels) when exploring the power mattering has on athlete mental health and wellbeing. Feeling we matter, or not, is a core part of building our 'best self'. Mattering is central to wellbeing. We are suggesting that it's something we need to better understand and a conversation that is worth having.

ATHLETE VOICE

C'mon Leggy Eggy – understanding the need to matter

'As fast as you can Eggy! Hold nothing back from your old man!'

The words rang in my ears. That was my dad, my hero. I can see him now, hands grasping his beloved bat, his sleeveless jumper proudly bearing the Invicta symbol. He stood in front of the wicket, goading me to hurl the ball with all my might – to topple those two bails he proudly and stubbornly protected.

Eggy was my pet name. 'Sunny side up – that's you', my dad would say. 'Always got a smile on your face for me'.

And I did have. All that mattered to me was being with my dad and all that mattered to him was being with me. It was quality time. If I had a sunny disposition, he had given it to me and together we were invincible.

I paced myself carefully. This run-up had to be perfect. If I pitched the ball correctly, line and length, or maybe a surprise bouncer, dad might be fooled. It was a real battle as he'd be reading my every move but I reckoned I had him this time.

I rubbed the ball one last time down the side of my trousers, felt my fingers grip the seam and started the run. Run smooth. Get everything moving in sync. My eyes were fixed on that corridor of uncertainty. The place dad had shown me many times and where he, himself, had got out so many players in his career.

I released the ball, propelled at top speed. I almost lost balance but righted myself just in time to see the outcome. The bails were in orbit! Off-stump, cartwheeling backwards. What a mess! Dad's bat was still in mid-air. The mighty shot that would have cleared the boundary had evaded him. He stood dumbfounded, a look of astonishment on his face. Or was it a look of admiration?

My heart raced, my pride burst through. I had defeated my dad! At last! The practice and the persistence had finally paid off. And, not only that . . . I was a GIRL and I was only SEVEN! Can you believe it? Eggy scrambled her dad's wicket!

It would be years before I could accept that dad allowed me to bowl him out! We laughed about it again when I was thirteen and had become the youngest female player to take 5 wickets for 24 runs in my County age squad. My nickname of 'Eggy' had morphed into 'Leggy-Eggy' by my teammates.

'You're a proper speedster aren't you?' my teammates would say.

This made me feel good, wanted even and valued by my team. And I guess that was true. Every wicket I took was greeted with hugs, back slapping and endless handshaking. They were confident in my ability to knock 'em over! With the fire in my belly to succeed and the dream of making it to the England squad always on my mind, I notched up 30, then 40 then the magic 50 wickets in a season haul. Cricket was great. Life was good.

Throughout the years, dad had been there for me, guiding, teaching and encouraging me. I wanted him to be so proud of me, to pat himself on the back for my achievements. Every wicket, every match and every trophy, I dedicated to him. Sunny side up days were all due to him.

Life couldn't have been much sweeter by the time I was seventeen. If I put my dad on a pedestal, he put me even higher! My performance went from strength to strength. When I walked out onto the field, I felt that welcome surge of adrenaline. The drive to excel and a sharpness of mind kicked in. And there was my dad, thumbs up, a broad grin on his face. Come rain or shine he took his place. Our worlds revolved around cricket and each other. Or so I thought.

The bombshell came a day after my eighteenth birthday. Dad had seemed on edge, different somehow over the past few months. I put it down to work pressures and running his own business. A couple of times he missed a match and I struggled to focus without him there. We sat on the sofa at home, the England women's team had just been victorious against their Aussie rivals.

'That will be you out there soon, Eggy', dad had said. 'You'll make it one step further than I ever did. You know you mean the world to me. I couldn't be more proud of you'.

'It's only because of you dad', I said. 'You make me play this way'.

'No . . . it's all you now. I might have fanned the flames but you're burning brightly because you're talented and gifted and you work harder than I ever did', he said. 'The sky's the limit for you'.

And then it came . . .

'I'm going away, Eggy. It's been the hardest decision I've ever made but I know it's the right one. Things haven't been good between your mum and me for some time now. I need to try to find happiness elsewhere. You're a beautiful, young woman, strong and resilient. You don't need your old dad hanging around all the time'.

My world imploded. My heart felt as though it had stopped. Feelings of nausea swept over me.

'I must try to find happiness elsewhere', he said.

Had I heard that right? Had those words really left my dad's lips? I couldn't EVER find happiness elsewhere. If my dad wasn't there, I wasn't either.

The following days and weeks passed in a blur. I begged, sobbed, shouted, screamed, wrung my hands in despair in front of him, but something stronger than me, more important and significant was compelling him to go. It had to be someone else. How could he break my heart, unless it meant he didn't want to break someone else's? After all these years, the sweat and the tears, it seemed I just didn't matter anymore. The rest of the season was insignificant. I felt so totally alone, vulnerable and cheated. Mum didn't know how to deal with me. It seemed that their separation had been brewing for years – just until I was eighteen, strong enough to cope! My teammates either had their own problems or my dip in form was seen as an opportunity, for one or two of them, to step up into my place. So much for team spirit I thought.

At first, my self-confidence went. Then my self-belief. My coaches knew there was something wrong. But I couldn't put words to how I was really feeling. There was pressure on me to be strong and focused. Not weak and pathetic. That's how I was feeling inside. They wanted the best of me. But this disappeared when my dad disappeared. No longer could I cripple the opposition because I was the cripple now. No one could know that I had been ripped inside out. And who really cared? There was nobody there who would be really proud of my accomplishments and saddened by my failures. My close daughter–dad relationship that was nourished by cricket gave my dad a sense of purpose, and me much strength, because dad's presence was necessary and helpful to me in so many ways.

As the season drew to a close, so did my performance. Mentally I couldn't cope. I couldn't express my insecurities and neither did I want to explain my vulnerabilities. I built a wall around me to try to protect myself. I lost the drive to go on and the will to succeed. To give him some credit, I guess my coach noticed much more than he ever said. I fumbled with excuses and promised a return to my old self in the new season but he clearly wasn't convinced. The pressure was on. Leggy-Eggy became scrambled egg head! 'We've got the England selectors at our next match, with winter tour selection on their minds', my coach reminded me nervously. 'We are counting on you – the team are all behind you'.

What difference did that make? If my dad was behind me, I could do it. Without him, it meant nothing.

Selectors' match day arrived. I struggled to get up that morning. The outcome would be the same, whether I played or not I thought. But something in me, pride or embedded discipline perhaps, got my bags packed. The train ride to the ground felt long and arduous. Best get it out the way and return to my misery. I walked the last ten minutes in despondency and rounded the corner by the yew tree. Dad used to wait there when I met him after school for practice at the Club. Now its evergreen branches just looked heavy and sad.

That's when I heard it. Just as I was walking past, a voice that made my heart skip and my pulse race. 'It's the big one today, Eggy! Sunny side up day'.

Nothing could have prepared me for the elation that I felt. And nothing could have prepared him for the mad rush of a teenage daughter into her father's arms. He held me tighter than ever, six words on repeat, as he soothed the sobs away.

'Forgive me, you're all that matters'.

After a full decade, there's still no feeling quite like that of knowing you matter. Mattering to your team? Your club and even mattering to your country? Or, perhaps there is?

Perhaps what matters most is seeing the face of the man who made it all possible.

SCHOLAR VOICE

Learning in moments that matter

In Leggy-Eggy's story, we can find many significant feeling components of mattering. For example, feeling important in her dad's life, the attention he gave her as she developed as a cricketer, her dad's appreciation of her progress and feelings they got from their inter-dependence. These feelings ideally need to be a two-way street. I matter to you and you to me. They are reciprocal. It requires both being active and receptive (Marshall, 2001). Feelings of mattering are often rooted in having someone recognise that we are 'special' to them in some way and that they 'get us'. Leggy-Eggy's story is highly personal and reflects how being focused upon, in positive ways, helps us feel like we matter. Additionally, there are also some significant action components of mattering in the story. The nature, intensity and frequency of actions are often ways of knowing the difference between real, perceived and imagined mattering. By actions, we mean actions between Leggy-Eggy and her dad that convey that they matter to each other. For example, there is the way her dad invests time and thoughtfulness into his daughter's wellbeing and progress. There are repeated examples of how her dad expressed his belief in his daughter's capabilities and how her dad, for the most part, went out of his way to 'be there' for Leggy-Eggy when she needed him.

There are many things we can do to help someone realise they matter and especially when these actions are repeated unconditionally. However, it is also important to appreciate the impact and potential destructiveness of not mattering to others, both real and imagined. The seminal work of Schlossberg (1989) is critical here. She describes two 'polar themes', one as mattering, the other as marginalisation, or as Flett (2018) puts it, anti-mattering. In Leggy-Eggy's story her dad's phrase, 'I'm going away Eggy' brought with it particularly intense feelings that she no longer mattered to her dad. Her positive motivational orientation together with her feelings of self-confidence and belief came crashing down. Her feelings of being connected and attuned were put under pressure. 'The best of me disappeared when my dad disappeared', says Leggy-Eggy. Losing the drive and will to go on and succeed together with a sense of vulnerability flooded Leggy-Eggy's whole being.

In moments like this it's hard to feel ok about ourselves, while at the same time acknowledging our pain. She says, 'I begged, sobbed, shouted, screamed, wrung my hands in despair in front of him . . . It seemed I just didn't matter anymore . . . The rest of the season was insignificant'. At times like this, which sadly are not uncommon, the role of family, friends, teachers, coaches and support staff can be, literally, a life saver. We are not specifically, or necessarily, referring to the work of sports lifestyle managers, sports psychologists, counsellors, buddies, mentors and others here. What we are pointing up is the necessity and significance of 'healing companions' in times like this. People who are empathetic, compassionate and attuned to listen to Leggy-Eggy's story and support them towards making wise future decisions and healthy relationships. In the moment Leggy-Eggy says:

> My mum didn't know how to deal with me . . . My team mates either had their own problems or my dip in form was seen as an opportunity, for one or two of them, to step up into my place.

Her coaches knew that something was wrong, but she felt she couldn't put into words how she was really feeling. 'The pressure on me was to be strong and focussed'. The most valuable contribution, arguably, we can make to someone like Leggy-Eggy who is hurting, is the gift of listening.

> It is not something we do. It is something we are. We become a listening presence, a way of being in which stillness and attentiveness provide space in which someone [Leggy-Eggy in this case] can speak authentically and know they have been heard.
> *(Whitney et al., 2019, p. 79)*

Leggy-Eggy and form of mattering

One contemporary mantra is, the only person you can change is yourself. Another is, 'we live and thrive in relationship' (Whitney et al., 2019, p. 15). U MATTER and the process of mattering are firmly in the realm of the latter. If you think about, or hear the words, 'that athlete is thriving/flourishing', what comes to mind? If you collected everyone's responses, it is very likely you would find reference to physical and emotional safety and security. Also, the ability for athletes to freely express themselves, where successes, no matter how small, are celebrated, together with reference to places and conversations where the athlete feels welcomed, valued, appreciated and respected. These things and more inspire young athletes to be their best. Taken together this relational richness can be seen as moments that energise, strengthen and uplift the best self. They generate feelings that we matter. Mattering is associated with human thriving. It is a very important source of wellbeing (Flett, 2018) and especially for adolescents (Rosenberg & McCullough, 1981).

In Table 2.1, we use examples of Leggy-Eggy's story to bring to sporting life the broader work of Elliot, Kao, and Grant (2004) and their three forms of mattering. As we have already suggested, mattering can take many forms. Arguably, it is fundamentally to do with two core aspects of athletes' sense of self, namely attention and relationships (see Table 2.1). Attention is the feeling that an athlete holds the interest of, is recognised or noticed by significant others, such as their coach, physiotherapist, strength and conditioner, nutritionist and lifestyle mentor. Family, friends, teammates and more broadly the attention of competitors, the media and attention on various social media platforms come into this first core aspect. Attention can, of course, be regarded by the athlete as good or bad, desirable or undesirable, positive or negative, focused or divided and shades in-between.

The second is relational, meaning a relationship between the athlete and others to whom the athlete matters and vice versa. This links with an appreciation of mattering as something external, rather than as an internal focus. As mattering relationships can be bi-directional, it's important to distinguish between its two forms. The first form is to do with importance. In general, and athletes are no different, we feel we matter to others if we are the object of their interest and concern. For example, a coach may listen to an athlete's worries, anxieties, dietary and sleep self-reports, mood, aspirations and make every effort to see that their athletes' needs are met. The second form is to do with reliance. For example, from a coach's perspective, a young athlete matters if they look to the coach for the co-construction and satisfaction of their personal needs or performance goals. Another expression of reliance is when a young athlete needs the reassurance, or focusing skills, from an older person, experienced teammate, trusted friend or coach when preparing for competition. Reliance can flow both ways and complements the essential capability of athletes to be self-reliant. Over-reliance can be dysfunctional of course like a young athletes' persistent reliance on parents to taxi them around without a thought of considering taking a bus or train and even to wash their kit!

The core question that gives this chapter meaning and purpose is, 'In what ways do you feel you matter to others and they to you?' The complementary question is, 'And how would you feel if you felt you didn't matter at all?' Leggy-Eggy's story speaks vividly to these questions. In Table 2.1, we focus only on mattering rather than NOT mattering.

TABLE 2.1 Forms, meanings and examples of mattering in the U MATTER project

Forms of mattering	Meanings of mattering from athlete/coach/family member perspectives	Illustration from Leggy-Eggy's cricketing story (attention and relationship with dad)
Awareness	• Being noticed by significant others. • Being remembered and addressed by name. • Being the focus of attention from family and peers. • Others being aware of athletes' presence both real and virtual.	Eggy was my pet name. 'Sunny side up – that's you', my dad would say. 'Always got a smile on your face for me'. And I did have. All that mattered to me was being with dad and all that mattered to him was being with me. 'You're a proper speedster aren't you?' my teammates would say. This made me feel good, wanted even and valued by my team.
Importance	• Athlete success is a source of pride for others. • The go-to 'healing companion'. • Coach/family member cares about what athlete achieves. • Athlete appreciates coach's experience.	It would be years before I could accept that dad allowed me to bowl him out! We laughed about it again and again when I was thirteen when I had become the youngest female player to take 5 wickets for 24 runs in my County age squad. 'We've got the England selectors at our next match, with winter tour selection on their minds', my coach reminded me nervously. 'We are counting on you – the team are all behind you'.
Reliance	• Athlete seeks coach advice. • Athlete has the support of the coach during times of challenge (e.g. failure to qualify for an event). • Coach values athlete views. • Athlete trusts coach to 'be there'.	Dad says, 'You know you mean the world to me. I couldn't be more proud of you'. 'It's only because of you dad', I said. 'You make me play this way'. My close daughter–dad relationship that was nourished by cricket gave my dad a sense of purpose and me much strength because dad's presence was necessary and helpful to me in so many ways.

Mattering, rationality and becoming

A point of entry to begin to appreciate the broader wellbeing space within which mattering is positioned are the twin notions of relationality and becoming (Pihkala & Karasti, 2018) and the associated processes of relational sensitivity and ways of noticing. Mattering is central to any concern we may have to provide a socio-psychological context for young athletes to thrive and flourish. It's a crucial part of youth development, social behaviours and athletic performance. Parental mattering plays a significant part too in enabling young athletes to become their best-self. Arguably, we need to matter to one another, not just because it is the right thing to do but also because we have evolved to be that way.

With regard to the first notion of relationality (Thapan, 2019), mattering is a crucial part of forming a valid picture of the relational or social self and is an integral part of identity theory. Chen, Boucher, and Kraus (2011) explain the relational self as having four parts. (1) It is self-knowledge that is linked in our memory to knowledge about significant others, such as other athletes, coaches and support staff; (2) It exists at multiple levels of specificity; (3) It is capable of being contextually or chronically activated; and (4) Is comprised of self-conceptions and a constellation of other self-aspects (e.g. motives, self-regulatory strategies, anxieties and self-debilitating beliefs) that characterise the self when relating to significant others. Given this depth of meaning, we can go on to postulate that the 'young athletic self' is not a singular, monolithic, cognitive structure. Instead, it is comprised of at least three fundamental components which have all been exposed in this chapter and which all play a part in feeling that you matter, or not! They are the individual self (Leggy-Eggy), relational self (in relation to her dad) and the collective self (in relation to her teammates and the sport of cricket) (Sedikides & Brewer, 2001). We should remember that we may feel we matter in different ways depending upon which self we have in our mind.

And onto a final point. One conclusion of the fascinating work of Sedikides, Gaertner, and O'Mara (2011) suggests that the individual (athletic) self is at the motivational core of the self-system. The collective self (i.e. in relation to team membership or feeling part of a community of an individual sport) is at the bottom of the three-tier motivational self-hierarchy. The positioning of the collective self is the outcome of how mattering (or not) impacts on the athletes' individual and relational selves. If you accept this finding, a big message for coaches emerges. That is to show how much the individual athlete matters by placing them front and central. If successful, then we suggest that the athlete should be high on self-disclosure and low on self-concealment (ref: 'I couldn't put into words how I was really feeling . . . I couldn't cope. I couldn't express my insecurities and neither did I want to explain my vulnerabilities. I built a wall around me to try to protect myself', explains Leggy-Eggy). This 'silencing of the self' is an indicator that all is not well and is something which those who support the athlete need to look out for.

A deep dive – mattering, self-criticism and self-assurance

If we take a deeper dive into this important field of mattering and youth athlete wellbeing, the work of Gilbert, Clark, Hempel, Miles, and Irons (2004) comes helpfully into view. Although again, yet to be used in sport, their Self-Criticism and Self-Reassurance Scale opens a new vista relevant to this chapter. Their Scale is an intriguing measure and has three sub-scales, namely (1) the inadequate self, (2) the hated self and (3) the reassured self. Given the context of competitive sport and the pressures on youth athletes to perform and stay well, the strengthening that comes from feeling you matter (and the weakening from not mattering) becomes essential and relevant to all three sub-scales. The use of this Scale, which forms part of the multi-method approach of the U MATTER project, together with a Compassionate Engagement and Action Scale (Gilbert et al., 2017), helps us explore different ways athletes feel they matter when things go wrong and is a rich source of promising practices for interventions that seek to sustain a positive mindset, when things are going well. Taken together all of this is central to feelings of mattering in relation to tendencies to be self-critical and/or self-reassuring when perceiving setbacks and failures. We suggest that mattering can act, at least, as a buffer, or as a sense of perspective to moderate being overly self-critical, and especially to feeling inadequate, self-hating and even contemptuous of one's self. Conversely and promisingly when associated with self-compassion, it has the potential to fuel an athlete's ability to self-reassure.

We suggest sport has much to learn from, for example, the application of this Scale and from the findings of its use in a range of different studies, in which self-criticism has been linked to depression and anxiety (Gilbert et al., 2004), self-harm (Gilbert et al., 2010), anger (Gilbert et al., 2005), debilitating beliefs (Mills, Gilbert, Bellew, McEwan, & Gale, 2007) and perfectionism (Gilbert, Durrant, & McEwan, 2006). In contrast, the evidence shows that greater self-reassurance is related to better psychological health (Gilbert et al., 2006), secure attachment (Irons, Gilbert, Baldwin, Baccus, & Palmer, 2006) and memories of warmth and security (Richter, Gilbert, & McEwan, 2009). In recent work reported by Flett (2018) with over 200 university-aged students, mattering was strongly related to an unwillingness to perceive the self as inadequate and much less willingness to hate the self. Mattering was related positively to reassuring the self. Given high-profile athlete self-disclosures over the years about their emotional, mental, physical, relational states, as aspects of their mental health, and especially how some reported sliding from feelings of inadequacy into 'hatred' (self-loathing, potential self-harming, etc.), understanding how mattering flows in/between an athlete and significant others becomes essential to know. To do better (e.g. coach better) we need to know better (Chambers, 2017). We suggest that between an athlete and coach, conversations about how far, and in what ways they feel, they matter, are conversations worth having. 'When you think of conversations worth having, think engagement, interweaving, co-creation, inspiration, respect, illumination, emergence, enriched relationships, trust empathy and bringing out the best' (Stavros & Torres, 2018, p. 6).

Towards an elevation and amplification of mattering in sport

In this chapter, we have tried to set out a case that mattering deserves much more attention in general given the publication of the seminal work of Rosenberg and McCullough (1981) and in youth sport, in particular. Mattering (or not) captures the powerful impact that others' have on an athlete's life and vice versa, it also reflects our general need to be valued and well regarded by others. Mattering is central to our sense of identity and purpose. But we should not forget that mattering is double-edged. The person who feels they matter, 'is a resilient and engaged person, but the person without a sense of mattering is someone prone to stress and distress' (Flett, 2018, p. 6).

We conclude with another proposition. This is one step on from simply initiating mattering conversations with youth athletes. It's a commitment to elevate and amplify them. To do this, we need to be open to the possibility that mattering conversations not only have the power to help the athlete perform, but they can also transform! Conversation linked to conversation to propel improvement? Aspiration touching aspiration? Hope touching hope? To do this, those in sport may have to bring in the meaningful outside! For example, Algoe (2012) specifically shows how gratitude builds socio-psychological resources. It is vividly illustrated in her 'find, remind and bind theory'. At its core, this theory is all about seizing and sustaining opportunities for connection with responsive and significant others. It's a small step to apply Algoe's work to add both reasons and justifications to conduct mattering conversations. For example, applying her work to sport illustrates how important it is to an athlete's wellness to find dyadic relationships that enhance their wellbeing. It helps remind us of the value of existing relationships that support an athlete's subjective wellbeing. And finally, it serves to assist in binding together meaningful social relationships, the ones that truly matter.

A practical turn – can you work the M.A.G.I.C.?

We propose that mattering conversations have the potential to amplify the signal strength of blessings in one's sporting life. Strengthening the feeling you matter, we suggest, enhances the signal strength of who and what is significant in one's life. We propose that the use of the acronym M.A.G.I.C. to help put mattering into practice. Here is an illustration of how coaches (and other staff) might, through their words and actions, work their M.A.G.I.C. with young athletes.

M = MEANINGFUL – Develop positively meaningful relationships with young athletes based on mutual trust and a clear commitment to each athlete's welfare and performance. This requires you to have the capability to empathise, show appropriate affection and that you care about them as people.

A = ANTICIPATORY – Athletes will know that they matter if you help them to feel that you are trying to create conditions for their future success. To do this, you need to communicate a compelling vision of a desired future state and have an ability to help each athlete see this horizon.

G = GENEROSITY – This is the need for coaches to demonstrate generosity of spirit. You need to do this by showing compassion, thoughtfulness, open-heartedness and selfless support towards each individual athlete. These are some of the powerful elements that forge positive human connections. It's about a coach who champions their athlete's willingness to try and demonstrates that you want them to succeed.

I = INDIVIDUATION – This is a coach's ability to help each athlete to feel unique, special and focused upon. It's helping athletes know they matter by conveying a feeling that 'you get me'! The critical skill for you is your ability to 'be present' with each athlete. There is 'being present' when the athlete is talking, by noticing facial and hand gestures, tone of voice and not jumping ahead because you think you already know what they are trying to say. Also 'being present' when you're talking! This is making your point appropriately whilst at the same time noticing the effect your words are having on the athlete.

C = CURIOSITY – Cultivating curiosity within the minds of each young athlete shows them that their future matters to you. It's about helping them hear a voice inside their head that says, 'I want to know more', 'that's interesting', 'that's challenging' and 'this is something new for me to learn'.

Framed in this way, mattering conversations are not just any kind of conversation but also life-giving ones that serve to open up new possibilities and elevate greatness in young athletes.

References

Algoe, S. B. (2012). Find, remind, and bind: The functions of gratitude in everyday relationships. *Social and Personality Psychology Compass, 6*(6), 455–469. https://doi.org/10.1111/j.1751-9004.2012.00439.x

Chambers, R. (2017). *Can we know better? Reflections for development*. Rugby, UK: Practical Action Publishing.

Chen, S., Boucher, H., & Kraus, M. (2011). The relational self. In S. J. Schwartz, K. Luyckx, & V. L. Vignoles (Eds.), *Handbook of identity theory and research* (pp. 149–175). London: Springer.

Elliot, G., Kao, S., & Grant, A. M. (2004). Mattering: Empirical validation of a social-psychological concept. *Self and Identity*, *3*(4), 339–354. https://doi.org/10.1080/13576500444000119

Flett, G. (2018). *The psychology of mattering: Understanding the human need to be significant*. London: Academic Press.

Gilbert, P., Catarino, F., Duarte, C., Matos, M., Kolts, R., Stubbs, J., . . . & Basran, J. (2017). The development of compassionate engagement and action scales for self and others. *Journal of Compassionate Health Care*, *4*, 4. https://doi.org/10.1186/s40639-017-0033-3

Gilbert, P., Cheung, M., Irons, C., & McEwan, K. (2005). An exploration into depression-focused and anger-focused rumination in relation to depression in a student population. *Behavioural and Cognitive Psychotherapy*, *33*(3), 273–283. https://doi.org/10.1017/S135246580400204

Gilbert, P., Clark, M., Hempel, S., Miles, J. N. V., & Irons, C. (2004). Criticising and reassuring oneself: An exploration of forms, styles and reasons in female students. *British Journal of Clinical Psychology*, *43*(1), 31–50. https://doi.org/10.1348/014466504772812959

Gilbert, P., Durrant, R., & McEwan, K. (2006). Investigating relationships between perfectionism, forms and functions of self-criticism, and sensitivity to put-down. *Personality and Individual Differences*, *41*(7), 1299–1308. https://doi.org/10.1016/j.paid.2006.05.004

Gilbert, P., McEwan, K., Irons, C., Bhundia, R., Christie, R., Broomhead, C., & Rockliff, H. (2010). Self-harm in a mixed clinical population: The roles of self criticism, shame, and social rank. *British Journal of Clinical Psychology*, *49*(4), 563–576. https://doi.org/10.1348/014466509X479771

Hampson, E., & Jacob, A. (2020). Mental health and employers: Refreshing the case for investment. *Deloitte*. Retrieved from https://www2.deloitte.com/uk/en/pages/consulting/articles/mental-health-and-employers-refreshing-the-case-for-investment.html

Irons, C., Gilbert, P., Baldwin, M. W., Baccus, J. R., & Palmer, M. (2006). Parental recall, attachment relating and self-attacking/self-reassurance: Their relationship with depression. *British Journal of Clinical Psychology*, *45*(3), 297–308. https://doi.org/10.1348/014466505X68230

Marshall, S. K. (2001). Do I matter? Construct validation of adolescents' perceived mattering to parents and friends. *Journal of Adolescence*, *24*(2), 473–490. https://doi.org/10.1006/jado.2001.0384

Mills, A., Gilbert, P., Bellew, R., McEwan, K., & Gale, C. (2007). Paranoid beliefs and self-criticism in students. *Clinical Psychology and Psychotherapy*, *14*(5), 358–364. https://doi.org/10.1002/cpp.537

Pihkala, S., & Karasti, H. (2018). Politics of mattering in the practices of participatory design. *Proceedings of the 15th Participatory Design Conference*, *2*(13), 20–24

Richter, A., Gilbert, P., & McEwan, K. (2009). Development of an early memories of warmth and safeness scale and its relationship to psychopathology. *Psychology and Psychotherapy: Theory, Research and Practice*, *82*(2), 171–184. https://doi.org/10.1348/147608308X395213

Rosenberg, M., & McCullough, B. C. (1981). Mattering: Inferred significance and mental health among adolescents. *Research Community and Mental Health*, *2*, 163–182.

Schlossberg, N. K. (1989). Marginality and mattering: Key issues in building community. *New Directions for Student Services*, *48*, 5–15.

Sedikides, C., & Brewer, M. B. (2001). Individual, relational, and collective self: Partners, opponents, or strangers? In C. Sedikides & M. B. Brewer (Eds.), *Individual self, relational self, collective self* (pp. 1–4). Abingdon, UK: Psychology Press.

Sedikides, C., Gaertner, L., & O'Mara, E. M. (2011). Individual self, relational self, collective self: Hierarchical ordering of the tripartite self. *Psychological Studies, 56*, 98–107. https://doi.org/10.1007/s12646-011-0059-0

Stavros, J., & Torres, C. (2018). *Conversations worth having: Using appreciative inquiry to fuel productive and meaningful engagement*. Oakland, CA: Berrett-Koehler.

Thapan, M. (2019). Self-knowledge and relatedness in everyday life. *Psychological Studies, 64*, 275–282. https://doi.org/10.1007/s12646-019-00520-3

Whitney, D., Adams Miller, C., Teller, T.C., Ogawa, M., Cocciolone, J., Moon, H., . . . & Leon de la barra, A. (2019). *Thriving women, thriving world, an invitation to dialogue, healing & inspired actions*. Chagrin Falls, OH: Taos Institute Publications.

3

THE ROLE OF PARENTS AND FAMILY IN THE WELLBEING OF ATHLETES

Camilla J. Knight, Katie S. Uzzell and Catherine Shearer

Introduction

Sport provides an opportunity for children, young people, and adults alike to develop physically, mentally, and socially. It provides an avenue through which friendships can be developed, skills can be learnt, and, perhaps most importantly, fun and enjoyment can be had. However, such positive outcomes are not guaranteed and, unfortunately, for some people they are never realised. Rather, for some, involvement in sport can actually threaten their wellbeing. The extent to which those involved in sport have an opportunity to gain the benefits associated with sport, while minimising any threats to wellbeing, is largely dependent upon the support, guidance, and involvement of those around them, particularly their parents and family.

Through this chapter, we first provide a narrative based on the applied experiences of a Senior Sport Psychologist, who will illustrate her experiences of working alongside parents of elite athletes to maximise health, wellbeing, and performance. Next, we provide a critical overview of the role parents and broader social support networks play in enhancing or challenging an individual's wellbeing, before considering how parental/familial involvement can directly and indirectly impact upon athlete wellbeing. From here, we examine literature to highlight how parents can work with athletes, as well as the wider support network, to enhance athlete wellbeing across the lifespan. Drawing on these recommendations, we will conclude the chapter with suggestions for best practice.

PRACTITIONER VOICE

Working with parents to enhance athlete wellbeing: experiences of a sport psychologist

During the last 18 years in my role as a Sport Psychologist, I have worked with over 20 sports and spent significant time in high-performance sporting environments. In these environments, I often meet parents and observe the interactions between them, coaches, and athletes. I am also exposed to any insight provided by coaches on interacting with parents. In the past, many sports believed that parents should be kept on the outside of the athlete environment. I believe the intention of such an approach was to support athletes to develop independence, ownership, and responsibility and minimise chances for conflict between parents/athletes/coaches. In applying this principle in practice, numerous sports I have worked with would, for example, publicly criticise athletes whose parents packed their bags for them. Although such an approach may facilitate the development of athletes' planning and interpersonal skills, experience tells me that such skills can still be achieved, and perhaps even more effectively, by integrating parents.

Parents are often a substantial part of an athletes' support network, and one of, if not the most consistent presence in an athlete's life. Athletes commit substantial time and effort to perform at their highest level and to manage the demands they encounter in this endeavour, it is essential that they are encouraged to draw on their broader support network, including parents. Moreover, ensuring that parents, athletes, and coaches are working together with the same aims will enable athletes to maximise their performance gains and enhance athletes' wellbeing. Recognising the importance of parents within the lives of athletes, I, along with different coaches, practitioners, and sports organisations, have sought to enhance our work with parents over the last few years. Based on these multitudes of experiences, the aim of this narrative is to provide insights into work I have carried out with parents, or pertaining to parents, to enhance athlete wellbeing. To protect the anonymity of individuals, examples from a variety of sports and individuals have been amalgamated.

In my experience, there are numerous benefits that arise when parents are appropriately integrated within athletes' sporting experiences. For instance, by working with parents, we can ensure that they have a full understanding of the context the athlete operates in and are aware of the demands, expectations, and motivations for their child's participation. For instance, coaches and performance directors often talk about the behaviours and skills required to deliver consistent high-level performances, such as good communication, injury management, and physiological monitoring.

If parents understand such expectations and demands, it facilitates more productive conversations across all stakeholders because parents are more likely to ask appropriate questions, provide appropriate support, and know when to get involved (and when to step back). Athletes whose parents understand their sporting context and goals report feeling understood, supported, and that discussions about their sport are productive. Consequently, conflict (and associated negative outcomes) within the home are often avoided. Additionally, athletes and coaches often establish goals for competitions, events, or seasons. If these goals are shared with parents, they can proactively support their athlete in achieving these and will be less likely to discuss inappropriate goals or expectations. In contrast, parents with little understanding of their child's sport or what they are trying to achieve are more likely to hold unrealistic or inappropriate expectations, particularly pertaining to results and selections. Overall, having sought to integrate and work with parents across a variety of sports, the general response has been extremely positive because not only can trust and communication be more open, but also parents can increasingly reinforce coach's messages, role model appropriate behaviours, and help the child to understand expectations and demands. Further, it can enhance parents' experiences, leading to them feeling more valued and better understood.

However, some negative wellbeing consequences can also arise from seeking to incorporate parents within high-performance environments. Understandably, parents want the very best for their child and in doing this, some parents might seek information from external sources and try to take more control of their child's experience. Unfortunately, this can result in some parents believing they can do the coach's job more effectively, and they may start questioning the coach's philosophy. This can have a detrimental effect on an athlete's wellbeing because they may become embarrassed or feel trapped in the middle of conflict. It may impact on a coach's wellbeing because they may feel their abilities are being questioned or challenged as well as adding to an already substantial to-do list. It may also impact on the wellbeing of parents (which can subsequently impact on athletes). Many parents have full-time jobs, additional children to consider, and other activities to fit into the weekly schedule. Expecting mums and dads to also be 'Performance Parents' can add to the already stressful and busy family schedules. Nevertheless, in my experience, the positive benefits of engaging with parents far outweigh such negatives, but only when appropriate, considerate, and thoughtful strategies are utilised to engage parents.

Common practice is changing, and within Wales, we have trialled numerous strategies to support parents, recognising this work as a key part of developing our performance pathway. For example, a strategy that many sports are increasingly engaging with is hosting parent meetings. Specifically, sports invite parents to meet with them at the start of the season so that they can increase their understanding around the pathway, funding, selection policies, expectations, and appropriate communication methods. Anecdotal conversations highlight that conflict is reduced between coaches, parents, and athletes due to parents' increased understanding of the context in which their child and the coach are operating. As such, the wellbeing of the athlete, coach, and parent is enhanced due to all stakeholders understanding the environment and how they function within that. Beyond these initial meetings, I have also often worked with athletes to encourage them to further discuss their environment and experiences with their parents, which can have a huge impact on wellbeing. For instance, one athlete I worked with expressed high levels of stress due to their parents not understanding how to best support them at major games. We responded by helping the athlete educate their parents on their daily schedule. This allowed all involved to understand the demands on the athletes and for the parent to support the athlete more appropriately, minimising their stress.

The outcomes have been even more substantial when I have supported athletes to talk to their parents about the impact their involvement and behaviours are having, not least because parents often do not realise the effect they have. This lack of understanding is often evident in the language used or conversations parents have. For example, a parent of an athlete I was working with expressed to their child that they (the parent) could retire if they made a living out of their sport, whilst another tried to encourage their child to stay in the sport (even when they wanted to stop) because it would open up more opportunities for them. The parents had good intentions, but athletes can interpret these comments very differently, and perceive increases in pressure. So, encouraging the athlete to talk to their parent, and the parent learning about more sensitive and supportive responses is important.

Working directly with parents either individually or in groups to help them understand their own experiences can also be useful. For instance, parents invest a huge amount of time, money, and emotion into their child's sport and also want to minimise the opportunities for their child to experience disappointment or upset. Consequently, it is not surprising that they may have an emotional reaction when the outcome that they or their child is hoping for is not achieved. If athletes witness such reactions from parents, it can add to their distress. Thus, supporting parents to help them understand their own reactions, as well as how to prepare for such situations, is something I have found particularly useful. Further, celebrating parents' contribution to their child's experience can be a great way to help them feel valued, appreciated, and increase their and subsequently their child's wellbeing. For example, I recently held a session with parents asking them what, if anything, they would like support with and acknowledged their contribution to their child's experience. The feedback received on this session was that they felt part of the environment and that they were excited about future support they could provide to their child. This also increased the confidence in the parents that the National Governing Body is focusing on all aspects of their child's development, which has a positive effect on their interactions with their child.

However, there are some challenges to prepare for when seeking to work with parents. The biggest challenge is the time required from everyone involved. The development of such a holistic support structure is still often perceived as an addition rather than a necessity and is often at low priority. Consequently, encouraging engagement and initial commitment can be difficult, irrespective of whether the sport understands the benefits. There have been instances where plans have not been delivered which can increase frustration and stress for parents and athletes. In such instances, the intended initiative becomes counterproductive, and interventions should only be promised if it can be delivered. Other reasons why the initiative can be pushed down the priority list is the amount of work it can take to fully integrate parents of all the athletes involved in a sport. If we consider that there are often upwards of 100 athletes on a performance pathway, that results in a lot of parents to support and consequently it can feel like too big a project to tackle. However, I have learnt that we do not need to be providing numerous information and education sessions to parents. Rather, I have learnt that focusing on changing perceptions regarding parents, focusing on supporting the development of a welcoming, positive environment, and being available informally to chat with parents, and support coaches and athletes around this topic is often more effective. Additionally, as we progress our work in this area, we are increasingly drawing on creative approaches such as vlogs and online discussions/forums for sharing information. However, such approaches are in their infancy and more consideration of the practicalities and limitations of this work continue to be needed.

SCHOLAR VOICE

Enhancing wellbeing: why do we need to consider social support?

Cath's experiences demonstrate that parents form a key element of an athletes' support network and working with them can have huge benefits for athletes. But why is it important to consider athletes' social support network when seeking to enhance athlete wellbeing? Despite the associated physical, social, and psychological benefits of sport and physical activity (see Eime, Young, Harvey, Charity, & Payne, 2013 for a review), the demands of elite level sport may lead to negative wellbeing and poor mental health outcomes for some athletes (Rice et al., 2016). Although the prevalence of certain mental illnesses, such as anxiety and depression, is reported to be similar for athletes as the general population (Schaal et al., 2011), the similarity of symptoms, alongside a culture of toughness in elite sport, may increase the likelihood of certain conditions, such as overtraining syndrome and burnout being diagnosed (Schwenk, 2000). Typically, initial onset of poor mental health (including clinical mental illnesses) occurs during the transition from adolescence into adulthood (Kessler, Berglund, Demler, Jin, & Walters, 2005). Considering the relatively young age at which many elite athletes reach peak performance (Allen & Hopkins, 2015), athletes may be particularly vulnerable to experience poor mental health during their careers. In order to minimise this risk, the wellbeing of athletes deserves considerable attention. The presence of wellbeing in itself may not imply a lack of mental illness or poor mental health, however, high levels of wellbeing may serve as a protective factor against such outcomes occurring (Keyes, 2002).

When considering how to enhance athletes' wellbeing, one consideration is the availability of social support, whereby social support may be considered as the provision of aid and assistance through interpersonal exchanges and within relationships (Beets, Cardinal, & Alderman, 2010). Social support has been shown to be significantly associated with wellbeing in children, adolescents, and older adults alike (Chu, Saucier, & Hafner, 2010; Rook, 2015). The provision of social support has been linked to numerous wellbeing and good mental health outcomes, such as reduced negative affect and vulnerability to clinical mental illness (Cohen & Wills, 1985; Keyes, 2002). For those who do experience poor mental health (including clinical mental illnesses), individuals with a larger social network have been shown to score more highly on certain recovery indicators, such as hope and goal orientation (Corrigan & Phelan, 2004). Conversely, a lack of social support has been associated with poor mental health and ill-being outcomes, such as cognitive decline, depression, and, in some cases, psychosis (see Hawkley & Cacioppo, 2010 for a review). In particular, Grav, Hellzèn, Romild, and Stordal (2012) reported a positive association between lack of social support and clinical depression. This association was present after controlling for age, gender, and support type, highlighting the important role social support plays in influencing individuals' wellbeing throughout the lifespan.

However, the relationship between social support and wellbeing is complex (see Shumaker & Brownell, 1984); not all social support is associated with wellbeing outcomes, and in some situations it appears that social support can actually have a negative effect on an individual's wellbeing, leading to outcomes of ill-being (Rook, 1984; Antonucci, Akiyama, & Lansford, 1998). The positive effects of social support may be particularly helpful during stressful situations. For instance, evidence suggests that social support has a direct effect on wellbeing, as well as a buffering effect on the negative consequences of stress on wellbeing (Cohen & Wills, 1985). In addition, the positive relationship between social support and good mental health is significantly enhanced in situations where the support provided is considered necessary (Melrose, Brown, & Wood, 2015). However, when support is deemed to be unnecessary by the recipient, wellbeing may be negatively affected (Williamson, Oliger, Wheeler, & O'Hara, 2019). One explanation for this is that excessive support (e.g. too much contact, giving unwanted advice, or making decisions on behalf of an individual) increases levels of stress, by undermining recipients' independence, which results in one feeling a lack of control (Boutin-Foster, 2005). Indeed, individuals who rate independence as more important display higher levels of depressive symptoms in response to support, compared to individuals who rate independence as less important (Martire, Stephens, Druley, & Wojno, 2002).

Various other factors may also determine the effect that social support has on wellbeing (Gariepy, Honkaniemi, & Quesnel-Vallée, 2016; Merz & Huxhold, 2010). For example, support provided by more salient sources (e.g. parental support for children) has a more significant effect on wellbeing outcomes than support provided by less salient sources (e.g. teachers, peers) (Gariepy et al., 2016). In addition, the effects of social support on wellbeing may also be determined by the type of support being offered by the provider, with Merz and Huxhold (2010) reporting differences in the effect that emotional or instrumental support (e.g. providing comfort or helping with practical tasks, such as cooking and cleaning) provided by family members or non-family members on wellbeing outcomes. To expand, emotional support provided by family members, as well as instrumental support provided by non-family members positively affected subjective wellbeing. However, instrumental support provided by family members negatively affected subjective wellbeing, although the study reported this effect was moderated by relationship quality. Interestingly, emotional support provided by non-family members did not have an effect on participants' subjective wellbeing in this study, highlighting the importance of emotional support provided by family members in relation to subjective wellbeing.

Enhancing wellbeing in sport: what is the value of working with parents?

For athletes, as with the general population, social support plays an important role in relation to wellbeing (Rees & Hardy, 2000; Rosenfeld, Richman, & Hardy, 1989). For instance, social support may enhance athlete wellbeing by promoting autonomy and enhancing athletes' enjoyment of sport (Gagné, 2003), while a lack of social support has been associated with athlete burnout; a condition that is thought to reflect low levels of psychological wellbeing caused by feelings of autonomy loss and social isolation (e.g. Coakley, 1992; Creswell, 2009). This importance has been highlighted by athletes themselves, who report utilising different types of support from various sources, to cope with the demands associated with sport (e.g. Brady & Shambrook, 2003; Rees & Hardy, 2000). Social support has been linked to various positive outcomes associated with athlete wellbeing, such as increased motivation, enhanced satisfaction, and decreased risk of burnout (Sheridan, Coffee, & Lavallee, 2014 for a review).

In particular, social support may be particularly important for enhancing the wellbeing of athletes who are injured or transitioning out of sport (e.g. Brown, Webb, Robinson, & Cotgreave, 2018; Lu & Hsu, 2013). For example, for athletes transitioning out of elite sport, whether as young athletes leaving a high-performance system (an academy or talent pathway programme) due to, for instance, deselection, or an established adult athlete retiring, social support has been shown to help alleviate distress (Brown et al., 2018; Neely, McHugh, Dunn, & Holt, 2017). However, providing appropriate support in such instances, particularly within high-performance youth sport environments, is not always easy (Burgess, Knight, & Mellalieu, 2016; Neely et al., 2017). Firstly, for social support to positively impact on athlete wellbeing in any given situation, the support provider needs to deliver the right type of support, as perceived by the athlete (Hassell, Sabiston, & Bloom, 2010). Secondly, the support provider should ensure that the type of support provided matches the stressor, as this has been shown to play a key role in mediating the effects of social support on athlete wellbeing (Mitchell, Evans, Rees, & Hardy, 2014). Finally, particularly within competitive youth sport settings, the main support provider is often parents who may find managing their child's distress and disappointment challenging (Harwood, Drew, & Knight, 2010) and consequently be unable to provide the necessary support to their child until they have been able to process their own emotional response (Neely et al., 2017).

Throughout their sporting career, athletes draw on support from a range of sources, including coaches, teammates, friends, and practitioners to help them manage demands and, hopefully, excel, within the sport environment (Wylleman & Lavallee, 2004). Beyond these individuals, parents, siblings, and other family members are a particularly important part of their support network (Bloom, 1985; Côté, 1999; Knight, Berrow, & Harwood, 2017). Although other individuals enter and leave an athlete's sporting journey at different times, the support and involvement of parents and family are (hopefully) enduring (Fredricks & Eccles, 2004; Harwood & Knight, 2015). Parents are usually responsible for introducing children to sport, encouraging their initial love of physical activity, and providing the resources needed to begin their initiate and continue their involvement (Côté, 1999; Lauer, Gould, Roman, & Pierce, 2010). As children progress in sport, parents usually provide a range of support to facilitate their involvement (Wolfenden & Holt, 2005; Wuerth, Lee, & Alfermann, 2004). For instance, parents continue to fund participation and commit time to transporting children to training and competitions, washing kit, and learning about their child's sport (Knight & Holt, 2014). Furthermore, parents often provide emotional support during periods of injury or disappointments, encouraging children from the sidelines, picking them up after poor performances, or celebrating with them when they do well (Knight & Holt, 2014). They also source information about aspects, such as the pathway for progression, competitions to enter, and nutritional demands, which they subsequently share with their children (cf. Knight & Holt, 2013). Throughout their child's athletic journey, the specifics of support needs might change, but no matter their age or stage of development, access to parental support seems necessary (Harwood & Knight, 2015).

Recognising the numerous types of support provided by (and needed from) parents within sport settings, it is widely accepted that without parental involvement, children would be unlikely to be able to participate (Knight & Holt, 2014). Moreover, studies have indicated that parental support can enhance or mediate athletes' self-esteem (Kang, Joen, Kwon, & Park, 2015), vitality (Felton & Jowett, 2013), perceptions of positive body image (Voelker & Reel, 2015), and enhance the overall psychological wellbeing (Nunomura & Santos Oliveira, 2013). Additionally, autonomy support from parents has been shown to positively influence athletes' motivation (Hein & Jõesaar, 2015; Keegan, Harwood, Spray, & Lavallee, 2014), increase athletes' sense of competence (Amado, Sánchez-Oliva, González-Ponce, Pulido-González, & Sánchez-Miguel, 2015), and enhance self-esteem and vitality (Gagné, 2010). In contrast, if athletes perceive a lack of support from their parents, it can result in symptoms of psychological ill-being (Van Yperen, 1998), while feelings of parental pressure or criticism can result in increases in perfectionistic worry (Ommundsen, Roberts, Lemyre, & Miller, 2006), concerns about making mistakes (McArdle & Duda, 2004) and decreases in self-esteem (Harrist & Witt, 2015). Moreover, if a parent adopts a more controlling parenting style, athletes report poorer motivation (Borman & Kurdek, 1987), as well as reductions in self-esteem and vitality (Gagné, 2010).

Unfortunately, although parents might seek to be an appropriate source of social support for their children, and engage in behaviours and practices that will result in positive outcomes such as those listed earlier, the line between appropriate and inappropriate is not always clear or consistent (Knight et al., 2017; Knight & Holt, 2014). It has been argued that it is an individual's *perception* of support, rather than simply the presence of support, that may have the greatest influence on wellbeing (e.g. Sarason, Pierce, & Sarason, 1990), such a finding is replicated within sport (DeFreese & Smith, 2014; Hassell et al., 2010). For example, athletes who perceive support providers to offer a preferred type of support report a positive effect on their wellbeing, whereas when the support offered by the provider is perceived as non-preferential, athletes report negative effects (Hassell et al., 2010).

Perceptions of support may be shaped by the specific environment in which an individual is situated, the relationship quality between the support provider and receiver, as well as the personal characteristics of the individual (Coyne & DeLongis, 1986; Diener & Seligman, 2002; Gallagher & Vella-Brodrick, 2008). For instance, adolescent athletes have indicated that they want their parents to be supportive without being pressuring at competitions and provided suggestions of ways in which parents can do this (e.g. not providing tactical advice, helping with physical preparation, encouraging both teams, respecting sporting etiquette, and providing honest but positive feedback after games) (Knight, Boden, & Holt, 2010). However, athletes have also indicated that the types of behaviours that are supportive from parents will vary depending upon the context (e.g. home, training, and competitions; Knight, Little, Harwood, & Goodger, 2016), the timing (e.g. before, during, or after competitions; Knight, Neely, & Holt, 2011), as well as their goals for sport and that specific competition (Knight & Holt, 2014), and the outcome of the game or competition (Knight et al., 2010, 2011; Knight & Holt, 2014).

Such specific needs and desires regarding parental involvement and behaviours are frequently witnessed by practitioners working in the field with athletes. For instance, as Cath shared, athletes can, understandably, experience heightened stress and demands in the lead-up to and during major competitions (e.g. Olympics and Commonwealth games). In such situations, behaviours that would have previously been desirable/welcomed by the athlete (such as regular conversations about a competition) may become undesirable and potentially have negative effects on athlete wellbeing. Therefore, less discussion about any upcoming competition may be welcomed more by the athlete. As Cath explained, ensuring that such changes in preferences are discussed and understood by all members of the athlete's support network, but particularly parents, will likely be extremely valuable.

Given such complexity, there is potential for parents to provide inappropriate types of support which may subsequently have a negative rather than the desired positive impact on wellbeing. Thus, it appears particularly important that parent(s) take time to talk to their individual child(ren) to learn about the types of support they find beneficial in different situations to maximise positive outcomes. Such conversations and communication between parents and their children regarding support are particularly important because, as Cath shared earlier in this chapter, parents do not always realise how their children are interpreting their behaviours with research indicating that parents and children can differ substantially regarding their perceptions of support within sport settings (Charbonneau & Camiré, 2019; Kanters, Bocarro, & Casper, 2008). For instance, in a recent cross-sectional study, Dorsch, Smith, and Dotterer (2016) sought to understand (among other aims), the concordance of parents and children's perceptions of a variety of parental influences as well as feelings of pressure or support. Data were collected from athletes aged 11–13 years of age and their parents, and the overall findings indicated a modest correspondence among fathers, mothers, and children. Such findings led the authors to conclude that, "The considerable lack of agreement across raters suggest that sport experiences fall on a continuum from more to less shared" (p. 139), reiterating the challenge parents may encounter in trying to provide the "right" types of support for their child.

The extent to which athletes perceive support positively and experience enhanced wellbeing outcomes may be influenced by the responsiveness of said support (Rouquette, Knight, Lovett, & Heuzé, under review). That is, the extent to which parents and family members are seen to be providing support that is sensitive and responsive to an athlete's needs and wishes may impact upon athletes' wellbeing (Reis, 2012). It is suggested that responsiveness is underpinned by three components: understanding, validation, and feeling cared for (Reis, 2012). Findings from a recent study examining the impact of athletes' perception of parental responsive support indicated that it increases athletes' self-perceptions and thriving (Rouquette et al., under review). The extent to which parents can provide responsive support may be related to the quality of the parent–athlete relationships (Clarke, Harwood, & Cushion, 2016; Knight & Holt, 2014), which can also impact on wellbeing (Melnick, Dunkelman, & Mashiach, 1981). Such findings reinforce the importance of parents regularly conversing with their child to gain a comprehensive understanding of their specific needs at different times in their athletic journey, an activity that has been well utilised and positively received by the parents that Cath has been working with.

Finally, it is important that parental support and involvement are considered within the broader social network. As previously indicated, the impact of social support on an individual's wellbeing depends not only on support provided by one individual but also the availability of such support from others. Within youth sport, the presence and involvement of others (i.e. coaches and peers) in the environment can alter the outcomes of parents' behaviours (Knight et al., 2017). For instance, the impact of parents' autonomy support on children's motivation is influenced by the autonomy support provided by children's peers and coaches (Gaudreau et al., 2016; Schwebel, Smith, & Smoll, 2016). In their two-part study, Gaudreau and colleagues (2016) sought to understand the impacts of parent and coach autonomy support on sport-related outcomes, such as motivation, need satisfaction, achievement, and flow. Their findings indicated that parental autonomy support moderated the effects of coaching autonomy support; that is, when higher levels of parental autonomy support were available, coach influence was reduced and vice versa. Thus, it appears that the impact parents have upon their children's wellbeing may, to some degree, be influenced by their access to support from others. Given such combined influences of the social support network on athlete's wellbeing, ensuring that work with parents and athletes does not happen in isolation is key. Rather, as Cath illustrated in her narrative, ensuring there is support from, and engagement with, not only athletes and parents but also coaches, performance directors, and the broader sports organisation is important to maximise the positive benefits that can arise from engaging with parents.

Strategies for optimising parental and family support to enhance wellbeing

As indicated by Cath, although the support that parents and family members provide to athletes can positively influence wellbeing, this support also has the potential to contribute to state of ill-being in certain circumstances. As such, it may be useful for parents and family members to consider strategies which may optimise the likelihood of support that they provide enhancing the wellbeing of the athlete. We offer some concluding strategies for putting this into practice when working with parents:

- Parents and family members may find it useful to remember the provision of support may not always be beneficial, particularly if the athlete does not perceive the support to be available (Hassell et al., 2010; Sarason et al., 1990). Therefore, it may help to be explicit about the support that is being offered to the athlete, to increase the likelihood that they will perceive the support to be available.
- Support provision that is perceived as excessive, unresponsive, inappropriately timed, or delivered in the incorrect contexts may also lead to outcomes associated with ill-being. Therefore, parents and family members may find it helpful to talk to the athlete to establish the amount and type of support they feel they require. As an athlete's support needs will vary throughout their career (Wylleman & Lavallee, 2004), it will be important that such conversations happen between parents, athletes, and the broader support network at regular intervals throughout a season and career.
- The development of quality relationships between family members and the athlete may not only increase athlete wellbeing but also buffer any detrimental wellbeing effects which may occur if support type is not perceived to be preferable (Merz & Huxhold, 2010). Thus, focusing on the broader quality of a parent–child relationship, not solely support provision, is also advised when seeking to enhance athletes' wellbeing.

Finally, within the athletes' social support network, the influence of parents is instrumental to athlete wellbeing. However, the amount of parental influence is moderated by others in the social support network (i.e. coaches, other athletes). Therefore, in order to provide optimum support for the athlete, it is essential that all members of the social support network are communicating, engaging, and working together. This final recommendation is key to sustaining enhanced experiences of wellbeing across the athlete's journey.

References

Allen, S. V., & Hopkins, W. G. (2015). Age of peak competitive performance of elite athletes: A systematic review. *Sports Medicine, 45,* 1431–1441. https://doi.org/10.1007/s40279-015-0354-3

Amado, D., Sánchez-Oliva, D., González-Ponce, I., Pulido-González, J. J., & Sánchez-Miguel, P. A. (2015). Incidence of parental support and pressure on their children's motivational processes towards sport practice regarding gender. *PLoS One, 10,* 1–14. https://doi.org/10.1371/journal.pone.0128015

Antonucci, T. C., Akiyama, H., & Lansford, J. E. (1998). Negative effects of close social relations. *Family Relations, 47*(4), 379–384. https://doi.org/10.2307/585268

Beets, M. W., Cardinal, B. J., & Alderman, B. L. (2010). Parental social support and the physical activity-related behaviors of youth: A review. *Health Education & Behavior, 37*(5), 621–644. https://doi.org/10.1177/1090198110363884

Bloom, B. (1985). *Developing talent in young people.* New York: Ballantine Books.

Borman, K. M., & Kurdek, L. A. (1987). Gender differences associated with playing high school varsity soccer. *Journal of Youth and Adolescence, 16,* 379–400. https://doi.org/10.1007/BF02138468

Boutin-Foster, C. (2005). In spite of good intentions: Patients' perspectives on problematic social support interactions. *Health and Quality of Life Outcomes, 3,* 52. https://doi.org/10.1186/1477-7525-3-52

Brady, A., & Shambrook, C. (2003). Towards an understanding of elite athlete quality of life: A phenomenological study. *Journal of Sports Sciences, 21,* 341–342.

Brown, C. J., Webb, T. L., Robinson, M. A., & Cotgreave, R. (2018). Athletes' experiences of social support during their transition out of elite sport: An interpretive phenomenological analysis. *Psychology of Sport and Exercise, 36,* 71–80. https://doi.org/10.1016/j.psychsport.2018.01.003

Burgess, N. S., Knight, C. J., & Mellalieu, S. D. (2016). Parental stress and coping in elite youth gymnastics: An interpretative phenomenological analysis. *Qualitative Research in Sport, Exercise, and Health, 8*(3), 237–256. https://doi.org/10.1080/2159676X.2015.1134633

Charbonneau, E. F., & Camiré, M. (2019). Parental involvement in sport and the satisfaction of basic psychological needs: Perspectives from parent-child dyads. *International Journal of Sport and Exercise Psychology,* 1–17. https://doi.org/10.1080/1612197X.2019.1570533

Chu, P. S., Saucier, D. A., & Hafner, E. (2010). Meta-analysis of the relationships between social support and well-being in children and adolescents. *Journal of Social and Clinical Psychology, 29*(6), 624–645. https://doi.org/10.1521/jscp.2010.29.6.624

Clarke, N. J., Harwood, C. G., & Cushion, C. J. (2016). A phenomenological interpretation of the parent-child relationship in elite youth football. *Sport, Exercise, and Performance Psychology, 5*(2), 125–143. https://doi.org/10.1037/spy0000052

Coakley, J. (1992). Burnout among adolescent athletes: A personal failure or social problem? *Sociology of Sport Journal, 9*(3), 271–285. https://doi.org/10.1123/ssj.9.3.271

Cohen, S., & Wills, T. A. (1985). Stress, social support, and the buffering hypothesis. *Psychological Bulletin, 98*(2), 310–357. https://doi.org/10.1037/0033-2909.98.2.310

Corrigan, P. W., & Phelan, S. M. (2004). Social support and recovery in people with serious mental illness. *Community Mental Health Journal, 40,* 513–523. https://doi.org/10.1007/s10597-004-6125-5

Côté, J. (1999). The influence of the family in the development of talent in sport. *The Sport Psychologist, 13*(4), 395–417. https://doi.org/10.1123/tsp.13.4.395

Coyne, J. C., & DeLongis, A. (1986). Going beyond social support: The role of social relationships in adaptation. *Journal of Consulting and Clinical Psychology, 54*(4), 454–460. https://doi.org/10.1037/0022-006X.54.4.454

Creswell, J. (2009). *Research design: Qualitative, quantitative, and mixed methods approaches* (3rd ed.). Thousand Oaks, CA: Sage.

DeFreese, J. D., & Smith, A. L. (2014). Athlete social support, negative social interactions, and psychological health across a competitive sport season. *Journal of Sport & Exercise Psychology, 36*(6), 619–630. https://doi.org/10.1123/jsep.2014-0040

Diener, E., & Seligman, M. E. (2002). Very Happy People. *Psychological Science, 13*, 81–84. https://doi.org/10.1111/1467-9280.00415

Dorsch, T. E., Smith, A. L., & Dotterer, A. M. (2016). Individual, relationship, and context factors associated with parent support and pressure in organized youth sport. *Psychology of Sport & Exercise, 23*, 132–141. https://doi.org/10.1016/j.psychsport.2015.12.003

Eime, R. M., Young, J. A., Harvey, J. T., Charity, M. J., & Payne, W. R. (2013). A systematic review of the psychological and social benefits of participation in sport for children and adolescents: Informing development of a conceptual model of health through sport. *International Journal of Behavioral Nutrition and Physical Activity, 10*, 98. https://doi.org/10.1186/1479-5868-10-98

Felton, L., & Jowett, S. (2013). Attachment and well-being: The mediating effects of psychological needs satisfaction within the coach–athlete and parent–athlete relational contexts. *Psychology of Sport and Exercise, 14*, 57–65. https://doi.org/10.1016/j.psychsport.2012.07.006

Fredricks, J. A., & Eccles, J. S. (2004). Parental influences on youth involvements in sports. In M. R. Weiss (Ed.), *Development sport and exercise psychology: A lifespan perspective* (pp. 145–164). Morgantown, WV: Fitness Information Technology.

Gagné, M. (2003). The role of autonomy support and autonomy orientation in prosocial behavior engagement. *Motivation and Emotion, 27*, 199–223. https://doi.org/10.1023/A:1025007614869

Gagné, M. (2010). Autonomy support and need satisfaction in the motivation and well-being of gymnasts. *Journal of Applied Sport Psychology, 15*(4), 372–390. https://doi.org/10.1080/714044203

Gallagher, E. N., & Vella-Brodrick, D. A. (2008). Social Support and Emotional Intelligence as Predictors of Subjective Well-Being. *Personality and Individual Differences, 44*(7), 1551–1561. https://doi.org/10.1016/j.paid.2008.01.011

Gariepy, G., Honkaniemi, H., & Quesnel-Vallée, A. (2016). Social support and protection from depression: Systematic review of current findings in Western countries. *British Journal of Psychiatry, 209*(4), 286–295. https://doi.org/10.1192/bjp.bp.115.169094

Gaudreau, P., Morinville, A., Gareau, A., Verner-Filion, J., Green-Demers, I., & Franche, V. (2016). Autonomy support from parents and coaches: Synergistic or compensatory effects on sport-related outcomes of adolescent-athletes? *Psychology of Sport and Exercise, 25*, 89–99. https://doi.org/10.1016/j.psychsport.2016.04.006

Grav, S., Hellzèn, O., Romild, U., & Stordal, E. (2012). Association between social support and depression in the general population: The HUNT study, a cross-sectional survey. *Journal of Clinical Nursing, 21*, 111–120. https://doi.org/10.1111/j.1365-2702.2011.03868.x

Harrist, C. J., & Witt, P. A. (2015). Calling the screens: Self-reported developmental outcomes in competitive basketball. *Journal of Adolescent Research, 30*(6), 751–778. https://doi.org/10.1177/0743558414561293

Harwood, C. G., Drew, A., & Knight, C. J. (2010). Parental stressors in professional youth football academies: A qualitative investigation in specializing stage parents. *Qualitative Research in Sport and Exercise Sciences*, 2(1), 39–55. https://doi.org/10.1080/19398440903510152

Harwood, C. G., & Knight, C. J. (2015). Parenting in youth sport: A position paper on parenting expertise. *Psychology of Sport and Exercise*, 16(1), 24–35. https://doi.org/10.1016/j.psychsport.2014.03.001

Hassell, K., Sabiston, C. M., & Bloom, G. A. (2010). Exploring the multiple dimensions of social support among elite female adolescent swimmers. *International Journal of Sport Psychology*, 41, 340–359.

Hawkley, L. C., & Cacioppo, J. T. (2010). Loneliness matters: A theoretical and empirical review of consequences and mechanisms. *Annals of Behavioral Medicine*, 40(2), 218–227. https://doi.org/10.1007/s12160-010-9210-8

Hein, V., & Jõesaar, H. (2015). How perceived autonomy support from adults and peer motivational climate are related with self-determined motivation among young athletes. *International Journal of Sport and Exercise Psychology*, 13(3), 193–204. https://doi.org/10.1080/1612197X.2014.947304

Kang, S., Jeon, H., Kwon, S., & Park, S. (2015). Parental attachment as a mediator between parental social support and self-esteem as perceived by Korean sports middle and high school athletes. *Perceptual and Motor Skills*, 120, 288–303. https://doi.org/10.2466/10.PMS.120v11x6

Kanters, M. A., Bocarro, J., & Casper, J. M. (2008). Supported or pressured? An examination of agreement among parent's and children on parent's role in youth sports. *Journal of Sport Behavior*, 31(1), 64–81.

Keegan, R. J., Harwood, C. G., Spray, C. M., & Lavallee, D. (2014). A qualitative investigation of the motivational climate in elite sport. *Psychology of Sport and Exercise*, 15(1), 97–107. https://doi.org/10.1016/j.psychsport.2013.10.006

Kessler, R. C., Berglund, P., Demler, O., Jin, R., & Walters, E. E. (2005). Lifetime prevalence and age-of-onset distributions of *DSM-IV* disorders in the National Comorbidity Survey Replication. *Archives of General Psychiatry*, 62(2), 593–602. https://doi.org/10.1001/archpsyc.62.6.593

Keyes, C. L. M. (2002). The mental health continuum: From languishing to flourishing in life. *Journal of Health and Social Behavior*, 43(2), 207–222. https://doi.org/10.2307/3090197

Knight, C. J., & Holt, N. L. (2013). Strategies used and assistance required to facilitate children's involvement in tennis: Parents' perspectives. *The Sport Psychologist*, 27(3), 281–291. https://doi.org/10.1123/tsp.27.3.281

Knight, C. J., & Holt, N. L. (2014). Parenting in youth tennis: Understanding and enhancing children's experiences. *Psychology of Sport and Exercise*, 15(2), 155–164. https://doi.org/10.1016/j.psychsport.2013.10.010

Knight, C. J., Berrow, S. R., & Harwood, C. G. (2017). Parenting in sport. *Current Opinion in Psychology*, 16, 93–97. https://doi.org/10.1016/j.copsyc.2017.03.011

Knight, C. J., Boden, C. M., & Holt, N. L. (2010). Junior tennis players' preferences for parental behaviors. *Journal of Applied Sport Psychology*, 22(4), 377–391. https://doi.org/10.1080/10413200.2010.495324

Knight, C. J., Little, G. C. D., Harwood, C. G., & Goodger, K. (2016). Parental involvement in elite junior slalom canoeing. *Journal of Applied Sport Psychology*, 28(2), 234–256. https://doi.org/10.1080/10413200.2015.1111273

Knight, C. J., Neely, K. C., & Holt, N. L. (2011). Parental behaviors in team sports: How do female athletes want parents to behave? *Journal of Applied Sport Psychology*, 23(1), 76–92. https://doi.org/10.1080/10413200.2010.525589

Lauer, L., Gould, D., Roman, N., & Pierce, M. (2010). How parents influence junior tennis players' development: Qualitative narratives. *Journal of Clinical Sport Psychology*, 4(1), 69–92. https://doi.org/10.1123/jcsp.4.1.69

Lu, F. J. H., & Hsu, Y. (2013). Injured athletes' rehabilitation beliefs and subjective well-being: The contribution of hope and social support. *Journal of Athletic Training*, 48(1), 92–98. https://doi.org/10.4085/1062-6050-48.1.03

Martire, L. M., Stephens, M. A. P., Druley, J. A., & Wojno, W. C. (2002). Negative reactions to received spousal care: Predictors and consequences of miscarried support. *Health Psychology*, 21(2), 167–176. https://doi.org/10.1037//0278-6133.21.2.167

McArdle, S., & Duda, J. L. (2004). Exploring social-contextual correlates of perfectionism in adolescents: A multivariate perspective. *Cognitive Therapy and Research*, 28, 765–788. https://doi.org/10.1007/s10608-004-0665-4

Melnick, M. J., Dunkelman, N., & Mashiach, A. (1981). Familial factors of sports giftedness among young Israeli athletes. *Journal of Sport Behavior*, 4(2), 82–94.

Melrose, K. L., Brown, G. D., & Wood, A. M. (2015). When is received social support related to perceived support and well-being? When it is needed. *Personality and Individual Differences*, 77, 97–105. https://doi.org/10.1016/j.paid.2014.12.047

Merz, E. M., & Huxhold, O. (2010). Wellbeing depends on social relationship characteristics: Comparing different types and providers of support to older adults. *Ageing and Society*, 30(5), 843–857. https://doi.org/10.1017/S0144686X10000061

Mitchell, I., Evans, L., Rees, T., & Hardy, L. (2014). Stressors, social support and the buffering hypothesis: Effects on psychological responses of injured athletes. *British Journal of Health Psychology*, 19(3), 486–508. https://doi.org/10.1111/bjhp.12046

Neely, K. C., McHugh, T.-L. F., Dunn, J. G. H., & Holt, N. L. (2017). Athletes and parents coping with deselection in competitive youth sport: A communal coping perspective. *Psychology of Sport and Exercise*, 30, 1–9. https://doi.org/10.1016/j.psychsport.2017.01.004

Nunomura, M., & Santos Oliveira, M. (2013). Parents' support in the sport career of young gymnasts. *Science of Gymnastics Journal*, 5(1), 5–17.

Ommundsen, Y., Roberts, G. C., Lemyre, P.-N., & Miller, B. W. (2006). Parental and coach support or pressure on psychosocial outcomes of pediatric athletes in soccer. *Clinical Journal of Sport Medicine*, 16(6), 522–526. https://doi.org/10.1097/01.jsm.0000248845.39498.5

Rees, T., & Hardy, L. (2000). An Investigation of the social support experiences of high-level sports performers. *The Sport Psychologist*, 14(4), 327–347. https://doi.org/10.1123/tsp.14.4.327

Reis, H. T. (2012). Perceived partner responsiveness as an organizing theme for the study of relationships and well-being. In L. Campbell & T. J. Loving (Eds.), *Interdisciplinary research on close relationships: The case for integration* (pp. 27–52). Washington, DC: APA.

Rice, S. M., Purcell, R., De Silva, S., Mawren, D., McGorry, P. D., & Parker, A. G. (2016). The mental health of elite athletes: A narrative systematic review. *Sports Medicine*, 46, 1333–1353. https://doi.org/10.1007/s40279-016-0492-2

Rook, K. S. (1984). The negative side of social interaction: Impact on psychological well-being. *Journal of Personality and Social Psychology*, 46(5), 1097–1108. https://doi.org/10.1037/0022-3514.46.5.1097

Rook, K. S. (2015). Social networks in later life: Weighing positive and negative effects on health and well-being. *Current Directions in Psychological Science*, 24(1), 45–51. https://doi.org/10.1177/0963721414551364

Rosenfeld, L. B., Richman, J. M., & Hardy, C. J. (1989). Examining social support networks among athletes: Description and relationship to stress. *Sport Psychologist*, 3(1), 23–33. https://doi.org/10.1123/tsp.3.1.23

Rouquette, O. Y., Knight, C. J., Lovett, V. E., & Heuzé, J.-P. (under review). The effect of parent-child responsive interactions in youth sport: An exploratory study.

Sarason, B. R., Pierce, G. R., & Sarason, I. G. (1990). Social support: The sense of acceptance and the role of relationships. In B. R. Sarason, I. G. Sarason, & G. R. Pierce (Eds.), *Social support: An interactional view* (pp. 97–128). Hoboken, NJ: John Wiley & Sons.

Schaal, K., Tafflet, M., Nassif, H., Thibault, V., Pichard, C., Alcotte, M., Guillet, T., El Helou, N., . . . & Toussaint, J-F., (2011). Psychological balance in high level athletes: Gender-based differences and sport-specific patterns. *PLoS ONE*, 6, 5. https://doi.org/10.1371/journal.pone.0019007

Schwebel, F. J., Smith, R. E., & Smoll, F. L. (2016). Measurement of perceived parental success standards in sport and relations with athletes' self-esteem, performance anxiety, and achievement goal orientation: Comparing parental and coach influences. *Child Development Research*. 1–13. https://doi.org/10.1155/2016/7056075

Schwenk, T. L. (2000). The stigmatization and denial of mental illness in athletes. *British Journal of Sports Medicine*, 34(1), 4–5. http://doi.org/10.1136/bjsm.34.1.4

Sheridan, D., Coffee, P., & Lavallee, D. (2014). A systematic review of social support in youth sport. *International Review of Sport and Exercise Psychology*, 7(1), 198–228. https://doi.org/10.1080/1750984X.2014.931999

Shumaker, S. A., & Brownell, A. (1984). Toward a theory of social support: Closing conceptual gaps. *Journal of Social Issues*, 40, 11–36. https://doi.org/10.1111/j.1540-4560.1984.tb01105.x

Van Yperen, N. W. (1998). Being a sport parent: Buffering the effect of your talented child's poor performance on his or her subjective well-being. *International Journal of Sport Psychology*, 29, 45–56.

Voelker, D. K., & Reel, J. J. (2015). An inductive thematic analysis of female competitive figure skaters' experiences of weight pressure in sport. *Journal of Clinical Sport Psychology*, 9(4), 297–316. https://doi.org/10.1123/jcsp.2015-0012

Williamson, J. A., Oliger, C., Wheeler, A., & O'Hara, M. W. (2019). More social support is associated with more positive mood but excess support is associated with more negative mood. *Journal of Social and Personal Relationships*, 36(11–12), 3588–3610. https://doi.org/10.1177/0265407519831771

Wolfenden, L. E., & Holt, N. L. (2005). Talent development in elite junior tennis: Perceptions of players, parents, and coaches. *Journal of Applied Sport Psychology*, 17(2), 108–126. https://doi.org/10.1080/10413200590932416

Wuerth, S., Lee, M. J., & Alfermann, D. (2004). Parental involvement and athletes' career in youth sport. *Psychology of Sport and Exercise*, 5(1), 21–33. https://doi.org/10.1016/S1469-0292(02)00047-X

Wylleman, P., & Lavallee, D. (2004). A developmental perspective on transitions faced by athletes. In M. R. Weiss (Ed.), *Developmental sport and exercise psychology: Research status on youth and directions toward a lifespan perspective* (pp. 503–523). Morgantown, WV: Fitness Information Technology.

4
DUAL CAREERS AND ATHLETE WELLBEING

Lindsay Woodford and Claire-Marie Roberts

Introduction

There is a growing body of literature supporting the importance of dual careers in assisting athletes to prepare for their athletic retirement. Indeed, many countries have developed dual career programmes to help athletes combine their sport and academic aspirations. However, the commitment to fulfilling a dual career for an athlete can lead to added anxieties and tensions caused by the likely entrenchment in two environments that are subject to high evaluation. This chapter explores some of the challenges of maintaining a dual career and the adverse effect that this can have on athlete wellbeing.

> **ATHLETE VOICE**
>
> **Grace's story**
>
> I'm a female beach volleyball player on a scholarship in an American University. I moved here not only to better my chances of reaching my goals of being a Commonwealth and Olympic Gold medallist but also to help lay foundations for a career post sport. Moving to America meant I could get a fully funded college degree plus access to some of the best trainers. There isn't really anywhere in the UK that has set up a programme where you can train every single day in my sport and get a college education at the same time. In America, there's definitely more support for athletes pursuing a dual career. At my university, you have access to coaches, assistant coaches and athlete support personnel. My coaches say that school comes first, so I was always told 'you are a student-athlete, and it is that way round for a reason'.

DOI: 10.4324/9780429287923-4

When I arrived in America, I originally enrolled in a sport science degree. Although I initially did well with my grades, I sensed that the course was going to get harder. This caused me fluctuating levels of stress once I realised what was expected of me academically. I was also stressed about the prospect of not getting good grades and all of the 'what ifs' associated with not doing well academically. I decided that I hadn't flown halfway across the world to be stressed about this. I also knew that I didn't want to come all the way out here to spend every day studying and not being able to get extra practice or enjoy living in a different country. So, as a lifestyle choice, I decided to change courses. And I felt that if I hadn't made that change, I would have spent a lot more time studying which was exactly what I didn't want to do, and as I have observed in other athletes, it had the potential to impact negatively on my wellbeing.

My second choice of course was a major in Communications and a minor in Psychology. Apart from my lifestyle choices, this course is a lot easier in terms of workload and it offers me a wider range of job options after I graduate. I'm not 100% sure of what I want to go into, I want to play volleyball as long as I can and then stay in the sport, probably coaching. As student-athlete, we are expected to achieve a minimum grade point average (GPA) in our studies. As a result, our academic performance is heavily scrutinised. If you continuously perform poorly in your academic work, you're given mandatory study hall hours or the requirement to see extra tutors or both. In a couple of instances, we have had girls who have not been allowed to practice with us because their schoolwork wasn't up to scratch. Some girls have had to leave the team because everything just slipped and they couldn't get it back. The constant threat of this is stressful and it impacts on your ability to socialise and relax. But then this year it irritated me that they were all happy because we had a really high GPA, it was like a 3.8 as a team, which is really good. But then we didn't achieve our goals volleyball-wise. And so, to me it's like 'well maybe if people didn't put so much focus on their homework, we might have achieved our volleyball goals'.

In general, although it's the right thing to do, pursuing a dual career is very stressful. I can only work so many hours on campus a week, due to being an international student and obviously I can't get a job outside of campus either. This adds an extra financial stress because you can't earn money, but you still have to spend it! Additionally, having such a busy existence impacts on my ability to socialise and have downtime. I tend to stay in my athletic group, which I think in a wellbeing sense is isolating. In class, I'm very friendly with people that sit next to me, but you don't have time to hang out with them unless you have to work on a group project. Their schedules just don't fit with mine.

Even within my athletic group of friends, there's a big difference between preseason and season. During the season, no one socialises because once you're done with practice, you have to do homework. In preseason, when you have a little bit more energy, and a little bit more time, people have time to socialise with each other more. I isolate myself a little bit, because I have so many things I have to do. I think it can have quite a negative impact on your wellbeing because it feels like the whole time you're not going to be making the mark. All my classmates are supportive although a lot of them typically don't understand what it takes. They just see the occasional practice and our games, but they don't understand all the hard work that goes on in between. They might see us play for an hour, but we had heavy training for this for months. They don't see us when we're dying in conditioning or lifting weights or waking up early to do rehab.

Since moving over here, I think that I emotionally distanced myself from my family. I've always been the very positive one and so when something negative happens I don't want to put that burden on them. Being a student-athlete, you have to learn how to effectively deal with these extra stresses in your life compared to people who are just students or just athletes. We're required to perform higher than the average person in both areas. However, I struggle sometimes as I predominately identify with being an athlete. If I'd stayed back home, I don't think I would have gone to university. And so, I moved all the way over here for beach volleyball – not necessarily to go to school. There are upsides to this dual focus. If I've had a bad day, I remind myself that I'm not just an athlete, I'm not just a student, I'm both. And I'm doing really well. I'm doing what everyone else does plus more. Additionally, I have definitely become more independent since I moved to America. Sometimes that's a very positive thing and sometimes it can be seen as a negative. I think it almost distances me, especially from my parents and friends back home because my life out here is very different from the life I had back home. The pressures and intensity of my lifestyle here. They ask me 'why do you look so tired?' and I'll say, 'I'm doing my best'. For me, the realisation that I can't be all things to all people is tough – I have to be the best version of myself – a good student, athlete, daughter, sister, girlfriend, best friend and stuff like that. Being a student-athlete also provides a good distraction when you're injured and can't practice. Then, I put in extra time into studying and socialising or go to extra rehab or get some extra treatment. And so, I think having the necessity of still keeping your grades high regardless of whether you're injured or not for me it was a good thing because it was a distraction, it helped me cope.

I cope with this high-pressure lifestyle by working hard to prioritise everyday things. Do I have time to go and see my friends or do I need to get my homework done first? Can I see my friends later or is it actually beneficial for me to hang out for a bit, to relax to switch my mind off and then maybe I'll be more efficient when I do my homework later on? Whether that's an assessment deadline or little things like sending like your brother or sister a birthday card in the post, does that need to be done now or can it wait? And it's just deciding like when it needs to be done and what can wait. I also get around this by compartmentalising things. If my practice is going bad or good – that's practice time. And it's like yes you can think about it, but you don't bring that into the classroom and it's the same thing with classroom stuff like you don't bring that out onto the court with you.

One of the things I am concerned about is what happens after I finish my degree at the University. It is like you have been the be all and end all of the college world, as a super high performer – excelling in your sport, excelling in your studies, picking up awards. Then you get into the real world and you don't really know what to do, I worry that I will feel lost, scared and depressed without my sport. You have this internal drive because you're so used to succeeding all the time and for a lot of not reaching those milestones every day can be depressing.

SCHOLAR VOICE

Theorising wellbeing within the dual career setting

To achieve a holistic development and allow athletes to be best prepared for their future role in society at the end of their athletic career, they are encouraged to combine their sport and academic aspirations (Park, Lavallee, & Tod, 2013; Roberts, Mullen, Evans, & Hall, 2015; Torregrosa, Ramis, Pallarés, Azócar, & Selva, 2015). This combination of aspirations is referred to as a 'dual career' and is briefly defined in the literature as 'a career with major foci on sport and studies or work' (Stambulova & Wylleman, 2015, p. 1). There is a growing body of literature supporting the importance of dual careers in assisting athletes to prepare for their athletic retirement and adaptation to their post-sport career (e.g. Aquilina & Henry, 2010; Ryba, Stambulova, Selänne, Aunola, & Nurmi, 2017). Dual career programmes and services are largely established in the United States of America, Australia, Canada and New Zealand. Although there are provisions in place in Europe, these range from flexible academic programmes, financial/service support and individually negotiated agreements, rather than fully established and structured provisions. In a way, a dual career does not mean the same for all athletes – it is dependent on the country you reside in, and to a certain degree, your sport. Although the benefits of a dual career approach to athletic and professional development are widely positively acknowledged, there are many challenges to this approach for the athletes on these pathways. For example, as Grace identifies, a dual career for an athlete can lead to added anxieties and tensions caused by the likely entrenchment in two environments that are subject to high evaluation (e.g. Christensen & Sørensen, 2009;

Gustafsson, Hassmen, Kentta, & Johansson, 2008; O'Neill, Allen, & Calder, 2013; Sorkkila, Aunola, & Ryba, 2017). Additionally, societal pressures as a result of dual career pursuits can lead to the pressure to make 'the right choice' of a post-sport career (Ryba et al., 2017). Grace highlights this in her repeated acknowledgement of 'moving half way around the world' for her desire to pursue beach volleyball.

Whilst athletes enrolled in higher education have the opportunity to compete at multi-sport international and continental university sport events (e.g. Universiade, World University Championships, Pan-American University Championships, European EUSA Games), considerable differences have been reported worldwide in the provision of dual career programmes and services, mainly due to country-specific cultural and organisational regulations in the field of sport and education (Amsterdam University of Applied Sciences, 2016). Australia (Australian Government, 2018), Canada (Canadian Sport Institute, 2018), New Zealand (Ryan, Thorpe, & Pope, 2017) and the United States (National Collegiate Athletic Association, 2018) have formalised dual career programmes, whereas African, Asian and European student-athletes are presented with a multiplicity of national approaches to dual career support ranging from flexible academic programmes and financial support to individually negotiated agreements when possible (e.g. Capranica & Guidotti, 2016). As Grace demonstrated, this difference in recognition and support of dual careers across the five continents has driven student-athletes to seek out the opportunity to fulfil their academic and sporting goals outside of their home country. Research by Condello, Capranica, Doupona, Varga, and Burk (2019) explored the global dual career experiences of student-athletes competing at the 2017 Summer Universiade in Taipei (Taiwan). They reported: (1) a difference between continents for the time spent in sport and university engagement and in transferring from home to the training venue; (2) a higher amount of time in sport engagement for individual sport student-athletes compared to their team sport counterparts; (3) a difference between university major categories on the time spent in university engagement; and (4) a difference between continents regarding the athletes' familiarity and awareness of dual career policies, programmes, measures, initiatives and availability of policy documents that facilitate their elite sports and studies pathways.

Grace spoke of how she felt she had no option but to seek out dual career opportunities in the United States as there was no comparable provision for student-athletes in Europe in her sport – beach volleyball. Whilst the dual career scholarship programmes on offer through the college system in the United States are attractive for international student-athletes like Grace, it meant that she had to relocate internationally, distancing herself from her primary support network – her family. She reflected on how this had encouraged her to become more independent and resilient, but that it had also had an adverse impact on her wellbeing as she had become self-reliant to the point of not asking for support when she needed it.

Once enrolled in her dual career programme, Grace illustrated the precarity of her position as a student-athlete on a scholarship at an American university and the constant pressure to make a minimum GPA to keep her place at the college and her scholarship. Ultimately, this pressure led her to change the course she was studying for – one that was 'easier' as a measure to protect her wellbeing. This approach to study by student-athletes is in fact a trend, identified by a number of journal articles. For example, Schneider, Ross, and Fisher (2010) observed that many college administrators believe that student-athletes choose the path of least resistance (less competitive majors) so they can maintain their eligibility on their programmes. In fact, it has been noted that academic administrators are complicit in this practice (e.g. Crepeau, 2006). Opting for the easy option of study is noted regularly in the student-athlete population. Whilst the majority of athletes in Navarro's (2015) study suggested that their academic endeavours were important, often their choice of major did not align with their career aspirations. Sadly, this tokenistic engagement with a field of studies is not what a dual career approach was aimed at, and ultimately this could impact on the long-term wellbeing of the athlete where they remain fundamentally unprepared for a life post sport (e.g. Cosh & Tully, 2014; Ryba, Stambulova, Ronkainen, Bundgaard, & Selänne, 2015). Arguably, the college system (or indeed any high-performance sport system) needs to ensure that the long-term wellbeing of athletes is appropriately served, and that the system does not simply serve to ameliorate the immediate circumstances to drive performance. A life-long duty of care is required.

Combining an athletic career with education is demanding even for the most talented student-athletes and since only a small proportion of athletes will obtain elite status, student-athletes need to strive for success in both domains to facilitate transition into the labour market (Stambulova & Wylleman, 2015). Grace spoke of how she was expected to perform at a higher level in both her sport and her studies in comparison to 'the average person' who was either a student or an athlete. Whilst she found this constant pressure stressful, she took great pride in successfully managing a dual career (although recognised this management was harder with a more challenging major, i.e., sport science) and in the recognition she received from her peers as being a 'super high performer'. She identified strongly as being a student-athlete and voiced her concern about how she would cope outside of the college system; although the notion that to 'cope' would be her default emotional strategy, this might indicate a need for Grace to develop and deepen her ability to consciously tolerate stress. This continual striving for success was Grace's modus operandi, and she was worried that without sport and academia as metrics to assess her progress she would feel 'lost, scared and depressed'. Whilst both volleyball and university provided a competitive arena in which Grace could realise these successes, there were times when she felt overloaded and the constant pressure to perform impacted on her wellbeing. This pressure can result in sport and academic burnout, which has been defined as sport/education-related exhaustion (i.e. chronic fatigue due to pressures in sport/studies), cynicism towards the meaning of sport/education (i.e. indifferent or distal attitude towards one's own sport/ studies) and inadequacy as an athlete/student (Sorkkila, Tolvanen, Aunola, & Ryba, 2019). It has been suggested that burnout can develop when the demands experienced (e.g. high training loads and competition/academic demands and assessments) constantly exceed the available resources such as social and family support (Smith, 1986). This may place student-athletes (who have high demands as they strive for success in two domains) at risk of experiencing burnout.

Research suggests that the domains of sport and education are highly intertwined and that one is likely to affect the other. For example, it has been reported that student-athletes' exhaustion in education spills over to sport (Capranica & Guidotti, 2016). Moreover, high success expectations in one domain have been shown to protect student-athletes from burnout symptoms in the same domain but be positively related to burnout symptoms in the other domain and a reduction in wellbeing (Amsterdam University of Applied Sciences, 2016). Indeed, Grace talked of the delicate balance of managing her academic and athletic commitments and her concerns that if this tipped one way or the other it would be very hard to get it back. She shared her teammates' experience, of falling behind in studies, the impact this subsequently had on her volleyball and that despite her best efforts she had to drop out of the scholarship programme.

The narrowing of post-sport career choices

Whilst dual careers may seem attractive to athletes in that they provide an opportunity to obtain a university degree whilst participating in high-performance sport, it has been suggested that sport narrows the influences necessary to explore a breadth of future career possibilities and that this can have a negative impact on athletes wellbeing after retirement (Ronkainen & Ryba, 2017) and on career readiness. Research suggests that athletes may stay in sport as a future career as it is a familiar environment or choose a career that shares characteristics with sport (Roberts et al., 2015). When asked about her career aspirations after graduation, Grace said that she wanted to remain in America to play beach volleyball professionally as long as her body would allow her to and that after she retired from playing, she would like to remain in the sport in a coaching capacity. Beach volleyball is not currently supported as a professional sport in the UK so both her athletic and coaching career aspirations would be limited if she returned; a weighty thought not conducive to good mental health. Whilst she was studying for a degree in communication, this was seen as a way of accessing support to further her volleyball career rather than as a conscious career choice. Studies of career-related challenges for graduating student-athletes have identified issues such as arrested career development and athletes' sense of uncertainty about the future (Webb, Nasco, Riley, & Headrick, 1998), grief and loss regarding the transition to a non-athletic career post college (Lally, 2007) and identity foreclosure (Linnemeyer & Brown, 2010). Indeed, universities, national governing bodies and student-athletes have become increasingly concerned about the readiness of student-athletes to enter the workforce after graduation.

Certainly, student-athletes invest a significant amount of time and energy into their sport which detracts from time they could commit to exploring and preparing for potential careers (Sandstedt, Cox, Martens, Ward, Weber, & Ivey, 2004). Student-athletes often dedicate up to twenty hours per week – the equivalent of a part-time job – in official practice time on their sport (National Collegiate Athletic Association, 2018). Although, this figure may be conservative as many athletes also spend additional hours on unofficial mental preparation and personal training to maintain or improve their performance (Wieberg, 2011). Given that fewer than two percent of college student-athletes in the United States actually go on to play sports at the professional level, the extensive hours spent on their practice rarely translate into post university employment (National Collegiate Athletic Association, 2018). This challenge of focusing extensive time and energy to achieve excellent sport and academic performances may disadvantage student-athletes in their ability to prepare themselves for a transition into a non-sports career (Heird & Steinfeldt, 2013; Parham, 1993). It could be argued that this is due to the time constraints the dual role presents, therefore, student-athletes are less likely to engage with valuable career development opportunities such as part-time employment and internships.

While significant attention has been given to professional athletes' transition out of sports, comparatively little research has focused on the transition of student-athletes into post university employment (Cummins & O'Boyle, 2015). Recent research by August (2020) suggested that career readiness was related to four key qualities: optimism, resilience, adaptivity and the recognition of overlapping skills, knowledge and personal strengths required for sports and work. Indeed, there are a growing number of 'performance lifestyle' practitioners in the UK that provide support to athletes to help them develop their careers outside of sport (e.g. Devaney, Nesti, Ronkainen, Littlewood, & Richardson, 2018). There is a call for more work on career exploration with athletes to help inform future career directions earlier (Di Maggio, Ginevra, Laura, Ferrari, & Soresi, 2015; Savickas et al., 2009).

Grace is one of approximately 400,000 student-athletes competing at a National Collegiate Athletic Association (NCAA) institution. In recent years, academic support centres have been created at universities across the United States in response to the outrage over the reported lack of academic resources for student-athletes (Huml, Hancock, & Bergman, 2014). Furthermore, the NCAA reform policies have introduced penalties for the athletic departments that fail to meet the required academic minimums. Indeed, Grace spoke of how her coaches told them that they were identified as 'student-athletes not athlete-students' for a reason, because their primary focus should be on their academic rather than athletic pursuits. Whilst Grace identified predominantly as an athlete, she felt under constant scrutiny – constant surveillance – to maintain a minimum GPA and the threat of not being allowed to train if her academic work slipped was a source of immense stress; it is unsurprising that Grace's wellbeing began to suffer.

Although the threat of penalties has encouraged athletic departments to increase their academic budgets, hire additional staff and build specialist academic centres, it may have had an adverse impact on the wellbeing of student-athletes (such as imposed isolation in Grace's situation). Whilst on the one hand they encourage student-athletes to focus on their studies and provide access to academic support, concerns have been raised around the separation of student-athletes from the student body (Rubin & Moses, 2017). Grace talked about how little interaction she had with the other students on her course because of her lack of spare time as she tried to manage both roles.

The coping mechanism that Grace had developed for managing the pressure of being a student-athlete was to follow a strict daily routine to ensure that she was giving her best in both her academic and athletic objectives. If she deviated from her routine, she would become increasingly anxious that her ability to maintain high levels of performance in both domains would be compromised. She spoke of the impact this anxiety had on her sleep, diet and mental health. However, it is worth acknowledging that this need for adherence to such a strict routine may have long-term implications for her wellbeing and place her at a higher risk of experiencing conditions such as overtraining syndrome and burnout. Decisions on whether or not to socialise with friends were determined by a cost-benefit analysis of the potential impact it would have on her academic and athletic commitments. She spoke of how isolating this was and the negative impact her lack of social support outside of her athletic group had on her wellbeing. She said that in her first year at university she 'emotionally distanced' herself from her family back home as she found this easier than telling them that she was struggling with the intense demands of being a student-athlete – this account mirrors the experiences of elite swimmers in Tekavc, Wylleman, and Cecić Erpič's (2015) study on dual careers. She always felt the need to present the 'best version of myself' and that she was always the positive person in the family and that being anything other than that was difficult to communicate. Furthermore, she felt that with being at university on the other side of the world there was little they could do to help, and she did not want to worry them.

Conclusion

As Grace has eloquently demonstrated, the need to constantly balance two significant areas of development and achievement (sport and higher education) has the potential to have a significant impact on the student-athlete's wellbeing – arguably presenting both times of thriving and times of surviving. The factors that Grace described had an impact on her dual career development and arguably caused additional threats to wellbeing in the short term over and above pursuing an athletic career in isolation. Those factors included the additional stress and opportunity of relocating to the USA to pursue a dual career, the concerns over the precarity of her position as a student-athlete, the delicate balancing of two distinctly important areas of her life which both attract equal amounts of evaluation and the social isolation and emotional distancing as an inherent consequence of such a pressurised existence. Whilst the evidence for the benefits of a dual career is strong in the long term, it is suggested that much more work is undertaken to ensure that athletes embarking on a dual career have their short-term wellbeing needs met to allow them to maximise the intended positive outcomes.

References

Amsterdam University of Applied Sciences, Birch Consultants, the Talented Athlete Scholarship Scheme, the Vrije Universiteit Brussel, & European Athlete as Student Network. (2016). *Study on the minimum quality requirements for dual career services.* Research Report. Retrieved from https://ec.europa.eu/sport/news/2016/study-minimum-quality-requirements-dual-careers-published_en

Aquilina, D., & Henry, I. (2010). Elite athletes and university education in Europe: A review of policy and practice in higher education in the European Union Member States. *International Journal of Sport Politics, 2*(1), 25–47. https://doi.org/10.1080/19406941003634024

August, R. A. (2020). Understanding career readiness in college student-athletes and identifying associated personal qualities. *Journal of Career Development, 47*(2), 177–192. https://doi.org/10.1177/0894845318793936

Australian Government. (2018). *Australian Institute of Sport, elite athlete friendly university program.* Retrieved from www.ausport.gov.au/ais/personal_excellence/university_network/elite_athlete_friendly_university_program

Canadian Sport Institute. (2018). *Education, career and transition: Sportsgrad program.* Retrieved from http://csicalgary.ca/life-services/education-career-and-transition

Capranica, L., & Guidotti, F. (2016). *Research for Cult Committee: Qualifications/dual careers in sports.* European Parliament, Directorate-General for Internal Policies. Policy Department B: Structural and Cohesion Policies: Cultural and Education. Retrieved from www.europarl.europa.eu/RegData/etudes/STUD/2016/573416/IPOL_STU(2016)573416_EN.pdf

Christensen, M. K., & Sørensen, J. K. (2009). Sport or school? Dreams and dilemmas for talented young Danish football players. *European Physical Education Review, 15*(1), 115–133. https://doi.org/10.1177/1356336X09105214

Condello, G., Capranica, L., Doupona, M., Varga, K., & Burk, V. (2019). Dual-career through the elite university student-athletes' lenses: The international FISU-EAS survey. *PLoS ONE, 14*(10), e0223278. https://doi.org/10.1371/journal.pone.0223278

Cosh, S., & Tully, P. J. (2015). Stressors, coping, and support mechanisms for student-athletes combining elite sport and tertiary education: Implications for practice. *The Sport Psychologist, 29*(2), 120–133. https://doi.org/10.1123/tsp.2014-0102

Crepeau, R. C. (2006, July 19). *Sport and society for arete*. The Sport Literature Association. Retrieved from www.uta.edu/english/sla/s&s060719.html

Cummins, P., O'Boyle, I. O. (2015). Psychosocial factors involved in the transitions from college to post-college careers for male NCAA Division-I basketball players. *Journal of Career Development, 42*, 33–47.

Devaney, D. J., Nesti, M. S., Ronkainen, N. J., Littlewood, M., & Richardson, D. (2018). Athlete lifestyle support of elite youth cricketers: An ethnography of player concerns within a national talent development program. *Journal of Applied Sport Psychology, 30*(3), 300–320. https://doi.org/10.1080/10413200.2017.1386247

Di Maggio, I., Ginevra, M. C., Laura, N., Ferrari, L., & Soresi, S. (2015). Career adaptabilities scale-Italian form: Psychometric proprieties with Italian preadolescents. *Journal of Vocational Behavior, 91*, 46–53. https://doi.org/10.1016/j.jvb.2015.08.001

Gustafsson, H., Hassmen, P., Kentta, G., & Johansson, M. (2008). A qualitative analysis of burnout in elite Swedish athletes. *Psychology of Sport and Exercise, 9*(6), 800–816. https://doi.org/10.1016/j.psychsport.2007.11.004

Heird, E. B., & Steinfeldt, J. A. (2013). An interpersonal psychotherapy approach to counseling student-athletes: Clinical implications of athletic identity. *Journal of College Counseling, 16*(2), 143–157. https://doi.org/10.1002/j.2161-1882.2013.00033.x

Huml, M. R., Hancock, M. G., & Bergman, M. J. (2014). Additional support or extravagant cost? Student-athletes' perceptions on athletic academic centers. *Journal of Issues in Intercollegiate Athletics, 7*, 410–430.

Lally, P. (2007). Identity and athletic retirement: A prospective study. *Psychology of Sport and Exercise, 8*(1), 85–99. https://doi.org/10.1016/j.psychsport.2006.03.003

Linnemeyer, R. M., & Brown, C. (2010). Career maturity and foreclosure in student-athletes, fine arts students, and general college students. *Journal of Career Development, 37*(3), 616–634. https://doi.org/10.1177/0894845309357049

National Collegiate Athletic Association. (2018). *Student-athlete*. Retrieved from www.ncaa.org/student-athletes

Navarro, K. M. (2015). An examination of the alignment of student-athletes' undergraduate major choices and career field aspirations in life after sports. *Journal of College Student Development, 56*, 364–379.

O'Neill, M., Allen, B., & Calder, A. M. (2013). Pressures to perform: An interview study of Australian high performance school-age athletes' perceptions of balancing their school and sporting lives. *Performance Enhancement & Health, 2*(2), 87–93. https://doi.org/10.1016/j.peh.2013.06.001

Parham, W. D. (1993). The intercollegiate athlete: A 1990s profile. *The Counseling Psychologist, 21*(3), 411–429. https://doi.org/10.1177/0011000093213005

Park, S., Lavallee, D., & Tod, D. (2013). Athletes' career transition out of sport: A systematic review. *International Review of Sport and Exercise Psychology, 6*(1), 22–53. https://doi.org/10.1080/1750984X.2012.687053

Roberts, C. M., Mullen, R., Evans, L., & Hall, R. (2015). An in-depth appraisal of career termination experiences in professional cricket. *Journal of Sports Sciences, 33*(9), 935–944. https://doi.org/10.1080/02640414.2014.977936

Ronkainen, N. J., & Ryba, T. V. (2017). Rethinking age in athletic retirement: An existential-narrative perspective. *International Journal of Sport and Exercise Psychology, 15*(2), 146–159. https://doi.org/10.1080/1612197X.2015.1079920

Rubin, L., & Moses, R. (2017). Athletic subculture within student-athlete academic centers. *Sociology of Sport Journal, 34*(4), 1–36. https://doi.org/10.1123/ssj.2016-0138

Ryan, C., Thorpe, H., & Pope, C. (2017). The policy and practice of implementing a student–athlete support network: A case study. *International Journal of Sport Policy and Politics, 9*(3), 415–430. https://doi.org/10.1080/19406940.2017.1320301

Ryba, T. V., Stambulova, N. B., Ronkainen, N. J., Bundgaard, J., Selänne, H. (2015). Dual career pathways of transnational athletes. *Psychology of Sport & Exercise, 21*, 125–134. https://doi.org/10.1016/j.psychsport.2014.06.002

Ryba, T. V., Stambulova, N., Selänne, H., Aunola, K., & Nurmi, J. E. (2017). Sport has always been first for me" but "all my free time is spent doing homework": Dual career styles in late adolescence. *Psychology of Sport and Exercise, 33*, 131–140. https://doi.org/10.1016/j.psychsport.2017.08.011

Sandstedt, S. D., Cox, R. H., Martens, M. P., Ward, D. G., Weber, S. N., & Ivey, S. (2004). Development of the Student-Athlete Career Situation Inventory (SACSI). *Journal of Career Development, 31,* 79–93. https://doi.org/10.1007/s10871-004-0566-5

Savickas, M. L., Nota, L., Rossier, J., Dauwalder, J., Duarte, M. E., Guichard, J., Soresi, S., Van Esbroeck, R., & van Vianen, A. E. M. (2009). Life designing: A paradigm for career construction in the 21st century. *Journal of Vocational Behavior, 75*(3), 239–250. https://doi.org/10.1016/j.jvb.2009.04.004

Schneider, R. G., Ross, S. R., & Fisher, M. (2010). Academic clustering and major selection of intercollegiate student-athletes. *College Student Journal, 44*(1), 64–70.

Smith, R. E. (1986). Toward a cognitive-affective model of athletic burnout. *Journal of Sport Psychology, 8*(1), 36–50. https://doi.org/10.1123/jsp.8.1.36

Sorkkila, M., Aunola, K., & Ryba, T. V. (2017). A person-oriented approach to sport and school burnout in adolescent student-athletes: The role of individual and parental expectations. *Psychology of Sport and Exercise, 28*(7), 58–67. https://doi.org/10.1111/sms.13422

Sorkkila, M., Tolvanen, A., Aunola, K., & Ryba, T. V. (2019). The role of resilience in student-athletes' sport and school burnout and dropout: A longitudinal person-oriented study. *Scandinavian Journal of Medicine and Science in Sports, 29*, 1059–1067.

Stambulova, N. B., & Wylleman, T. V. (2015). Dual career development and transitions. *Psychology of Sport and Exercise, 21*, 1–134. https://doi.org/10.1016/j.psychsport.2015.05.003

Tekavc, J., Wylleman, P., & Cecić Erpič, S. (2015). Perceptions of dual career development among elite level swimmers and basketball players. *Psychology of Sport & Exercise, 21*, 27–41. https://doi.org/10.1016/j.psychsport.2015.03.002

Torregrosa, M., Ramis, Y., Pallarés, S., Azócar, F., & Selva, C. (2015). Olympic athletes back to retirement: A qualitative longitudinal study. *Psychology of Sport & Exercise, 21*, 50–56. https://doi.org/10.1016/j.psychsport.2015.03.003

Webb, W. M., Nasco, S. A., Riley, S., & Headrick, B. (1998). Athletic identity and reactions to retirement from sports. *Journal of Sport Behavior, 21*(3), 338–362.

Wieberg, S. (2011). NCAA survey delves into practice time, coaches' trust. *USA Today.* Retrieved from http://usatoday30.usatoday.com/sports/college/2011-01-14-ncaa-survey_N.htm

5
THE ROLE OF COACH LEADERSHIP IN PROMOTING ATHLETE WELLBEING AND PERFORMANCE

James Matthews and David Passmore

Introduction

Leadership behaviour can have a considerable impact on the behaviour, performance and wellbeing of athletes. In this chapter, we will focus on how leadership can influence athlete wellbeing in elite sport. First, using a case study, we will outline the challenges in promoting athlete wellbeing observed by a highly experienced coach across different elite sport settings. Then, we will briefly look beyond elite sport to other high-performance domains such as the military and emergency medicine. Next, we will examine the role of the leader and leadership behaviours in high-performance domains and how it relates to follower wellbeing. In doing so, we will briefly examine the theoretical perspectives of transformational leadership and shared leadership and the empirical literature across selected high-performance domains. Reflecting on practices outside of sport and selected leadership theories, we make a number of practical recommendations and propose two theoretically derived interventions to address the athlete wellbeing challenges observed by the coach.

> ### PRACTITIONER VOICE
>
> #### The coach's observations
>
> I have had the great fortune to work with athletes and teams at an elite level of field hockey for a number of years including international teams competing at European, World and Olympic levels. These experiences have shown me that many elite level coaches tend to focus on athlete performance through the technical, tactical and physical aspects of their sport. However, like human performance in any field, athlete development and performance

DOI: 10.4324/9780429287923-5

are also impacted by the performer's psychological and emotional wellbeing. Simply put, if an athlete's psychological and emotional needs are not satisfied within the sporting environment or in other areas of their life, in my experience, they will almost always underperform on the pitch. The coaching environment and, in particular, the actions and behaviours of the coach can contribute significantly to satisfying these needs and supporting an athlete's wellbeing. Where coaching environments are maladaptive, they not only potentially limit athlete development and constrain performance, but also I firmly believe that they put an athlete's health and wellbeing at risk. Indeed, in recent times, we have seen a number of high-profile examples of elite sport environments and specifically questionable leadership practices within those environments that put athletes' health and wellbeing at risk. It is incumbent on all people working in high-performance sport to ensure that these risks are minimised.

From my experience in elite sport, I have noticed that many of the challenges around coaches and athlete wellbeing are similar across the environments I have coached in or observed as a coach developer. These challenges include:

1 Many high-performance coaches perceive their role as needing to push and drive athletes to maximise performance rather than challenging and supporting athletes. A coaching environment that is unrelenting and where there is little consideration for wellbeing can lead to maladaptive outcomes such as burnout. I have witnessed numerous examples of where this type of coach behaviour and a coach attitude of "sink or swim" can lead athletes to feel that their only option to "get away" is to stop competing or even to prematurely retire.

2 Many coaches do not prioritise good coach–athlete relationships and do not see the importance of having positive relationships. Positive relationships between coaches and athletes are fundamental in helping athletes to thrive within elite sport. When these positive relationships are absent, I have seen how this can lead to a culture of fear, isolation, and/or avoidance, and are often a precursor for athlete or team underperformance.

3 A number of coaches I have worked with frequently highlighted their discomfort with the concept of emotional intelligence and how awareness of one's own and others' emotions might enhance their coaching practice. From my experience, this discomfort came from a lack of knowledge as to how an athlete's feelings and emotions can influence their ability to engage in sport or a perception that is not part of the coach's role to consider an athlete's feelings. However, a lack of consideration of athletes' emotional needs by a coach or coaching team can lead to athlete ill-being and underperformance.

4 Some coaches are unwilling or unable to trust athletes sufficiently to hand over ownership to them or even involve them in the decision-making

process. This unwillingness not only disempowers athletes which may influence their wellbeing but also reduces the likelihood of the athletes "working things out" in pressure moments. Indeed, I have seen on numerous occasions throughout my career how coaches overestimate their ability to impact performance during highly pressurised competitive situations. As a result, teams fail to deal with, or work their way out of challenging scenarios in competition play; in many instances, this is due to not being given sufficient autonomy in practice settings.

5   Some coaches I have observed are not willing to tailor their coaching approach to the particular group of athletes they are working with. For example, the coaching approach required to work with an elite junior team is different from the approach required when working with an elite senior team. I believe adaptability in coaching practice is needed and if there is a gap between the approach being used by the coach and where the team is at, it can lead to reduced enjoyment and a lack of athlete satisfaction.

6   There is often a disconnect between what some coaches espouse in terms of values and the behaviours they demonstrate. This can lead to a lack of trust in coaches by athletes. In my experience, this disconnect is exemplified by the statement, "Do as I say . . . Not as I do" and can lead to a culture where there is frustration, uncertainty and ultimately conflict between coach and athletes.

There is an opportunity to address these challenges through a shift in how coaches interact with athletes in and around the sport setting. From my many years as an elite coach, I believe this opportunity is through a person-centred and holistic approach to coaching. This approach seeks to engage athletes by inspiring or motivating them and highlighting their agency in both training and competition environments. This form of leadership behaviour by a coach can facilitate high levels of wellbeing and psychological functioning in athletes. In terms of behaviours, I believe this involves an investment of time by a coach in getting to know their athletes within and outside of the sport setting. For example, from understanding their life story, family background, previous experiences and interests outside of the sport, to what they feel makes them perform to the best of their ability and their preferences in terms of recovery and rest. By making this investment and building a regular dialogue with their athletes, coaches can develop a deeper insight into the whole person and gain a clearer insight into the athlete's wellbeing at any time.

National governing bodies and national high-performance centres need to build coach development programmes that introduce this person-centred approach to overcome these challenges. This will enable coaches to develop their knowledge and more importantly develop their skills in how to utilise a leadership style in elite sport environments that promote athlete wellbeing and performance. In particular, the use of theoretical approaches such as transformational or shared leadership may be particularly relevant. Coaches first need to be educated in why athlete-centred environments can enhance athlete development, and coaches should then be supported in developing such an environment. Underpinning all coaching environments is the leader's personal values and beliefs. Through my work with the Irish Institute of Sport coach development programme, we found that in order for coaches to generate a culture characterised by positive leadership practice, coaches needed to understand their own values and beliefs. By aligning their values with positive leadership (being athlete centred) and then ensuring their practice reflected those values, it enabled athletes to strive for greater performance whilst maintain their wellbeing.

SCHOLAR VOICE

Overview

As illustrated earlier, the role of the coach in a high-performance setting is particularly important in influencing athletes' wellbeing. The challenges observed across different high-performance environments are similar with many coaches heavily focused on the technical aspects of their role rather than the relational elements. In the following sections, we will consider the challenges posed in this case study within the context of the literature and how this might inform recommendations to help overcome these challenges.

Learning from high-performance settings

There is an increasing body of literature highlighting the similarities between elite sport and other performance domains such as surgery, emergency medicine and military operations (Hays, 2009). These domains can be described as high-stress, high-demand performance settings in which the individuals require not only the psychological capabilities but also the environmental supports to manage the potential risks involved and perform effectively (Salas, Driskell, & Hughes, 2013). While these performance domains have different structures and specific characteristics, individuals within each of these settings are likely to experience similar leadership related stressors such as maladaptive leader–follower interactions (Arnold & Fletcher, 2012), low managerial support (Basu, Qayyum, & Mason, 2017) value misalignment and poor team or unit culture (Harms, Krasikova, Vanhove, Herian, & Lester, 2013). The consequence of these stressors is the same across each of the domains, that is, poor performance and poor wellbeing. For example, limited or ineffective leader support has been linked with poor wellbeing in soldiers with higher levels of combat engagement (Adler, Saboe, Anderson, Sipos, & Thomas, 2014). While in a medical setting, mistreatment by those in positions of authority is linked with increased levels of physician burnout (Cook, Arora, Rasinski, Curlin, & Yoon, 2014). Therefore, there is merit in examining the role of the leader and wellbeing in domains that closely align with elite sport and applying the learnings from these domains to some of the challenges observed in the case study.

Theories of leadership and leadership–wellbeing relationships

While leadership has been studied in sport, the bulk of the research in this area has been conducted in the organisational psychology or management domains. Recent reviews of literature within these domains suggest that leadership can have a significant impact on the wellbeing of followers (Inceoglu, Thomas, Chu, Plans, & Gerbasi, 2018). Positive leadership behaviours such as inspiring and motivating are linked to both hedonic (e.g. positive affect and satisfaction) and eudaimonic forms of wellbeing (e.g. engagement, purpose, meaning) in followers (Inceoglu et al., 2018). While destructive leadership behaviours such as aggression and authoritarianism are associated with lower levels of wellbeing and psychological functioning (Montano, Reeske, Franke, & Hüffmeier, 2017). These findings reinforce our observations across different high-performance settings. While a review of leadership theories is beyond the scope of this chapter, we will briefly introduce two theories that have shown promise in promoting follower wellbeing from both hedonic and eudaimonic perspectives which have particular relevance for this case study. These theories are Transformational Leadership and Shared Leadership.

Transformational leadership

Central to the theory of Transformational Leadership (TL) is the suggestion that a leader's behaviour inspires and motivates followers to exceed performance expectations by shaping followers' beliefs and attitudes (Bass, 1985). Bass' (1985) model detailed four behaviours that positively impact on follower outcomes. These were idealised influence, inspirational motivation, intellectual stimulation and individualised consideration. Idealised influence refers to a leader behaving in admirable ways that cause followers to identify with the leader. Leaders who provide inspirational motivation articulate a vision that inspires followers and challenges them with high standards. Intellectual stimulation refers to the leader seeking follower input. Leaders who give individualised consideration listen to followers' concerns and attend to their needs (Judge & Piccolo, 2004). Two further behaviours were added to Bass' conceptualisation of TL based on the work of others, that is, high-performance expectations and fostering acceptance of group goals (Podsakoff, MacKenzie, Moorman, & Fetter, 1990). High-performance expectations relate to leaders highlighting the need for excellence, while fostering acceptance of group goals is where leaders promote cooperation among their followers to achieve group goals. A number of narrative reviews have concluded that TL is also strongly associated with lower levels of stress and burnout and higher levels of wellbeing (Montano et al., 2017).

Despite the widespread interest in TL in organisational psychology, the empirical exploration of transformational leaders in sport is relatively recent. Most of the studies have been cross-sectional in nature and conducted with a non-elite youth population (Arthur, Bastardoz, & Eklund, 2017). A notable exception to this is the work by Smith, Young, Figgins, and Arthur (2017) who highlighted TL behaviours that might enhance elite performance in cricket. Specifically, they detailed how coaches are responsible for setting high-performance expectations, and how they demonstrate individual consideration for players in training. By contrast, Smith et al. (2017) suggested how formal leaders such as the head coach are supported by the captain and/or senior players in delivering TL behaviours. For example, while coaches may set high expectations, it is the captain or senior players who reinforce this by modelling the required behaviours. With respect to wellbeing, Stenling and Tafvelin (2014) reported how TL behaviour was linked to athlete wellbeing. They showed that athletes who perceived their coach as displaying TL behaviours were more likely to have their basic psychological needs satisfied and in turn improve their wellbeing. Given the limited body of TL and wellbeing research in sport settings, it is helpful to examine evidence from other high-performance domains.

Transformational Leadership has been used regularly as an underlying framework for leadership research in military settings. In a longitudinal study, Arthur and Hardy (2014) demonstrated that TL can positively impact the organisational climate and organisational efficiency in a military context. Alongside this focus on performance-related outcomes, a small body of studies within a military setting have examined leadership behaviour and its effects on follower wellbeing. For example, in the 2008 report of the Mental Health and Advisory Team MHAT-5 (2008), evidence showed that a positive leadership climate was associated with almost halving the rates of psychological and emotional problems in United States soldiers who had experienced combat. These findings were reinforced by Jones et al. (2012; Jones, Campion, Keeling, & Greenberg, 2018) who studied members of the United Kingdom Armed Forces and found that perceived "good leadership" behaviours such as showing concern for unit members (i.e. individual consideration), being interested in what unit members thought (i.e. intellectual stimulation) and acting in a supportive manner (i.e. idealised influence) were associated with better psychological health in soldiers (as measured by the General Health Questionnaire; Goldberg & William, 1988).

Applying transformational leadership to the case study

In considering the challenges put forward in our case study, we can see how TL could help to overcome some of these challenges. The first relevant challenge is the lack of balance shown by coaches between pushing athletes to maximise performance and showing concern and care for athletes' needs. Transformational leadership theory could be applied here through inspirational motivation, high-performance expectations and individual consideration. In doing so, the coach creates a vision for the athletes and then provides the appropriate level of challenge and support to enable the athletes to achieve that vision, for example, through the provision of information-rich feedback. Furthermore, we heard in our case study how there is often a disconnect between what coaches espouse in terms of values and the behaviours they demonstrate, and the negative impact this can have on the environment. Transformational leadership could be applied through idealised influence whereby coaches must ensure that their behaviours align with the espoused values of the particular high-performance environment. By clearly modelling these behaviours, coaches can connect with athletes in the environment, building a sense of trust and strengthening the team culture. Finally, how coaches do not consider athletes' emotional needs was considered a key challenge in our case study as was their potential lack of knowledge regarding emotional awareness. Therefore, there is a need to educate coaches as to the importance of building positive relationships with athletes through personal and emotional exchanges. This may be achieved by coaches adopting TL behaviours such as showing concern for athletes' feelings and needs (i.e. individual consideration) and fostering an environment of cooperation among athletes towards group goals. These positive relationships may help to cultivate an environment that develops athletes' resilience and ultimately promotes and protects their wellbeing.

Shared leadership

In recent years, there has been a shift from a top–down vertical leadership process to a horizontal and shared leadership process among team members across different settings (Lord, Day, Zaccaro, Avolio, & Eagly, 2017). Shared Leadership (SL) is distinct from other theories of leadership as it highlights the agency of team members in the leadership process and has been described as a condition where teams collectively exert leadership influence (Cox, Pearce, & Perry, 2003). SL has three distinct characteristics: the source of the leadership, unit of analysis, and the distribution of influence. To elaborate, the source of leadership is horizontal, lateral leadership from team members rather than a top–down approach. The unit of analysis considers shared leadership as the pooled leadership influence of all the team rather than residing solely in the formal leader. While the distribution of influence is situated broadly across team members rather than centralised with one person (Zhu, Liao, Yam, & Johnson, 2018). Shared Leadership can have a considerable effect on the performance of teams with a recent meta-analysis highlighting a significant positive relationship between this form of leadership and team performance (D'Innocenzo, Mathieu, & Kukenberger, 2014). Indeed, Serban and Roberts (2016) showed that SL is positively related to team member satisfaction (hedonic wellbeing).

Much like TL, there has been a growing interest in SL within the sport domain (Cotterill & Fransen, 2016). Morgan, Fletcher, and Sarkar (2015) and Hodge, Henry, and Smith (2014) explored how successful teams function, specifically the English and New Zealand teams who won the Rugby World Cup in 2003 and 2011, respectively. Both studies demonstrated how the leadership model adapted over time from a primarily transformational approach led by the management to a SL model between management and players. This shared approach may have many benefits ranging from team functioning to wellbeing and performance (Cotterill & Fransen, 2016). To understand this form of distributed leadership within a team, social network analysis may be a valuable diagnostic tool as it enables a deep understanding of how leadership is shared among group members (Fransen et al., 2015). Indeed, using this tool, Fransen et al. (2017) reported that high-quality athlete leadership in which different players took on different leadership roles within the team (i.e. the roles of task leadership, motivational leadership, social leadership, external leadership) was positively related to team effectiveness in professional sport with team members displaying increased commitment to the task and enhanced confidence in team abilities. Furthermore, coaches who empower their athletes to share the leadership role may be perceived by their followers as being more effective (Fransen et al., 2019). An SL approach has also been explored in other high-performance domains such as acute healthcare and is linked to team member wellbeing within this domain (Aufegger, Shariq, Bicknell, Ashrafian, & Darzi, 2019). This is exemplified by Brandstorp, Kirkengen, Sterud, Haugland, and Halvorsen (2015) who examined leadership practices in primary care emergency team training and found that a distribution of influence approach led to improved performance and an enhanced focus on functioning and wellbeing in team members.

Applying shared leadership to the case study

Through the lens of an SL approach, there are again clear links to some of the challenges outlined in our case study. Specifically, we have the challenge of coaches being unwilling to engage athletes in the decision-making process. From an SL perspective, coaches should give athletes a voice in the decision-making process as this will not only empower athletes but might also influence team functioning and performance, therefore, acting in accordance with source of leadership. Alongside this, coaches should consider how to create a structure whereby different groups within the team environment take on different leadership roles. For example, some athletes can focus on task leadership (i.e. taking charge on the pitch), while others can focus on social leadership (i.e. creating good relationships among the team), therefore, acting in accordance with distribution of leadership (Fransen et al., 2017). This approach may not only be "intellectually stimulating" for athletes but can also enhance trust between coaches and athletes. In creating this shared leadership approach, social network analysis may prove a useful diagnostic tool that gives players their voice, and the performance leader to select leaders that are accepted by their teammates (Fransen et al., 2015, 2019). Finally, in our case study, we have seen how coaches can rigidly stick to a coaching approach and not consider the particular profile of the group of athletes they are working with or perhaps the situation or context. It is important to challenge this perspective. For example, a transformational approach may be more appropriate when a team is newly formed, whereas a horizontal, shared leadership approach may be more effective as the team matures (Morgan et al., 2015). However, it must be noted that the use of both transformational and shared leadership approaches is not mutually exclusive. These perspectives can co-exist and act in a reciprocal fashion to promote team performance and wellbeing (Hodge et al., 2014).

Applying theory-based leadership approaches to promote follower wellbeing and performance

In our case study, we discuss how there is an opportunity to educate coaches on the importance of a holistic approach to coaching, one that looks beyond the technical and tactical competencies of being a high-performance coach to the relational elements of the role which considers the person as well as the performance. It is important that educational programmes designed to promote adaptive leadership behaviours are evidence-based. In this section of the chapter, we describe two such interventions, one from elite sport and one from a military setting.

Hardy et al. (2010) designed a programme to enhance the TL behaviours of military trainers and assessed its effect on military recruits in the United Kingdom. The programme was situated within the training process for Royal Marine Commando recruits. Initially, the research team worked with a select group of military personnel (known as the coaching advisory team; CAT), who then trained the section commanders who worked with the Royal Marine recruits. The intervention focused on specific TL behaviours such as fostering acceptance of group goals and teamwork, inspirational motivation, appropriate role modelling and individual consideration (Hardy et al., 2010). To facilitate the training process and make these concepts more acceptable to the CAT, a three-component model was developed: vision, support and challenge. This model allowed each of the particular TL behaviours to be described in the context of how vision, support and challenge could be provided to recruits. In describing the intervention, Hardy et al. (2010) detailed how modelling may be used to provide a vision (i.e. behaviours and characteristics of the leader that the follower wants to emulate), or support (i.e. the leader acting in a way that is consistent with the values they espouse), and even challenge (i.e. the followers' perception of their leader's behaviours is so high that the followers may feel extremely challenged in trying to emulating them). The use of these key leadership behaviours was also applied to four commonly occurring coaching activities that military trainers engage in with recruits goal-setting; observation of behaviour; giving motivational and/or developmental feedback; and asking effective questions of recruits to enhance their engagement and ownership. After receiving this training, the CAT delivered the training programme to the military trainers who were then required to apply their leadership behaviours within the 15-week recruit training programme Royal Marine recruits undertake. The study results demonstrated that the intervention had a significant effect on the TL behaviours as perceived by the recruits and produced corresponding impact increases in follower variables. Specifically, the trainers who underwent the intervention were perceived to be more transformational than those that did not, and the programme enhanced recruits' confidence, resilience and satisfaction (hedonic wellbeing). Coaches could be educated to utilise TL through the model of vision, challenge and support espoused in this intervention (Arthur, Hardy, & Woodman, 2012; Hardy et al., 2010).

From a SL perspective, Duguay, Loughead, and Munroe-Chandler (2016) devised a programme to develop athletes' leadership capabilities. The programme targeted female varsity athletes and was delivered over a period of three months. It entailed four 1-hour workshops, each focused on developing both human capital (intrapersonal development) and social capital (interpersonal development). The targeted leadership principles were guided by multidimensional model of leadership and the full range leadership model. They included democratic behaviour, positive feedback, social support, training and instruction, fostering of group goals and high-performance expectations. The workshops aimed to promote good practice through the provision of information on these leadership principles, a demonstration of these leadership principles by the facilitators and, finally, providing athletes the opportunity to put these leadership principles into practice. Specific workshop activities included athletes exploring the expectations they hold for themselves and their teams (linked to high-performance expectations) and creating a "toolbox" of skills they feel comfortable using when teaching or mentoring their teammates (linked to training and instruction). In addition to these workshops, athletes were given a leadership handbook that expanded on the materials presented at the workshop and a "take home" activity to complete after each workshop to help put these principles into practice. The results demonstrated that the programme had a positive impact on leadership behaviours with athletes reporting using the leadership behaviours significantly more often after completing the leadership programme than before it. Furthermore, athletes reported positive increases in social capital variables such as satisfaction (hedonic wellbeing) and peer motivational climate. Social validation interviews reinforced the positive results of this leadership programme with athletes detailing how they developed a shared understanding of leadership, and how each member can contribute to team leadership even when not holding a formal leadership role. Once more, coaches could be educated as to how to develop this shared approach to leadership within a high-performance environment.

These two evidence-based interventions offer promise in educating coaches as to how to apply a more holistic approach with their athletes. However, it is important to note that educating high-performance coaches on their own may be insufficient to increase their engagement in TL or SL behaviours. Therefore, consideration should be given to other determinants of behaviour change and how they might influence coaches' engagement in these behaviours. For example, from an environmental perspective, does the high-performance culture in which a coach operates advocate for and support the use of these behaviours? Sport and Exercise Psychologists may have a key role to play not only in providing support to coaches in how to implement these behaviours but also in facilitating high-performance sport units to adapt their organisational or team cultures (Collins & Cruickshank, 2015) to support and reinforce these adaptive leadership behaviours. Indeed, Fletcher and Wagstaff (2009) have highlighted the potential impact organisational or team culture can have on the wellbeing and performance of individuals. However, cultural change within elite sport environments can be very challenging. High-performance teams (and the leaders within these teams) are under pressure to get things right quickly due to the outcome-based funding models applied to elite sport by many countries in recent years (Cruickshank, Collins, & Minten, 2014). However, successful cultural change is a complex dynamic process that takes time and requires input from many stakeholders. This is illustrated by Cruickshank, Collins, and Minten (2014, 2015) in their model for cultural change in elite sport. These researchers propose that the cultural change process requires a period of initial evaluation, planning and impact, in which performance leaders refrain from engaging in actions that would not be appropriately received by stakeholders and must reinforce optimal immediate results. They also suggest that performance leaders must continually engage with internal and external stakeholders to promote long-term acceptance of these changes. Therefore, while education is an important step in changing coaches' leadership behaviours to promote athlete wellbeing, it must be situated within a supportive and reinforcing organisational or team culture to ensure long-term success.

Conclusion

In summary, this chapter explores how elite coaches can support athlete wellbeing. In trying to understand this issue and the related challenges, we looked beyond elite sport to other high-performance domains and considered leadership theories that have demonstrated efficacy in promoting follower wellbeing. Drawing on theory, we developed evidence-based recommendations which could be used to overcome some of the coach behaviours that may prevent elite coaches from supporting athlete wellbeing. Finally, we examined two theoretically framed interventions targeting leadership behaviour to understand how these behaviours can be implemented within high-performance environments to support performance and wellbeing.

References

Adler, A. B., Saboe, K. N., Anderson, J., Sipos, M. L., & Thomas, J. L. (2014). Behavioral health leadership: New directions in occupational mental health. *Current Psychiatry Reports*, *16*(10), 484. https://doi.org/10.1007/s11920-014-0484-6

Arnold, R., & Fletcher, D. (2012). A research synthesis and taxonomic classification of the organizational stressors encountered by sport performers. *Journal of Sport and Exercise Psychology*, *34*(3), 397–429. https://doi.org/10.1123/jsep.34.3.397

Arthur, C. A., Bastardoz, N., & Eklund, R. (2017). Transformational leadership in sport: Current status and future directions. *Current Opinion in Psychology*, *16*, 78–83. https://doi.org/10.1016/j.copsyc.2017.04.001

Arthur, C. A., & Hardy, L. (2014). Transformational leadership: A quasi-experimental study. *Leadership and Organization Development Journal*, *35*(1), 38–53. https://doi.org/10.1108/LODJ-03-2012-0033

Arthur, C., Hardy, L., & Woodman, T. (2012). Realising the Olympic dream: Vision, support and challenge. *Reflective Practice*, *13*(3), 1–8. https://doi.org/10.1080/14623943.2012.670112

Aufegger, L., Shariq, O., Bicknell, C., Ashrafian, H., & Darzi, A. (2019). Can shared leadership enhance clinical team management? A systematic review. *Leadership in Health Services*, *32*(2), 309–335. https://doi.org/10.1108/LHS-06-2018-0033

Bass, B. M. (1985). *Leadership and performance beyond expectations*. New York: Free Press.

Basu, S., Qayyum, H., & Mason, S. (2017). Occupational stress in the ED: A systematic literature review. *Emergency Medicine Journal*, *34*(7), 441–447. https://doi.org/10.1136/emermed-2016-205827

Brandstorp, H., Kirkengen, A. L., Sterud, B., Haugland, B., & Halvorsen, P. A. (2015). Leadership practice as interaction in primary care emergency team training. *Action Research*, *13*(1), 84–101. https://doi.org/10.1177/1476750314566660

Collins, D., & Cruickshank, A. (2015). Take a walk on the wild side: Exploring, identifying, and developing consultancy expertise with elite performance team leaders. *Psychology of Sport & Exercise, 16*(1), 74–82. https://doi.org/10.1016/j.psychsport.2014.08.002

Cook, A. F., Arora, V. M., Rasinski, K. A., Curlin, F. A., & Yoon, J. D. (2014). The prevalence of medical student mistreatment and its association with burnout. *Academic Medicine: Journal of the Association of American Medical Colleges, 89*(5), 749–754. https://doi.org/10.1097/ACM.0000000000000204

Cotterill, S. T., & Fransen, K. (2016). Athlete leadership in sport teams: Current understanding and future directions. *International Review of Sport and Exercise Psychology, 9*(1), 116–133. https://doi.org/10.1080/1750984X.2015.1124443

Cox, J. F., Pearce, C. L., & Perry, M. L. (2003). Toward a model of shared leadership and distributed influence in the innovation process. In C. A. Pearce & J. A. Conger (Eds.), *Shared leadership: Reframing the hows and whys of leadership* (pp. 69–102). Thousand Oaks, CA: Sage.

Cruickshank, A., Collins, D., & Minten, S. (2014). Driving and sustaining culture change in Olympic sport performance teams: A first exploration and grounded theory. *Journal of Sport & Exercise Psychology, 36*(1), 107–120. https://doi.org/10.1123/jsep.2013-0133

Cruickshank, A., Collins, D., & Minten, S. (2015). Driving and sustaining culture change in professional sport performance teams: A grounded theory. *Psychology of Sport & Exercise, 20*, 40–50. https://doi.org/10.1016/j.psychsport.2015.04.007

D'Innocenzo, L., Mathieu, J. E., & Kukenberger, M. R. (2014). A meta-analysis of different forms of shared leadership–team performance relations. *Journal of Management, 20*, 1–28. https://doi.org/10.1177/0149206314525205

Duguay, A. M., Loughead, T. M., & Munroe-Chandler, K. J. (2016). The development, implementation, and evaluation of an athlete leadership development program with female varsity athletes. *The Sport Psychologist, 30*(2), 154. https://doi.org/10.1123/tsp.2015-0050

Fletcher, D., & Wagstaff, C. R. D. (2009). Organizational psychology in elite sport: Its emergence, application and future. *Psychology of Sport and Exercise, 10*(4), 427–434. https://doi.org/10.1016/j.psychsport.2009.03.009

Fransen, K., Haslam, S. A., Mallett, C. J., Steffens, N. K., Peters, K., & Boen, F. (2017). Is perceived athlete leadership quality related to team effectiveness? A comparison of three professional sports teams. *Journal of Science and Medicine in Sport, 20*(8), 800–806. https://doi.org/10.1016/j.jsams.2016.11.024

Fransen, K., Mertens, N., Cotterill, S. T., Vande Broek, G., & Boen, F. (2019). From autocracy to empowerment: Teams with shared leadership perceive their coaches to be better leaders. *Journal of Applied Sport Psychology, 32*(1), 1–23. https://doi.org/10.1080/10413200.2019.1617370

Fransen, K., Van Puyenbroeck, S., Loughead, T. M., Vanbeselaere, N., De Cuyper, B., Vande Broek, G., & Boen, F. (2015). Who takes the lead? Social network analysis as a pioneering tool to investigate shared leadership within sports teams. *Social Networks, 43*, 28–38. https://doi.org/10.1016/j.socnet.2015.04.003

Goldberg, D., & Williams, P. (1988). *A user's guide to the General Health Questionnaire*. Windsor: NFER-Nelson.

Hardy, L., Arthur, C. A., Jones, G., Shariff, A., Munnoch, K., Isaacs, I., & Allsopp, A. J. (2010). The relationship between transformational leadership behaviors, psychological, and training outcomes in elite military recruits. *The Leadership Quarterly, 21*(1), 20–32. https://doi.org/10.1016/j.leaqua.2009.10.002

Harms, P. D., Krasikova, D. V., Vanhove, A. J., Herian, M. N., & Lester, P. B. (2013). Stress and emotional well-being in military organizations. *Research in Occupational Stress and Well Being, 11*, 103–132. https://doi.org/10.1108/S1479-3555(2013)0000011008

Hays, K. F. (2009). *Performance psychology in action.* Washington, DC: American Psychological Association.
Hodge, K., Henry, G., & Smith, W. (2014). A case study of excellence in elite sport: Motivational climate in a world champion team. *The Sport Psychologist. 28*(1), 60. https://doi.org/10.1123/tsp.2013-0037
Inceoglu, I., Thomas, G., Chu, C., Plans, D., & Gerbasi, A. (2018). Leadership behavior and employee well-being: An integrated review and a future research agenda. *The Leadership Quarterly, 29*(1), 179–202. https://doi.org/10.1016/j.leaqua.2017.12.006
Jones, N., Campion, B., Keeling, M., & Greenberg, N. (2018). Cohesion, leadership, mental health stigmatisation and perceived barriers to care in UK military personnel. *Journal of Mental Health, 27*(1), 10–18. https://doi.org/10.3109/09638237.2016.1139063
Jones, N., Seddon, R., Fear, N. T., McAllister, P., Wessely, S., & Greenberg, N. (2012). Leadership, cohesion, morale, and the mental health of UK armed forces in Afghanistan. *Psychiatry: Interpersonal and Biological Processes, 75*(1), 49–59. https://doi.org/10.1521/psyc.2012.75.1.49
Judge, T. A., & Piccolo, R. F. (2004). Transformational and transactional leadership: A meta-analytic test of their relative validity. *Journal of Applied Psychology, 89*(5), 755–768. https://doi.org/10.1037/0021-9010.89.5.755
Lord, R. G., Day, D. V., Zaccaro, S. J., Avolio, B. J., & Eagly, A. H. (2017). Leadership in applied psychology: Three waves of theory and research. *Journal of Applied Psychology, 102*(3), 434–451. https://doi.org/10.1037/apl0000089
Montano, D., Reeske, A., Franke, F., & Hüffmeier, J. (2017). Leadership, followers' mental health and job performance in organizations: A comprehensive meta-analysis from an occupational health perspective. *Journal of Organizational Behavior, 38*(3), 327–350. https://doi.org/10.1002/job.2124
Morgan, P. B. C., Fletcher, D., & Sarkar, M. (2015). Understanding team resilience in the world's best athletes: A case study of a rugby union World Cup winning team. *Psychology of Sport and Exercise, 16,* 91–100. https://doi.org/10.1016/j.psychsport.2014.08.007
Podsakoff, P. M., MacKenzie, S. B., Moorman, R. H., & Fetter, R. (1990). Transformational leader behaviors and their effect on followers' trust in leader, satisfaction, and organizational citizenship behaviors. *The Leadership Quarterly, 1,* 107–142.
Salas, E., Driskell, J. E., & Hughes, S. (2013). Introduction: The study of stress and human performance. In J. E. Driskell & E. Salas (Eds.), *Stress and human performance* (pp. 1–46). Mahwah, NJ: Erlbaum.
Serban, A., & Roberts, A. J. B. (2016). Exploring antecedents and outcomes of shared leadership in a creative context: A mixed-methods approach. *The Leadership Quarterly, 27*(2), 181–199. https://doi.org/10.1016/j.leaqua.2016.01.009
Smith, M. J., Young, D. J., Figgins, S. G., & Arthur, C. A. (2017). Transformational leadership in elite sport: A qualitative analysis of effective leadership behaviors in cricket. *The Sport Psychologist, 31*(1), 1–15. https://doi.org/10.1123/tsp.2015-0077
Stenling, A., & Tafvelin, S. (2014). Transformational leadership and well-Being in sports: The mediating role of need satisfaction. *Journal of Applied Sport Psychology, 26*(2), 182–196. https://doi.org/10.1080/10413200.2013.819392
Zhu, J., Liao, Z., Yam, K. C., & Johnson, R. E. (2018). Shared leadership: A state-of-the-art review and future research agenda. *Journal of Organizational Behavior, 39*(7), 834–852. https://doi.org/10.1002/job.2296

6

SUPPORTING ATHLETES FROM DIFFERENT CULTURES AND NATIONALITIES

The case of women's football

Claire-Marie Roberts and Katie Rood

Introduction

In professional team sports, a global market for the buying and selling of players has emerged and is currently thriving. In a sport like women's football, this is out of necessity due to the lack of a sustainable talent pool in the 22 countries that currently run professional leagues. The movement of athletes from different nationalities and cultures to a new club overseas brings with it common challenges for the individual, such as loneliness, homesickness, difficulties associated with a change in living circumstances, the stress of relocation and the emotional consequences of the negative impact the move has on the athlete's family. Add to this, challenges with language barriers, a loss of cultural and personal identity and social support networks, problems with basic logistics and a culture shock – this is a common recipe for significant threats to the athlete's wellbeing. This chapter examines the athletic and cultural transitions of a professional female footballer who moved from her home in New Zealand to become a member of the first women's football team at Juventus in Italy. The athlete's story is presented first followed by a discussion of the extant research through the lens of a quasi-normative career transition requiring effective coping mechanisms to allow the individual to continue to function in their personal and professional life. The chapter concludes with ideas of how best to support the cultural transitions of athletes with a focus on individual holistic wellbeing.

DOI: 10.4324/9780429287923-6

ATHLETE VOICE

Katie Rood – professional footballer, Lincoln Ladies F.C., Juventus Women's F.C., Bristol City Women's F.C. and Lewes F.C. Women

I have been a professional footballer all of my adult life. I hold New Zealand and British dual nationality, and I've played for four professional international clubs (Lincoln Ladies F.C., Juventus Women's F.C., Bristol City Women's F.C. and Lewes F.C. Women) outside of my antipodean base. I have represented the New Zealand National team, having scored 5 goals in 8 caps, and I'm in the running to make the New Zealand Tokyo Olympic women's football team for 2020. As an individual, I hold strong environmental values and I am a passionate vegan. Due to my various international moves, I have been required to make a number of cultural athletic career transitions, overcoming many challenges to perform at my best as an athlete. What I have found during the course of my career is that these challenges often go unnoticed by football clubs, coaches, support staff and players' unions. Here, I provide an account of how these cultural transitions have challenged me as an individual and as an athlete.

I had moved away from home to pursue football, with the objective of being selected for the New Zealand Football team. The coach told me that because women's football in New Zealand isn't professional and not played at a high enough standard, I'd need to play overseas to have a chance of being selected. I took them at their word, and as I turned 18, I decided to take up the offer of a trial at Lincoln Ladies' F.C. – a professional football club in the small English East Midlands town of Lincoln. As an 18-year-old, this was my first ever long-haul journey. It took me 35 hours to reach my destination. Along the way, I had lost my luggage and I had been interrogated by immigration, because of my foreigner status. Apparently, because I couldn't tell them whether I was staying for 4 weeks or 11 months and, therefore, didn't have a return ticket, they were reluctant to let me through the border. The day I arrived, I had landed on U.K. soil at 0900, and by 1930, I was training with the team – after a 35 hour flight, and a traumatic experience at immigration. My mind-body connection was completely out of whack – this is not good when you're trialling for your first professional team.

Overcoming extreme fatigue and disorientation, I ended up being selected for the Lincoln Ladies' team. Unfortunately, I got injured at the end of my first season. At this time, I was more than ready to get back to New Zealand. The Club told me that they wouldn't pay for me to return, and I certainly couldn't afford the flight home. Luckily, they finally relented and gave me some money towards the flight – just before they went into administration! After my rehabilitation, I decided the time was right to try to join an overseas club again. This time, my agent found an opportunity at Juventus Women's F.C. in Italy. Within three days of the invite to trial I had packed my life up and was on a plane to Europe – this was really tough for me emotionally to leave all of my family and friends behind at such short notice.

When I landed in Turin, I had 2 to 3 days before I was expected to trial for the team. I was put up in an average quality club-owned hotel in a tiny village and had to share my small room with another trialist. The facilities were a far cry from my home environment. What I did find though is that people whose English was not particularly strong didn't really engage with me. On many occasions, I was lost and confused at some of the instructions the coach gave during sessions. I also found that when staff were emotional, they spoke almost entirely in Italian and rarely in English. I would have to ask for players to translate but at times it was awkward because I knew the coach was mad, but I wasn't entirely sure why and that made me feel very excluded. On a more practical level, I found it really hard to do simple things like walk down the street and buy fruit. I found the whole issue of food in Italy very difficult to cope with. There is a strong cultural focus on food – especially meat. During one of my first team meals, plates of veal hit the table all around me and all I could think of was baby cows. Literally, nobody was aware of what they were eating. I was so upset. It was often a challenge to find vegan food and to be catered for in Italy so I often ended up, especially in team settings, eating very bland food and an unbalanced diet because they didn't make an effort to cater for me.

There were additional logistical issues that were associated with the team being the first Juventus women's squad – for example, the club didn't know how to deal with us foreigners! I remember needing to find an apartment to live in when I signed my contract. Juventus allocated the men's accommodation manager to us to help us in our search. He started sending us details of huge mansion-like properties as if we were able to afford them on our small salaries! I think it's fair to say that extended the time it took us to find somewhere suitable. Practicality-wise, it took me 3 months to get a bank account and associated debit card sorted. It was also a nightmare to lose anything as a foreigner – bank cards, phone, I.D., etc. This was beyond frustrating and took much time and emotional effort to get things sorted – not good when you're trying to focus on training and playing football. Additionally, the concept of time seems to be thought of differently in Italy. We would more often than not start our training sessions 30–45 minutes late and this took some getting used to. We had to laugh when our first competitive game we played as a team kicked off late!

We found at times that although our teammates had a lack of understanding as to what it was really like to be living in a foreign country. For example, we didn't have our own transport for the first 6 months, so we relied heavily on public transport. We would get back really late from away games and have to run to make sure we caught the last tram home because no one would offer us a ride – even though they were heading in the same direction! This was common, as was a distinct preference for, and favouritism towards the home-grown players. They would always get selected over the foreigners, and the club rules were flexed for them on a regular basis.

Then, there was the issue of communication. I had a lot of difficulty communicating with the coach – I had a feeling that she wouldn't understand where I was coming from and as a result the level of communication needed wasn't there. I never fully understood what my role was in the team and as a result I often felt misunderstood and underappreciated. I was concerned that the potential language and communication barrier with the staff could risk me making my situation worse if I had been misinterpreted, so that meant that I wouldn't attempt to communicate properly with them.

During my time in Italy, I was often envious of my teammates being able to go home often and spend time with their families – because I was so far away from home this wasn't possible for me. If we had a couple of days off, the European players would fly home and the Italian-based players would go and see their families. It was okay the first few times as the weather was nice, and I was bold enough to travel on my own but as winter approached it became harder and lonelier. It was really difficult to integrate into the community outside of football because of the limitations that come with not knowing the language properly. Thankfully, halfway through the season, my boyfriend came over to Italy for a couple of months, but it didn't work out for him there. I became his only source of support and this was difficult on both of us. We couldn't manage his moods and it got dark for some time; he knew I was struggling too – without question, this impacted on my performance on the pitch. I can imagine in the men's game, the spouses and families would be helped and accommodated when they move to a new place. A further cultural consideration was the patriarchal nature of Italian society, so the concept of a woman playing football for them was odd and they weren't aware that it was a "thing". There were old patriarchal views voiced regularly and even some of the staff at the training facility admitted that they had never seen females playing sport before.

I was signed by Bristol City Women's F.C. for the 2018/2019 season and subsequently Lewes F.C. Women for the 2019/2020 season – making a return to England to play football. Due to my previous experiences in England and Italy, I found the cultural transition much easier to deal with. For my return, I had become more resilient as an individual. Having said that, I still continue to see foreign players struggling with adapting to the new culture they find themselves in and I think football clubs need to do more to support them. As a more experienced player, I can help mentor them having been through the same experience myself. However, while support provided by teammates is important, there is an urgent need for more professional structured support from professionals at the club – especially when there are language barriers.

SCHOLAR VOICE

Exploring Katie's experiences

Throughout their sporting careers, athletes' transition through many different stages to develop and maintain their sporting expertise. Indeed, an athlete's career is punctuated by transitions specific to the developmental lifecycle in sport (e.g. junior to senior representation) including the end of their career, as well as to other elements of the athletes' life (Roberts & Davis, 2017). Transitions have been defined as a turning phase in athletes' development that brings about a set of demands (usually appraised as stressors) and requires adequate coping processes to continue athletic and parallel careers such as education or work (Stambulova & Wylleman, 2014; Wylleman, Reints, & De Knop, 2013). Transitions can be both sport and developmentally related and can be categorised as 'normative', 'non-normative' and 'quasi-normative' (Stambulova, 2016). Normative transitions are predictable turning points in the course of an athletic career such as a progression from one competitive level to the next, or the transition from adolescence to adulthood. Non-normative transitions on the other hand are less predictable, more idiosyncratic events such as injury or deselection during an athletic career, or atypical and major lifetime events, which do not follow the predictable developmental pattern of the lifecycle such as participation at the World Cup or the Olympic/Paralympic Games (Koulenti & Anastassiou-Hadjicharalambous, 2011). Non-normative transitions by their very nature are difficult to prepare for and consequently difficult to cope with. Quasi-normative transitions, however, are predictable but only for certain groups of athletes, for example, cultural transitions for transnational athletes.

Katie describes her experience as a transnational athlete earlier. Transnational athletes are defined by Ryba and Stambulova (2013) as mobile subjects whose athletic and non-athletic development spans international borders. The frequency of the transnational migration of athletes has been on the increase across a number of sporting contexts (Maguire & Falcous, 2011; Ronkainen, Harrison, & Ryba, 2014; Ryba, Haapanen, Mosek, & Ng, 2012; Ryba & Stambulov, 2013) but significantly so in professional team sports, such as football, cricket and rugby. In professional team sports specifically, a global market for the buying and selling of players has emerged and is currently thriving (Kalén, Rey, Sal de Rellán-Guerra, & Lago-Peñas, 2019). In football, for example, the unhindered migration of players has increased substantially during the last 25 years, as limits on the number of foreign players in the European leagues have been lifted and clubs have become more commercially minded (Milanovic, 2005).

There are a number of factors that drive athlete migration from their home countries into a host country. As Katie alludes, these include a lack of sufficient indigenous talent in the host country, plus the relative status and reputation of the sport in different countries, including the quality and styles of play, characteristics of players and economic prowess of clubs and leagues. Indeed, some leagues and clubs seek to attract the best talent from overseas to enhance their likelihood of competitive success (Maguire, 2011). Perhaps, one of the most salient examples of this is in women's football as Katie illustrates. Across the 22 countries that now run professional leagues, rarely is there a sustainable domestic talent pool to populate their teams, and, therefore, an unprecedented number of female footballers are moving into domestic leagues from overseas.

The experience of migrating to play sport in a host country differs between genders (Maguire, 2011). Although there is growth in the migration of female athletes internationally, the trend remains male-dominated in part due to the social structure of gender norms (Maguire, 2011) and the relative infancy of female professional sport worldwide. It is evident that female professional athletes earn significantly less than their male counterparts (Koller, 2019), however, the large distinction in wages is not the only difference female athletes face when making a cultural transition. The degree to which athletes are exploited, dislocated and require cultural adjustment varies across gender too (Maguire, 2011). In fact, how gender is perceived culturally in the host nation can shape a migrant athlete's experience. In countries where there are significant levels of gender inequality, the cultural transition may bring about significant risks to the athlete's wellbeing. Katie refers to this eloquently in her account of playing football in the heavily patriarchal Italian society (Medaglia, 2001).

Published research supports Katie's accounts of the challenges and stressors she faced as an athlete moving to a foreign country with a different culture. Indeed, the common challenges highlighted in research suggests loneliness (Fry & Bloyce, 2017), homesickness (Baghurst, Fiaud, Tapps, Bounds, & LaGasse, 2018), difficulties associated with a change in living circumstances, the stress of relocation and the impact the move has on the athlete's family (Bahdur & Pruna, 2017) are all threats to athlete wellbeing. In addition, there are often logistical challenges associated with language barriers, communication problems, religious or spiritual differences and cultural mismatches (Schinke, McGannon, Battochio, & Wells, 2013). Migration may also bring with it a loss of cultural and personal identity and social support networks. These common challenges (or stressors) present a significant risk to the athlete's wellbeing and require effective coping mechanisms to allow the individual to continue to function in their personal and professional life.

Based on transition taxonomy, cultural transitions for athletes are classed as quasi-normative – a predictable period of change – but only for athletes that experience geographic mobility. Transnationalism is a term that encapsulates the living of everyday life across numerous physical and discursive borders (i.e. geographic, linguistic and socio-political), being simultaneously embedded in multiple cultural locations and social networks, and having a fluid mobile identity (Glick Schiller, Basch, & Szanton Blanc, 1992; Vertovec, 2001). Being a transnational athlete brings with it the requirement to face, and successfully adjust to a number of challenges, that when played out alongside an athletic career can be extremely challenging and disruptive to wellbeing (Ryba, Stambulova, Ronkainen, Bundgaard, & Selänne, 2015). As a coach or a practitioner working in sport, it is fundamental that the interconnectedness or intersection of the variety of transitions (both sport and non-sport) the transnational athlete encounters is fully understood to recognise how best to support them (Wylleman & Lavallée, 2004). It is, therefore, important to view the transnational athlete as someone who is developing athletically and personally in "a fluid, shifting, and often culturally ambivalent social field beyond national borders" (Ryba et al., 2015). While athletes' development admittedly encompasses the athletic, psychological, psychosocial and academic/vocational domains described in the Wylleman and Lavallée's (2004) model, central to understanding transnational (career) development is the cultural transition backdrop that either facilitates or constrains it.

To recap, female football players are often required to migrate to a host country out of need rather than want. Currently, female footballers can only make a living out of playing football in 22 out of 147 countries in the world (Tiesler, 2016). Therefore, in order for them to progress in their sport, it is suggested that migration to a professional footballing nation is fundamental to their athletic development. With this need comes many challenges. As discussed earlier, the transition to a new country and a new culture brings with it many stressors that require effective coping including the overriding requirement to settle into a new club and perform athletically at the highest level. The following sections will examine these challenges and their impact on wellbeing in greater detail, concluding with suggested solutions for the future management of cultural transitions in athletes.

Loneliness, homesickness and a change in living circumstances

The loneliness and homesickness that result from arriving in a new country and getting used to a new culture can lead to difficulties for athletes in transition (Bahdur & Pruna, 2017). As Katie explains, leaving close friends and family overseas can fracture an athlete's social support provision and hamper the coping process needed to adapt to a new cultural environment. Apart from the reality of leaving family and friends behind, the individual may find themselves living in very different circumstances. Katie described being housed in a hotel temporarily, although many migrating athletes encounter this living arrangement for an extended period of time while a more permanent home is found. In some circumstances, athletes may house share with strangers or with a host family if the individual is a minor. Either way, this is often a departure from the living arrangements the individuals left at home, and the adjustment to the new way of living, whether permanent or temporary is not always straightforward. As athletes can be signed by professional clubs from the age of 16, their relocation may be the first time they have travelled out of their home country. For those living alone for the first time, they may have no idea of how to perform basic tasks. The new living arrangements all require adjustment which can bring about increased stress and pressure on the player – with consequences for them both on and off the pitch. The arrival and immediate immersion in a new country and environment can result in a "culture shock" (Baghurst et al., 2018). Homesickness is considered to be a component of a culture shock – defined as "a search for familiar environments and means to create a belonging feeling" (Baghurst et al., 2018, p. 78). If the athlete is unable to achieve the feeling of belonging in their new surroundings, this may result in depression, a sense of rejection and isolation (Archer, Ireland, Amos, Broad, & Currid, 1998; Constantine, Kindaichi, Okazaki, Gainor, & Baden, 2005; Pedersen, 1995).

Care in a challenging football club culture

On the basis that caring relationships may be possible and even conducive to high-performance sport, Cronin, Knowles, and Enright (2020) explore care within a case study of a Premier League Football Club. The study unpacked the experiences of a single strength and conditioning coach as he sought to care for an injured athlete. Consistent with Noel's experiences, the case study illustrated how caring relationships can be difficult to establish in performative settings because of an emphasis on short-term results. The individuals (e.g. coaches) within the football club were also subject to wider economic and social pressures to win games. Their employment was linked to these results and was thus insecure. Additionally, the case study identified how undefined notions of care and micro-political actions may constrain good athlete wellbeing practices. For example, working in a high-performance context is often an interdisciplinary activity. This requires interaction between key personnel, such as coaches, players, medical staff and sport science staff. Thus, caring relationships cannot solely be dyadic but need to include a wide range of individuals. As Cronin et al. (2020) illustrate, however, the power dynamics between these individuals can inhibit the care provided to athletes. Cronin et al. (2020) conclude that an emphasis on short-term results and micro-political actions that are heightened by the precarious nature of employment can contribute to a culture in which it is challenging to establish and maintain caring relationships.

Of course, this does not mean that care cannot happen in football. Rather as Noel illustrates, there are examples of good caring practices within football. Furthermore, the aforementioned research (e.g. Cronin & Armour, 2018; Knust & Fisher, 2015) illustrates that caring can actually be a part of successful high-performance environments; indeed, Noddings' concepts (engrossment, motivational displacement and reciprocity) may be of interest to managers and owners who seek to develop more caring cultures. Moreover, this evidence may provide a powerful motive for stakeholders to invest in and support athlete wellbeing. Nonetheless, in contexts, which have limited financial and human resources, it can be a challenge to care for athletes. This is because as Noddings (2013) explains, care is a demanding form of emotional labour. In the absence of resources, for example, allocated time, there is a risk that this labour is either provided by staff in addition to, or instead of their existing duties, or perhaps not at all. Thus, Noel suggests that it is important that (1) senior staff support athlete wellbeing by allocating resources, and that (2) athlete wellbeing does not become a topic discussed solely in meetings but a behaviour, which is valued and modelled by these senior staff on a daily basis. In considering the successful implementation of wellbeing strategies centred upon the creation of caring cultures, football clubs must recognise the arising challenges faced by all organisations tasked with instilling change and consider the most appropriate approach to overcome such challenges.

Culture shock

In an extension of the loneliness, homesickness and a change in living circumstances, foreign athletes like Katie may experience a wider "culture shock" (Oberg, 1960) when relocating to a host country. It relates to a response characterised by "the anxiety that results from losing all of the familiar signs and symbols of social intercourse" (p. 177). It may involve the distortion of self-reflections that happen as a result of responses from naturalised inhabitants of the host country and an overriding expectation to adapt behaviour to suit. In some host countries, the culture shock may result from sport-specific issues, such as different training methods, talent identification and financial models (e.g. Schinke et al., 2013). The process by which migrant athletes adopt the cultural patterns of the host country is known as "acculturation", which for the individual refers to a change in attitudes, beliefs, behaviours and values (Szapocznik & Kurtines, 1980). The larger the contrast between the immigrant athlete's original and host cultures, the more difficult acculturation will be. Indeed, previous studies have found a positive relationship between psychological distress and acculturation (e.g. Kaplan & Marks, 1990).

Language barriers

Katie described one of the most common challenges associated with adjustment to a new country and culture – the language barrier (Bahdur & Pruna, 2017). She portrayed a distinct loss of communication competence (Zaharna, 1989) and the problems this generated on a day-to-day logistical level but also in generating a feeling of isolation. Even a school-level grasp of a host language is seldom sufficient enough to help orientate the athlete in the culture and day-to-day life of their host culture. Although some of the more affluent sports will employ player liaison officers, or professional translators, the type of conversations held with these individuals is anecdotally transactional, and often does not include feelings or emotions, instead focused at a practical level "my TV doesn't work" or "I'm not sure which appliance is the dishwasher". Realising you have a complete inability to express yourself can add to the frustrations encountered on being dropped into another space and time, albeit on the same planet. For some, the regional variations of a host country can challenge even the most fluent individual. Most notably, a lack of host language competence becomes critical when it affects the athlete's ability to communicate with coaches, support staff and teammates. This presents a number of risks to wellbeing including a lack of role clarity, a reduction in athletic development and a lack of assimilation into the team which may generate feelings of isolation and problems with team dynamics (e.g. Battochio et al., 2013; Ryba et al., 2012; Schinke, Yukelson, Bartolacci, Battochio, & Johnstone, 2011).

Logistics

Clearly, the logistics of living in a different country with a different culture require adjusting to as Katie illustrated in her account of moving to Italy. This often involves a lengthy period of information gathering, some trial and error, and ultimately adjustment as the athlete compares these practices in their host country to those they are accustomed to. For example, anecdotally, immigrant athletes report problems with fundamental financial processes, such as the setting up of bank accounts, the logistics of direct debits, paying bills and money exchange. In addition, in some circumstances, getting used to driving on the opposite side of the road, negotiating public transport, understanding general opening hours of shops and where to obtain goods are all arrangements that may require adaption by the athlete. In addition, certain countries are often associated with different styles of play, depending on the sport in question; therefore, the migrant athlete will need to adapt to a style of play that diverges from one that they are used to.

These logistical stressors presented to transnational athletes migrating to a foreign country to play their sport adds to an already extensive list of stressors present in the sport performance environment (Roberts, Faull, & Tod, 2016). The continuous presence of these and so many other stressors has led academics and practitioners alike to conclude that they present threats to wellbeing and in many cases lead to mental ill-health (Arnold & Fletcher, 2012; Roberts et al., 2016).

Discrimination

In her account, Katie described a situation where her domestic teammates were prioritised for selection over foreign players. Although there are few accounts of the topic of discrimination in the migrant athlete population specifically, athletes from different ethnic or religious backgrounds to their host country may be at risk. Empirical evidence provides an inconclusive picture at the elite end of the spectrum of sport, but when professional clubs in host countries are tasked with developing home-grown talent, there is the likelihood that indigenous athletes are given preferential treatment over migrant athletes. Indeed, a 2014 analysis from the National Basketball Association (NBA) in America concluded that wage discrimination existed for foreign players (Hoffer & Freidel, 2014). There is also the likelihood of discrimination on the basis of religion, spirituality or personal values if this differs significantly from that of the host country – as Katie illustrated when she spoke of the lack of accommodation for vegan athletes in Italy. As expected, discrimination has a powerful negative influence on wellbeing, especially for immigrants (Noh, Beiser, Kaspar, Hou, & Rummens, 1999; Schmitt, Branscombe, Postmes, & Garcia, 2014). It has been reported as the single biggest detriment to life satisfaction and mental health (Berry & Hou, 2017).

"hitting the ground running"

As Katie aptly describes when she talks about her experiences playing for foreign clubs, it is not uncommon for migrating athletes to arrive into their new host country, and be expected to train immediately, or even play a full match/feature in a competition. The teammates, fans and even sport science support staff may not always know that the player/athlete has just stepped off a long-haul flight only hours beforehand, and the normal standard of expectations is rarely lowered to take this into account. Generally, most of the people in the host country, and at the host club will not be familiar with the characteristic performances of the migrating player, and, therefore, there is an expectation that these athlete migrants should be able to adapt and culturally perform to make a measurable impact almost straight away on arrival. Naturally, this expectation places a great deal of stress on the athlete as they are forced to impress their hosts after (in some cases) long, arduous journeys and sleep deprivation. In isolating the sleep deprivation aspect of long distance travel, numerous studies have demonstrated the detrimental effects on both physical and cognitive performance, including impaired reaction time and negative influences on memory (Banks & Dinges, 2007; Reynolds & Banks, 2010). In fact, the impact of poor sleep is magnified in athletes due to the likelihood of the high-performance demands of their sport highlighting any small amount of negative influences on physical and emotional wellbeing (Ryswyk et al., 2017).

Food

The general quality of food and availability of cuisine may present a problem for some athletes during migration. In many cases, due to the significance of dietary practices in sport, and the clear cultural influences of diet, "dietary acculturation" (Satia-Abouta, 2010) is necessary. "Dietary acculturation" specifically refers to the process that occurs when members of a migrating group adopt the eating patterns/food choices of their new environment (Satia-Abouta et al., 2001). For some athletes, this means that their dietary practices may become less healthy (Satia-Abouta, 2010) or more difficult to manage – especially for those athletes with specific dietary requirements such as food allergies, or those who adopt a vegetarian or vegan diet. This was certainly true for Katie as a vegan with strong core environmental values. In her case, the lack of respect and associated accommodation for her special diet not only led to emotional problems as her teammates were fed large plates of meat in front of her at team dinners but also had a detrimental physical impact as she ended up eating an unbalanced diet. The link between a good, balanced diet and mental and physical wellbeing is long-established (Owen & Corfe, 2017), not to mention the criticality of diet in the maintenance of superior athletic performance (Khan, Khan, Khan, Khan, & Khan, 2017).

Solutions

Overall, there is a myriad of different challenges that require a wide range of coping resources to help increase the likelihood of a successful cultural transition for the athlete in question. These are grouped into individual, group level and organisational approaches or interventions. On an individual level, problem and emotion-focused coping, positive reframing and acceptance and seeking social support (Aroian et al., 2009; Crockett et al., 2007; Jibeen & Khalid, 2010; Kloek, Peters, & Sijtsma, 2013) can help bring about adaptation. Certainly, access to appropriate social support is key in bringing about successful adaptation. In some sports, a system where the migrant athlete is mentored by an indigenous athlete can be a useful intervention. In addition, migrant athletes often form unofficial support groups, to help combine resources to face collective challenges faced. At the organisational level, awareness of the issues referred to in this chapter is the first step in understanding the challenges faced by migrant athletes in cultural transition. The provision of cultural adaptation programmes may help expedite athletes' transition into their role in their host country. It may also helpfully reinforce the view that you cannot learn a new culture in days, so an extended intervention may be effective in bring about lasting change and increase the likelihood of greater levels of inclusion within the host sport, club, neighbourhood or country. Increased inclusion is associated with higher levels of wellbeing (e.g. Battochio et al., 2013). At the very least, engaging the services of a translator and providing lessons in the official language of the host nation would serve the athlete well as tangible support. Certainly, when coping is effective and successful acculturation leads to adaptation, this is likely to result in psychological and emotional wellbeing and enhanced athletic performance.

References

Archer, J., Ireland, J., Amos, S.-L., Broad, H., & Currid, L. (1998). Derivation of a homesickness scale. *British Journal of Psychology, 89*(2), 205–221. https://doi.org/10.1111/j.2044-8295.1998.tb02681.x

Arnold, R., & Fletcher, D. (2012). A research synthesis and taxonomic classification of the organizational stressors encountered by sport performers. *Journal of Sport & Exercise Psychology, 34*(3), 397–429. https://doi.org/10.1123/jsep.34.3.397

Aroian, K. J., Hough, E. S., Templin, T. N., Kulwicki, A., Ramaswamy, V., & Katz, A. (2009). Model of mother- child adjustment in Arab Muslim immigrants to the U.S. *Social Science and Medicine, 69*(9), 1377–1386. https://doi.org/10.1016/j.socscimed.2009.08.027

Baghurst, T., Fiaud, V., Tapps, T., Bounds, E., & LaGasse, A. (2018). Considerations when coaching the International athlete. *International Journal of Kinesiology in Higher Education, 2*(3), 76–86. https://doi.org/10.1080/24711616.2018.1425936

Bahdur, K., & Pruna, R. (2017). The impact of homesickness on elite footballers. *Journal of Novel Physiotherapies, 7*, 1–7. https://doi.org/10.4172/2165-7025.1000331

Banks, S., & Dinges, D. F. (2007). Behavioral and physiological consequences of sleep restriction. *Journal of Clinical Sleep Medicine, 3*(5), 519–528. https://doi.org/10.5664/jcsm.26918

Battochio, R. C., Schinke, R. J., McGannon, K. R., Tenenbaum, G., Yukelson, D., & Crowder, T. (2013). Understanding immigrated professional athletes' support networks during post-relocation adaptation through media data. *International Journal of Sport and Exercise Psychology, 11*(1), 101–116. https://doi.org/10.1080/1612197X.2013.748996

Berry, J. W., & Hou, F. (2017). Acculturation, discrimination and wellbeing among second generation of immigrants in Canada. *International Journal of Intercultural Relations, 61*, 29–39. https://doi.org/10.1016/j.ijintrel.2017.08.003

Constantine, M. G., Kindaichi, M., Okazaki, S., Gainor, K. A., & Baden, A. L. (2005). A qualitative investigation of the cultural adjustment experiences of Asian international college women. *Cultural Diversity and Ethnic Minority Psychology, 11*(2), 162–175. https://doi.org/10.1037/1099-9809.11.2.162

Crockett, L. J., Iturbide, M. I., Torres Stone, R. A., McGinley, M., Raffaelli, M., Carlo, G. (2007). Acculturative stress, social support, and coping: Relations to psychological adjustment among Mexican American college students. *Cultural Diversity & Ethnic Minority Psychology, 13*(4), 347–355. https://doi.org/10.1037/1099-9809.13.4.347

Cronin, C., & Armour, K. (Eds.). (2018). *Care in sport coaching: Pedagogical cases.* Oxon, UK: Routledge.

Cronin, C., Knowles, Z. R., & Enright, K. (2020). The challenge to care in Premier League Football Club, *Sports Coaching Review, 9*(2), 123–146, https://doi.org/10.1080/21640629.2019.1578593

Fry, J., & Bloyce, D. (2017). 'Life in the travelling circus': A study of loneliness, work stress, and money issues in touring professional golf. *Sociology of Sport Journal, 34*(2), 148–159. https://doi.org/10.1123/ssj.2017-0002

Glick Schiller, N., Basch, L., & Szanton Blanc, C. (1992). *Toward a transnational perspective on migration.* New York: New York Academy of Sciences.

Hoffer, A. J., & Freidel, R. (2014). Does salary discrimination persist for foreign athletes in the NBA? *Applied Economics Letters, 21*(1), 1–5. https://doi.org/10.1080/13504851.2013.829183

Jibeen, T., & Khalid, R. (2010). Predictors of psychological well-being of Pakistani immigrants in Toronto, Canada. *International Journal of Intercultural Relations, 34*(5), 452–464. https://doi.org/10.1016/j.ijintrel.2010.04.010

Kalén, A., Rey, E., Sal de Rellán-Guerra, A., & Lago-Peñas, C. (2019). Are soccer players older now than before? Aging trends and market value in the last three decades of the UEFA Champions League. *Frontiers in Psychology, 10,* 76. https://doi.org/10.3389/fpsyg.2019.00076

Kaplan, M., & Marks, G. (1990). Adverse effects of acculturation: Psychological distress among Mexican American young adults. *Social Science & Medicine, 31*(12), 1313–1319. https://doi.org/10.1016/0277-9536(90)90070-9

Khan, S. U., Khan, A., Khan, S., Khan, M. K., & Khan, S. U. (2017). Perception of athletes about diet and its role in maintenance of sports performance. *Journal of Nutrition & Food Sciences, 7*(2), 592. https://doi.org/10.4172/2155-9600.1000592

Kloek, M. E., Peters, K., & Sijtsma, M. (2013). How Muslim women in the Netherlands negotiate discrimination during leisure activities. *Leisure Sciences: An Interdisciplinary Journal, 35*(5), 405–421. https://doi.org/10.1080/01490400.2013.831285

Knust, S. K., & Fisher, L. A. (2015). NCAA Division I female head coaches' experiences of exemplary care within coaching. *International Sport Coaching Journal, 2*(2), 94–107.

Koller, D. (2019). The new gender equity in elite women's sports. In N. Lough & A. N. Geurin (Eds.), *Routledge handbook of the business of women's sport.* Abingdon, UK: Routledge.

Koulenti, T., & Anastassiou-Hadjicharalambous, X. (2011). Non-normative life events. In S. Goldstein & J. A. Naglieri (Eds.), *Encyclopaedia of child behavior and development.* London: Springer.

Maguire, J. A. (2011). 'Real politic' or 'ethically based': Sport, globalization, migration and nation-state policies. *Sport in Society, 11*(4), 1040–1055. https://doi.org/10.1080/17430430802019375

Maguire, J. A., & Falcous, M. (2011). *Sport and migration: Borders, boundaries and crossings.* Abingdon, UK Routledge.

Medaglia, A. (2001). *Patriarchal structures and ethnicity in the Italian community in Britain.* Abingdon, UK: Routledge.

Milanovic, B. (2005). Globalization and goals: Does soccer show the way? *Review of International Political Economy, 12*(5), 829–850. https://doi.org/10.1080/09692290500339818

Noddings, N. (2013). *Caring: A relational approach to ethics and moral education*. Oakland, CA: University of California Press.

Noh, S., Beiser, M., Kaspar, V., Hou, F., & Rummens, J. (1999). Perceived racial discrimination, depression, and coping: A study of Southeast Asian refugees in Canada. *Journal of Health and Social Behavior, 40*(3), 193–207. https://doi.org/10.2307/2676348

Oberg, K. (1960). Culture shock: Adjustment to new cultural environments. *Practical Anthropology, 7*(4), 170–179. https://doi.org/10.1177/009182966000700405

Owen, L., & Corfe, B. (2017). The role of diet and nutrition on mental health and wellbeing. *The Proceedings of the Nutrition Society, 76*(4), 425–426. https://doi.org/10.1017/S0029665117001057

Pedersen, P. (1995). *The five stages of culture shock: Critical incidents around the world*. Westport, CT: Greenwood Press.

Reynolds, A. C., & Banks, S. (2010). Total sleep deprivation, chronic sleep restriction and sleep disruption. *Progress in Brain Research, 185*, 91–103. https://doi.org/10.1016/B978-0-444-53702-7.00006-3

Roberts, C.-M., & Davis, M. (2017). Career transition. In J. Taylor (Ed.), *Assessment in applied sport psychology*. Champaign, IL: Human Kinetics.

Roberts, C.-M., Faull, A. L., & Tod, D. (2016). Blurred lines: Performance enhancement, common mental disorders and referral in the U.K. athletic population. *Frontiers in Psychology, 7*, 1067. https://doi.org/10.3389/fpsyg.2016.01067

Ronkainen, N. J., Harrison, M., & Ryba, T. V. (2014). Running, being and Beijing – An existential exploration of a runner identity. *Qualitative Research in Psychology, 11*(2), 189–210. https://doi.org/10.1080/14780887.2013.810796

Ryba, T. V., Haapanen, S., Mosek, S., & Ng, K. (2012). Towards a conceptual understanding of acute cultural adaptation: A preliminary examination of ACA in female swimming. *Qualitative Research in Sport, Exercise and Health, 4*(1), 80–97. https://doi.org/10.1080/2159676X.2011.653498

Ryba, T. V., & Stambulova, N. (2013). Turn to a culturally informed career research and assistance in sport psychology. In N. Stambulova & T. V. Ryba (Eds.), *Athletes' careers across cultures* (pp. 1–16). Abingdon, UK: Routledge.

Ryba, T. V., Stambulova, N., Ronkainen, N. J., Bundgaard, J., & Selänne, H. (2015). Dual career pathways of transnational athletes. *Psychology of Sport & Exercise, 21*, 125–134. https://doi.org/10.1016/j.psychsport.2014.06.002

Ryswyk, E. V., Weeks, R., Bandick, L., O'Keefe, M., Vakulin, A., Catcheside, P., . . . & Antic, N. A. (2017). A novel sleep optimisation programme to improve athletes' wellbeing and performance. *European Journal of Sport Science, 17*(2), 144–151. https://doi.org/10.1080/17461391.2016.1221470

Satia-Abouta, J. (2010). Dietary acculturation and the nutrition transition: An overview. *Applied Physiology, Nutrition & Metabolism, 35*(2), 219–223. https://doi.org/10.1139/H10-007

Satia-Abouta, J., Patterson, R. E., Kristal, A. R., Hislop, T. G., Yasui, Y., & Taylor, V. M. (2001). Development of dietary acculturation scales among Chinese Americans and Chinese Canadians. *Journal of the American Dietary Association, 101*(5), 548–553. https://doi.org/10.1016/S0002-8223(01)00137-7

Schinke, R. J., McGannon, K. R., Battochio, R. C., & Wells, G. D. (2013). Acculturation in elite sport: A thematic analysis of immigrant athletes and coaches. *Journal of Sports Sciences, 31*(15), 1676–1686. https://doi.org/10.1080/02640414.2013.794949

Schinke, R. J., Yukelson, D., Bartolacci, G., Battochio, R. C., & Johnstone, K. (2011). The challenges encountered by immigrated elite athletes. *Sport Psychology in Action, 2*(1), 1–11. https://doi.org/10.1080/21520704.2011.556179

Schmitt, M. T., Branscombe, N. R., Postmes, T., & Garcia, A. (2014). The consequences of perceived discrimination for psychological well-being: A meta-analytic review. *Psychological Bulletin, 140*(4), 921–948. https://doi.org/10.1037/a0035754

Stambulova, N. (2016). Olympic Games as career transitions. *Revista De Educado Fisica, 85*(2), 121–123.

Stambulova, N., & Wylleman, P. (2014). Athletes' career development and transitions. In A. G. Papaioannou & D. Hackfort (Eds.), *International perspectives on key issues in sport and exercise psychology. Routledge companion to sport and exercise psychology: Global perspectives and fundamental concepts* (pp. 605–620). New York: Routledge.

Szapocznik, J., & Kurtines, W. (1980). Acculturation, biculturalism, and adjustment among Cuban Americans. In A. M. Padilla (Ed.), *Acculturation: Theory, models, and some new findings*. Boulder, CO: Westview.

Tiesler, N. C. (2016). Three types of transnational players: Differing women's football mobility projects in core and developing countries. *Revista Brasileira de Ciências do Esporte, 38*(2), 201–210. https://doi.org/10.1016/j.rbce.2016.02.015

Vertovec, S. (2001). Transnationalism and identity. *Journal of Ethnic and Migration Studies, 27*(4), 573–558. https://doi.org/10.1080/13691830120090386

Wylleman, P., & Lavallée, D. (2004). A developmental perspective on transitions faced by athletes. In M. Weiss (Ed.), *Developmental sport and exercise psychology* (pp. 503–524). Morgantown, WV: Fitness Information Technology.

Wylleman, P., Reints, A., & De Knop, P. (2013). A developmental and holistic perspective on athletic career development. In P. Sotiriadou, & V. D. Bosscher (Eds.), *Managing high performance sport* (pp. 159–182). New York: Routledge.

Zaharna, R. S. (1989). Self-shock: The double-binding challenge of identity. *International Journal of Intercultural Relations, 13*(4), 501–525. https://doi.org/10.1016/0147-1767(89)90026-6

7
THE IMPACT OF SELECTION AND DESELECTION ON ATHLETE WELLBEING

Australian women's cycling

Jenny McMahon, Kerry R. McGannon and Chris Zehntner

Introduction

This chapter contributes to sport, sociology and athlete wellbeing literature by outlining issues associated with selection, non-selection and deselection of athletes in the sport of Australian Women's cycling. In particular, this chapter delves into the tortuous and unpredictable nature that is associated with selection in the Australian Women's cycling team (e.g. a survival of the fittest and elimination approach is adopted). A humanisation framework is used as a lens to critically reflect and analyse practices relating to selection, deselection and non-selection in this high-performance sporting context. The humanisation framework has been previously used in high-performance sport research to critically reflect on practices, policies and procedures that athletes are subjected to and the subsequent impact of these practices. Applying the humanisation framework to athletes' experiences is important because when the athlete is considered as a whole personal and their humanness recognised, then she/he is most likely to thrive and flourish within and beyond sport. This chapter provides insight into the dehumanising and often unpredictable nature of selection and the impact on athlete welfare. It offers suggestions in regard to how athletes could be better supported by coaches and national sporting bodies not only during the selection process but also after, whatever the outcome may be.

ATHLETE VOICE

Sarah's story

Here I go. I hand over my mobile phone to coaches as I enter the Australian Institute of Sport (AIS) premises for the first day of the selection camp. This means no contact with my boyfriend or parents. No Facebook, Snapchat or Instagram either. I am in isolation with no connection to the outside world. I am given a placard with the number 7 on it by coaches soon after I arrive. I am no longer Sarah, I am now number 7. I sit down for what feels like my mugshot. I am not allowed to smile as I hold the placard with my number in the middle of my chest. My photo is then placed on a large wall in the testing lab with 20 other female athletes who are also vying for Australian team selection. All the photos look the same. Each of the girls is holding their identifying number in the middle of their chest and none are smiling.

For the duration of the camp, cycling staff will only refer to us athletes as the number that we are given rather than by our names. We are also told that for the duration of the camp, we are being monitored and assessed 24 hours per day. After my mugshot, I hear my number called, I have to drop off my bags and be back in 20 minutes for a VO2 max test. I don't bother unpacking my gear because if I fail this test, I am out.

It is at this moment that I realise that I am now running on the precision time of the coaches, with only so much as a breath in between each challenge. I quickly drop off my bags and put on my cycling kit ready for the VO2 max test. I smash down an energy drink. When I arrive at the testing room, the physiologists, scientists and coaches are busily doing their thing around me in preparation for my test. I mount the stationary bike and a breathing mask is attached to my face along with a heart rate monitor to my chest. The physiologists organise needles ready to prick me as part of the lactic acid test. I suck in full and deep breaths as I know the pain that awaits me ahead – I have endured this hellish test so many times before. The physiologist gives me the nod and the test commences. I start pedalling. I settle into a rhythm cycling at 200 watts. I do exactly as the physiologist asks and my body responds to each increment that is imposed on it. The staff are standing so close to me that I can feel their breath blowing on my face. It is annoying and distracts me momentarily. After about 20 minutes, the test is finally over. My body is shaking with exhaustion, and my heart rate is sitting just over 200 beats per minute. I am breathing in as much oxygen as I can to try and recover. Physiologists flurry around me collating all my numbers and pricking my skin for my blood. Nobody says great job. Nobody cares about how I am feeling. They just work around me in silence. I feel like an object that is being poked and prodded for my output numbers. I wonder if I have done enough to pass. Are my results enough to be one of the cyclists they are looking for? Finally, I hear my number called, I can warm down and go back to my room. That is all I hear at the completion of the test. Nobody else says anything to me as I walk off.

That evening as I climb into bed, my body is totally exhausted. My chances of making the team remain alive for another day. I wonder what is in store for us tomorrow. We never know until the last minute as they don't want us to prepare too much mentally. When I think about tomorrow, I feel uneasy. It is like I cannot truly relax because, any hour, any minute, I must be ready to perform, and it may not be enough, and I will be out.

Around 11 pm, I am suddenly awoken to loud banging on my bedroom door. As I sit up wondering what the loud noise was, I also hear the banging on my teammates' doors echoing down the hallway. I then hear yelling from one of the coaches as he walks past my door.

> 'Wake up Number 7', you need to be kitted up and ready to ride. Your suitcase must be packed in preparation for elimination. We are doing the midnight mountain challenge! Last one back from the mountain is out.

I quickly pack my suitcase. My body feels weary as I am still recovering from the massive first day. I go downstairs as requested and most of the girls are already there ready to go. At midnight, we roll out of the AIS in the darkness on our bikes, taillights flashing. From the onset, the pace is on. The silence across the peloton highlights what is at stake for each of us. I smash down a caffeine gel to try and lift me. I am not known as a climber as I am not small in stature. Instead, I am known more for my power in criterion format races. As we approach the climb, I try and sit on Gilly's wheel. I can feel my heart rate climbing as we approach halfway up the mountain. I am trying desperately to hang on to her, but I can feel myself slipping off the back of the pack. I know that I can make up some lost time descending the mountain, but I must not let them get too far away from me otherwise I will never be able to catch them. As I am climbing the last part of the mountain, all the fast hill climbers are descending on the opposite side of the road. I try not to panic. Because it is so dark, I cannot see how far Gilly has gotten in front of me. I can still hear her though, so I assume she cannot be that far ahead. I am relieved when I hit the summit and turn ready to descend. I work every corner of the mountain as I descend. I take risks as I know I must make up for lost time. I work every element of the road until I arrive back at the AIS. I can see all the girls are already there and I realise that I have finished last. They are all looking at me as I roll in and have sympathetic looks on their faces. Numbers were called, none of them mine. They know what this means for me. I know what it means, no Australian team for me this year.

Tears start to well in my eyes, I feel like a failure. I quickly pack up my bike and then go back to my room to retrieve my packed suitcase. I get changed and I am back in the foyer of the AIS for the requested 'debrief' within 30 minutes of me finishing the hill climb. By this time, it is nearly 3 am and I am emotionally exhausted. Although I pass several other girls and team managers during this time, nobody says a word to me, not so much as even a side glance towards me. As I enter the foyer, the coaches take me into the testing room. Although this is the first camp where I have been eliminated early, I know what is about to come as many of my teammates have had to endure the 'debrief'. One of the coaches starts to speak. His tone is blunt, and his face is emotionless. The debrief is intense and follows the 'silent running' mode of, no positive or negative feedback, where I have to assess my own weaknesses for the coach and show that I understand how I don't fit the category of cyclist they are looking for.

As I pick my performance apart, I can feel the torch being extinguished and that was it, I was 'deselected'. At the end of the debrief, the coach walks to the wall of athlete photos and removes number 7. I walk outside, a car and driver are waiting for me.

SCHOLAR VOICE

Contextualising Sarah's story: creative non-fiction

Sarah's story is a form of 'creative analytical practice' (CAP), whereby the researchers have produced a tale from 'research data' as a story in an evocative and accessible form (McMahon, 2016; Smith, 2016). As such, the story presented is not an identity of one athlete, but the culmination of the analysis of multiple sources of media data from a larger project (Zehntner, McGannon, & McMahon, 2019). CAP is an umbrella term for research practices that embrace creative forms of representation to show the layers of lived experience, emotion and theory in research findings (McMahon, 2016; Smith, McGannon, & Williams, 2016). The research findings, in this case, were from a larger study that extended understanding of how athletes and coaches in a women's cycling talent development and selection programme negotiate and normalise athlete abuse in the digital landscape (see Zehntner et al., 2019). The data corpus in that study included public forms of media (e.g. Twitter feed of the Australian Development Team, news reports, personal blog posts, press releases and online cycling magazine articles). Through the creation of Sarah's story, we shifted from that of story analysts to that of 'storytellers' (Smith, 2016) by selecting compelling passages from the digital data to communicate the layers of power, complicity and control prevalent in our media analysis findings (Zehntner et al., 2019). This 'creative non-fiction' process involved the creation of a composite character (i.e. Sarah) whose experiences and interactions with coaches were centralised through creating fictional and compelling storylines from the public forms of digital data gleaned from larger project (Smith et al., 2016;

Spalding & Phillips, 2007). Although we used creative licence as storytellers, we enhanced rigour by integrating paraphrased quotes from the digital data corpus as much as possible to centralise the athlete's experience (Spalding & Phillips, 2007). The authenticity and value of this creative non-fiction lie in the potential emotions invoked in reader/listener, with a range of possible interpretations and reactions (Frank, 2010). Sarah's story is not a window into 'what really happened', or is it put forward not as form of truth to be member checked, but instead is a socially constructed and culturally infused account with naturalistic generalizability (Smith & Sparkes, 2009).

Introducing the Australian women's cycling section camp

The focus of Sarah's storied experiences – and our larger study – comes from the Australian women's cycling selection camp. This camp was initiated as a result of High5 Nutrition Pro cycling team manager, Cycling Australia (Australia's peak cycling body) and the AIS, as a way of identifying the strongest and toughest of female riders (Zehntner, McGannon, & McMahon, 2018). The AIS is Australia's high-performance sport agency and operates under the Australian Sports Commission (ASC), which is a unit within the Australian Government's Department of Health portfolio (ASC, 2017). The AIS is claimed to be the "cradle of Australia's national sports system . . . recognised the world over for its ability to identify, develop and produce world, Olympic and Paralympic champions" (ASC, 2017).

Since 2011, when the cycling selection camp started (Duffy & Moore, 2015), secret army techniques have underpinned every element of the camp. High5 Nutrition cycling team manager describes the selection camp as both a "brutal [and] highly scientific program designed to mentally and physically break the girls" (High5 Nutrition, 2015, para. 3). The camp is purposely made brutal, so the athletes feel like they are in a living hell (Gilmore, as cited in Palmer, 2015). Cycling Australia as an organisation put more of a positive spin on the camp, claiming that while it is highly demanding, it is a very rewarding activity (Barras, 2015). From the perspective of the head coach of the Australian women's cycling team, the selection camp is "designed to increase the efficiency of the transition of athletes selected domestically into international competition" (Barras, 2015).

The methodology used for the women's cycling selection camp is based on the selection methodology employed by Australia's Special Air Service Regiment. Collectively, the camp seeks to evaluate: "cyclists' physiological capacities in the lab and on road, basic bike skills, racing skills, tactical and strategic knowledge, mechanical skills, mindset, leadership, decision-making, team work, emotional and physical resilience and ability to learn"

(Barras, 2015; Zehntner et al., 2018). Australian female cyclists are limited in the ways that they can gain selection into the European professional ranks, for example, teams available due to their gender (Zehntner et al., 2018). Therefore, as a consequence, many of the female cycling contenders have no other choice but to attend this training camp as a way of not only obtaining/maintaining their individual funding (i.e. money that comes from Australian government, Australian cycling and High5 Nutrition) but also to be considered for Australian team selection.

Introduction

Critical enquiry into the selection, non-selection and deselection of athletes in high performance (HP) sport remains underrepresented in sport-related research. This is surprising given that across all sports, athletes must participate in selection processes to be considered for individual and/or team selection and to obtain/maintain their individual funding. Increasing evidence (e.g. Beamish & Ritchie, 2006; Brackenridge & Rhind, 2010; David, 2005; Hoberman, 1992; Kavanagh & Brady, 2014; McMahon, Penney, & Dinan-Thompson, 2012) has revealed that the pursuit of excellence in sporting contexts has come to greatly influence cultural practices which includes selection, deselection and non-selection procedures amongst other things (e.g. coaching practices centring on win at all costs mentality). Such practices and procedures are associated with particular culturally driven ideological discourses (e.g. meritocracy, technocentrism), and some approaches (e.g. slim to win, hell week camps) have been challenged for their inappropriateness, dehumanising nature and compromising of health and wellbeing (Beamish & Ritchie, 2006; Brackenridge & Rhind, 2010; David, 2005; Hoberman, 1992; Kavanagh & Brady, 2014; McMahon et al., 2012; UNICEF, 2010). It is, therefore, crucial for researchers in athlete wellbeing to make known the processes and practices in sport associated with un/desirable outcomes by applying suitable frameworks with which to review and scrutinise them (Kavanagh & Brady, 2014).

Humanisation framework

Within this section of the chapter, the humanisation framework is introduced which was developed by Todres, Galvin, and Holloway (2009). The humanisation framework (Todres et al., 2009) will be used to analyse the practices associated with selection, deselection and non-selection for athletes in the Australian Women's cycling context. This framework was originally developed for application in a healthcare setting by Todres et al. (2009) who were interested in the examination of what it means to be 'human'. While the humanisation framework has been successfully used to analyse practices in the healthcare sector, Kavanagh and Brady (2014) recently proposed that this framework can be applied to a HP sport setting due to its many parallels. In response to the calls made by Kavanagh and Brady (2014), we have adapted the original framework developed by Todres et al. (2009, p. 7) to better reflect sporting culture research and sport terminology. For example, insiderness (an original element included in Todres et al., 2009, framework) has been found to be problematic in sport research (see McMahon & Barker-Ruchti, 2017), because athletes who were achieving competitively and meeting coaches' and team managers' expectations were socially rewarded with an insider status, while those who did not meet coaches' and team managers' expectations were ostracised or isolated.

Consideration of the dimensions of humanisation and dehumanisation within the HP sport context is important as it allows researchers to utilise these concepts as a way with which to examine the sporting policies and practices that athletes are subjected to. Kavanagh and Brady (2014) explain that when the athlete is considered as a whole person and their humanity is recognised, then she/he is most likely to thrive and flourish both within and beyond sport. In Table 7.1, the seven essential constituents of what it is to be human within the framework are presented (Todres et al., 2009). Kavanagh and Brady (2014) explain how each constituent is heuristically expressed as a continuum, stretching from the term that characterises humanisation in a positive sense through to the term that characterises the barrier to such a possibility. Applying these seven constituents to sporting contexts can assist researchers to gain new insights into athlete wellbeing and humanisation within sport practices (Kavanagh & Brady, 2014).

To demonstrate the theoretical application of the dimensions, three constituents of the humanisation framework are expanded upon in reference to

TABLE 7.1 Dimensions of humanisation and dehumanisation

Forms of humanisation	Forms of dehumanisation
Whole person or sentient being	Technocentric object (i.e. treating athlete body as a machine/object of performance)
Agency	Obedience
Individuality	Sameness
Connectedness	Segregation
Learning	Loss of meaning
Personal journey	Loss of personal journey
Embodiment	Disembodiment

Source: Adapted from Todres et al., original work in healthcare (2009, p. 70) to align better with sport terminology and sport research

Sarah's story of selection and deselection in the Australian women's cycling team. While each of the seven constituents is relevant to and can be applied to Sarah's story, the three most salient elements of the framework will be discussed which include Sentient being/Technocentric object, Agency/ Obedience and Individuality/Sameness.

Sentient being/technocentric object

Individual and team selection is physically, mentally and emotionally challenging for athletes, so it is important for coaches and team managers to understand what athletes are experiencing, rather than seeing them as objects of performance. Looking at an athlete as a whole person or sentient being with feelings and emotions signifies the importance of respecting them as being human. Kavanagh and Brady (2014) explain that to be human is to make sense of one's own personal world based upon subjective interpretation of experience through the lenses of thoughts, feelings and emotions at the time. In contrast, technocracy occurs when a person is viewed as a human resource (Bain, 1990) and indeed viewed as objects, or parts of a system, statistical model or a strategy to be labelled, classified and processed accordingly. Sport, and sport science, often seeks to objectify athletes and label them statistically. Although this practice may be viewed as an essential aspect for achieving competitive performance, technocracy is one such form of objectification that potentially 'dehumanises' the athlete (Kavanagh & Brady, 2014).

Applying the whole person/technocracy constituent to Sarah's creative non-fiction story, it becomes evident that cycling personnel treated her as a technocentric object in several ways. Sarah revealed that she, along with the other athletes vying for selection, were subjected to gruelling physical tests (e.g. VO2 max test and Mountain climbing test) where their performance results were subsequently 'labelled' and 'classified' by coaches, team managers and physiologists. Coaches, team managers and physiologists would then scrutinise these results and decide which athletes were eligible to 'make the cut' and proceed to the next day of the selection camp. Consequently, with cycling staff placing a precedence on athletes' physical test results or outputs rather than considering their feelings, emotions and thoughts (i.e. sentient being/whole person), athletes were viewed as technocentric objects of performance. Ball (2004) describes technocentrism as:

> A technology; a culture and a mode of regulation, or even a system of terror that employs judgements, comparisons and displays as a means of control, attrition and change. The performances of individual subjects or organisations serve as measures of productivity or output, or

> displays of 'quality', or moments of promotion or inspection. They stand for, encapsulate or represent the worth, quality and value of an individual or organisation within field of judgement.
>
> *(p. 143)*

Later, an extract from Sarah's story highlights her experiences with objectification and potential impact and consequences on her health and wellbeing.

> *Nobody says great job. Nobody cares about how I am feeling. They just work around me in silence. I feel like an object that is being poked and prodded for my output numbers. I wonder if I have done enough to pass. Are my results enough to be one of the cyclists they are looking for? Finally, I hear my number called, I can warm down and go back to my room. That is all I hear at the completion of the test. Nobody else says anything to me as I walk off.*

Sarah's experience as outlined with the story excerpt earlier, further shows how cycling staff failed to recognise that the athletes vying for selection were human beings with feelings, thoughts and emotions that should be nurtured and individually understood in terms of their sentience (Crossley, 1996). Instead, they were viewed as technocentric objects of performance which could be manipulated, tested and controlled.

Agency/obedience

In this next section, the agency/obedience constituent is applied to further make sense of Sarah's creative non-fiction story of experience in the selection camp. Athlete agency involves the freedom to not only be an active participant in one's sport whereby they can make choices and decisions but also be responsible for their decisions and actions (Kavanagh & Brady, 2014). In contrast, obedience refers to when the athlete is controlled by others (e.g. coach) and/or their actions are limited due to others' decision-making and rigidity. Kavanagh and Brady (2014) warn that obedience can lead to athletes feeling disempowered, a loss of dignity and perceived lack of control over their decision-making.

Through the construction of Sarah' story, it was shown how a variety of techniques were used by cycling staff to exercise power over the athletes which in turn limited athlete agency. The first technique drawn from Sarah's story was her de-identification. The process of de-identification is best illustrated using the numbered mugshots of athletes entering the programme. Through this tactic of publicly posting such pictures, Sarah was no longer Sarah (the person/human) but instead referred to as 'number 7' highlighting how she was positioned to become obedient by cycling staff, thus reducing her to an item of data.

Another technique shown through Sarah's story during the selection camp was the strict control of her time, space and actions which limited her agency and choices. The first encounter that exemplifies this point within Sarah's story when she was photographed within minutes of arriving at the camp and subjected to her first physical challenge – a VO2 max test in the lab:

> *After my mugshot, I hear my number called, I have to drop off my bags and be back in 20 minutes for a VO2 max test.*
> *It is at this moment that I realize that I am now running on the precision time of the coaches, with only so much as a breath in between each challenge.*

The constant monitoring of Sarah exemplifies another technique (i.e. gaze) employed by cycling staff, limiting her agency. *We are also told that for the duration of the camp, we are being monitored and assessed 24 hours per day.* Foucault's concepts of disciplinary power have been used to examine the power dynamics occurring in sporting contexts and the impact of these. One of the power techniques that Foucault discussed is 'the gaze'. Foucault (1979) explains how the gaze is an inspecting gaze, a gaze that individual internalise, to the point that she is her own overseer (Foucault, 1980). The gaze of cycling staff was a grand formula – a superb power that was exercised continuously throughout the selection camp for what turns out to be minimal cost (Foucault, 1980). Within Sarah's story one can see that she knew she was being watched (gazed upon), and it was ensured that she behaved in a way deemed acceptable by cycling staff to keep her selection chances alive. Sarah thus accepted the overt gazing and monitoring by staff and in this way normalised it. Foucault (1991) explains how power produces reality and rituals of truth in and through the practices that 'the gazer' and the 'gazed upon' enact. Sarah's acceptance and taken for grant use of such approaches show how these forms of power are productive.

Cycling staff not only had control over Sarah's time and space but also had control over her ability to communicate with the outside world, thus restricting her ability to make contact with her network and receive emotional and mental support. *I hand over my mobile phone to coaches as I enter the Australian Institute of Sport (AIS) premises for the first day of the selection camp.* Passivity was shown – and power continued to be productive – when Sarah did what staff wished and performed as they wanted, with the techniques, the speed and the efficiency that they determined (Foucault, 1991; Theberge, 1987). The practices of cycling staff were promoted through the concepts of productivity, efficiency and performance which were inscribed on Sarah, thus becoming normative within the culture of the training camp (Foucault, 1991). As a result of the cycling staff's rules and approach, a docile, passive and obedient athlete was produced, who had internalised these rules, practices and cultural norms without question. Denison (2007, p. 376) explains how sport staff are agents of normalisation and thus contribute to the obedience or passivity of athletes, which in this case was Sarah. One of the reasons why Sarah became an obedient object during the selection camp is primarily because the coaches were also the gatekeepers of the selection. Athletes ultimately had little choice but to *submit* themselves to coaches' procedures if they wanted to be considered for selection and obtain/maintain funding. In so doing, they embodied obedience due to the constant techniques of power and surveillance demonstrated during the camp. Obedience was thus productive and solidified by the social structures and lack of opportunities for women within the sport (e.g. scarcity of funding, few spots for women, less options for training within the sport). As the head coach stated when asked about the selection camp, it will not just be the biggest engine that gains selection (Barras, 2015) but rather the candidate that best responds, in our opinion, to the selection camp throughout the week.

Individuality/sameness

In sporting contexts – and particularly when it comes to selection processes and performance testing – it is important for coaches and sporting team staff to view athletes as individuals rather than focusing on their results or characteristics which fit into a particular category (i.e. sameness) most likely to achieve competitive performance. In other sporting contexts (e.g. elite swimming), it has been revealed that when athletes have been reduced to their results and outputs which have seen them placed into specific categories, a number of serious emotional effects have resulted such as depression and self-withdrawal (McMahon et al., 2012). In this respect, athlete individuality can never be reduced to a list of characteristics because athletes are always more than the sum of their various parts (Kavanagh & Brady, 2014).

Sameness (also known as homogenization) deemphasises uniqueness and individuality in athletes by focusing on the ways they fit into specific groups and categories (e.g. those most likely to achieve performance because of particular outputs). Sameness (i.e. homogenization) is practised via the use of descriptors that serve to categorise through cultural or subcultural value-based characteristics (Kavanagh & Brady, 2014). When applying the individuality/sameness constituent to Sarah's story, homogenization/sameness was practised in a number of ways. The first way that Sarah and the other athletes experienced sameness/homogenization was through the way they were treated by cycling staff. As outlined earlier, athletes were not referred to by their name but rather by a number. Furthermore, every athlete was subjected to the same testing regimes (e.g. VO2 max test) with no individual considerations or approaches implemented. Those athletes who met specific figures, categories and outputs remained in contention for team selection, while those who did not fit within the desired categories were out (i.e. deselected).

> *I have to assess my own weaknesses for the coach and show that I understand how I don't fit the category of cyclist they are looking for.*

The focus on the athletes' outputs, figures and numbers exemplifies Sluggett's (2011) notion of the coded body whereby athletes' bodies are conceptualised as [performance] databases or data storage. Indeed, Sarah was represented by her 'data' which carried performance values of what was good and what was bad according to a rigid set of criteria set by cycling staff (Sluggett, 2011). When Sarah's data did not fit into the category that cycling staff were looking for (i.e. sameness through numbers), she was dropped and her opportunity within the sport ended. Shogan (1999) has long explained how high-performance sport works to homogenise athletes to produce a 'hybrid' performing athlete.

Sameness occurs in sporting contexts as a consequence of the "constant pressures [for athletes] to conform to the same model" (Foucault, 1979, p. 182). However, Shogan (1999) argues that it is impossible to homogenise athletes because they enter sporting environments with diverse identities, skills, backgrounds and embodied experiences (Shogan, 1999, as cited in Sinden, 2010, 2012). Consequently, homogenising athletes can have dire consequences for the athlete in terms of their mental health, particularly as they strive to conform to 'one' model that is culturally accepted in high-performance sport (Shogan, 1999, as cited in Sinden, 2010, 2012).

Summary

Practices developed as part of this selection camp highlighted within this chapter and with Sarah's creative non-fiction story sit in stark contrast to the humanisation constituents. This chapter brings to fore how selection, deselection and non-selection practices in Australian women's cycling were found to be dehumanising but were justified and normalised in the pursuit of selection. These practices implemented by cycling staff centred on technocracy, homogenization/sameness, isolation, control, obedience and technocracy and show clear examples of dehumanising practices. The approaches of cycling staff failed to recognise that athletes vying for selection were human beings with feelings, thoughts and emotions (i.e. sentient beings) that should be nurtured and individually catered for and understood. Sarah's wellbeing was compromised when she experienced sadness, loss and isolation during this selection camp – all of which are triggers that can negatively affect the mental health and adjustment of an individual.

Indeed, the practices of cycling staff can be viewed as non-accidental violence as characterised by Mountjoy et al. (2016). They explain that when sporting practices have psychological and/or physically damaging effects on athletes, they are considered as maltreatment or abuse [i.e. non-accidental violence] (Mountjoy et al., 2016). What is of concern in Sarah's story is that selection camp and the coaching practice embedded within it was done purposely to both "mentally and physically break the girls down and get them to their breaking point" (Gilmore cited by Palmer, 2015).

Only time will tell if these experiences will impact Sarah's wellbeing in the long term (and the wellbeing of her fellow athletes). In this closing section, we provide some recommendations to ensure selection, deselection and non-selection practices in HP sport consider the human first and the athlete second.

Selection camp recommendations

1. Athletes should be considered as humans first and foremost rather than objects of performance (i.e. being called by their name, not an identification number).
2. As selection processes can be arduous physically and mentally, athletes need to be given some choice and freedom throughout the process (rather than having their phones taken off them and their time/space controlled).
3. It is important to get to know athletes and their individual contexts to build trusting relationships (rather than ignoring them throughout the selection process).
4. It is important to offer support at all times (no support was given to Sarah when she was deselected).
5. It is important for athletes to be aware of what is happening. Further, athletes' parents/relatives need to understand fully their situation, so they can provide support.
6. The selection camp environment can be unsettling for athletes, therefore, sporting personnel need to do their best to mitigate this and reduce their sense of dislocation (from their home environments).
7. Every athlete is unique and valuable and need to be treated with respect and dignity. Thus, athletes should be treated with a dignified and respectful approach in any situation.
8. Athletes are more than the sum of the parts that produce performance outputs. They are humans with thoughts, feelings, emotions and ideas.

References

Australian Sports Commission. (2017). *Role of the AIS*. Retrieved from www.ausport.gov.au/ais/about

Bain, L. (1990). A critical analysis of the hidden curriculum in physical education. In D. Kirk & R. Tinning (Eds.), *Physical education, curriculum and culture: Critical issues in the contemporary crisis* (pp. 23–41). Hampshire, United Kingdom: Falmer Press.

Ball, S. (2004). Performativities and fabrications in the education economy: Toward the performative society. In S. Ball (Ed.), *The Routledge Falmer reader in sociology of education* (pp. 143–155). London: Routledge Falmer.

Barras, M. (2015). In defence of the AIS selection camp process. *Cycling Tips*. Retrieved from https://cyclingtips.com/2015/05/in-defence-of-the-ais-selection-camp-process/

Beamish, R., & Ritchie, I. (2006). *Fastest, highest, strongest a critique of high-performance sport*. London: Routledge.

Brackenridge, C. H., & Rhind, D. (2010). *Elite child athlete welfare*. Uxbridge, UK: Brunel University Press.

Crossley, N. (1996). Body-subject/body-power: Agency, inscription and control in Foucault and Merleau-Ponty. *Body and Society*, 2(2), 99–116. https://doi.org/10.1177/1357034X96002002006

David, P. (2005). *Human rights in youth sport*. London: Routledge.

Denison, J. (2007). Social theory for coaches: A Foucauldian reading of one athlete's poor performance. *International Journal of Sports Science and Coaching*, 2(4), 369–383. https://doi.org/10.1260/174795407783359777

Duffy, C., & Moore, T. S. (2015). Australian Institute of Sport turns to SAS commando training to select future cycling gold medallists. *ABCNews*. Retrieved from www.abc.net.au/news/2015-05-11/commando-program-inspires-aiscycling-selection-boot-camp/6461536

Foucault, M. (1979). *Discipline and punish: The birth of the prison*. New York: Vintage Books.

Foucault, M. (1980). Body power. In C. Gordon (Ed.), *Power/knowledge: Selected interviews and other writings, 1972–1977* (pp. 109–133). New York: Pantheon Books.

Foucault, M. (1991). *The Foucault reader*. London: Penguin.

Frank, A. W. (2010). *Letting stories breathe: A socio-narratology*. Chicago, IL: University of Chicago Press.

High5 Nutrition. (2015). *High5 Australian women's road development team to be selected at military style camp* [Press release]. Retrieved from http://us10.campaign-archive2.com/?u=9508ff6b8c20fa59c9c2f9657&id=1ba3259c7f&e=66306af7b6

Hoberman, J. (1992). *Mortal engines: The science of performance and the dehumanization of sport*. Caldwell, NJ: The Blackburn Press.

Kavanagh, E., & Brady, A. (2014). A framework for understanding humanization and dehumanization in sport. In. D. Rhind & C. Brackenridge (Eds.), *Researching and enhancing athlete welfare* (pp. 34–43). London: Brunel University Press.

McMahon, J. (2016). *The coach never arrived back at its destination*. Manchester: Manchester University Press. https://doi.org/10.7228/manchester/9780719096310.003.0007

McMahon, J., & Barker-Ruchti, N. (2017). Assimilating to a boy's body shape for the sake of performance: Three female athletes' body experiences in a sporting culture. *Sport, Education and Society*, 22(2), 157–174.

McMahon, J., Penney, D., & Dinan-Thompson, M. (2012). Body practices – Exposure and effect of a sporting culture? Stories from three Australian swimmers. *Sport, Education and Society*, 17(2), 181–206. https://doi.org/10.1080/13573322.2011.607949

Mountjoy, M., Brackenridge, C., Arrington, M., Blauwet, C., Carska-Sheppard, A., Fasting, K., & Starr, K. (2016). International Olympic committee consensus statement:

Harassment and abuse (non-accidental violence) in sport. *British Journal of Sports Medicine*, *50*(17), 1019–1029. http://doi.org/10.1136/bjsports-2016-096121

Palmer, T. (2015). The extreme methods and measures at the Australian women's development team selection camp. *Cycling Tips*. Retrieved from https://cyclingtips.com/2015/04/extreme-methods-australian-womens-selectioncamp/

Shogan, D. (1999). *The making of high-performance athletes: Discipline, diversity, and ethics*. Toronto, ON: University of Toronto Press.

Sinden, J. L. (2010). The normalization of emotion and the disregard of health problems in elite amateur sport. *Journal of Clinical Sport Psychology*, *4*(3), 241–256. https://doi.org/10.1123/jcsp.4.3.241

Sinden, J. L. (2012). The elite sport and christianity debate: Shifting focus from normative values to the conscious disregard for health. *The Journal of Religion and Health*, *52*, 335–349. https://doi.org/10.1007/s10943-012-9595-8

Sluggett, B. (2011). Sport's doping game: Surveillance in the biotech age. *Sociology of Sport Journal*, *28*(4), 387–403. https://doi.org/10.1123/ssj.28.4.387

Smith, B. (2016). Narrative analysis in sport and exercise: How can it be done? In B. Smith & A. Sparkes (Eds.), *Routledge handbook of qualitative research in sport and exercise* (pp. 260–273). New York: Routledge.

Smith, B., & Sparkes, A. C. (2009). Narrative analysis and sport and exercise psychology: Understanding lives in diverse ways. *Psychology of Sport and Exercise*, *10*(2), 279–288. https://doi.org/10.1016/j.psychsport.2008.07.012

Smith, B., McGannon, K., & Williams, T. (2016). Ethnographic creative nonfiction: Exploring the what's, whys and how's. In G. Molnar & L. Purdy (Eds.), *Ethnographies in sport and exercise research*. London: Routledge.

Spalding, N. J., & Phillips, T. (2007). Exploring the use of vignettes: From validity to trustworthiness. *Qualitative Health Research*, *17*(7), 954–962. https://doi.org/10.1177/1049732307306187

Theberge, N. (1987). Sport and women's empowerment. *Women's Studies International Forum*, *10*, 387–393.

Todres, L., Galvin, K. T., & Holloway, I. (2009). The humanisation of healthcare: A value framework for qualitative research. *International Journal of Qualitative Studies on Health and Wellbeing*, *4*(2), 68–77. https://doi.org/10.1080/17482620802646204

UNICEF. (2010). *UNICEF annual report*. Retrieved from www.unicef.org/publications/files/UNICEF_Annual_Report_2010_EN_052711.pdf

Zehntner, C., McGannon, K. R., & McMahon, J. (2019). Control, consent and complicity in the coaching of elite women's cycling in Australia: A media analysis. *Sport, Education and Society*, *24*(5), 520–532. https://doi.org/10.1080/13573322.2017.1417257

8
SUPPORTING THE WELLBEING FOR ATHLETES OF FAITH

Charles H. Wilson, Jr., Christina M. Gipson and Natalie Campbell

Introduction

This chapter examines issues relating to supporting athletes of faith, or in a broader sense, spiritual athletes. Faith can be difficult to clearly define, similar to other terms describing human behaviour and beliefs like "leadership." The term "spirituality" encompasses the potentially overlapping concepts of faith and religion. Some athletes self-identify as spiritual, religious, or as a person of faith, while others ignore, deny, or compartmentalise it out of their athletic identity. It is the responsibility of the sport organisation to create a culture that recognises and values the identities of all athletes, whether they are spiritual or not. This chapter focuses on three interrelated aspects of effective sport organisations: organisational culture, holistic, athlete-centred coaching, and the concept of respectful pluralism. In fact, recognising and supporting an individual's faith and spirituality is a duty in providing holistic care. For example, this support may include adjustments to training times, locations, uniforms, and nutrition. It is imperative that administrators, coaches, and anyone supporting athletes recognise each athlete as an individual and allow them to express their individual spiritual beliefs while still respecting the rights and beliefs of others.

PRACTITIONER VOICE

What's faith got to do with it?

When I became a performance lifestyle advisor (PLA), I initially began working with a number of teams Great Britain National Governing Bodies of Sport (NGBs). After being in post only a week the performance director (PD)

DOI: 10.4324/9780429287923-8

of one of the sports asked that I discuss the "lifestyle" of a particular athlete. I asked for more detail and was told that there were some concerns about the amount of training sessions the athlete was missing, the types of food they were eating, possible disordered sleeping patterns, a lack of engagement in team activities, and their dismissal of sports psychology. As a rule, I am hesitant to take the word of Person A about Person B to be true and absolute (I will make my own mind up thank you), but it was important for me to understand what the PD was thinking, and even more so that they felt I heard their concern. The role of a PLA treads a precarious line between ensuring the NGB feels supported in their mission of producing elite athletes, whilst also ensuring the athletes we work with feel confident in our mission to support, develop, and stand with them as people.

As part of my "getting to know you" period with the athletes, there was nothing in my meeting with this particular athlete that illuminated the concerns of the PD. They were a full-time university student (a dual career athlete); however, they lived at home, they did not do any part-time work, they did not drink or smoke, they did not go out to socialise much, they did not have a significant other, and they often reported themselves to be physically and mentally well. Importantly, they believed that they were progressing positively on the programme. I was obviously missing something.

When catching up with the NGB support staff (the S&C coach, the nutritionist, the physiotherapist, the team manager, etc.) to discuss the needs and progressions of all the athletes as part of their periodic performance lifestyle plan, I would push a little more for them to elaborate on their concerns about this particular athlete. As I listened, it became clear to me that these concerns were contextualised against the backdrop of the athlete's religion.

I must be clear though – at no point did any member of staff explicitly say *The problem is that the athlete is Sikh*. No. And I do not believe that they cognised of the issues in this way. Instead, I interpreted the context of the concerns as "The athlete is making choices that go against what the program is prescribing." This was critical to my understanding of the presentation of the problem. I asked if any of the concerns had been openly discussed with the athlete in relation to the athlete's religious beliefs, but the overwhelming concern from the staff was *Surely that is discrimination?*

It was clear that there were multiple compounding issues. Why was the NGB conflating religion with lifestyle? Why did staff think simply having a conversation with an athlete about their religious practices was discrimination? Why was the athlete so unaware of the tensions felt by the support staff regarding certain decisions? This issue was complex – intimate yet global – and required a careful approach if I was to maintain any sort of fulfilling relationship with the athlete moving forwards.

The next week I approached the athlete and said:

> *You know what, I don't know anything about Sikhism – I'd love to learn more about it so that I can do a better job of understanding how you balance all these huge things that are important to you in your life!*

As the athlete discussed Sikhism with me in great detail, I began to join the dots of why the PD had brought this to my attention, and I could see how some of their religious practices might be seen as being counter to the evidence in elite sport of professional behaviours – even if I did not necessarily agree with this myself.

Their diet was lacto-vegetarian (not an issue in itself); however, the athlete practised *langar* for every meal (e.g. iron utensils only, traditional meals cooked by baptised Sikhs, meditating whilst cooking, those eating needing to be at equal sitting heights). At times this meant that the athlete would join teammates at the canteen but often would not eat with them (seen as disrespectful by the PD), would need specially prepared food for international competitions (seen as an inconvenience by the team manager), and struggled to keep lean (seen as an obstacle by the nutritionist). In addition, the athlete would observe *nitnem* – everyday they would get up three hours before dawn to pray (seen as poor sleep hygiene by the Head Coach and disruptive to teammates when sharing rooms on camps/competitions). Furthermore, they would often use one of their five daily prayers to focus on their athletic performance instead of engaging in the sport psychology sessions (interestingly the psychologist had no issue with this as they understood it to be an integral part of the athlete's performance needs). Furthermore, the athlete actively practised *seva* – delivering selfless acts of charity work and service to others to people within and outside of the Sikh community considered to be in need. Whilst the athlete would rarely miss technical sessions, they would often engage in other services outside of the scheduled day (e.g. S&C, physiotherapy, and performance analysis) to ensure that they fulfilled *seva* daily (seen by the majority of the support staff as incorrect prioritising and dictating their own timetable). Finally, the athlete discussed the importance of *panth* and *sangat* – the deep and meaningful holy connections and expectations as a member of the Sikh community. Their weekends were routinely filled with congregations and celebrations with extended family and friends (seen by the Head Coach as significant block to the athlete's progression on the programme). And this – I concluded – was why the PD wanted me to talk to the athlete about their "lifestyle."

The NGB had expressed that the athlete had potential to perform as a senior international athlete, but this increasing dissonance between performance expectations and religious practice was compromising the professional behaviours of the staff, and often resulted in the athlete being overlooked in training, and not selected for camps and competitions. To me, it appeared that the athlete was becoming increasingly ignored; that the

NGB was just sort of waiting for the athlete to take themselves off the programme, or waiting for an opportunity to officially release them.

I considered the crux of the problem to be the perception from NGB that the athlete was refusing to follow the requirements of the programme – and yet they had never seemed to have had an explicit discussion with the athlete for fear of seeming discriminatory. My role as the PLA was to have an honest, authentic, coached, and meaningful conversation with the athlete about the reality of the situation and to explore what – if anything – could be negotiated with both the staff and the athlete moving forwards. Did the athlete understand the concerns of the staff? How could the programme better accommodate the athlete's faith? What were the non-negotiables for each person involved? How did the staff and the athlete think progress on the programme could be made?

It was beyond evident that the athlete gained their purpose in life from their faith, not from their sporting achievements. After weeks of discussion on choice, consequence, and intention with myself, their family, and the Sikh community, the athlete made the conscious decision that they would not be making any changes to their behaviours that might compromise their dedication to their faith. If this resulted in them no longer being part of the programme then this their *dharma* – the divine truth.

My interpretation of the situation was that the NGB was problematizing the core of the athlete's wellbeing. However, it got me thinking about how other elite athletes of faith explore and manage the competing (and at times conflicting) values and requirements of high-performance sport.

With absolutely no training or experience in working through situations like this, I found myself asking the question "How can an athlete be committed to God and committed to elite sport?"

SCHOLAR VOICE

Research insights into supporting athletes of faith

Coaches, managers, performance directors, and athletic administrators all share the responsibility of creating an atmosphere, or organisational culture, which is inclusive and welcoming to athletes of all backgrounds. One of the beautiful aspects of sport is that it unites people of disparate backgrounds in a mutual, if competitive, quest for excellence. While the world, at times, may seek to subdivide people by arbitrary distinctions, such as primary language, geography, abilities, ethnicity, gender, or worldview, sport has the ability to unite any and all people who are willing to come together under the rules of the competition. Speaking on the power of sport in 2000, the late Nelson Mandela famously declared that "It has the power to inspire. It has the power to unite people in a way that little else does ... It laughs in the face of all types of discrimination" (Laureus, 2012).

However, this unity does not happen by accident, sport must be intentionally leveraged for its positive potential. Some examples of this include the growing opportunities for athletes with disabilities, the recent spike in attention to the equal pay movement in elite sport, and the National Football League's Rooney Rule which requires candidates of color to be interviewed for head coaching positions. Yet one subgroup that has arguably received relatively little specific support beyond legislation is the athlete of faith. In an era of expanding diversity and inclusion, supporting athletes of faith is an area that can help athletes and organisations move from potential to maximum performance. This support may simultaneously create richer and more enjoyable experiences for those athletes that affirm the value of each athlete irrespective of their performance, which paradoxically may improve their performance. Furthermore, demonstrating support for athletes of faith may help organisations recruit and retain the best candidates from a global pool of athletes.

This chapter examines issues relating to supporting athletes of faith, or in a broader sense, spiritual athletes. While the term "faith" has been broadened in recent years to be almost synonymous with religions, such as Buddhism, Christianity, Hinduism, Islam, Judaism, and Sikhism, we prefer the term "spirituality" to encompass the often overlapping concepts of faith, religion, and spirituality. Some athletes self-identify as spiritual, religious, and/or as a person of faith, while others may deny or compartmentalise this aspect of their life out of their athletic identity. To compartmentalise their spirituality means to detach their athletic and spiritual identities into different "compartments" of their lives, keeping them separate and distinct from each other. For example, an athlete may attend religious services on a particular day of the week and believe in specific teachings of a particular faith but might not intentionally carry those teachings into competition. Among the reasons this may happen are to try and fit in with the beliefs of a majority of a team or club, because they do not see the relevance of the spirituality to their sport, and/or because they have not been allowed to freely express their spirituality (as can be seen with the experience Natalie provided). It is this last reason – that they have not been allowed to freely express their spirituality – that this chapter will focus on through discussion of organisational culture, holistic, athlete-centred coaching, and respectful pluralism.

Spiritualty within organisational culture

Organisational culture is critical for success in the management of people both in and out of sport. Individuals in management roles regularly aim to create environments that increase productivity, work-life balance, and interconnectedness through positive organisational culture (Ashmos & Duchon,

2000). Generally, organisational culture is defined as the shared values, beliefs, and assumptions that guide organisational behaviours and decisions (Lewis, 2002; Louis, 1985; Schein, 1991). Leaders form, reinforce, and share the desired culture. Five-time National Champion and three-time Olympic Gold Medal winning basketball coach Mike Krzyzewski (2000), or Coach K, puts it this way: "Every year, we create a brand new culture for Duke basketball ... how we grow that culture – how we develop communication, how we care for our people – means everything" (p. 52). It is important to note his point that organisational culture is not a static entity and must be consistently and intentionally nurtured.

One way to attempt to codify and replicate organisational culture is through policies and practices (Fink & Pastore, 1999). However, these policies and practices are best created through two-way communication. Consistent negotiation among group members leads to the establishment of acceptable and unacceptable behaviours and practices (Kusluvan & Karamustafa, 2003; Tyrrell, 2000). Coach K demonstrated this "negotiation" when he took over as Head Coach of the US Senior Men's National Basketball Team: he asked the players for their input on the team standards. As Krzyzewski (2009) puts it, "you have to give your team the opportunity to contribute to your collective identity" (p. 70). Intentionally seeking athlete input increases their sense of autonomy, improves communication, and deepens the relationship with the coaching staff; all of which enhance organisational culture, athlete commitment, and athlete satisfaction.

More broadly, as the workforce is becoming more diverse through a variety of personal characteristics such as age, gender, race, ethnic background, religion, sexual orientation, physical ability, and marital and parental status (Mai-Dalton, 1993), organisations are becoming more reflective of society (Loden & Rosener, 1991). Such cultural diversity means that individuals bring in their own unique set of values, beliefs, attitudes, expectations, languages, symbols, customs, and behaviours (Adler, 1991; DeSensi, 1995). Organisations, therefore, have to identify how to address diversity, and this is often done through the established organisational culture which dictates the acceptance and valuing (or rejection) of differences from the top management level that is then funnelled down through the whole organisation. Natalie's narrative explained that this spiritual diversity was perhaps lacking within that particular sport.

Sport organisations are different from traditional organisations because they are represented in educational institutions (schools, colleges, and universities); professional sport teams; nonprofit organisations (YMCA and Boys and Girls Club of America); profit-oriented firms (dealing with sport, fitness, and wellness services or consulting, legal, and marketing); governmental agencies (city recreational departments and state parks and recreation departments); national and international sport-governing bodies (United States Basketball Association and International Federation of Football Association); and umbrella sport organisations (National Collegiate Athletic Association and the U.S. Olympic Committee) (Chelladurai, 1999). Therefore, the make-up of sport organisations is diverse and their focuses vary. For example, high schools and universities have multiple sport focuses yet educating individuals is the main purpose and activity. In contrast, a professional team's focus is the team, which is singular-focused instead of broad. More specifically, Chelladurai (1999) noted that an athletic team has all the attributes of an organisation while also differing because of the "constant roster size of members across teams in the same sport, the codification of the activities of the team in rule books, and the public and precise record of performances of the team" (p. 60). Scholars have treated teams as organisations to understand satisfaction of athletes (Riemer & Chelladurai, 1998), satisfaction of coaches (Chelladurai & Ogasawara, 2003), commitment to occupation (Turner & Chelladurai, 2005), and general comparisons to non-sport organisations (Drucker, 1995).

DeSensi (1995) recognised the lack of diversity and called for sport organisations to value diversity, varied perspectives, and multicultural teams that hold power. Doherty and Chelladurai (1999) proposed a theoretical framework – The impact of cultural diversity as a function of organisational culture framework (p. 290) – for managing cultural diversity as it increases respect for differences, a tolerance of risk and ambiguity, and a person orientation. Fink and Pastore (1999) highlighted that when sport organisations are proactive in adopting an organisational culture that supports diversity, acceptance, and respect, it is practised at all levels. Athletes should benefit from an organisational culture that honours and values diversity because they also bring in their own personal characteristics, value systems, and beliefs – such as Sikhism in Natalie's example. Ideally, the organisational culture that values diversity and inclusion should be reflected by coaches to the athletes. Scott (1997) explained the process in a little more detail using intercollegiate athletics. He highlighted that athletic directors are responsible for creating and managing the optimal culture that should then be practised at all levels of the organisation. Teams (or programmes) will create their own belief system as a subculture of the larger organisations. Five-time NBA Champion basketball coach Greg Popovich of the San Antonio Spurs explained it this way, "You have to have a culture. You have to have a pipeline not just talent-wise, but idea-wise, emotion-wise, camaraderie-wise, I'm responsible to you, you're responsible to him, we're responsible to each other. I don't want to let you down. That's what it's all about" (personal communication, July 22, 2016). The subculture (in this case the Spurs team) should reflect the larger organisational culture (the Spurs organisation), but it will be specific to the team's needs and dynamics – and spirituality may very well form part of this culture.

A key part of effective organisational culture in the modern sporting world is holistic, athlete-centred care for athletes. Holistic care is, of course, based on the ancient Greek concept of holism that holds that a whole (or team) is greater than the sum of its parts (or players) (Mallett & Rynne, 2010). Even for individual sports, an athlete is more than just their physical conditioning, technical skill level, tactical, and strategic acuity, and how full they keep their mental skills toolbox. The topic of holistic care is dissected much more deeply in other chapters, but for our purposes we will focus on the coaches' role.

Holistic athlete-centred care and spirituality

For coaches to fully commit to holistic, athlete-centred coaching, they must know that they have the support of their superiors as part of the organisational culture. Academic calls for caring and compassionate coaching (Burton & Peachey, 2013; Rieke, Hammermeister, & Chase, 2008; Vella, Oades, & Crowe, 2010) mean little if the coaches know they are being primarily evaluated on, and their continued employment dictated by, wins and losses. Furthermore, research has shown that the higher the level of competition, the more pressure coaches must handle (Frey, 2007; Kelley & Gill, 1993; Olusoga, Butt, Hays, & Maynard, 2009; Richman, 1992; Wang & Ramsey, 1998), which can cause some coaches to lose sight of a well-intentioned, holistic, athlete-centred coaching philosophy in pursuit of short-term glory. Natalie's narrative demonstrates this insofar as the Performance Director was seeming genuinely concerned about the athlete's lifestyle and its potential effect on performance.

Martinkova and Parry (2011) argued that coaches have two primary duties and responsibilities: non-maleficence, including avoiding the psychological impact of stress, and benevolence, including protecting personal identity. A holistic, athlete-centred perspective addresses each of these. In the International Sport Coaching Framework, the International Council on Coaching Excellence and Association of Summer Olympic International Federations (2012) explained that "the premise of an athlete-centred approach is the protection and respect for the integrity and individuality of those with whom coaches work" (p. 13). This individuality may include the athletes' spiritual beliefs, which may impact such things as their commitment to competing by the rules. In addition, respecting an athlete's integrity includes not asking them to act counter to their convictions.

Furthermore, an athlete-centred philosophy recognises that athletes are more than just their performance. 11-time NBA champion coach Phil Jackson was famous for trying to connect with each player individually on and off the court. Jackson wrote, "That's why I like to introduce them to ideas outside the realm of the game, to show them that there's more to life than basketball – *and more to basketball than basketball*" (Jackson, 1995, p. 124). This approach places the athletes' experience in the forefront of a coach's actions through the "application of a questions-based pedagogy with the intention of identifying and working toward shared goals ... associated with the need to maintain a positive, cheerful, caring, coaching front at all times" (Nelson, Potrac, & Marshall, 2010, p. 467). Employing a questions-based pedagogy engages the athletes' mind, builds trust, and improves communication. Natalie did this when she asked the athlete to openly discuss their faith with them by asking questions, showing interest, and listening with intent. NFL Super Bowl champion coach Doug Pederson explained it this way: "I pay attention to the feelings of my players. When guys are smiling as they walk out to practice, that's a good thing" (Pederson, 2018, p. 110). This emphasis on positivity is yet another aspect of a strong organisational culture that values the holistic, athlete-centred model.

Wilson and Burdette (2019) noted four key steps in implementing Holistic, Athlete-Centred Coaching: (1) Redefine success; (2) Set proper goals that focus on personal progression and the process; (3) Include democratic processes; and (4) Provide proper feedback that finds the positive and is information rich. The redefinition of success does not mean that winning is not important, just that winning is not all that is important. A concept of success that includes goals for self-improvement, task mastery, and competence may assist with long-term athlete motivation and confidence, which hopefully leads to more wins while not sacrificing integrity. Including athletes in the development of the organisational culture through democratic processes increases athletes' sense of autonomy, which may positively impact their commitment to the organisation through the elusive athlete "buy-in." Successful coaches, like the example of Coach K soliciting player input earlier, value and seek athlete opinions on the games that they themselves are playing.

When researchers observed legendary Coach John Wooden's basketball practices, they found that he often gave instructions in a right way – wrong way – right way pattern (Gallimore & Tharp, 2004). In that vein, we will move from the "right way" of Holistic, Athlete-Centred Coaching discussed earlier to a "wrong way" example. Former National Collegiate Athletic (NCAA) athlete Sarah Hillyer – whose Christian faith is very important to her – shared the devastating impact of an abusive coach who would not allow Sarah to integrate her spiritual and athletic identity. Hillyer wrote about her painful experience as a collegiate basketball player where she felt that differing worldviews fuelled controlling and abusive behaviour by her coach. For example, Hillyer shared this reflection, "My Christian faith and conservative upbringing seemed to cause a great deal of animosity between us" (2010, p. 16). Hillyer believes that the abuse she faced contributed to an eating disorder and deep depression. Sadly, she recounted in painful detail how her coach attacked her for her beliefs, such as this exchange the day after she set the school record for three-pointers in a game: "And as of today, if I ever see you with another Christian t-shirt on underneath your practice jersey, you'll be running sprints until you are begging your 'God' to save you from my wrath. Do I make myself clear?" (p. 17). Hillyer felt singled out and targeted for her spiritual identity, despite her excellent performance on the basketball court. In fact, despite being named runner-up for the Conference Freshman of the Year, she wrote, "I hated my life. I felt alone. I was afraid. I was confused. My coach hated me" (p. 17–18). Though the coach did not share Hillyer's spiritual beliefs, she should have created an environment that allowed Hillyer to feel supported and certainly not attacked. But what exactly does that support look like? That question leads us into the "right way" to integrate spiritual and athletic identities by employing the concept of respectful pluralism.

Respectful pluralism in sport

Douglass Hicks' (2003a) work on respectful pluralism in the workplace can be easily applied to the sporting context and ties together our discussions on organisational culture and holistic, athlete-centred care of athletes. In fact, Hicks (2003b) argued that "all organisations have an organisational culture; some scholars will call any such culture a functional equivalent of a religion. Respectful pluralism is itself a set of ideas for creating a culture that models, as the name suggests, mutual respect amidst diversity" (p. 37). This mutual respect is a key aspect of holistic, athlete-centred care of athletes.

There are three key tenets of Hicks' respectful pluralism that should be applied in sport: (1) non-degradation, (2) non-coercion, and (3) non-establishment. First, neither the organisation nor any leader should degrade the spiritual beliefs of someone under their authority (as was seen in the Hillyer example earlier). Likewise, someone cannot attack the dignity of a fellow athlete, coach, or employee under the guise of religion. Second, there must not be an attempt to coerce someone under their authority, or a teammate, to believe in and/or act with the same spiritual beliefs as theirs. Third, non-establishment requires that a sport organisation, team, and coach should not establish that there is only one acceptable spiritual worldview allowed in that group. Importantly, this does not mean that all spiritual expression should be banned. On the contrary, spiritual expression should be encouraged that meets non-degradation, non-coercion, and non-establishment. Learning from teammates and/or co-workers with different spiritual beliefs can strengthen bonds, improve understanding, bolster communication, and improve player satisfaction.

Some examples of spiritual expression include dress, diet, prayer, and calendars – as Natalie described earlier in the case of her athlete practicing Sikhism. Athletes with sincerely held beliefs should be allowed to wear religious clothing, such as an Islamic hijab, Sikh dastar, or Jewish kippah, without fear of degrading comments from their own team and/or leaders. Stephen Curry, the only unanimous Most Valuable Player award winner in NBA history, and a devout Christian, had "4:13" and "I can do all things" included in the design of his shoes to represent one of his favourite Bible verses: Philippians 4:13, "I can do all things through Christ who strengthens me." However, leagues may have the power to prevent some similar expressions, such as the NCAA banning overtly religious messages after the winner of the prestigious Heisman Trophy, Tim Tebow wrote Bible verses on his eye black.

Similarly, religious dietary customs should be respected. For example, players that follow kosher Jewish laws should have those beliefs not only respected but also proactively sought out and considered in planning team meals. This may include daily dietary guidelines, such as some Hindu or Jewish beliefs, or during special times of year, such as not eating or drinking from dawn to dusk as part of Islam's Ramadan. In fact, devout Muslim and NBA Hall-of-Fame player Hakeem Olajuwon famously observed the Ramadan traditions, despite his strenuous game and travel schedule.

Prayer and/or worship – regardless of the religion – is a fundamental practice for most of the believers. Providing an appropriate location and time for prayer and/or worship might include pre-competition chapel service for Christians or noon prayers for Muslims. Stephen Curry has spoken of the importance of pre-game prayer and chapel services to his routine and peace of mind. This could be considered similar to Natalie's athlete using prayer in place of their sport psychology session. Furthermore, days of the week have significance, and restrictions, in several religions, and some religions would not condone competition on special holy days. One of the most famous examples is all-time-great, Major League Baseball pitcher Sandy Koufax not playing in the 1965 World Series Game 1, which fell on Yom Kippur – the Day of Atonement on the Jewish Calendar. Koufax shared that "Man is entitled to his belief and I believe I should not work on Yom Kippur. It's as simple as all that and I have never had any trouble on that account since I've been in baseball" (as quoted in Rothenberg, n.d.). Similarly, when the Church of Jesus Christ of Latter-day Saints' Brigham Young University (BYU) makes the NCAA basketball tournament known as March Madness, the NCAA makes sure not to schedule BYU to play on Sundays in accordance with their religious beliefs.

Conclusion

Returning once again to organisational culture, it is imperative that organisations either produce their own materials, such as the Football Association's Belief in the Game, or seek out materials already available, such as the UK's Sporting Equals information sheets on inclusion and diversity in sport (including religion). Coaches, performance directors, and administrators should make an intentional effort to become more culturally competent in their knowledge of belief systems that may be very different from their own or the majority of the people in their community. The jacket analogy is useful here: if a coach or leader's spiritual beliefs were a jacket, they do not have to leave that jacket in the parking lot when they come to work or play. They can remain authentic to their beliefs and wear that jacket into the building. However, they may not force someone else to wear their jacket! Each person needs to have the freedom to be themselves and not be forced to hide their beliefs.

This balance of dignity and respect for all in respectful pluralism is a wonderful way for sport organisations to affirm athletes of faith as individuals and allow them to express their individual beliefs while still maintaining an organisational culture that values the holistic, athlete-centred care of all members of the team or organisation. Hicks (2003b) argued that respectful pluralism effectively walks the fine line between "resisting company-sponsored religion and spirituality while allowing employees to bring their own religions to work" (p. 2). Returning to our earlier discussion of organisational culture, Hicks noted that the research and literature in leadership, organisational culture, human resource management, and even religious studies have overlooked the importance of religious beliefs and practices at work. While most of the athletes are not employees, the concept still fits well into high-performance sport. Furthermore, there is often little formal training made available to sports employees to upskill them in understanding how to correctly and appropriately enfold the needs of spiritual athletes into their athletic programmes.

Athletes are often removed from the social support structures that they grew up with when they advance in their athletic careers. This makes supporting athletes of faith even more important for their mindset and wellbeing. In his first NBA MVP acceptance speech, Stephen Curry shared, "I can't say enough how important my faith is to how I play the game and who I am" (ASAP Sports, 2015). Travelling extensively, team and performance-orientated time commitments, and the lack of privacy elite athletes often encounter can make continuing religious traditions such as church, mosque, or temple attendance more difficult. Having a sport organisation and personnel that recognise this is one way to care for the whole athlete and not just the physical specimen. This holistic care may encourage increased commitment from the athlete and potentially better performance. However, if the organisation includes religious and/or spiritual expression solely to get more production out of the person then it misses the point of those beliefs (Wilson, 2014).

As seen in Natalie's opening example, many organisations and individuals deal with religion and spirituality in athletics by not addressing it at all. Some are afraid that bringing it up will cause more problems than it solves, but this is not the case. It is crucial that the organisation implement a clear philosophy that supports all athletes' rights to express their beliefs, as with respectful pluralism. If the organisation does implement a clear policy, this will embolden personnel such as coaches and performance directors to proactively and positively address spirituality when appropriate.

Effective leadership and coaching really come down to relationships. Getting to know athletes individually is a productive principle of athletic leadership that strengthens relationships and creates an environment conducive to high performance. If a coach, performance director, or other organisational employee is able to connect with an athlete beyond their sport, then they will probably learn if spirituality is important to that athlete. This knowledge will allow for the creation of an individual plan for athletic success that not only incorporates the latest scientific advances but also respects and honours the dignity of the individual by adjusting training for their spiritual convictions.

However, the reality is that difficult decisions may have to be made, in which an athlete might have to miss out on an athletic opportunity to maintain their religious practices. On the other hand, a spiritual athlete also might be willing to consult their religious leaders to explore if there can be flexibility in their practices, such as with Moe Shibi (a Muslim Great Britain Rower) and Jonathan Edwards (a Christian Great Britain Triple Jumper).

Supporting athletes of faith is an important part of modern sport organisational culture. Elite sport organisations have become global enterprises, recruiting the best athletes from around the world. Having an organisational culture that values and respects individuals for who they are and allows them to respectfully express their identities as part of holistic, athlete-centred care will have an advantage in recruiting and retaining the best of the best from around the world.

References

Adler, N. J. (1991). *International dimensions of organizational behaviour* (2nd ed.). Boston MA: PWS-Kent.

ASAP Sports. (2015). *Golden State Warriors media conference*. Retrieved from http://asapsports.com/show_conference.php?id=108794

Ashmos, D. P., & Duchon, D. (2000). Spirituality at work: A conceptualization and measure. *Journal of Management Inquiry, 9*(2), 134–145. https://doi.org/10.1177/105649260092008

Burton, L., & Peachey, J. W. (2013). The call for servant leadership in intercollegiate athletics, *Quest, 65*(3), 354–371. https://doi.org/10.1080/00336297.2013.791870

Chelladurai, P. (1999). *Human resource management in sport and recreation*. Champaign, IL: Human Kinetics.

Chelladurai, P., & Ogasawara, E. (2003). Satisfaction and commitment of American and Japanese collegiate coaches. *Journal of Sport Management, 17*(1), 62–73. https://doi.org/10.1123/jsm.17.1.62

DeSensi, J. T. (1995). Understanding multiculturalism and valuing diversity: A theoretical perspective. *Quest*, *47*(1), 34–43. https://doi.org/10.1080/00336297.1995.10484143

Doherty, A. J., & Chelladurai, P. (1999). Managing cultural diversity in sport organizations: A theoretical perspective. *Journal of Sport Management*, *13*(4), 280–297. https://doi.org/10.1123/jsm.13.4.280

Drucker, P. (1995). *Managing in a time of great change*. Oxford, UK: Butterworth-Heinemann.

Fink, J. S., & Pastore, D. L. (1999). Diversity in sport? Utilizing the business literature to devise a comprehensive framework of diversity initiatives. *Quest*, *51*(4), 310–327. https://doi.org/10.1080/00336297.1999.10491688

Frey, M. (2007). College coaches' experiences with stress – "problem solvers" have problems, too. *The Sport Psychologist*, *21*(1), 38–57. https://doi.org/10.1123/tsp.21.1.38

Gallimore, R., & Tharp, R. (2004). What a coach can teach a teacher, 1975–2004: Reflections and reanalysis of John Wooden's teaching practices. *The Sport Psychologist*, *18*(2), 119–137. https://doi.org/10.1123/tsp.18.2.119

Hicks, D. A. (2003a). *Religion and the workplace: Pluralism, spirituality, leadership*. Cambridge: Cambridge University Press.

Hicks, D. A. (2003b). Religion and respectful pluralism in the workplace: A constructive framework. *Journal of Religious Leadership*, *2*(1), 23–51.

Hillyer, S. J. (2010). *Women's softball in Iran: An autoethnographic journey* [Doctoral dissertation]. Retrieved from https://trace.tennessee.edu/utk_graddiss/702

International Council for Coaching Excellence & Association of Summer Olympic International Federations. (2012). *International sport coaching framework*. Champaign, IL: Human Kinetics.

Jackson, P. (1995). *Sacred hoops: Spiritual lessons of a hardwood warrior*. New York: Hyperion.

Kelley, B. C., & Gill, D. L. (1993). An examination of personal/situational variables, stress appraisal, and burnout in collegiate teacher-coaches. *Research Quarterly for Exercise and Sport*, *64*(1), 94–102. https://doi.org/10.1080/02701367.1993.10608783

Krzyzewski, M. (2000). *Leading with the heart: Coach K's successful strategies for basketball, business, and life*. New York: Warner Books.

Krzyzewski, M. (2009). *The gold standard: Building a world-class team*. New York: Business Plus.

Kusluvan, Z., & Karamustafa, K. (2003). Organizational culture and its impact on employee attitudes and behaviours in tourism and hospitality organizations. In S. Kusluvan (Ed.), *Managing employee attitudes and behaviors in the tourism and hospitality industry* (pp. 453–485). New York: Nova Science.

Laureus. (2012). Nelson Mandela, Laureus World Sports Awards 2000, Monaco [Video]. *YouTube*. Retrieved from www.youtube.com/watch?v=GdopyAFP0DI

Lewis, D. (2002). Five years on – The organizational culture saga revisited. *Leadership & Organization Development Journal*, *23*(5), 280–287. https://doi.org/10.1108/01437730210435992

Loden, M., & Rosener, J. B. (1991). *Workforce America: Managing employee diversity as a vital resource*. Homewood, IL: Business One Irwin.

Louis, M. (1985). *An investigator's guide to workplace culture*. Beverly Hills, CA: Sage.

Mai-Dalton, R. R. (1993). Managing cultural diversity on the individual, group, and organizational levels. In M. M. Chemers & R. Ayman (Eds.), *Leadership theory and research: Perspectives and directions* (p. 189–215). Cambridge, MA: Academic Press.

Mallett, C. J., & Rynne, S. B. (2010). Holism in sports coaching: Beyond humanistic psychology: A commentary. *International Journal of Sports Science & Coaching*, *5*(4), 453–457. https://doi.org/10.1260/1747-9541.5.4.439

Martinkova, I., & Parry, J. (2011). Coaching and ethics of performance enhancement. In A. Hardman & C. Jones (Eds.), *The ethics of sports coaching* (pp. 165–184). Abingdon, UK: Routledge.

Nelson, L., Potrac, P. A., & Marshall, P. (2010). Holism in sports coaching: Beyond humanistic psychology – A commentary. *International Journal of Sports Science & Coaching, 5*(4), 465–468. https://doi.org/10.1260/1747-9541.5.4.439

Olusoga, P., Butt, J., Hays, K., & Maynard, I. (2009). Stress in elite sports coaching: Identifying stressors. *Journal of Applied Sport Psychology, 21*(4), 442–459. https://doi.org/10.1080/10413200903222921

Pederson, D. (2018). *Fearless: How an underdog becomes a champion*. New York: Hachette Books.

Richman, J. M. (1992). *Perceived stress and well-being in coaching: Impact of hassles, uplifts, gender, and sport* [Unpublished doctoral dissertation]. The Ohio State University.

Rieke, M., Hammermeister, J., & Chase, M. (2008). Servant leadership in sport: A new paradigm for effective coach behaviour. *International Journal of Sports Science & Coaching, 3*(2), 227–239. https://doi.org/10.1260/174795408785100635

Riemer, H. A., & Chelladurai, P. (1998). Development of the athlete satisfaction questionnaire (ASQ). *Journal of Sport and Exercise Psychology, 20*(2), 127–156. https://doi.org/10.1123/jsep.20.2.127

Rothenberg, M. (n.d.). *Sandy Koufax responded to a higher calling on Yom Kippur in 1965*. Retrieved from https://baseballhall.org/discover/sandy-koufax-sits-out-game-one

Schein, E. H. (1991). *Organizational culture and leadership*. San Francisco, CA: Jossey-Bass.

Scott, D. K. (1997). Managing culture in intercollegiate athletic organizations. *Quest, 49*(3), 403–415. https://doi.org/10.1080/00336297.1997.10484257

Turner, B. A., & Chelladurai, P. (2005). Organizational and occupational commitment, intention to leave, and perceived performance of intercollegiate coaches. *Journal of Sport Management, 19*(2), 193–211. https://doi.org/10.1123/jsm.19.2.193

Tyrrell, M. W. D. (2000). Hunting and gathering in the early silicon age. In N. M. Ashkanasy, C. P. M. Wilderom & M. F. Peterson (Eds.), *Handbook of organizational culture and climate* (pp. 85–99). Thousand Oaks, CA: SAGE Publications.

Vella, S. A., Oades, L. G., & Crowe, T. P. (2010). The application of coach leadership models to coaching practice: Current state and future directions. *International Journal of Sports Science & Coaching, 5*(3), 425–434. https://doi.org/10.1260/1747-9541.5.3.425

Wang, J., & Ramsey, J. (1998). The relationships of school type, coaching experience, gender and age to new coaches' challenges and barriers at the collegiate level. *Applied Research in Coaching and Athletics Annual*, 1–22.

Wilson, C. H. (2014). *Peace under pressure: Portraits of Christian leadership in college basketball coaches* [Doctoral dissertation]. Retrieved from https://trace.tennessee.edu/utk_graddiss/2905/

Wilson, C. H., & Burdette, T. (2019). Holistic, athlete-centered coaching orientation. In K. Dieffenbach & M. Thompson (Eds.), *Coach education essentials*. Champaign, IL: Human Kinetics.

9

THE ABLEISM OF ATHLETE WELLBEING SUPPORT

Additional needs of the paralympic athlete

Natalie Campbell and Danielle Brown

Introduction

This chapter will explore the additional challenges that are met by an elite athlete with a disability when competing in high-performance sport. Supporting a person with a disability in a high-performance training structure can often present issues that National Governing Bodies neglect to consider – for example, the impact of funding on disability allowances, mediating medication, accessing health care in new towns and finding fully accessible housing. The majority of Paralympic sports operate from elite training centres, and for some athletes with disabilities the physical, psychological and emotional difficulties experienced through 'becoming' an elite para-athlete can be overwhelming – especially if this becoming takes them away from trusted and relied upon social and medical networks. This chapter provides significant insight into the wellbeing needs of the Paralympic athletes, is framed in consideration with various sociological models of disability and details examples of best practice for how sporting organisations can ensure the structures and systems to support para-athletes are successfully in place from the beginning their elite journey through to the end.

ATHLETE VOICE

Danielle Brown (Team GB para-archery)

I was a member of Team GB for 9 years, and it is interesting to see how athlete wellbeing has slowly been prioritised. I think there is still a concern amongst Paralympic athletes that to ask for support is considered a weakness. Perhaps the same could be said for non-disabled athletes; Paralympians are a stubborn bunch. We often resist asking for help because there is

DOI: 10.4324/9780429287923-9

some sort of need to prove how capable and independent we are, even if this is at the cost of our own wellbeing. I think it can be especially hard to ask for support when the vast majority of the support staff do not have disabilities themselves. Disability is extraordinarily complex – people with the same disability will live, act and respond very differently to every situation, and this can make it challenging for support staff to know how to help at both the human and performance level.

The general topic of disability was not really ever discussed in terms that were not medical. The majority of the questions would come from the physiotherapist or the team doctor and were usually asked as *Can you physically do this? Can you physically do that?* – and I think this was done because of two particular reasons. Firstly, so the coaching staff could try to figure out how they could take what the non-disabled athletes were doing and try some sort of copy and paste training methodology to the Para-athletes. There always seems to be a lot of trial and error type coaching in Paralympic sports that does not seem to happen in Olympic sports. Secondly, I think this is because classification is such an important aspect of being a Paralympic athlete.

My own experiences with classification are of a process that was physically and emotionally painful, as well as humiliating and career ending. I had my first classification in 2009, and it was a bittersweet moment because I thought *Yes I can become a Paralympic athlete* but at the same time I was thinking *OK – so you are actually labelling yourself as disabled now*. This was quite challenging for me because I acquired my disability as a teenager – and I think sometimes the psychology of how this can affect how someone sees them self needs thought. I don't actually remember anyone asking me how I felt about this really big change to my life – asking me if I was 'OK' with it all. I began to notice how classification can be experienced very differently between people who acquired their disability (like me) and people who have had their disability since birth (or from a very young age). The word 'disabled' is definitely contentious amongst Paralympians – some embrace it, some resist it, some reject it. For me, classification was most difficult because it went against my life narrative of consistently trying to show how 'able' I am, but in classification you are sort of thinking *please see how disabled I am!* In 2013, new classification rules were introduced – which I had some knowledge of, but not much – and I was re-classified at a World Championships in Taiwan. I remember the classifier twisting my foot saying *If your condition is real you shouldn't be able to feel this*. They put me through so much pain that I was unable to get myself off of the medical bench – the classifier then looked at me and said *Why are you pretending to be paralysed?* My career ended the very next day when I was classified out of the sport. So there I was – thousands of miles from home, with no one there to support me through this intense and immediate shock. Suddenly, I was not disabled enough! Was I making my disability up? The possibility of this situation had never been discussed with me. I remember saying to my coaching team *So what am I supposed to do now?* and the response I got was something like *With a CV like yours you won't have any difficulty finding work*. When I got back to the UK, I appealed the classification decision but I was unsuccessful. Without question, my mental wellbeing was at one of the lowest points I have ever experienced.

During my time in elite disability sport, I have heard of some truly awful experiences that other Paralympians have faced. These challenges place additional unwanted stress on para-athletes and are often things that non-disabled athletes have the privilege of living without. Some examples include my teammates taking the doors off of bathrooms in hotels to make them (actually) accessible the night before a major competition. Another athlete won a competition meaning her funding increased, but this resulted in losing her specially adapted car after her finances were subsequently re-assessed by the Department for Work and Pensions. This meant that she had to get public transport to training which took nearly an hour longer each way (not forgetting the need to call the council 24 hours in advance to request that the bus actually made the stop in her remote village). On their way to Paralympic qualification, a group of para-athletes had their suitcases lost for over 72 hours and many of them had their medication, catheters, feeding pegs, etc. in there so they had to go immediately to the hospital after a 13-hour flight to get emergency supplies. Some athletes have been told that their NGB did not have the funds to support paying for a personal assistant to accompany them to training camps or competitions abroad and so the athlete is left having to find the finances to pay the additional cost or lose the opportunity to complete. These continuous little difficulties then simply build and build and will have detrimental effects on the wellbeing of a para-athlete, as well as potentially damaging an athlete's performance if they are not managed appropriately.

There is also the issue of cultural differences or understandings of disability – for example, disability in the UK is different to disability in China or Russia or India, so you have to think hard about, and prepare yourself for, instances such as if you have a competition in country that has poor standards of accessible facilities or has poor standards of equality laws. The non-disabled athletes take a lot for granted and also support staff too. I've even noticed that many practitioners work with Paralympic sports with little knowledge or experience of the upskilling required to be fully aware of the daily difficulties, and the sport-specific situations that can impact the physical wellness and the mental wellbeing of Paralympic athletes – this could be anything from nutrition to performance lifestyle to strength and conditioning. But people seem reluctant to ask us the 'big' questions which means quick wins can get easily missed.

Small things could make such a huge difference to para-athletes – like knowing ahead of time any potential changes to Personal Independent Plans (PIPs) that the government might bring in, or ensuring all communication is sent in accessible formats. Para-athletes shouldn't have to ask for simple everyday things like these! For me, disability was only discussed in two ways – disability as a function of your performance and disability as your story for a media hook or platform. No one seemed to care about 'me'. Honestly, it's exhausting . . . and that's before you add in the full-time training programme we all do!

SCHOLAR VOICE

Towards an understanding of ableism in Paralympic sport

This chapter explores some of the most salient issues presented by Danielle and theorises these against contemporary critical disability studies (CDS) literature. The sociological domain of CDS calls for transparency with regard to a lived experience of the phenomenon being researched or written about. Indeed, a number of academics have highlighted the ethical and empirical challenges that can arise when non-disabled academics take up space within the CDS arena, discussing the nuances of empathy, positionality and reflexivity in research produced with disabled athletes (Brighton, 2015; Brighton & Williams, 2018; Campbell, 2019; Howe, 2018). Therefore, it is important to note that the author of this chapter is non-disabled. In addition, the author is another non-disabled person working in Paralympic sport, contributing to the problem observed by Danielle that non-disabled people may occupy roles in Paralympic sport by default, chance or opportunity (rather than by design or desire) (Bush, 2017; Campbell, 2017; Duarte & Culver, 2014; Fairhurst, Bloom, & Harvey, 2017; Townsend, Huntley, Cushion, & Fitzgerald, 2018). This in itself can be problematic and supports Danielle's concern that (at times) much of the working performance-based practices in Paralympic sports are understood through 'trial and error' – something Danielle states is not often tolerated in Olympic sports (Townsend, Cushion, & Morgan, 2019). By unpacking the binary of Olympic and Paralympic as a starting point, we can begin to explore a number of concerns that highlight the realities and associated challenges of achieving wellbeing as a disabled person (para-athlete or not).

A number of models exist within CDS that attempt to theorise the phenomenon that is 'disability'; something deeply challenging in its concept as disability is simultaneously uniquely individual yet globally experienced. However, Danielle's narrative can be explored through four particular models that serve to demonstrate the complexities of the terms 'disabled' and 'disability' and show how such theories can be both complementary and contradictory to understanding wellbeing. These models are (1) the Medical model, (2) the Social model, (3) the Social-Relational model and (4) the Psycho-Emotional model.

The medical model

Perhaps the earliest attempt to theorise disability came from the pathologising of people considered to be physically or psychologically 'abnormal'. The model purports that the state of abnormality is internal to the individual, and that such abnormality may reduce the individual's quality of life and cause clear disadvantages to their state of living. The medical model of disability exacts that curing, or at least managing illness or disability, revolves around identifying the illness or disability from an in-depth clinical and scientific perspective by understanding it, classifying it and learning to control and/or alter its course in an attempt to provide some semblance of assumed 'normality' to the individual. Critically, the consideration of classifying the abnormality is often an overt topic when CDS literature collides with high performance (HP) sport. It would be remiss to explore the ableism of wellbeing in Paralympic settings without drawing explicit attention to the requirement of the classification system. A number of scholars have written about the paradoxical nature of the Paralympic Games and the challenges that classification presents for disabled people (e.g. Bredahl, 2011; Howe & Silva, 2018; McNamee, 2017; Purdue & Howe, 2012a) – presenting to the world how physically able a person is through a system that specifically exposes how disabled they are.

Danielle recalls how the vast majority of her conversations with support staff were medicalised, specifically around performance – with this in itself being an example of the immediate and constant compromising of her presence within her sport. She is first and foremost required to be a disabled athlete. This notion of being a disabled athlete and announcing oneself as such can be exceptionally detrimental to an individual's wellbeing. Danielle discusses the impact of her first classification and the conscious decision to become a Paralympic athlete, knowing that in doing so she was committing to regular medical classification testing and labelling herself as disabled – a 'bittersweet' experience for her, that unquestionably affected and altered her self-identity forever. When an individual gets accepted onto an Olympic programme, this occasion is often joyous, exhilarating and long awaited. However, it is critical to understand that whilst classification for some individuals can be seen as affirming and rewarding, for others, fully accepting the ensuing medicalisation of oneself can bring with it exceptionally unpleasant (and in Danielle's case 'humiliating') experiences (Van Dornick & Spencer, 2019). As if, somehow, classification legitimises an individual's affinity with disability. The paradoxical conundrum of the classification system is the requirement of an individual to proclaim disability to be accepted in a mega sporting event that, in its intents, celebrates ability. As a monolithically oppressive system whereby already marginalised individuals are further reduced to a state of physical functioning – classification highjacks agency. Paramount to the experience is the reality that classification can engender as well as abjure the formal certification of the disabled. As Danielle recalls, her career as a Paralympic athlete ended within 24 hours of a reclassification event, leaving her feeling powerless, ashamed and lost – emotions consistent with chronic feelings of ill-being. Worryingly, she discusses the lack of immediate support to help her cope with declassification, with her rationally emotional reaction to this clinically driven situation seemingly quickly dismissed. Whilst non-voluntary retirement from elite sport (i.e. through injury or funding cuts) has long been of interest to sport psychology researchers, little attention has been paid to the retirements of elite athletes with disabilities (Bundon, Ashfield, Smith, & Goosey-Tolfrey, 2018), especially in regards to medically determined dismissing.

Classification is a complex and problematic arrangement entrenched within the purpose and principles of Paralympic sport. However, the psychological exposure this mandatory medicalising requirement imposes upon an individual and their relationship to being or not being disabled needs academic scrutiny. The confounding effects that 'becoming' disabled might have on an individual's wellbeing should not be overlooked; nor should the potential lasting dissonance of self-identity if an individual is later announced as medically 'not disabled enough' to continue on their Paralympic journey. Saliently, Danielle shares that her 'lowest point' with regard to mental wellbeing came not from losing a competition but from losing her right to be considered disabled within HP sport.

The social model

With its roots in political activism, the 'social model' of disability – established by the Union of the Physically Impaired Against Segregation (UPIAS) in the United Kingdom (UK) in 1976 – sought to reframe impairment as biological and disability as a social construction. Placing emphasis on the everyday structural and material barriers disabled people encounter, the notion of impairment is situated as only pertinent in specific settings – such as classification (e.g. Oliver, 1992; Barnes & Mercer, 2003). Sociologically considered against critiques of oppression and capitalism, the social model was, and remains, instrumental in contesting the "systemic removal of disabled people from mainstream economic and social life" (Barnes, 2020, p. 15).

Danielle's narrative illuminates the prevalence of such removal through everyday ableist interactions, both within and outside of the HP sport setting. Such interactions demonstrate the constant physical and mental micro-traumas absorbed by disabled athletes and support the consideration that non-disabled athletes hold 'privilege' in so easily avoiding such societal stressors and oppressors. These micro-traumas identified by Danielle, as supported by Arnold, Wagstaff, Steadman, and Pratt (2017), serve to underline the extent to which disabled athletes are simply expected to flex, cope and accept avoidable situations that have detrimental effects on both performance and wellbeing. From discommoding experiences of hotel accessibility, to life-threatening consequences of lost luggage, through to changes in governmental essential living assistance, it is evident that para-athletes – regardless of impairment – are fundamentally disabled from experiencing elite sport in the same tenor as non-disabled athletes.

The constant and consistent situations that expose the ableist notions of elite sport are often hidden in the taken-for-grantedness of everydayness (Berger, 2011); the tacit knowledge of the additional compromises to wellbeing being held only by those who experience it daily. Although not exclusive to para-sports, the lack of funding available to athletes to compete globally is felt more so by athletes that require personal assistants – from reducing physical stressors such as carrying equipment, through to aiding biological requirements such as toilet transference, the need for additional support can impact heavily on both performance and wellbeing. Danielle explains the challenges the majority of para-athletes face when needing to secure additional funding for personal assistants, and that these financial burdens are often overlooked when para-sport NGBs are devising business plans and budget spends to win medals. Personal assistants are not considered essential to performance; rather, a luxury if a willing (and financially secure) volunteer can be sourced. Although it is not unusual for some sports clubs to depend entirely on volunteers (Partington, 2018), Netting (2008) reflects that marginalised communities are often dependent on 'donated talent'; reliant upon the collective behaviours of the non-oppressed to mobilise access to denied essential life opportunities. To think that this would even be a consideration at the highest level of competitive sport serves to demonstrate the invisible, yet increasingly prevalent, barriers to paralleled experiences of wellbeing between para- and non-disabled athletes.

The issue of securing a personal assistant for competitions is not the only financial pressure faced by para-athletes. Bundon et al. (2018) argue that para-athletes retiring from sport due to declassification (such as Danielle) experience unique and difficult challenges, and that uncertainty regarding post-sport employment opportunities for people with disabilities simply compounds the inevitable. Despite an attempt to comfort Danielle that she 'would not have any trouble' finding work after her declassification, the seriousness of the financial difficulties imposed on disabled people should not be overlooked; indeed, this should be central to the learning and development undertaken by individuals with responsibility of supporting the mental health and wellbeing of the para-athlete. In the UK, the migration of the Disability Living Allowance to the Personal Independent Payment (PIP) has been controversial, with a quick internet search revealing a multitude of individual stories of embarrassment, humiliation and suffering. Since its introduction in 2013, a number of Team GB para-athletes have spoken out about the reform and have vocalised the detrimental effects of a PIP assessment on their mental health and overall wellbeing. Specifically, knowing that any changes to their physical capabilities incurred through training (despite this being the objective of training) could result in both a de/reclassification from their sport, as well as a fundamental change to the financial support they receive. Brittain, Biscaia, and Gérard (2020) argue that ableism acts as a regulatory mechanism to deny disabled people equal social practice and participation in sport and physical activity, a concept Activity Alliance coin 'The Activity Trap' (Activity Alliance, 2018) – that disabled people 'fear' being fit (p. 5). Despite physical activity helping people to manage impairments and pain, improve mental health, gain autonomy over their own health and facilitate social opportunities, disabled people are fearful of losing access to governmental financial support, as well as being fearful of being seen as too independent to be disabled (Activity Alliance, 2018). Chronic fear is not conducive to good mental health. This dichotomy of impaired body and elite performance in disabling social structure is – as Danielle explains – 'exhausting' and yet serves as another example of the micro-trauma inflicted upon para-athletes.

The social-relational model

While the Medical model and the Social model of disability have been the more widely recognised and debated models within CDS, it is argued that they do not adequately reflect the views of many people who experience disability and thus are of limited use in reality (Shakespeare, 2004; Shakespeare & Watson, 2001). Although the defining distinction between the two models is the separation of disability from impairment, this distinction has not been without substantial criticism (Barnes, 2012; Barnes, Oliver, & Barton, 2002; Shakespeare, 2004; Shakespeare & Watson, 2001; Thomas, 1999, 2001, 2004a, 2007). The work of Thomas (1999, 2001, 2004a, 2004b, 2007, 2010) explicitly addresses this criticism by developing a social-relational understanding of disability. Thomas argues the need to acknowledge that an individual will live with two discrete experiences – the personal experience of impairment and the socially constructed experience of disability. Thus, a social-relational understanding of disability holds that "disability is a form of social oppression involving the social imposition of restrictions of activity on people with impairments and the socially engendered undermining of their psycho-emotional well-being" (Thomas, 1999, p. 60).

An important consideration towards the social-relational model of disability is the fluidity of the social oppression a disabled person might experience. The interplay of society and body within shifting contexts allows a disablism that is in flux; a disablism that constitutes direct and unavoidable impact on the physical, sensory, social and emotional functioning of an individual's lifeworld. Danielle gives a prominent example of this when she highlights 'cultural differences or understandings of disability' and that athletes should 'prepare' for such experiences of othering and oppression outside of the Paralympic training centres. Scholars have debated the concept of disability as an (non)accepted state of humanness across world cultures for many years – from recordings of infanticide in Ghana (Oti-Boadi, 2017), to inaccessible infrastructure in Russia (Hartblay, 2017), to multidimensional poverty in Mexico (Pinilla-Roncancio, 2018). Recently, athlete (and fan) activism has been increasingly visible; voicing disagreement and resistance with hosting sporting mega-events in countries that deny fundamental human rights (such as Ghana, Russia and Mexico). For example, a number of international teams threatened to boycott the 2014 Sochi Olympic Games due to the anti-lesbian, gay, bisexual and transgender (LGBT) legislation passed by Russia just months before the start of the competitions (Davidson & McDonald, 2018). However, the same level of advocacy was not afforded to the para-athletes at the Rio de Janeiro 2016 Games, despite widespread coverage of the abuse of human rights (especially those of disabled people) in Brazil (Horne, 2018). Non-disabled athletes were not threatening to boycott attending the Games to succour the progression of disability rights in Brazil. The lived experience for many para-athletes is that when an event is announced as being held in a country that has 'poor standards of equality laws', or a country exposed as denying the human rights of disabled people, they must consciously and resolutely plan for potential episodes of discrimination, discomfiture and humiliation. Practitioners must ask themselves to what extent does a non-disabled athlete encounter such feelings on account of how their body is socially interpreted? The consideration that para-athletes may regularly absorb such adverse and damaging emotions to compete on the international stage is without question an exceptional example of ableism preponderating the macro-hierarchical power structures of elite sport.

The psycho-emotional dimensions model

The final model that can help to further understand the complexities of ableism discussed by Danielle is the Psycho-Emotional Dimensions model. First introduced by Reeve (2004), the concept builds upon the Social-Relational model to include both structural and psycho-emotional dimensions of disability; "seeing disability as a form of social oppression that operates at both the public and personal levels, affecting what people can do as well as who they can be" (p. 83). This notion of what disabled people can do and be is deeply entrenched within CDS and serves to be a cornerstone of identity construction within the disabled community as a whole. As Danielle points out, 'some embrace it, some resist it, some reject it'. There remains heavy debate considering the hypocrisy of employing a single encompassing term to typecast all individuals with impairments, whilst simultaneously acknowledging the individual right to self-identify (or not) using the term. Indeed, an athlete might choose to identify as a Paralympian but not as a disabled person. The daily navigations of negotiating to what extent an individual should be disabled can cause immense emotional exhaustion and quickly lead to feelings of ill-being. Asking someone to read a leisure centre menu out loud, or needing to request a particular space on the bus to training practice, for example, describes the emotional costs of moving within 'landscapes of exclusion' (Kitchin, 1998, p. 351). Reeve (2004) considers this psycho-emotional dimension a response to experiences of structural disability; in that, an identity of being disabled is socially imposed on an individual even if the individual may initially resist or reject the term as part of their identity. Experiences of being disabled by society are in constant flux for para-athletes, requiring continuous emotional and physical effort to participate in the everydayness that non-disabled athletes would give no regard to.

Other ways in which para-athletes may experience disability is through social interaction with others. Reeve (2004) suggests that non-disabled people may feel that they have the right to be curious about an individual's impairment, especially if that individual is in 'their public space' (p. 86). The Paralympic Games is an acute example of this. The deluge of information regarding classification systems and the meaning to each category underscores the predominant commentary from non-disabled people – audiences want to know 'what's wrong with him/her' first and foremost, to judge a particular sporting performance on physical merit. As discussed previously, the classification process can be a significant source of stress for a para-athlete. However, the formality of publicly being a para-athlete can engender significant feelings of psycho-emotional disablism through social interactions from both non-disabled and disabled people. Indeed, the concept of being a Paralympian but not being disabled is a conundrum. Danielle comments that people with similar impairments will 'live, act and respond very differently' to societal narratives of what they can be and what they can do – especially with regard to bodily performance such as sport and physical activity. Literature within CDS highlights the dissonance that exists within the athlete and non-athlete disabled community, and how the Paralympic Games can impose a psycho-emotional disablism to non-athlete disabled people through a continuously ableist narrative. The Games have been blasted as a mockery of equality (Braye, 2016; Braye, Dixon, & Gibbons, 2013), that they serve to disempower non-athletic disabled people (Purdue & Howe, 2012b), failing to provide a tangible legacy for disabled people (Brittain & Beacom, 2016; Howe & Silva, 2018) and set unrealistic expectations of impairment to non-disabled people (McGillivray, O'Donnell, McPherson, & Misener, 2019). This constant moral obligation of displaying what a disabled person can both be and do through the medium of elite sport can weigh heavy, an unquestioned assumption that para-athletes represent all disabled people. It is an emotional microburden that is not represented in other marginalised groups in society and can affect the wellbeing of a para-athlete simply through the inability to escape both praise and prejudice in equal measures.

The final element of psycho-emotional disablism is that of internalised oppression; when individuals within a marginalised group in society internalise the prejudices held by the dominant group – the acceptance and incorporation of 'their values about our lives' (Morris, 1991, p. 29; emphasis in original). Reeve (2004) explains that this form of oppression is most effective when it is acting at the subconscious level, "affecting the self-esteem of the individual in addition to shaping their thoughts and actions" (p. 87). Danielle points out that para-athletes may often 'resist asking for support or help' in a need to prove capability and independence; however, this preservation of autonomy may be detrimental to the wellbeing of the person. Reeve (2004) discusses how disabled people (especially as children due to their holding less agency) may conflate value and worth with use and dependence; to ask for help would be to accept the prejudices and assumptions of 'invalidness' held by non-disabled people. The compounding element of this stigma is the expected (but unsubstantiated) mental toughness and emotional resilience married to being an elite athlete (Gucciardi, Hanton, & Fleming, 2017). Thus, a para-athlete asking a non-disabled support staff member for help (whatever that help might be) might, sub-consciously, bring to the fore accompanying internalised feelings of weakness and shame. Additionally, Reeve (2004) argues that internalised oppression is unconscious and insidious, and that it profoundly affects the psycho-emotional wellbeing of disabled people in its restriction of who an individual can be. Danielle makes the powerful statement that her disability was only ever discussed as a function of performance or 'as your story for a media hook'. Paralympic athletes are often sought to engage in public appearances that seek to champion messages of breaking down barriers, overcoming adversity and finding meaning in tragedy – trained in how to develop a narrative of 'being' that places their disability at the centre of its legitimacy and purpose. The late Stella Young (a disability activist and comedian) coined this 'inspiration porn' – the objectification of disabled people for the benefit of non-disabled people – with the explicit intent being to inspire and motivate through a narrative of 'life could be worse, you could be disabled'.[1] The perpetuated selling of para-athletes as a conduit for meaning making situates the depiction of people with impairment in a way that both devalues and fetishises their experiences (Grue, 2016). Therefore, the extent to which a para-athlete has agency to determine if and how and why their impairment should lead their public engagement is crucial to holistically developing a multidimensional and flourishing individual.

Recommendations towards inclusive holistic care

The future of holistic development and wellbeing support for para-athletes is ripe for development. The need to move beyond a tokenistic nod to inclusion via a mandatory online training module is paramount – especially if NGBs are to be held truly accountable in putting athlete wellbeing at the very centre of their policies and processes. Danielle recalls how she felt practitioners would enter the Paralympic space 'with little knowledge or experience of the upskilling' required to authentically support a para-athlete through their entire sporting journey. It is imperative that the athlete remains the expert on their lived experience of disability – and that support staff be mindful and appreciative of the unique approach each individual athlete will have in their relationship with their impairment and their relationship with society. By valuing these complexities and differences, practitioners can create early on psychologically safe environments that will facilitate conversations which may, initially, be considered challenging, intrusive or even taboo.

It is important for support practitioners to advocate for the upskilling they may require when working with a para-athlete for the first time; as this may not necessarily be offered immediately, and what may be offered might not be sufficient or appropriate. Practitioners should be proactive in enhancing their general disability awareness – read up on the national equality laws and acts within your country of practice, explore the websites of different disability rights and information groups and find robust statistics about the state of quality, diversity and inclusion in your country and in the sport you are working in. Danielle claims that practitioners should 'ask the big questions', however, consider this with a cautious approach, especially if you are working with athletes new to the Paralympic system or with an individual who has recently acquired their impairment. Indeed, small gestures that demonstrate awareness and empathy can quicken the athlete–practitioner relationship, such as asking what format they prefer to communicate in, asking how they to get to and from training, or letting them know that you have your ear to the ground regarding changes to Government support.

The quality of wellbeing support offered to elite level performers is improving reflected in the emergence of dedicated practitioner roles, professional standards of practice, newly developed qualifications and duty of care charters demonstrate this. However, the ableism of such support is rooted in wider systemic political and cultural systems that precede systems of elite sport, meaning proactive and purposeful change-making practitioners are needed. Therefore, the progress of wellbeing support provided to para-athletes hinges on future support staff recognising their own ableist practice, and reflecting on how their own prejudices, biases and misunderstandings of disability can shape a more equitable landscape of holistic development.

Note

1 Stella Young (2014). I am not your inspiration thank you very much. Ted Talk. Available from https://www.ted.com/talks/stella_young_i_m_not_your_inspiration_thank_you_very_much

References

Activity Alliance. (2018). *The activity trap: Disabled people's fear of being active*. Retrieved from http://www.activityalliance.org.uk/how-we-help/research/the-activity-trap

Arnold, R., Wagstaff, C. R., Steadman, L., & Pratt, Y. (2017). The organisational stressors encountered by athletes with a disability. *Journal of Sports Sciences, 35*(12), 1187–1196. https://doi.org/10.1080/02640414.2016.1214285

Barnes, C. (2012). Understanding the social model of disability: Past, present and future. In N. Watson, A. Roulstone, & C. Thomas (Eds.), *Routledge handbook of disability studies*, (pp. 12–29). London: Routledge.

Barnes, C. (2020). Understanding the social model of disability: Past present and future. In N. Watson & S. Vehmas (Eds.), *The Routledge handbook of disability studies* (pp. 14–31). London: Routledge.

Barnes, C. M., & Mercer, G. (2003). *Disability: Key concepts*. Cambridge: Polity Press.

Barnes, C. M., Oliver, M., & Barton, L. (2002). *Disability studies today*. Oxford, UK: Blackwell Publishing Company.

Berger, P. L. (2011). *Invitation to sociology: A humanistic perspective*. New York: Open Road Media.

Braye, S. (2016). 'I'm not an activist': An exploratory investigation into retired British Paralympic athletes' views on the relationship between the Paralympic games and disability equality in the United Kingdom. *Disability & Society, 31*(9), 1288–1300. https://doi.org/10.1080/09687599.2016.1251392

Braye, S., Dixon, K., & Gibbons, T. (2013). 'A mockery of equality': An exploratory investigation into disabled activists' views of the Paralympic Games. *Disability & Society, 28*(7), 984–996. https://doi.org/10.1080/09687599.2012.748648

Bredahl, A. M. (2011). Coaching ethics and Paralympic sports. In A. Hardman & C. Jones (Eds.), *The ethics of sport coaching* (pp. 135–146). London: Routledge.

Brighton, J. (2015). Researching disabled sporting bodies: Reflections from an 'able'-bodied ethnographer. In I. Wellard (Eds.), *Researching embodied sport* (pp. 163–177). London: Routledge.

Brighton, J., & Williams, T. L. (2018). Using interviews to explore experiences of disability in sport and physical activity. In R. Medcalf & C. Mackintosh (Eds.), *Researching difference in sport and physical activity* (pp. 25–40). London: Routledge.

Brittain, I., & Beacom, A. (2016). Leveraging the London 2012 Paralympic Games: What legacy for disabled people? *Journal of Sport and Social Issues, 40*(6), 499–521. https://doi.org/10.1177/0193723516655580

Brittain, I., Biscaia, R., & Gérard, S. (2020). Ableism as a regulator of social practice and disabled peoples' self-determination to participate in sport and physical activity. *Leisure Studies, 39*(2), 209–224. https://doi.org/10.1080/02614367.2019.1694569

Bundon, A., Ashfield, A., Smith, B., & Goosey-Tolfrey, V. L. (2018). Struggling to stay and struggling to leave: The experiences of elite para-athletes at the end of their sport careers. *Psychology of Sport and Exercise, 37*, 296–305. https://doi.org/10.1016/j.psychsport.2018.04.007

Bush, A. J. (2017). From Melksham to Rio: A coach's 20-year journey in Para-Swimming. In D. Peters & G. Kohe (Eds.), *High performance disability sport coaching* (pp. 163–185). London: Routledge.

Campbell, N. J. (2017). Creating a high performance para-rowing programme in the USA: From the geography of the land to the generosity of the spirit (and everything in between). In D. Peters & G. Kohe (Eds.), *High performance disability sport coaching* (pp. 34–54). London: Routledge.

Campbell, N. J. (2019). Gatekeepers, agency and rhetoric: An academic's reflexive ethnography of 'doing' a (failed) adaptive CrossFit project. *Qualitative Research in Sport, Exercise and Health, 12*(4), 612–630. https://doi.org/10.1080/2159676X.2019.1645727

Davidson, J., & McDonald, M. G. (2018). Rethinking human rights: The 2014 Sochi Winter Olympics, LGBT protections and the limits of cosmopolitanism. *Leisure Studies, 37*(1), 64–76. https://doi.org/10.1080/02614367.2017.1310284

Duarte, T., & Culver, D. M. (2014). Becoming a coach in developmental adaptive sailing: A lifelong learning perspective. *Journal of Applied Sport Psychology, 26*(4), 441–456. https://doi.org/10.1080/10413200.2014.920935

Fairhurst, K. E., Bloom, G. A., & Harvey, W. J. (2017). The learning and mentoring experiences of Paralympic coaches. *Disability and Health Journal, 10*(2), 240–246. https://doi.org/10.1016/j.dhjo.2016.10.007

Grue, J. (2016). The problem with inspiration porn: A tentative definition and a provisional critique. *Disability & Society, 31*(6), 838–849. https://doi.org/10.1080/09687599.2016.1205473

Gucciardi, D. F., Hanton, S., & Fleming, S. (2017). Are mental toughness and mental health contradictory concepts in elite sport? A narrative review of theory and evidence. *Journal of Science and Medicine in Sport, 20*(3), 307–311. https://doi.org/10.1016/j.jsams.2016.08.006

Hartblay, C. (2017). Good ramps, bad ramps: Centralized design standards and disability access in urban Russian infrastructure. *American Ethnologist, 44*(1), 9–22. https://doi.org/10.1111/amet.12422

Horne, J. (2018). Understanding the denial of abuses of human rights connected to sports mega-events. *Leisure Studies, 37*(1), 11–21. https://doi.org/10.1080/02614367.2017.1324512

Howe, P. D. (2018). Athlete, anthropologist and advocate: Moving towards a lifeworld where difference is celebrated. *Sport in Society, 21*(4), 678–688. https://doi.org/10.1080/17430437.2016.1273628

Howe, P. D., & Silva, C. F. (2018). The fiddle of using the Paralympic Games as a vehicle for expanding [dis]ability sport participation. *Sport in Society, 21*(1), 125–136. https://doi.org/10.1080/17430437.2016.1225885

Kitchin, R. (1998). 'Out of place', 'knowing one's place': Space, power and the exclusion of disabled people. *Disability & Society, 13*(3), 343–356. https://doi.org/10.1080/09687599826678

McGillivray, D., O'Donnell, H., McPherson, G., & Misener, L. (2019). Repurposing the (super) crip: Media representations of disability at the Rio 2016 Paralympic Games. *Communication & Sport*. https://doi.org/10.1177/2167479519853496

McNamee, M. J. (2017). Paralympism, Paralympic values and disability sport: A conceptual and ethical critique. *Disability and Rehabilitation, 39*(2), 201–209. https://doi.org/10.3109/09638288.2015.1095247

Morris, J. (1991). *Pride against prejudice: Transforming attitudes to disability*. London: Women's Press.

Netting, F. E. (2008). Including and excluding volunteers: Challenges of managing groups that depend on donated talent. In R. A. Cnaan & C. Milofsky (Eds.), *Handbook of community movements and local organizations* (pp. 410–425). Boston, MA: Springer.

Oliver, M. (1992). Changing the social relations of research production? *Disability, Handicap and Society, 7*(2), 101–104. https://doi.org/10.1080/02674649266780141

Oti-Boadi, M. (2017). Exploring the lived experiences of mothers of children with intellectual disability in Ghana. *Sage Open, 7*(4). https://doi.org/10.1177/2158244017745578.

Partington, N. (2018). Volunteering and EU sports law and policy. In *Research handbook on EU sports law and policy* (pp. 98–119). Cheltenham, UK: Edward Elgar Publishing. https://doi.org/10.4337/9781784719500.00014

Pinilla-Roncancio, M. (2018). The reality of disability: Multidimensional poverty of people with disability and their families in Latin America. *Disability and Health Journal, 11*(3), 398–404. https://doi.org/10.1016/j.dhjo.2017.12.007

Purdue, D. E. J., & Howe, P. D. (2012a). See the sport, not the disability: Exploring the Paralympic paradox. *Qualitative Research in Sport, Exercise and Health, 4*(2), 189–205. https://doi.org/10.1080/2159676X.2012.685102

Purdue, D. E. J., & Howe, P. D. (2012b). Empower, inspire, achieve: (Dis)empowerment and the Paralympic Games. *Disability & Society, 27*(7), 903–916. https://doi.org/10.1080/09687599.2012.695576

Reeve, D. (2004). Psycho-emotional dimensions of disability and the social model. In C. Barnes & G. Mercer (Eds.), *Implementing the social model of disability: Theory and research* (pp. 83–100). Leeds, UK: The Disability Press.

Shakespeare, T. (2004). Social models of disability and other life strategies. *Scandinavian Journal of Disability Research, 6*(1), 8–21. https://doi.org/10.1080/15017410409512636

Shakespeare, T., & Watson, N. (2001). The social model of disability: An outdated ideology? In S. Barnartt & B. Altman (Eds.), *Exploring theories and expanding methodologies: Where we are and where we need to go*, (pp. 9–28). Bingley, UK: Emerald Group Publishing Limited.

Thomas, C. (1999). *Female forms: Experiencing and understanding disability*. Buckingham, UK: Open University Press.

Thomas, C. (2001). Feminism and disability: The theoretical and political significance of the persona and the experiential. In L. Barton (Ed.), *Disability, politics and the struggle for change* (pp. 48–58). London: David Fulton.

Thomas, C. (2004a). How is disability understood? An examination of sociological approaches. *Disability & Society, 19*(6), 569–583. http://doi.org/10.1080/0968759042000252506

Thomas, C. (2004b). Disability and impairment. In J. Swain, S. French, C. Barnes, & C. Thomas (Eds.), *Disabling barriers – enabling environments* (2nd ed., pp. 21–27). London: SAGE Publications.

Thomas, C. (2007). *Sociologies of disability and illness: Contested ideas in disability studies and medical sociology*. Hampshire, UK: Palgrave Macmillan.

Thomas, C. (2010). Medical sociology and disability theory. In G. Scambler & S. Scambler (Eds.), *New directions in the sociology of chronic and disabling conditions: Assaults on the lifeworld* (pp. 37–56). Basingstoke, UK: Palgrave Macmillan.

Townsend, R. C., Cushion, C., & Morgan, D. (2019). Coaching in disability sport. In E. Cope & M. Partington (Eds.), *Sports coaching: A theoretical and practical guide*. London: Routledge.

Townsend, R. C., Huntley, T., Cushion, C. J., & Fitzgerald, H. (2018). 'It's not about disability, I want to win as many medals as possible': The social construction of disability in high-performance coaching. *International Review for the Sociology of Sport, 55*(3), 344–360. https://doi.org/10.1177/1012690218797526 https://doi.org/1012690218797526.

Van Dornick, K., & Spencer, N. L. (2019). What's in a sport class? The classification experiences of paraswimmers. *Adapted Physical Activity Quarterly, 37*(1), 1–19. https://doi.org/10.1123/apaq.2019-0007

10
THE IMPLEMENTATION OF AN INTEGRATED PSYCHOLOGICAL SUPPORT PROGRAMME FOR INJURED ATHLETES

'Stopping athletes from falling off the edge of the cliff'

Misia Gervis

Introduction

This chapter explores the mental health challenges that surround long-term injury. While there is a wealth of evidence that clearly demonstrates long-term injury leaves athletes psychologically vulnerable to a range of psychological issues including depression, anxiety and eating disorders, current practice is to simply treat the physical injury. However, there is an alternative approach that can be taken which offers athletes better rehabilitation experiences and integrates psychological support with physical recovery. The case study presented the RETURN protocol seen through the eyes of three experienced practitioners who have delivered it for a number of years in a professional academy football club.

Introduction to the programme

It has been well documented over many years that long-term injury poses a threat to athletes' psychological health and wellbeing. Indeed this can often be the time of greatest psychological struggle which can go unnoticed and unsupported (Gervis, Pickford, Hau, & Fruth, 2019). When an athlete's identity is compromised and they feel devalued and worthless, they can spiral into psychological difficulties including depression, addiction or eating disorders. Traditionally, the method to support athletes through their rehabilitation has been through physical rehabilitation and physiotherapy with little or no psychological support.

However, there is evidence that some sport psychologists are working to improve the experiences of injured athletes by implementing psychological support programmes throughout an athlete's rehabilitation until they transition to

DOI: 10.4324/9780429287923-10

138 Misia Gervis

competitive match play. This chapter explores one such programme created by the author, as the solution to offering athletes an alternative rehabilitation experience, namely RETURN. This is explored through the lens of three experts who have delivered it as they share their lived experiences. These are: the Head of Sport Psychology (HoSP), Head Physiotherapist (HP) and Head of Academy Performance (HoAP) who have delivered RETURN for a number of years within a football academy. The narrative later summarises a reflective conversation about RETURN in a football academy, and how it has been implemented. RETURN is an intra-disciplinary programme that relies on sharing of expert knowledge at every phase of rehabilitation. The rehabilitation phases are: Phase 1 – Acute, Phase 2 – Repair, Phase 3 – Remodelling (or Return to training) and Phase 4 – Return to Competition. The length of time that a player spends in each phase of recovery is injury and individually specific. Throughout rehabilitation players receive one-to-one support with the sport psychologist using Acceptance Commitment Therapy (ACT) as the underpinning psychological theory. The success of the programme is reliant on physiotherapists working collaboratively with the sport psychologist. The physiotherapists determine what phase of rehabilitation the player is in and inform the sport psychologist accordingly. In the Academy, all long-term injured players receive the RETURN protocol regardless of age. Thus, these core principles can be summarised by the acronym RETURN (see Figure 10.1).

R- Physical Rehabilitation
- Phase based physical rehabilitation
- Medics determine the physical rehabilitation procedures

E- Emotional/ Psychological recovery
- Present throughout recovery
- Delivered by sport psychologist with expertise in injury

T- Team Based
- An open sharing collaborative approach
- Physiotherapists, sport psychologist, sport scientist, nutritionist and coach

U- Unique
- Unique to each individual player
- Consideration is given to each individual's physical and psychological needs

R- Readiness, physical and psychological
- Players only return to competition when they are both physically and psychologically fit

N- Normalised
- Every longterm injured player receives psychological support
- Removes stigma

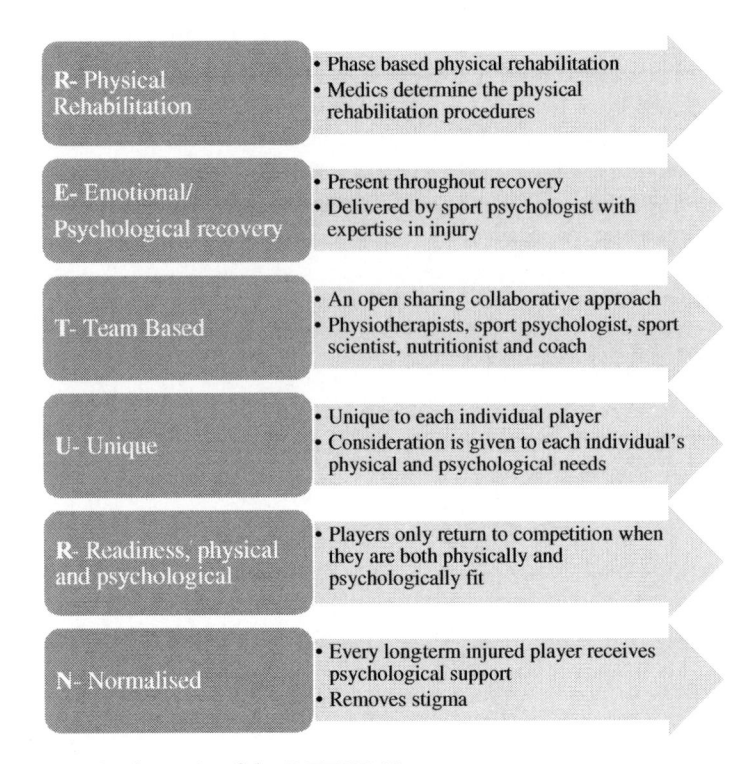

FIGURE 10.1 A schematic of the RETURN programme

PRACTIONER VOICES

The narrative later is a summary of a reflective conversation, guided by some critical questions, between three experts from different professional domains who work collaboratively to support injured players within an academy football setting. Thus, this case study draws on their experiences of working with many players and offers a unique inside perspective. Each voice is heard using their words as we explore their lived experiences and the challenges of delivering RETURN.

What was it like before RETURN?

HoAP: *Before we had an awareness of how the players were feeling but the in-depth psychological side wasn't really thought about. We just didn't really think about the extra psychological support that they would need.*

HP: *As a physio, it is embedded in you to have awareness of the emotional and psychological side of the player. But the only thing is what do you do with that when you find a psychological problem. Because as a physio you have your limitations. We don't have the knowledge or techniques to deal with emotional stress or fear of re-injury so we were lacking in that.*

How do we work together in Phase 1?

HP: *The RETURN protocol begins with a CPD meeting with all critical staff responsible for rehabilitation of players. Initially, the medical staff inform all support staff if a player will be long-term injured. This triggers the RETURN protocol. The sport psychologist discusses the injury status with the medical staff and the diagnosis to get a sense of what the recovery journey is going to look like. Players could be out for many months with injuries such as a broken leg or Anterior Cruciate Ligament (ACL) injury. Some players may need an operation or the expected outcome could be a return within 6–8 weeks.*

HoSP: *So different people have control of different aspects at different times through rehabilitation. But the overseeing and control of the process is managed by you (physio), and we are working to support that.*

HoSP: *In instances where a player needs an operation, my role is always trying to address any concern or fear they might have about having an operation, especially if this is the first one. There have been a couple of instances where players have been really scared about it and needed reassurance. I try and allow them to say that they're scared. Because sometimes the environment doesn't allow them to express these feelings. So I give them permission to own those feelings, explore and normalise them.*

HoAP: *So a phone call from you (psych) is a staple especially if they are not at the club. It is really good for them to know there is support that goes a long way.*

What happens in Phase 2?

HoSP: *The second phase is quite hard, especially when they aren't doing very much. They could be inactive for months with some injuries.*

HP: *This is where you start getting the frustration and boredom. And seeing your teammates move past you and going out on the pitch.*

HoSP: *There is a balance between keeping them connected (with teammates) and recognising that there are moments of extreme difficulty. I remember seeing a player who was standing at the window wistfully looking out and his whole body was saying 'Why is this so hard?' He looked totally dejected and lost.*

HP: *In the early stages progress is slow, at times it is so slow and small that progress is not recognised. That is where you (psych) have given us some skills to help us identify that.*

HoSP: *It is about creating mindfulness rehabilitation, having awareness and being present. We are trying to work with the player towards committed action to keep players engaged and to value every step they take however small. I work with the player to see where the opportunities lie, and we discuss the concept of mindful rehabilitation which seeks to ensure that they are fully present when doing exercises that can be very boring when done over and over again. Sometimes, I'll do their exercises with them to get them to have an awareness, notice and be present. One of the challenges is to help players find acceptance of the journey – once they stop fighting, recovery begins to happen.*

HoSP: *For me, this is when they are most vulnerable to depression. We had a player who was very vulnerable and who was walking his way into depression. His roommate actually alerted us to how he was at home, which was great because it shows how we have created an environment where there is awareness amongst the players. He recognised that his roommate was struggling and called me which allowed me immediately to respond and support the injured player.*

HP: *An unintended consequence is that all sorts of people are now talking about things in very different ways – which changes the whole environment.*

HoSP: *When you are working with a player you have to understand the environment, context and the pressures that are on them. There have been two or three players who were suffering with sub-clinical mental health problems without a doubt. And one player was walking himself into a clinical issue with his disordered eating that was becoming dangerous. However, this was picked up very early and addressed with appropriate support. The result was that he recovered psychologically before the eating disorder had taken hold of him.*

HP: *So we monitor players using a couple of psychometrics including BRUMS.*

HoSP: *I find the BRUMS really helpful as it gives me an early warning system about significant mood disturbances which can be a precursor to more serious psychological issues.*

What happens in Phase 3?

HoSP: *So now we are all involved in a different way. So they are now out on the pitch.*

HoAP: *So Dave and I are working very closely together. To write the programme and to make sure that everything is working, like the correct load assessing the limitations, identifying how we can progress the player. I think the player then gets an instant sense of achievement in that they are now back on the pitch with everyone else. They are no longer isolated and away from the action.*

HoSP: *So there is an immediate elevation of mood.*

HoAP: *It's hard on you (physio) because as soon as they start working with me, it is perceived as a reward and there is a willingness to work with me. I don't get the struggle that you get when they are working indoors and are plateauing. We do get it if they are on the pitch and then break down again. This is very hard psychologically for them as they have to go backwards. When things aren't right, the players become frustrated.*

HP: *I think that when they're working on the pitch there is a memory of what happened and at times this can linger.*

HoSP: *A lot of the work that I do with them then is help them understand that their brain is hardwired to say 'Alert' 'Alarm', and that automatically the brain is trying to protect you. So it will exacerbate anything that you feel and it will magnify it and you will be distracted by it. If this is not discussed, it can develop into re-injury fear which really holds them back. Or in some cases, this can expand into more generalised anxiety disorder.*

HP: *The key word is catastrophe; players perceive things differently and respond with worry. I remember player X had this when he started outdoors. He came in and said I'm feeling it – when clinically she/he was functioning well.*

HoSP: *So they catastrophise things that they are feeling. So they'll feel something and get anxious that it is something bigger, and question what does this mean. Am I injured again? So a lot of the conversations I have with them are around this narrative and this is where ACT is really powerful as I can help them accept that these thoughts will come, but they can change their relationship with them. So an example of how we work really well together is with player Y where I had done this work with him in the morning prior to him working with you on the pitch, and then I stood and was watching what he was doing with you and there were little moments where I was able to reinforce what we had been talking about. And also I was able to give you some psychological insights so you had a greater awareness of what might be helpful and what to reinforce. But this is where you get that complete integrated care which is the essence of RETURN.*

HP: *It is this collaboration, that is sometimes unseen that truly makes the difference and keeps players on the pitch. You have your consultation with the player and we see a change. We have examples of players who weren't progressing and then you (psych) spoke to him and then the following week he is flying.*

What happens in Phase 4?

HoSP: *One of the biggest challenges of this stage is managing expectations. The player is desperate to get back and start playing games again, and sometimes they expect to be exactly where they have left off. So together we identify what success looks like, and this will constantly evolve as they play more games. I also make sure that I manage the expectations of the coach so that they can recognise success differently in the returning player.*

HP: *The most challenging was X, when he did his knee. I felt that there was a big element of fear about returning to matches.*

HoSP: *You were absolutely right, and that fear never really left him and it started to develop into more generalised anxiety. And when we screened him using the Generalised Anxiety Disorder Assessment (GAD) this is what came up and this is what we worked with him to address. This was in tandem with his General Practitioner (GP) who had prescribed very low dose of anti-depressants but with no talking therapy.*

What impact do you think the RETURN programme has had on players?

HoAP: *First of all, I think they are more ready, and we are more aware of their ability to handle the next stage. Before this was considered in just physical terms and so some of them might not have been ready psychologically to progress to team training or matches but we progressed them anyway. I also think that the culture and the environment have changed, it's okay for them to speak their mind and tell us what they are feeling.*

HoSP: *So it isn't odd for anyone to be talking to me, there is no stigma attached. It is understood that psychological support is just part of normal rehabilitation. This makes it easier for players to be open about what they are going through.*

HP: *The support helps the player rehabilitate more holistically, and we get better results and quicker.*

So what have we learnt from each other?

HP: *It comes down to trust and respect to set something up. I have to trust the psychologist and in what they are doing. The psychologist has to come into a club with an open mind willing to learn about the environment. And the physio has to use their skills to adapt to the environment. We have to understand each practitioner's role, and how everyone's skills can synthesise together. Ultimately it is about working in harmony so that everyone feels comfortable.*

HoSP: *Now I have a much better understanding of the physical demands of rehabilitation, the four phases. I understand how you as a physio are navigating through that and how sometimes you're having to go two steps forward and one step back. I also feel that I can ask you any questions about the injury, or why you are prescribing some exercises. That openness is great for me. I have also understood how you (SC) are working to develop functional fitness and your role is more about transition back into play. And managing them when they want to go too fast. Seeing that whole process has really helped me see how I need to deliver my support at the different phases.*

HP: *Obviously, it has given me a better understanding of how the mind can affect injury. Or how the mind can affect getting injured. I have always believed that the mind and body have to be in synchrony but you have reinforced that. And you have actually shown me and seeing it live makes it really created a lot of awareness. Working as a team makes life easier for everyone.*

HoAP: *I think we all complement each other really well. Progress in the gym is all about the detail and being in the moment and that is what you have taught me, and using purposeful practice in rehabilitation.*

HoSP: *An unintended consequence is that all sorts of people are now talking about things in very different ways – which changes the whole environment.*

HP: *Ultimately what we want is a process that is very simple – but effective and that is what we've got.*

HoSP: *It is also a slow process where trust is built up. You have to allow for it to evolve through constant critical reflection and testing the waters, but also having an aspiration of what you are ultimately aiming for.*

SCHOLAR VOICE

Supporting injured performers: guidance from current research

It has been over 20 years since Heil (1993) first proposed his model of injury which established that injury impacts an athlete's physical, social, emotional and psychological wellbeing. Yet, for most of the athletes who are injured the focus is only on their physical recovery, the other aspects are often ignored (Gervis, Pickford, Hau et al., 2019; Hsu, Meierbachtol, George, & Chmielewski, 2017). The recovery strategies that are almost exclusively used are physiotherapy and physical rehabilitation. In my experience rarely is the psychological trauma associated with long-term injury given equal weight to the physical suffering. Moreover, it has been suggested that successful rehabilitation is connected to the degree to which the psychological needs of a long-term injured athlete are met by medics (Heijne, Axelsson, Werner, & Biguet, 2008). Despite research demonstrating that psychological interventions are effective in enhancing recovery, the evidence shows that this is far from the customary approach taken.

Research exploring current practices of supporting long-term injured players in professional football were found to be almost exclusively anchored in the physical medical domain delivered by people with little/no input from experts in psychological recovery. Interestingly, a contributing factor to this was the absence of psychologists available in their club able to deliver an integrated, psychologically orientated rehabilitation programme. Consequently, by solely addressing the physical symptomology, current practices are leaving players vulnerable to the risk of mental health problems (Gervis, Pickford, Hau et al., 2019).

During injury, there has been found to be an increased vulnerability to experiencing challenging mental health problems and a general decline in their mental health. Indeed there is considerable evidence demonstrating that psychological responses to injury can trigger or reveal a range of mental health issues, such as depression, anxiety, eating disorders, addiction and suicidal ideation (Gervis, Pickford, Hau et al., 2019; Gouttebarge, Frings-Dresen, & Sluiter, 2015; Putukian, 2016). However, this is often ignored or not recognised (Grindstaff, Wrisberg, & Ross, 2010; Walker, Thatcher, & Lavellee, 2010). The International Olympic Committee statement on mental health in elite athletes (2019) cited injury as a risk factor for the development of major depressive disorder and depressive symptomology, as well as suicide. Athletes can also be at risk of developing eating disorders while they are injured. It is not uncommon for athletes to restrict their food intake while injured because they are fearful of gaining weight when they are inactive. Elite athletes have also reported feeling they do not deserve to indulge or eat well whilst being injured (Putukian, 2016). This enhances their vulnerability as such behaviour can be the precursor to developing an eating disorder (Arthur-Cameselle & Baltzell, 2012).

The IOC (2019) recommends screening for mental health disorders following injury to mitigate against an athlete developing a range of co-morbid symptoms. This gives considerable support to the approach taken in the RETURN protocol whereby all players are carefully monitored for the emergence of any mental health issues. It is my belief that current practice is still to wait until someone has metaphorically 'fallen off the edge of the cliff' and is tumbling into deep psychological problems. By working as we do, the player never even 'walks to the edge of the cliff'. We recognise very early if any psychological difficulties are showing up and work with the player to help them navigate through this before it becomes a mental health crisis. Consequently, the recommendation is that there is a need to provide psychological screening and support for athletes suffering from severe injuries to mitigate the risk of mental health problems developing.

All injured athletes go through different phases of recovery, and it is important from a psychological perspective to have an understanding of these. It has been found that there are different psychological impacts, dependent upon the phase of rehabilitation (Clement, Arvinen-Barrow, & Fetty, 2015; Prentice & Arnheim, 2011). During Phase 1, the athlete is coming to terms with the knowledge that they will be unable to train and compete. This phase is often accompanied by debilitating, and sometimes extreme, emotional reactions, such as shock, fear, anger, confusion and helplessness (Carson & Polman, 2008; Tracey, 2003). These reactions can play out in a number of ways, and it is important that the psychologist working with the athlete allows these feelings to be voiced to help them begin the healing process. Indeed, it has been found that when people display elevated anger and aggression their body produces heightened levels of cytokine which impairs the immune responses resulting in slower healing (Takahashi, Flanigan, McEwen, & Russo, 2018).

Phase 2 can be the longest phase of recovery for some players when the focus is on repairing the physical damage (Heijne et al., 2008). During this time, rehabilitation is mostly in the physio room away from teammates. This can be extremely challenging when an athlete faces months and months of rehab and progress is very slow. During this phase, athletes have been found to experience feelings of loss of identity, feelings of exclusion, isolation and depression (Clement et al., 2015; Ruddock-Hudson, O'Halloran, & Murphy, 2012; Tracey, 2003). It is very clear that when athletes experience prolonged debilitative emotional reactions, the people who are working with them should be hypervigilant and not underestimate the increased risk of this spiralling into significant mental health issues. In this phase, the athlete is often isolated from teammates or training partners which further adds to the psychological challenge as often their daily contact with their network of social support is diminished.

A distinctive psychological issue that emerges in Phases 3 and 4 is fear of re-injury. This presents itself as anxiety surrounding the reoccurrence of the injury when the athlete returns to full training and competing (Ardern, Taylor, Feller, & Webster, 2012). Fear of re-injury is the specific fear about the injury which can result in muscular guarding and heightened sensitivity surrounding the injury and increased risk of re-injury (Hsu et al., 2017). It is important that a distinction is made between fear of re-injury and re-injury anxiety, as fear of re-injury is often used as a global term to describe both constructs (Hsu et al., 2017). Re-injury anxiety is any negative thinking or worry about the consequences of the injury such as the end of a sporting career, or deselection. Forced retirement of this nature has been shown to be traumatic in itself (Fortunato & Marchant, 1999). Moreover, poor rehabilitation adherence has been found to be characteristic of athletes experiencing fear of re-injury which often prevents a successful return to sport (Arvinen-Barrow, Hemmings, Weigand, Becker, & Booth, 2007; Hsu et al., 2017).

In the final stages of recovery, athletes need to demonstrate a psychological readiness to return, as characterised by Podlog, Banham, Wadey, and Hannon (2015), in order for there to be a successful transition back into competitive sport. These key attributes are: confidence to return, realistic expectations of capability and motivation to regain previous performance standards. In RETURN the decision to return to fully competitive play is a collaborative one whereby the physio, coach and psychologist consider the player from their expert perspectives. Thus, there could be a player who is physically ready but not psychologically ready. In this instance, the player will not go into a match situation until the psychologist has indicated psychological readiness. This mitigates against a player going into a match situation with anxiety about re-injury, which in turn reduces the likelihood of re-injury.

Thus, it is important to consider rehabilitation from this phased perspective, as a lack of understanding of the different psychological challenges potentially can be problematic for practitioners. Understanding how athletes respond psychologically to each phase would enhance the quality of treatment during rehabilitation. Further, there is a lack of evidence in sport of purposefully creating constructive psychological coping mechanisms for injured athletes when compared to other populations (Akhtar, 2012; Seligman, Steen, Park, & Peterson, 2005). The psychological support delivered in the RETURN protocol is delivered by psychologists with expert knowledge and understanding of the psychology of injury and awareness of the different presentations of psychological issues at each stage of rehabilitation. It is critical that the psychologist understands this to ensure the focus of the support aligns with the phase of recovery. So, for example, there is no point in working on fear of re-injury at Phase 1 because it doesn't manifest until Phase 3 or 4.

The overall responsibility for the rehabilitation of the players lies with the medical department, and in particular the Head Physiotherapist. The physiotherapist determines when the player moves from one phase to the next. The medical team determines all physical rehabilitation procedures. For example, if an operation is required, what type of exercises the player will need to do and when the player is ready to manage the physical demands associated with the transition to the next phase of recovery. Critically, the core principle of our protocol is that we take a holistic approach to supporting the rehabilitation of the players whereby all practitioners work with the injured player bringing their expertise and knowledge for the benefit of the best possible recovery of the player.

However, the contribution of each expert changes as the player progresses through rehabilitation. The critical principle of this approach is that all practitioners maintain open and regular communication with each other. Without this the RETURN protocol diminishes to experts working in silos, reducing the opportunity for important learnings to transpire. Given each practitioner views the injury through their lens of expertise by ensuring regular collaborative conversations, all practitioners gain an appreciation of the different professional perspectives. By adopting a holistic and integrated approach to rehabilitation, which includes a psychological component (Gervis, Pickford, & Hau, 2019; Grey-Thompson, 2017; Moesch et al., 2018; NICE Guidance, 2009), the best possible recovery and potential for psychological growth are achieved. Effective psychological support could present an opportunity for facilitating post-traumatic growth following a difficult injury (Turner & Cox, 2004).

In RETURN, every injured player has one-to-one sessions with the psychologist throughout rehabilitation, not just players who are identified as having psychological 'problems'. The importance of this is twofold: first, this approach reduces stigma about working with the sport psychologist; second, it ensures that every player is regularly monitored which means it is less likely for significant psychological problems to go undetected.

The psychological framework adopted to deliver this support is ACT. This is used for a number of reasons. First, it is congruent with the practice philosophy of the sport psychologist. Second, there is substantial evidence demonstrating ACT to be efficacious in supporting injury in other contexts (Gauntlett-Gilbert, Connell, Clinch, & McCracken, 2012).

Appropriate psychometric assessment is used across the phases to serve as 'barometer' checks for psychological readiness and vulnerability. These assessments help inform the nature of the psychological support as well as informing the other staff of the psychological state of the injured players. Different instruments are used at different phases of recovery to ensure relevant data are collected at appropriate phases. The medical staff trigger the psychometric assessment by informing the sport psychologist when the player moves to the next phase of rehabilitation. These include Brunel Mood Scale (BRUMS; Terry, Lane, Lane, & Keohane, 1999), Emotional Responses of Athletes to Injury Questionnaire (ERAIQ; Smith, Scott, O'Fallow, & Young, 1990) and adapted Re-injury Anxiety Inventory (RIAI; Walker et al., 2010).

Critical learnings

The critical findings from implementing RETURN lend weight to the following practical implications:

- The collaborative support approach to rehabilitation offers players the best outcome for complete recovery and should be adopted for every long-term injury as the norm.
- Appropriate psychological screening should be undertaken throughout the rehabilitation process.
- Current practice using the traditional medical support approach suggests that athletes should seek psychological support only if they need it, this, however, is insufficient. Our experiences clearly demonstrate that when psychological support is normalised as part of rehabilitation protocols, it acts as a preventative mechanism to mitigate against psychological difficulties and achieve psychological growth, in accordance with the recommendations by Gervis and colleagues (2019).

- Sport psychologists must be trained in the psychology of injury and be able to deliver a phased support programme.
- As a duty of care to the players, it is incumbent upon sport psychologists to engage in dialogue with physiotherapists, and other medical support staff, as change in practice to rehabilitation can only come about with their cooperation.

References

Akhtar, M. (2012). *Positive Psychology for overcoming depression: Self-help strategies for happiness, inner strength and well-being*. London: Watkins Media Limited.

Ardern, C. L., Taylor, N. F., Feller, J. A., & Webster, K. E. (2012). Fear of re-injury in people who have returned to sport following anterior cruciate ligament reconstruction surgery. *Journal of Science and Medicine in Sport, 15*(6), 488–495. https://doi.org/10.1016/j.jsams.2012.03.015

Arthur-Cameselle, J. N., & Baltzell, A. (2012). Learning from collegiate athletes who have recovered from eating disorders: Advice to coaches, parents, and other athletes with eating disorders. *Journal of Applied Sport Psychology, 24*(1), 1–9. https://doi.org/10.1080/10413200.2011.572949

Arvinen-Barrow, M., Hemmings, B., Weigand, D., Becker, C., & Booth, L. (2007). Views of chartered physiotherapists on the psychological content of their practice: A follow-up survey in the UK. *Journal of Sport Rehabilitation, 16*(2), 111–121. https://doi.org/10.1123/jsr.16.2.111

Carson, F., & Polman, R. C. J. (2008). ACL injury rehabilitation: A psychological case study of a professional rugby union player. *Journal of Clinical Sport Psychology, 2*(1), 71–90. https://doi.org/10.1123/jcsp.2.1.71

Clement, D., Arvinen-Barrow, M., & Fetty, T. (2015). Psychosocial responses during different phases of sport-injury rehabilitation: A qualitative study. *Journal of Athletic Training, 50*(1), 95–104. https://doi.org/10.4085/1062-6050-49.3.52

Fortunato, V., & Marchant, D. (1999). Forced retirement from elite football in Australia. *Journal of Personality and Interpersonal Loss, 4*(3), 269–280. https://doi.org/10.1080/10811449908409735

Gauntlett-Gilbert, J., Connell, H., Clinch, J., & McCracken, L. M. (2012). Acceptance and values-based treatment of adolescents with chronic pain: Outcomes and their relationship to acceptance. *Journal of Pediatric Psychology, 38*(1), 72–81. https://doi.org/10.1093/jpepsy/jss098

Gervis, M., Pickford, H., & Hau, T. (2019). Professional Footballers' Association Counsellors' perceptions of the role long-term injury plays in mental health issues presented by current and former players. *Journal of Clinical Sport Psychology, 13*(3), 451–468. https://doi.org/10.1123/jcsp.2018-0049

Gervis, M., Pickford, H., Hau, T., & Fruth, M. (2019). A review of the psychological support mechanisms available for long-term injured footballers in the UK throughout their rehabilitation. *Science and Medicine in Football, 4*(1), 1–8. https://doi.org/10.1080/24733938.2019.1634832

Gouttebarge, V., Frings-Dresen, M. H. W., & Sluiter, J. K. (2015). Mental and psychosocial health among current and former professional footballers. *Occupational Medicine, 65*(3), 190–196. https://doi.org/10.1093/occmed/kqu202

Grey-Thompson, T. (2017). *Duty of care in sport: Independent report to government.* Retrieved July 2018, from www.gov.uk/government/publications/duty-of-care-in-sport-review

Grindstaff, J. S., Wrisberg, C. A., & Ross, J. R. (2010). Collegiate athletes' experience of the meaning of sport injury: A phenomenological investigation. *Perspectives in Public Health, 130*(3), 127–135. https://doi.org/10.1177/1757913909360459

Heijne, A., Axelsson, K., Werner, S., & Biguet, G. (2008). Rehabilitation and recovery after anterior cruciate ligament reconstruction: Patients' experiences. *Scandinavian journal of medicine & science in sports, 18*(3), 325–335. https://doi.org/10.1111/j.1600-0838.2007.00700.x

Heil, J. (1993). *Psychology of sport injury.* Champaign, IL: Human Kinetics Publishers.

Hsu, C. J., Meierbachtol, A., George, S. Z., & Chmielewski, T. L. (2017). Fear of re-injury in athletes: Implications for rehabilitation. *Sports Health, 9*(2), 162–167. https://doi.org/10.1177/1941738116666813

Moesch, K., Kentta, G., Kleinert, J., Quignon-Fleuret, C., Cecil, S., & Bertollo, M. (2018). FEPSAC position statement: Mental health disorders in elite athletes and models of service provision. *Psychology of Sport & Exercise, 38*, 61–71. https://doi.org/10.1016/j.psychsport.2018.05.013

NICE Guidance. (2009, October). *Depression in adults with a chronic physical health problem: Recognition and management.* Retrieved from www.nice.org.uk/guidance/cg91

Podlog, L., Banham, S. M., Wadey, R., & Hannon, J. C. (2015). Psychological readiness to return to competitive sport following injury: A qualitative study. *The Sport Psychologist, 29*(1), 1–14. https://doi.org/10.1123/tsp.2014-0063

Prentice, W. E., & Arnheim, D. D. (2011). *Arnheim's principles of athletic training: A competency-based approach* (14th ed.). New York: McGraw-Hill Higher Education.

Putukian, M. (2016). The psychological response to injury in student athletes: A narrative review with a focus on mental health. *British Journal of Sports Medicine, 50*(3), 145–148. https://doi.org/10.1136/bjsports-2015-095586

Ruddock-Hudson, M., O'Halloran, P., & Murphy, G. (2012). Exploring psychological reactions to injury in the Australian Football League (AFL). *Journal of Applied Sport Psychology, 24*(4), 375–390. https://doi.org/10.1080/10413200.2011.654172

Seligman, M. E. P., Steen, T. A., Park, N., & Peterson, C. (2005). Positive psychology progress: Empirical validation of interventions. *American Psychologist, 60*(5), 410–421. https://doi.org/10.1037/0003-066X.60.5.410

Smith, A. M., Scott, S. G., O'Fallon, W. M., & Young, M. L. (1990). Emotional responses of athletes to injury. *Mayo Clinic Proceedings, 65*(1), 38–50. https://doi.org/10.1016/S0025-6196(12)62108-9

Takahashi, A., Flanigan, M. E., McEwen, B. S., & Russo, S. J. (2018). Aggression, social stress, and the immune system in humans and animal models. *Frontiers in Behavioral Neuroscience, 12*, 56. https://doi.org/10.3389/fnbeh.2018.00056

Terry, P. C., Lane, A. M., Lane, H. J., & Keohane, L. (1999). Development and validation of a mood measure for adolescents. *Journal of Sports Sciences, 17*(11), 861–872. https://doi.org/10.1080/026404199365425

Tracey, J. (2003). The emotional response to the injury and rehabilitation process. *Journal of Applied Sport Psychology, 15*(4), 279–293. https://doi.org/10.1080/714044197

Turner, D. S., & Cox, H. (2004). Facilitating post traumatic growth. *Health and Quality of Life Outcomes, 2*, 34. https://doi.org/10.1186/1477-7525-2-34

Walker, N., Thatcher, J., & Lavallee, D. (2010). A preliminary development of the Re-Injury Anxiety Inventory (RIAI). *Physical Therapy in Sport, 11*(1), 23–29. https://doi.org/10.1016/j.ptsp.2009.09.003

11
DEVELOPING CARING CULTURES IN FOOTBALL
A model for practice and change

Colm Hickey and Colum Cronin

Introduction

Contextualised by the shared experiences of Noel (pseudonym), a former professional footballer, the following chapter considers the creation and implementation of meaningful change within professional and elite sporting environments to refocus athlete wellbeing strategies. The chapter calls for such strategies to place central importance upon three elements central to care: (1) understanding the needs of athletes/players, (2) working to meet these needs, and (3) appreciating the importance of working with athletes who are themselves committed to such relationships. Acknowledging the resistance and obstacles faced while implementing such a strategy, the chapter proposes a move away from traditional linear planned change management approaches towards a more progressive emergent model. In order to create more effective wellbeing strategies, sporting organisations must acknowledge the unpredictable nature of change and endeavour to become open continuous learning environments that have the ability to react and evolve as different and new challenges present themselves.

ATHLETE VOICE

But can we do better?

> The athlete narrative provided for this chapter has been provided by a former professional football player. Although a pseudonym (Noel) has been applied, the story told is the real life experiences of an individual striving for excellence in both personal and professional domains.

DOI: 10.4324/9780429287923-11

As a younger footballer, I had an unusual path to a full-time professional career as a player. During university, I played semi-professionally throughout my degree. After graduating, I went back to full-time football. I played for a number of clubs in the lower leagues. As the end to my playing career came closer, I was able to draw upon my previous experiences as an aspiring apprentice and later my experiences of playing for the first team. Combined with the knowledge I had gained from my university studies and corporate experiences, I believed that I was well positioned to contribute as part of a player welfare charity. This led me to work for the charity for several years and secure an influential position amongst the senior leadership. At the core of the charity's concerns is the wellbeing of players, from what happens on the pitch and training grounds to more specific issues surrounding mental health, gambling, and addiction.

There are a number of good examples of athlete wellbeing and care in football. This support may be in the form of language skills for players, housing, supporting families through schooling, or integrating into a community. The nature of this support is regularly bespoke and involves specialist staff meeting the needs of individual players. As part of such tailored assistance, steps are taken to consider the wellbeing of players and then help them adapt and cope with the respective challenges they face as part of their career. While such support is highly commended and offers an example for others, it tends to be confined to a *number of* but *not all* high-profile clubs with considerable financial means (though one should note, there are exceptions). At the lower levels of football (where the majority of players make their living), player wellbeing may not be supported to the same extent. This is not to say that individuals working within such clubs care about their players any less; rather, it can be linked to the size and maturity of the organisation. More commercially successful clubs tend to have larger workforces that often come from, or draw upon, the insights of different industries. Lower league clubs have less full-time staff, and the clubs will certainly have smaller budgets to devise and implement athlete wellbeing plans and structures. Additionally, such staff members may hold other roles across the clubs; meaning that if a wellbeing policy *is* devised, it often remains as text on a shelf and unfortunately not implemented in practice.

Moving further away from high-level football, I am not sure that improved athlete wellbeing is likely to occur through policies alone. Change to any strategy or daily practice in football is difficult and often not successfully implemented or maintained. Rather, the decision-making and support of powerful individuals within clubs are key to better athlete wellbeing. Indeed, at the lower levels of the game, change is unlikely to occur without the support of key individuals and stakeholders. For example, as a form of support, a manager may introduce and encourage players to access a sport psychologist. Indeed, some clubs have full-time 'in-house' support staff, whereas clubs with less financial resources may refer players to part time or external psychologists on an ad-hoc basis. The challenge with this, however, is that football is an industry with a high degree of staff turnover. This occurs because appointments and dismissals are driven by success on the field. When a team loses a few games, owners will often replace a manager. The support staff including the sport psychologist around the manager may also leave. This means that an owner, or at the higher levels a CEO, is a very important stakeholder in terms of long-term planning. Without 'buy in' from the owner or CEO, any lasting change in areas like athlete wellbeing is unlikely.

Football by its very nature is a competitive industry that places a lot of importance on short-term results. Long-term planning is unlikely to occur because the culture is often dominated by the previous and upcoming games. With this in mind, the support of owners and CEOs can best be achieved by linking changes and new practices to results. For instance, changes in sport psychology, sport science, or support for players to engage in outside studies needs to be linked to, or at least accompanied by, improved sporting performance. If changes in areas such as athlete wellbeing are not seen to improve performance, then they are not likely to be supported or sustained by the key stakeholders (owners and CEOs). For example (and speaking from personal experience), I was criticised for undertaking my law degree and for not concentrating on full-time professional football. This is a bit bizarre because I actually think that period of study helped me grow overall as a person and helped my football – I believe that it improved my problem-solving, my sport processes, and independent thinking, all of which transferred onto the pitch. It also gave me the skills and confidence to take more control over my career, make decisions for myself, to analyse my performance more objectively, identify areas where I could improve, and decide where to invest my time and training. Reflecting upon wider attitudes within football, I can appreciate many managers would not hold the same opinion. Often the link between other interests and performance is lost, with players often being criticised for such undertakings. In order to have more clubs consider the wellbeing of their players, owners, CEOs, and managers must recognise and appreciate its potential to improve results. If not, improving and reforming athlete wellbeing is unlikely to receive sustained authentic support.

In addition to the support of senior high-level stakeholders, athlete wellbeing and support must have some level of independence and autonomy. Again, because clubs are primarily focused on short-term results, players can often be reluctant to use support staff for fear that their concerns or comments are not kept confidential and might later be shared with managers or coaches who perceive such behaviours as weaknesses. Revisiting the sport psychologist example; if a club offers such support, due to the nature of football, an ever-present suspicion (whether founded or not) about confidentiality between the psychologist and the manager can easily exist. Some players will naturally have confidence in the privacy of those situations while others will not. It is essential that players know that specific wellbeing staff are working in the best interest of the individuals they support. Ensuring wellbeing staff work independently of managers would go a long way in building a credible relationship with players. In some parts of the game, there are also typically archaic views about issues such as mental health, and we need to address this. We need to build up trust with players about these support services.

When I have seen changes in football done well, it has come through key stakeholders providing simple messages that are not only explained but also consistently implemented through behaviours. Living the messages daily through such behaviours is key and is much more important than buzzwords, images on the wall, or meetings. Meetings can help, as can consultants, but consistently living the behaviours (e.g. listening, noticing, and empathising) regardless of wins and losses is key. If athlete wellbeing is important, it should be important every day and regardless of the result. That said, as mentioned earlier, getting some relative success can help buy time to effect change. This is important because if you lose a few games, you will need support from the owner and supporters.

For support staff such as coaches and technical trainers, their job security is also heavily dependent on successful performances on the pitch. They are unlikely to buy into athlete wellbeing training and changes to current practices if they do not think it will be beneficial in achieving results. In terms of the hiring and selection of the staff responsible for the planning and implementation of athlete wellbeing and support, organisations need knowledgeable individuals who are appropriately qualified in areas such as mental health, addiction, and education and who are primarily motivated to help players. At the player welfare charity, we have support available and there are also other organisations who can help, but I think clubs need athlete wellbeing officers on a day-to-day basis. In an ideal world, these would be qualified people in their fields but also people who have an understanding of football environments. People who have empathetic understanding as to what players are going through. This could be very useful and perhaps there is a lack of talent in this area. To be clear, if athlete wellbeing staff are to work with the type of independence mentioned earlier, and hold positions of such importance to players, then the selection and hiring of such individuals must be undertaken with the utmost care. Such individuals must possess the necessary professional qualifications paired with a genuine understanding of football. This is because football and football clubs have cultures that are influenced by a variety of bespoke factors such as specific histories, geographic features, differing concerns and expectations of supporters, media coverage, and industry-specific economic structures. Clubs and organisations need to think about how they can recruit and train wellbeing officers that are really well qualified, have not only experiences outside of football, but also an in-depth understanding of football so that they can connect and relate to players.

SCHOLAR VOICE

Introduction to care

Research has highlighted that high-performance environments may not always be conducive to athlete wellbeing. For example, from a psychological perspective, Lebrun and Collins (2017) have argued that elite sport environments both require and develop singular athletic identities. Such an identity may lead athletes to have an overly self-critical attitude, low self-esteem in the face of defeat, and an inability to cope with wider life stressors, when such stressors are encountered, for example, post retirement (Doherty, Hannigan, & Campbell, 2016). Across Europe, footballers have reported symptoms of common poor mental health conditions including distress (12%), anxiety (37%), and adverse alcohol use (14%) (Nixdorf, Raphael, Hautzinger, & Beckman, 2013). In the UK, a more recent study revealed a high incidence (47.8%) of anxiety and/or depression amongst athletes (Foskett & Longstaff, 2017).

Beyond wider poor mental health challenges, concerns also exist about a host of areas relevant to athlete wellbeing such as concussion (McCrory et al., 2017) and overuse injuries (Soligard et al, 2016). Additionally, concerns abound about the prevalence of dementia in retired footballers (Rutherford, Stewart, & Bruno, 2019; Mackay et al., 2019) and the issue of sexual abuse of footballers in the UK also remains prevalent (Dixon, 2020). This research has been supported by wider media coverage that has reported elite athletes' experiences. These reports include negative accounts of athletes experiencing verbal, physical, and sexual abuse. Such reports have occurred across a range of cultural and international contexts. When such instances do occur, sporting cultures are often described as toxic, maladaptive, or unhealthy. Indeed, elite football, the focus of this chapter has been described as a cutthroat, micro-political, and uncaring environment (Roderick, 2006; Thompson, Portrac, & Jones, 2013; Roderick & Schumacker, 2017). Thus, both research evidence and media coverage support Noel's calls for better athlete wellbeing in football.

Care and performance

Beyond the wellbeing imperative for high-performance sport to be a caring environment (discussed earlier), there are also performance justifications for developing a more caring approach to elite athletes. For example, the well-established psychological work of Jowett and colleagues demonstrates that effective coach–athlete relationships are key to sport performance (Jowett & Poczwardowski, 2006; Jowett, 2007; Davis, Jowett, & Tafvelin, 2019). More specifically, close and committed relationships between coaches and athletes appear fundamental to successful performance. From a socio-pedagogical perspective, it has also been established that caring relationships can be a part of successful coaching. Specifically, researchers (e.g. Cronin & Armour, 2018) have used Nel Noddings' Ethic of Care as a theoretical framework to illustrate how high-performance coaches care for athletes. Noddings' care theory argues that relationships between carers (i.e. coaches and support staff) and the cared for (i.e. athletes) are essential to help individuals flourish. To be more precise, Noddings (2013) defines caring relationships by drawing upon three key concepts. Firstly, 'engrossment' requires that individuals pay repeated attention to others to understand their needs. This attention could be provided through actions such as observation, or dialogue. Secondly, once carers understand the needs of others, they must act on behalf of the cared for, rather than in their own self-interest. Noddings terms this 'motivational displacement'. Finally, in order to confirm that caring relationship exists, it is necessary for the cared for to 'reciprocate' by engaging in the relationship. This may involve accepting care, committing to the relationship, or simply expressing gratitude. The three concepts (engrossment, motivational displacement, and reciprocity) have been recorded in high-performance environments. For example, they have been observed in Swedish handball (Annerstedt & Lindgren, 2014), US Collegiate Sport (Knust & Fisher, 2015), and athletics and basketball in the UK (Cronin & Armour, 2018). Across these cases, coaches have developed relationships characterised by dialogue and a concern for the other. Indeed, it is not surprising that caring relationships help individuals flourish because it is within caring relationships that coaches can understand players' needs (engrossment), act to meet these needs (motivational displacement), and work with players who accept and are committed to these relationships (reciprocity). Thus, although many high-performance contexts may not be caring, nonetheless it is possible to have both high-performing athletes and caring relationships. Moreover, caring relations may even be a contributory factor to high-quality performances.

Care in a challenging football club culture

On the basis that caring relationships may be possible and even conducive to high-performance sport, Cronin, Knowles, and Enright (2019) explore care within a case study of a Premier League Football Club. The study unpacked the experiences of a single strength and conditioning coach as he sought to care for an injured athlete. Consistent with Noel's experiences, the case study illustrated how caring relationships can be difficult to establish in performative settings because of an emphasis on short-term results.

The individuals (e.g. coaches) within the football club were also subject to wider economic and social pressures to win games. Their employment was linked to these results and was, thus, insecure. Additionally, the case study identified how undefined notions of care and micro-political actions may constrain good athlete wellbeing practices. For example, working in a high-performance context is often an interdisciplinary activity. This requires interaction between key personnel, such as coaches, players, medical staff, and sport science staff. Thus, caring relationships cannot solely be dyadic but need to include a wide range of individuals. As Cronin, Knowles et al. (2019) illustrate, however, the power dynamics between these individuals can inhibit the care provided to athletes. Cronin, Knowles et al. (2019) conclude that an emphasis on short-term results and micro-political actions that are heightened by the precarious nature of employment can contribute to a culture in which it is challenging to establish and maintain caring relationships.

Of course, this does not mean that care cannot happen in football. Rather as Noel illustrates, there are examples of good caring practices within football. Furthermore, the aforementioned research (e.g. Cronin & Armour, 2018; Knust & Fisher, 2015) illustrates that caring can actually be a part of successful high-performance environments; indeed, Noddings' concepts (engrossment, motivational displacement, and reciprocity) may be of interest to managers and owners who seek to develop more caring cultures. Moreover, this evidence may provide a powerful motive for stakeholders to invest in and support athlete wellbeing. Nonetheless, in contexts, which have limited financial and human resources, it can be a challenge to care for athletes. This is because as Noddings (2013) explains, care is a demanding form of emotional labour. In the absence of resources, for example, allocated time, there is a risk that this labour is either provided by staff in addition to, or instead of their existing duties, or perhaps not at all. Thus, Noel suggests that it is important that (1) senior staff support athlete wellbeing by allocating resources, and that (2) athlete wellbeing does not become a topic discussed solely in meetings but a behaviour, which is valued and modelled by these senior staff on a daily basis. In considering the successful implementation of wellbeing strategies centred upon the creation of caring cultures, football clubs must recognise the arising challenges faced by all organisations tasked with instilling change and consider the most appropriate approach to overcome such challenges.

Implementing changes to player wellbeing and care strategies

As Noel and existing research suggest (Miller, 1990; Kondra & Hinings, 1998; Parent, O'Brien, & Slack, 2012), building an athlete care strategy based on football clubs understanding the needs of their players, acting to meet these needs, and working with players who accept and are committed to these relationships may be an uphill struggle. Balogun and Hailey (2004) explain that an estimated 70% of all change management strategies fail in achieving their desired outcomes. Such a low success rate is the result of a lack of meaningful and effective structures that outline how to implement and manage organisational change (Burnes, 2004), reflecting the often conflicting analysis and understanding provided by existing assumptions that frequently underestimate the very nature of organisational cultures and over emphasizes a top–down linear approach. These foundations provide the necessary reasoning to draw upon theoretical tools to better understand how organisations resist change. In the workday environment of a professional football club, patterns of behaviour, workplace norms, and cultural values are reinforced over time and become institutionalised. This institutionalisation of structure leads to increased organisational *momentum* (Miller & Friesen, 1980), referring to the resistance of organisations to deviate from dominant organisational practices, existing conditions, and entrenched cultural norms. The ever-present precarious employment status experienced by staff within football clubs, as described by Noel, also results in conditions that need to be understood to develop a strategy for sustainable change within their clubs. Investigations examining organisational structures in high-performance football and successful change management in sport more broadly do exist (Cruickshank & Collins, 2012; Cruickshank, Collins, & Minten, 2014; Gibson & Groom, 2017; Relvas, Littlewood, Nesti, Gilbourne, & Richardson 2010). However, Gibson and Groom (2017) rightfully highlight the limited empirical work that reflects the complexities faced when implementing organisational change within football.

Emergent change modelling

In response to such criticism, Emergent Change Modelling offers a meaningful solution (Greenwood & Hinnings, 1988; Miller & Friesen, 1980; Nadler & Tushman, 1989). Unlike traditional planned approaches to change (Elrod & Tippert, 2002; Lewin, 1947; Senior, 2002) that have come under increasing criticism for their top–down nature, linear methodology, and assumptions that organisations operate under constant conditions (Bamford & Forrester, 2003; Kanter, Stein, & Jick, 1992; Senior, 2002), the emergent approach emphasises that change should not be perceived as a sequence of linear measures within a particular period of time. Rather, emergent models see change as a continuous, open–ended process of adaptation to fluid circumstances and varying conditions (Burnes, 1996, 2004; Dawson, 1994). The emergent approach stresses the need to account for the unpredictable nature of change and views it as a process that develops through the relationship of a multitude of variables within an organisation. Accounting for the uncertainty of both the external and internal environment in football, emergent change models are more pertinent than the planned approach. Burnes (1996) reasons that a key factor in successful change is dependent on reaching a shared understanding of the complexity of the issues and implications concerned with the change process. This observation supports Noddings' notion of care as a reciprocal activity and the observation in Cronin, Knowles et al. (2019) that care needs to be discussed and defined by all actors involved. Furthermore, to cope with such complexity, it is suggested that organisations need to become open learning systems where strategy development and change emerge from the way a company acquires, interprets, and processes information about its environment, structures, systems, staff, and cultures (Altman & Iles, 1998; Davidson & De Marco, 1999; Dunphy & Stace, 1993). Pettigrew and Whipp (1993) highlight that a play-by-play rulebook, simply does not exist when leading and managing change. However, By (2005) identifies three models that organisations are able to observe when undertaking the change process (Kanter et al., 1992, *Ten Commandments for Executing Change*; Kotter, 1996, *Eight-Stage Process for Successful Organisational Transformation*; Luecke, 2003, *Seven Steps*) and provides a helpful guide in understanding and comparing these models.

Continual change – an emergent model for developing care in football clubs

When examining the shared similarities and differences between these models, it is worth noting Noel's observation that no two football clubs are the same. Related to this, Dunphy and Stace (1993) recognise that organisations will not always face similar challenges and hurdles to overcome. Keeping this in mind and addressing the original critique of the linear structure belonging to a planned approach, we (the authors) offer the proposed *Continual Change Model for Caring Cultures* (see Figure 11.1), as an amalgamation of existing theories.

If a change to player wellbeing is to be realised, then the emergent change model suggests a need for in-depth knowledge and understanding of club workplace environments via *Organisational Analysis*. Such an understanding goes beyond the traditional notions of analysis (e.g. SWOT, SOAR). While these tools are still valuable to organisations, emergent change strategies must be grounded in the social interactions within clubs. Accordingly, the *Vision* created must consider how Noddings' (2013) key concepts (engrossment, motivational displacement, and reciprocity) can and do manifest within the day-to-day workings of a given organisation. Identifying potential resistance and obstacles that a new wellbeing strategy will have to overcome is important, as is an understanding of the cultural attitudes, practices, and norms of those staff and individuals that will be influenced by such a change.

Developing caring cultures in football 159

Organisational Analysis
Identifying need to change.

Monitor key Performance Indicators
Adapt strategy and framework in response to problems in the change process.

Create Vision
Develop strategy and change framework. Consider engrossment, motivational displacement and reciprocity.

Generate Short Term Wins
Consolidate learning and progress, focus on results not activities.

Situational Analysis
Evaluate how well engrossment, motivational displacement are enacted. Include the perspectives of the cared for (reciprocity).

Create a "Guiding Coalition"
Cultivate political support from senior management.

Identify key stakeholders who work daily within the framework of new strategy. Include the 'cared for'.

Create Continual Learning Environments
More than "occasional seminars", communicate with colleagues, staff and players. Empower those who will contribute to and receive care.

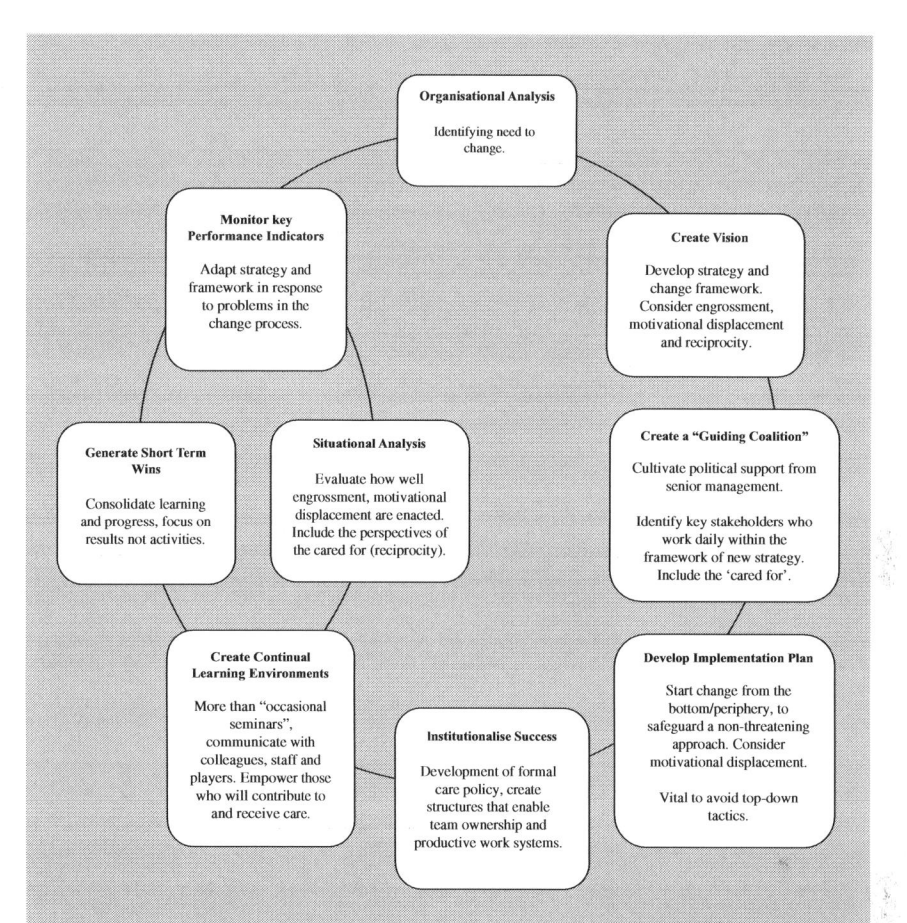

Institutionalise Success
Development of formal care policy, create structures that enable team ownership and productive work systems.

Develop Implementation Plan
Start change from the bottom/periphery, to safeguard a non-threatening approach. Consider motivational displacement.

Vital to avoid top-down tactics.

FIGURE 11.1 The Continual Change Model for Caring Cultures

Noel highlighted multiple times the need to have the support of senior club officials. He honestly points out the problematic nature of high staff turnover in football results in a club's CEO, board, or owner often being the only organisational positions that experience relative security. Acknowledging that for change to be successful, organisations must avoid a top–down approach and those responsible for the development and initiation of change strategies must endeavour to cultivate the support of senior management. To gain support of such individuals, a change strategy must not merely involve, but work in partnership *with* the key stakeholder as part of a *Guiding Coalition*. However, such support must be balanced, and working with everyday staff is equally as important. As highlighted by Noel, player facing employees who will be most affected and responsible for the sustained implementation of player wellbeing reform must be heavily involved in the formulation of such strategy.

Working in close partnership with staff (including players themselves) who are involved in the daily operations of player wellbeing and care, gives ownership to those most affected by the change, and to those who will *Implement the Plan* and *Institutionalise Success* (as the Continual Change model outlines). It also ensures a top–down framework is avoided. In the development and implementation of a club's new formal policy, safeguarding this non-threatening grassroots approach will create productive structures to effectively facilitate changes to wellbeing and care systems. This form of 360-degree feedback facilitates the empowering of staff to play an active role in the change process (Cope, Eys, Schinke, & Bosselut, 2010). For example, Mamatoglu (2008) reported how the introduction of this process within the manufacturing industry increased workers' perceptions of support and achievement culture. One can, therefore, make the assumption that involvement in a *Guiding Coalition* encourages and reinforces adherence to the change strategy by ensuring all stakeholders are provided with the opportunity to contribute and have their needs met and discussed (Cruickshank & Collins, 2012).

Noel alluded to the potential risk that once a new wellbeing policy is developed, it might simply 'sit on the shelf', never reaching a meaningful implementation phase. Noel further described how changes to player wellbeing – like any other change in football – must go beyond notions of buzzwords, images on a wall or occasional seminars. Consistently communicating with colleagues and staff via a two-way dialogue creates space for insight and feedback and, in turn, empowers the very stakeholders that will have to contribute to the implementation of sustained change. This dialogue may help staff such as coaches understand the players' needs (engrossment), act to meet these needs (motivational displacement), and work with players who accept and are committed to these relationships (reciprocity). Such a discourse creates a *Continual Learning Environment*, allowing for an agile change strategy that has the ability to listen and react as time goes on and different scenarios present themselves (rather than rigorously sticking to plan that may become obsolete). Thus, the principles of new wellbeing strategies will have a higher probability of becoming the shared behaviours and common cultural values within clubs. As staff turnover is high in football, a continual process of learning may ensure that key insights are retained by staff who remain in the organisation.

In order to ensure sustained support for change strategies, making senior managers aware of one's activities and efforts is not sufficient. Rather, a change framework must have clearly defined short-term *Key Performance Indicators* (KPIs) to consolidate learning and provide evidence of progress. Much like the strategy itself, these KPIs should be flexible and have the ability to change over time as the strategy progresses. As no two organisations are identical, football clubs will of course have performance indicators specific to their own environment. Drawing upon organisation-focused change management theory, Cruickshank and Collins (2012) described how an improved level of performance and/or outcome of success also indicates successful change within sport organisations.

As indicated by Noel and common to any sport organisation where success is judged on winning, one of the most significant challenges faced by player wellbeing change strategies is how the strategy contributes to winning on the pitch. In the development of such strategies, those involved must be mindful to *Generate Short Term Wins* by:

- Ensuring considerable effort be made to identify how players are positively influenced by such caring relationships.
- Establish how these influences effect match day results and league table outcomes.
- Determine how such influence can be measured and defined by KPIs.
- Fix realistic goals that are both achievable and illustrate the positive correlation between player wellbeing and performance.

Conclusion

Previous sections have outlined the tenets of a wellbeing strategy that focuses on the development of more caring cultures within football clubs for players. Specifically, Noddings' (2013) concepts of (1) engrossment (understanding players' needs, e.g. through noticing and listening); (2) motivational displacement (acting to meet these needs); and (3) reciprocity (supporting players to accept and commit to care) promote caring relationships that are both centred on the needs of the 'cared for' and also respect their autonomy. In sport, such relationships have been observed in physical education contexts (e.g. McCuaig, Öhman, & Wright, 2013), adult recreation contexts (Cronin, Walsh, Quayle, Whittaker, & Whitehead, 2019), and across a range of high-performance environments (Annerstedt & Lindgren, 2014; Cronin & Armour, 2018; Knust & Fisher, 2015). That said, recently it has been observed that developing caring relationships in high-performance football clubs can be challenging due to the wider socio-economic conditions, precarious nature of employment, and micro-political relationships within interdisciplinary teams (Cronin, Walsh et al., 2019). Additionally, Noel's insights suggest that caring cultures in football are difficult to establish without the support of key stakeholders such as owners and without a correlation with successful results on the field of play.

With the challenge of developing caring cultures in mind, this chapter has drawn upon emergent change theory (Greenwood & Hinnings, 1988; Kanter et al., 1992; Kotter, 1996; Luecke, 2003) to explore how caring cultures could be sustainably developed within football clubs. Specifically, an epistemological position, which conceives of change as dynamic and non-linear, has been adopted. This has been useful in identifying how caring cultures could be developed in varied and contextually situated football clubs. To that end, change theory suggests that individuals should engage necessary stakeholders as part of developing their care policy, vision and implementation of a care strategy; create an open learning environment, where all stakeholders can learn about care; measure and assess performance; and continually monitor the organisation's situational analysis to adjust and grow the necessary elements of the desired care strategy. Such actions move away from the traditional linear framework and take a cyclical approach to change management. Indeed, the *Continual Change Module for Caring Cultures* does not have a beginning or end, rather it is the commitment to continuous processes over an extended period that is necessary to manage and implement change strategies to achieve desired cultural and organisational goals (Cruickshank & Collins, 2012; Graetz & Smith, 2010, Higgs & Rowland, 2010). Thus, the efficacy of the model lies in its implementation. Nonetheless, in combining care theory with change management theory, this chapter has made a significant contribution that may be relevant to practitioners who are tasked with developing cultures conducive to athlete wellbeing and performance. Furthermore, the chapter calls upon and also challenges future research to support such work and to further embed care in football cultures.

References

Altman, Y., & Iles, P. (1998). Learning, leadership, teams: Corporate learning and organisational change. *Journal of Management Development, 17*(1), 44–55. https://doi.org/10.1108/02621719810368682

Annerstedt, C., & Lindgren, E.-C. (2014). Caring as an important foundation in coaching for social sustainability: A case study of a successful Swedish coach in high-performance sport. *Reflective Practice, 15*(1), 27–39. https://doi.org/10.1080/14623943.2013.869204

Balogun, J., & Hailey, V. H. (2004). *Exploring strategic change*. Harlow, UK: Pearson Education.

Bamford, D. R., & Forrester, P. L. (2003). Managing planned and emergent change within an operations management environment. *International Journal of Operations & Production Management, 23*(5), 546–564. https://doi.org/10.1108/01443570310471857

Burnes, B. (1996). No such thing as . . . a "one best way" to manage organizational change. *Management Decision, 34*(10), 11–18. https://doi.org/10.1108/00251749610150649

Burnes, B. (2004). *Managing change: A strategic approach to organisational dynamics*. Harlow, UK: Prentice Hall.

By, R. T. (2005). Organisational change management: A critical review. *Journal of Change Management, 5*(4), 369–380. https://doi.org/10.1080/14697010500359250

Cope, C. J., Eys, M. A., Schinke, R. J., & Bosselut, G. (2010). Coaches' perspectives of a negative informal role: The 'Cancer' within sport teams. *Journal of Applied Sport Psychology, 22*(4), 420–436. https://doi.org/10.1080/10413200.2010.495327

Cronin, C., & Armour, K. (2018). *Care in sport coaching pedagogical cases*. London: Routledge.

Cronin, C., Knowles, Z. R., & Enright, K. (2019). The challenge to care in a Premier League football club. *Sports Coaching Review*, 1–24. https://doi.org/10.1080/21640629.2019.1578593

Cronin, C., Walsh, B., Quayle, L., Whittaker, E., & Whitehead, A. (2019). Carefully supporting autonomy: Learning coaching lessons and advancing theory from women's netball in England. *Sports Coaching Review*, 8(2), 149–171. https://doi.org/10.1080/21640629.2018.1429113

Cruickshank, A., & Collins, D. (2012). Change management: The case of the elite sport performance team. *Change Management*, 12(2), 209–229. https://doi.org/10.1080/14697017.2011.632379

Cruickshank, A., Collins, D., & Minten, S. (2014). Driving and sustaining culture change in Olympic sport performance teams: A first exploration and grounded theory. *Journal of Sport and Exercise Psychology*, 36(1), 107–120. https://doi.org/10.1123/jsep.2013-0133

Davidson, M. C., & de Marco, L. (1999). Corporate change: Education as a catalyst. *International Journal of Contemporary Hospitality Management*, 11(1), 16–23. https://doi.org/10.1108/09596119910250355

Davis, L., Jowett, S., & Tafvelin, S. (2019). Communication strategies: The fuel for quality coach-athlete relationships and athlete satisfaction. *Frontiers in Psychology*, 10, 2156. https://doi.org/10.3389/fpsyg.2019.02156

Dawson, P. (1994). *Organizational change: A processual approach*. London: Paul Chapman.

Dixon, K. (2020). Sexual abuse and masculine cultures: Reflections on the British football scandal of 2016. In R. Magrath, J. Cleland & E. Anderson (Eds.), *The Palgrave handbook of masculinity and sport* (pp. 73–93). London: Palgrave Macmillian.

Doherty, S., Hannigan, B., & Campbell, M. J. (2016). The experience of depression during the careers of elite male athletes. *Frontiers in Psychology*, 7, 1069. https://doi.org/10.3389/fpsyg.2016.01069

Dunphy, D., & Stace, D. (1993). The strategic management of corporate change. *Human Relations*, 46(8), 905–920. https://doi.org/10.1177/001872679304600801

Elrod, P. D., & Tippett, D. D. (2002). The "death Valley" of change. *Journal of Organizational Change Management*, 15(3), 273–291. https://doi.org/10.1108/09534810210429309

Foskett, R. L., & Longstaff, F. (2017). The mental health of elite athletes in the United Kingdom. *Journal of Science and Medicine in Sport*, 21(8), 765–770. https://doi.org/10.1016/j.jsams.2017.11.016

Gibson, L., & Groom, R. (2018). Ambiguity, manageability and the orchestration of organisational change: A case study of an English Premier League Academy Manager. *Sports Coaching Review*, 7(1), 23–44. https://doi.org/10.1080/21640629.2017.1317173

Graetz, F., & Smith, A. C. (2010). Managing organizational change: A philosophies of change approach. *Journal of Change Management*, 10(2), 135–154. https://doi.org/10.1080/14697011003795602

Greenwood, R., & Hinnings, C. R. (1988). Organizational design types, tracks and the dynamics of strategic change. *Organization Studies*, 9(3), 293–316. https://doi.org/10.1177/017084068800900301

Higgs, M., & Rowland, D. (2010). Emperors with clothes on: The role of self-awareness in developing effective change leadership. *Journal of Change Management*, 10(4), 369–385. https://doi.org/10.1080/14697017.2010.516483

Jowett, S. (2007). Interdependence analysis and the 3 + 1 Cs in the coach-athlete relationship. In S. Jowett, D. Lavallee, S. Jowett, & D. Lavallee (Eds.), *Social psychology in sport* (pp. 15–27). Champaign, IL: Human Kinetics.

Jowett, S., & Poczwardowski, A. (2006). Critical issues in the conceptualization of and future research on coach-athlete relationship. In S. Jowett, & D. Lavalee (Eds.), *Social psychology in sport* (pp. 69–81). Champaign, IL: Human Kinetics.

Kanter, R. M., Stein, B. A., & Jick, T. D. (1992). *The challenge of organizational change.* New York: The Free Press.

Knust, S. K., & Fisher, L. A. (2015). NCAA Division I female head coaches' experiences of exemplary care within coaching. *International Sport Coaching Journal, 2*(2), 94–107. https://doi.org/10.1123/iscj.2013-0045

Kondra, A. Z., & Hinings, C. R. (1998). Organizational diversity and change in institutional theory. *Organization Studies, 19*(5), 743–767. https://doi.org/10.1177/017084069801900502

Kotter, J. P. (1996). *Leading change.* Boston, MA: Harvard Business School Press.

Lebrun, F., & Collins, D. (2017). Is elite sport (really) bad for you? Can we answer the question? *Frontiers in Psychology, 3*(8), 324–330. https://doi.org/10.3389/fpsyg.2017.00324

Lewin, K. (1947). Concept, method and reality in social science: Social equilibria and social change. *Human Relations, 1,* 5–41.

Luecke, R. (2003). *Managing change and transition.* Boston, MA: Harvard Business School Press.

Mackay, D. F., Russell, E. R., Stewart, K., Maclean, J. A., Pell, J. P., & Stewart, W. (2019). Neurodegenerative disease mortality among former professional soccer players. *New England Journal of Medicine, 381,* 1801–1808. https://doi.org/10.1056/NEJMoa1908483

Mamatoglu, N. (2008). Effects on organizational context (culture and climate) from implementing a 360-degree feedback system: The case of Arcelik. *European Journal of Work and Organizational Psychology, 17*(4), 426–449. https://doi.org/10.1080/13594320802281094

McCrory, P., Meeuwisse, W., Dvorak, J., Aubry, M., Bailes, J., Broglio, S., . . . & Vos, P. E. (2017). Consensus statement on concussion in sport – the 5th international conference on concussion in sport held in Berlin, October 2016. *British Journal of Sports Medicine, 51*(11), 838–847. https://doi.org/10.1136/bjsports-2017-097699

McCuaig, L., Öhman, M., & Wright, J. (2013). Shepherds in the gym: Employing a pastoral power analytic on caring teaching in HPE. *Sport, Education and Society, 18*(6), 788–806. https://doi.org/10.1080/13573322.2011.611496

Miller, D. (1990 [2012]). The Icarus Paradox: How exceptional companies bring down their own downfall. In L. Trenbeth & D. Hassan (Eds.), *Managing sport business.* Abingdon, UK: Routledge.

Miller, D., & Friesen, P. (1980). Archetypes of organizational transitions. *Administrative Science, 25*(2), 269–299. https://doi.org/10.2307/2392455

Nadler, D. A., & Tushman, M. L. (1989). Organizational frame-bending: Principles for managing reorientation. *Academy of Management Perspectives, 3*(3), 194–204. https://doi.org/10.5465/ame.1989.4274738

Nixdorf, I., Raphael, F., Hautzinger, M., & Beckman, J. (2013). Prevalence of depressive symptoms and correlating variables among German elite athletes. *Journal of Clinical Sport Psychology, 7*(4), 313–326. https://doi.org/10.1123/jcsp.7.4.313

Noddings, N. (2013). *Caring: A feminine approach to ethics and moral education.* Berkeley, CA: University of California Press.

Parent, M., O'Brien, D., & Slack, T. (2012). Organisation theory and sport management. In L. Trenbeth & D. Hassan (Eds.), *Managing sport business* (pp. 99–120). Abingdon, UK: Routledge.

Pettigrew, A. M., & Whipp, R. (1993). *Managing change for competitive success.* Cambridge: Blackwells.

Relvas, H., Littlewood, M., Nesti, M., Gilbourne, D., & Richardson, D. (2010). Organizational structures and working practices in elite European Professional Football Clubs: Understanding the relationship between youth and professional domains. *European Sport Management Quarterly, 10*(2), 165–187. https://doi.org/10.1080/16184740903559891

Roderick, M. (2006). A very precarious profession: Uncertainty in the working lives of professional footballers. *Work, Employment and Society, 20*(2), 245–265. https://doi.org/10.1177/0950017006064113

Roderick, M., & Schumacker, J. (2017). 'The whole week comes down to the team sheet': A footballer's view of insecure work. *Work, Employment and Society, 31*(1), 166–174. https://doi.org/10.1177/0950017016672792

Rutherford, A., Stewart, W., & Bruno, D. (2019). Heading for trouble: Is dementia a game changer for football. *British Journal of Sports Medicine, 53*(6), 321–322. http://doi.org/10.1136/bjsports-2017-097627

Senior, B. (2002). *Organisational change*. London: Prentice Hall.

Soligard, T., Schwellnus, M., Alonso, J-M., Bahr, R., Clarsen, B., Dijkstra, H.P., . . . & Engebretson, L. (2016). How much is too much? (Part 1) International Olympic Committee consensus statement on load in sport and risk of injury. *British Journal of Sports Medicine, 50*(17), 1030–1041. https://doi.org/10.1136/bjsports-2016-096581

Thompson, A., Portrac, P., & Jones, R. (2013). 'I found out the hard way': Micro-political workings in professional football. *Sport, Education and Society, 20*(8), 976–994. https://doi.org/10.1080/13573322.2013.862786

12
SUPPORTING AN ATHLETE THROUGH LEGAL ACTION

Seema Patel, Samantha Rippington and Pam Boteler

Introduction

This chapter evaluates the role of the law in the support of athletes in sport. The inclusion or exclusion of athletes based on personal characteristics potentially conflicts with the protection of their human rights. These rights can become lost within the complex relationship between sport and the law. This chapter will be centred on British female canoeist, Samantha Rippington, who launched a legal challenge against the London Organising Committee of the Olympic and Paralympic Games (LOCOG), because of the absence of women's canoe racing events in the programme. Sam is an elite British female canoeist, who competed at an international level in sprint canoe events. She was supported by Women-CAN International, a leading global advocate for equality and equity in Olympic canoeing. The President of WomenCAN, Pam Boteler, will also feature, offering unique insights into the role that her organisation played in this action. Sam's case illustrates the conflict between sport and the law, the challenges presented to athletes in the protection of their rights and the implications for individuals who support athletes.

ATHLETE AND PRACTITIONER VOICES

Samantha Rippington, female canoeist

The challenge all started in 2006 when I was introduced to a high kneeling canoe. My racing partner and I were keen to train and compete, but we discovered that the only competitions were at national regattas, racing against men. Despite these setbacks, we successfully won medals in several events against men. The male canoeists were very supportive.

With limited competitions for women in canoe, I quickly realised that British Canoeing (BC) was miles behind other countries when developing the sport. As one of only a few women competing at an elite level in canoe, I felt it was down to me to do something. I realised that part of the issue was a lack of funding because women's canoe was not in the Olympics. When I approached BC and the International Canoe Federation (ICF), I was told that women's canoe would not appear in the Olympics because it did not meet the International Olympic Committee (IOC) criteria, due to the lack of women competing in international events. I realised that I had to force governing bodies to give women the same rights and access to training and competing as men, by getting women's canoe into the Olympics by any means.

Between 2010 and 2011, I worked hard to increase the number of women in canoe in our country through several initiatives, such as becoming a racing officer at my canoe club, being elected onto the BC sprint committee and leading a workshop on developing women's canoe. In this time, women's canoe was introduced as formal events at all the World Cup events and World Championships. However, BC did not select us to race at those events, despite our race times equalling third place at the World Championship. I was devastated and couldn't understand their logic. How are we to develop a sport when countries don't send their best athletes to compete? This was the start of the uphill battle for me and my racing partner to compete in the sport we loved. I didn't know where to turn. I tried the ICF, but they pushed the responsibility onto BC.

In September 2011, I connected with WomenCAN International founder, Pam Boteler, who was already campaigning to get women's canoe into the Olympics. WomenCAN brought together the global canoe community and linked me to various training camps and competitions around the world which I was not aware of.

Pam suggested that I explore the possibility of legal action to secure female inclusion. We approached solicitors to help us, but none felt that the case had legal merit. We eventually found barristers who did believe in me and our cause. At the time, I was apprehensive about getting the law involved, and the possible backlash from BC, but deep down I knew something had to change. BC had no interest in developing women's canoe, and female athletes were being left on the side lines.

Eventually, in July 2012, I filed a legal claim for Judicial Review. I targeted the London Organising Committee for the Olympic Games (LOCOG), because they organised the Olympic Games and my aim was to highlight that women's canoe was not included in the Olympics, which was having a negative impact upon funding eligibility and the sport's development. I argued that LOCOG had a public duty to carry out an equality impact assessment (EIA) of the Olympic programme, in accordance with the Equality Act

2010 (EA). I had to raise £2000 to cover LOCOG's costs. WomenCAN offered to cover some of those costs, along with various international female canoeists, because I was representing all the other females who were fighting to get women's canoe recognised. Once the legal claim started, WomenCAN were in regular contact with me, offering moral support and informal advice.

A press release, drafted by my barristers, came out the following day which led to a media wildfire. On the one hand, I had canoeists from around the world congratulating me, yet on the other hand, people were telling me that I was jeopardising the sports future. LOCOG disagreed that they were a public body, so we knew it was going to be tricky. Permission to apply for Judicial Review was rejected by the court, and I was told by LOCOG's legal team that I would potentially be drowned in over £21,000 court costs if I appealed the decision. After taking legal advice, I decided not to renew my request for judicial review, and so the claim was withdrawn. Although I did not win the case, I felt I partly won the battle of highlighting to the public that women's canoe was not in the Olympics.

Shortly after, I continued the pressure by sending a letter to the ICF to include women's canoe in the Olympics. WomenCAN started a petition that received 6731 supporters. In November 2013, I was invited to an ICF Canoeing Summit at the headquarters in Switzerland to explore women's participation in canoe. Following that, the ICF proposed inclusion of women's canoe into the Olympics for 2020. In 2015, the ICF approved proposals directly related to IOC recommendations, including securing gender equity in the Olympic programme for 2020. As soon as this was confirmed, BC set up a talent identification scheme to promote women's canoe.

I do not regret taking on LOCOG and feel that the legal claim was imperative in achieving equity in the canoe and kayak programme at the Olympics. That said, I did feel isolated and overwhelmed by the experience. At the time, I felt that legal action was the only option. Although I fortunately found WomenCAN and received their full support during the claim, I would have liked more knowledge about the general legal process. It would have been useful to have access to, for example, a website, an organisation or an athlete body/committee who provide athletes with guidance on pursuing a legal claim, and who could have suggested other approaches that I could have taken to support female canoe athletes and ultimately get women's canoe into the Olympics.

Pam Boteler, WomenCAN International, athlete support

Since 2001, WomenCAN International has been a leading advocate in the fight for gender equality in Olympic canoeing. In addition to advocacy work, we have continued our philanthropic mission by financially assisting women canoeists around the world and donating funds and equipment to organisations dedicated to developing female and male canoeists equally. There were no Olympic events for women canoeists which meant limited opportunities. Athletes cannot reach high-performance levels when they are not provided equal access to the elite environment for success.

After a decade of little progress and continued resistance, in July 2011, I convened a working group of women advocates, including legal contacts, to explore legal options for female inclusion. We knew it was too late for events to be added to London 2012, but there was still time to apply pressure for Rio 2016. We decided to target LOCOG since the UK has strong human rights laws. Consequently, with the support of our working group, we drafted a letter to LOCOG, requesting that three British female canoeists are permitted to serve as forerunners and do demonstration runs at the London 2012 Canoe Slalom Test Event in July 2011. Senior ICF and London 2012 officials were copied in. Although the request was dismissed because women's canoe events were not in the Olympic programme, the backlash was immense, and we struck a chord.

We were keen to find a British athlete to be the face of a possible legal action against LOCOG, and it was fortuitous that Sam's situation with BC was incidentally running parallel to this initiative. Although initially hesitant because she did not want to destroy her career, Sam finally moved forward with her request for Judicial Review. I supplied her with extensive documents in support of her case. She argued that LOCOG was subject to the Equality Act 2010, since they were a public entity who needed to comply with requirements. Sam's legal representatives made it clear that her case was not a discrimination lawsuit and she was not asking for events at the London Olympics, but the media picked it up as such. From the beginning, legal action was always a last resort. However, there was a historic opportunity to challenge the Olympic movement's immunity to human rights laws. Sam and I were very disappointed that her case was ultimately "dismissed on papers" by the court. As a long-time advocate for gender equality in canoe, I found the legal realm very complex to navigate, with competing voices from sport and law, in different countries and with different agendas. Supporting Sam in her legal case and writing to LOCOG was a big risk and it costs me personally in a significant way, but I do not regret it. The law may have failed us, but the court of public opinion and subsequent media coverage helped move the needle forward for gender equality in Olympic canoeing.

Legal action probably made Sam's life a living hell too. But she stood for tens of thousands of athletes – women and girls, men and boys. Because of this, the pendulum swung.

SCHOLAR VOICE

Inclusion and exclusion in sport

Sam's story raises several pertinent issues about the ability of athletes to pursue a legal claim and access a legal remedy when they feel that they have been treated unfairly, and when there is a lack of available support for them. Her case reflects the imbalance between canoe events offered for men and women, the discrimination that athletes face when challenging the sport norms and the seemingly insurmountable financial and legal hurdles that athletes are forced to overcome.

The success of high-performance athletes is often determined by their mental and physical characteristics which distinguish them from other less successful performers. The essence of sporting activity is about challenging our human differences by creating conditions that separate athletes according to these differences. Sport organises competition by dividing men and women as a way of protecting that essence (Patel, 2015a). That said, the traditional world of sport was regarded as a male space and female participation was discouraged because it was presumed that only men possess physical characteristics suited to sport (Lemmon, 2019). The landscape of modern sport has transformed significantly, influenced by a positive shift in the gender regime (Patel, 2015b). Securing female participation is driving agendas and policies, and women's sport has become a lucrative product in an evolving market of commercial opportunity (Petty & Pope, 2018).

Despite these developments, the traditionally perceived differences between men and women continue to impact upon women's engagement and acceptance in female events or competing with men. Sam's early experiences of a sport organised for men are reflective of the wider struggles of women attempting to compete in male-dominated sports (Edwards, Davis, & Forbes, 2016).

The restrictive sporting boundaries faced by women are slowly being challenged in modern society (Patel, 2015b), particularly as our understanding of sex, gender and identity evolves. In 2012, Sam was encouraged to launch a legal challenge against the organisers of the London Olympics, LOCOG, because of the absence of women's canoe racing events in the Olympic programme. This is distinct from the Paralympic programme, which introduced canoe events for men and women at the Rio Olympics in 2016.

At the time of Sam's case, men had five canoe events, with no canoe events for women, and this was indicative of the wider gender imbalance in the Olympic events (Donnelly & Donnelly, 2013). The programme for the Olympics is determined by the IOC, in consultation with international sports federations, and the criteria for determining programme selection at the time of Sam's challenge was governed by Rule 47 of the IOC Olympic

Charter 2004 (International Olympic Committee, 2004), which states that "to be included in the programme of the Olympic Games, events must have a recognised international standing both numerically and geographically, and have been included at least twice in world or continental championships" (Rule 47 3.2). Furthermore, "Only events practised by men in at least fifty countries and on three continents, and by women in at least thirty-five countries and on three continents, may be included in the programme of the Olympic Games" (Rule 47 3.3). The absence of female canoe events was justified by the ICF on the grounds that the event did not satisfy these criteria. As reflected in Sam's account, there was a clear reluctance to support the inclusion of women's canoe and whilst there were limited world-level opportunities at the time, their ability to receive funding, develop, train or compete to an international standard was significantly constrained in the absence of Olympic recognition.

Since Sam's case, increasing attention has been paid to the validity of eligibility rules in sport and the rights of athletes as will be explored later (Court of Arbitration for Sport, 2019; Varnish v British Cycling Federation, 2019). However, the sport and legal remedies available to athletes in Sam's position remain unclear. Varied causes of action have been taken by athletes, with mixed outcomes (Court of Arbitration for Sport, 2019; Sagen v VANOC, 2010). The impact of the professional status of an athlete, on their ability to bring a legal action, has been analysed in other sport cases (Varnish v British Cycling Federation, 2019; Gardiner, O'Leary, Welch, Boyes, & Naidoo, 2012, p. 116).

Over a period of approximately six years, Sam recalls how she persistently but unsuccessfully appealed to the national and international canoe governing bodies for support, before resorting to legal action. Instead, WomenCAN championed her to pursue a legal claim. Initially, Sam struggled to secure legal representation through a solicitor, with firms declining to assist her. In order to bring a claim before a court, there must be a legal and rational basis for the challenge (Ministry of Justice, 2019, CPR Part 54). The case progressed with the support of a barrister who was willing to act for her on a pro bono (public access) basis. The barrister felt that there was legal merit in the case and an opportunity to draw media attention to the issue.

The relationship between sport and the law

Sport is a powerful global commercial enterprise that influences society and culture and contributes to economic growth (see Horne, Tomlinson, Whannel, & Woodward, 2012). Furthermore, the actions of sports bodies affect the rights of the participants. Given this dominant position, the relationship between sport and the law and its involvement in sport regulation receives increasing attention (Boyes, 2017). On the one hand, it is argued that sport serves a public function, given its societal impact, and thus the state has a central responsibility to regulate this area through the enforcement of legislation (Lewis & Taylor, 2014, pp. 4–5). In comparison, sport is viewed as an autonomous self-regulating private sphere, which is immune from government intervention (Lewis & Taylor, 2014, pp. 6–7). Contributing to this autonomy is the existence of the Court of Arbitration for Sport (CAS), the supreme global arbitration tribunal for settling sport-related disputes. Created in 1984 and operating independently since 1994, CAS is based in Lausanne, Switzerland, where they frequently hear cases concerning commercial or disciplinary disputes linked to sport.

Although there has been a shift to a more "public-private" supervisory role in the legal regulation of sport (Lewis & Taylor, 2014, pp. 7; Gardiner et al., 2012, p. 134; Ellson & Lohn, 2005), the courts have been mindful of this "sport exceptionalism" in the way it treats sports matters (Lenskyj, 2018, p. 41). Particularly in the area of discrimination, there has been a reluctance to hold private sports bodies legally accountable, where domestic equality legislation tends to only apply to public bodies (Boyes, 2017; Patel, 2015a). In the UK, whilst the courts have considered that sports bodies may be quasi-public authorities, that is, private bodies that exercise public functions, for the purpose of legal scrutiny, the position remains limited and narrow in the context of human rights (Boyes, 2000; Gardiner et al., 2012, p. 136). This impacts upon the ability of the courts to offer a remedy to athletes in Sam's position.

Out of the sporting context exists a robust framework of international, regional and domestic non-discrimination provisions which prohibit sex and gender discrimination and promote principles of equality (Patel, 2015a, p. 37). Of key importance are the United Nations Guiding Principles on Business and Human Rights (2011; UN GPs), which are aimed at all states and businesses, irrespective of their size, sector, location, ownership and structure (United Nations, 2011). The UN GPs seek to set an expected global standard for remedying human rights abuses linked to business activity. Sports bodies now make explicit reference to the UN GPs, detailed later.

The subject of Sam's legal claim was the UK Equality Act 2010 (EA) which shields individuals from discrimination based on their protected characteristics including sex and gender. The public sector equality duty under s.149 EA requires a public authority, in the exercise of its functions, to have due regard to the need to eliminate discrimination, harassment, victimisation, advance equality of opportunity and foster good relations. The Act applies to a public authority (s.150 EA) and clarifies that where a person may not be a public authority but exercises public functions, they must have due regard to these matters in the exercise of those functions.

Yet it is unclear to what extent non-discrimination provisions apply to sport, to what extent sports bodies are held accountable under them and how the human rights of an athlete can be guaranteed. In order to become an elite athlete, individuals agree to comply with regulations and rules that are specific to sport and often not in accordance with law. Whilst the work of athletes is, therefore, different from any other industry, it could be argued that the protection of their rights and their opportunity to pursue a legal case should be no less prioritised (Roberts & Sojo, 2019; Varnish v British Cycling Federation, 2019).

Sam's case[1]

The characterisation of sports bodies as public or private entities is one of the central issues in Sam's case. She sued LOCOG by way of judicial review which is a mechanism through which a judge can review the lawfulness of a decision by a public body. The basis of the action was the refusal by LOCOG to conduct an EIA of the Olympic programme, asserting that as a body exercising public functions in the hosting and staging the Games, it was bound by the public sector equality duty under s.149 EA. Sam's case was that there was a close connection between the LOCOG and the performance of public functions because they were providing a public service, since the Olympics are a public symbol of sports participation (R (Samantha Rippington) v LOCOG Claimant's Judicial Review Grounds 18 July 2012).

Conversely, LOCOG claimed to be exempt from the EA since they are a private body who do not exercise a public function and are not, therefore, amenable to judicial review. LOCOG dissolved in 2013, but were a private limited company, contractually bound to organise the Games. Even if their functions were of a public nature, the EA would only apply "in the exercise of those functions" (R (Samantha Rippington) v LOCOG Defendant's Summary Grounds of Defence 14 November 2012). LOCOG claimed not to exercise the function in issue, namely the selection of events for inclusion. When a participant seeks to challenge the actions of a sports body, the courts have evaluated the appropriate legal mechanisms that could be applied (Boyes, 2017; Lewis & Taylor, 2014, p. 7). As highlighted, the determination of whether sport body decisions are subject to equality legislation or amenable to judicial review has mostly hinged upon the characterisation of sports bodies, whatever their corporate form, as public or private (BBC News, 2015). The second legal issue in the case was the targeting of LOCOG who argued that they were the wrong defendants for this challenge. It is assumed that the barristers were faced with a difficult task of seeking a way in which a claim could be brought to entitle Sam to an appropriate remedy. LOCOG argued that they were the wrong targets since it is not part of their function to select events for inclusion in the Games. As highlighted earlier, the IOC were responsible for the Olympic programme. Subsequently, any challenge was out of time and should have been made in 2009 (three years before the case) when the IOC decided on the content of the Olympic sports programme.

Sam argued that the claim was not out of time because they were not seeking an alteration of the sports programme and were not challenging the lawfulness of LOCOG's decision to implement the IOC's selection of sports, but rather an in-depth examination of the gender bias in the Olympic programme by way of an EIA. The EIA was sought because it would assist Sam to lobby for greater inclusion of women's canoe. However, LOCOG considered this objective to be unconnected to their role. Regrettably for Sam, the court refused permission to apply for judicial review and the case was dismissed. The judge supported the decision of the IOC not to include women's canoe since it did not meet the selection requirements. The judge concluded that LOCOG are a sport organising body who do not exercise public functions and are, therefore, not amenable to judicial review (R (Samantha Rippington) v LOCOG, 2012). This is consistent with previous decisions where the courts have been reluctant to extend judicial review to the private contractual relationship between a sports body and its participants (Lewis, Taylor, De Marco, & Segan, 2016, p. 46).

Whilst LOCOG were not necessarily the appropriate target for this claim because they had no power to alter the sports programme and were, therefore, not directly responsible for excluding female athletes, the approach of the court to defer to sport bodies in these matters leaves athletes unsupported. Although Sam's counsel felt that there were merits for requesting reconsideration of this decision at an oral hearing, Sam was deterred by the possibility of being liable for significant costs if she pursued the case further. In the circumstances, Sam ultimately elected to withdraw the claim.

Other athlete challenges

Only in rare circumstances have the courts upheld an athlete's rights on the grounds of sex and gender (see Dr Renee Richards v United States Tennis Association, 1977). Sam's experience is analogous with the Canadian case of Sagen v VANOC (Sagen v VANOC, 2009). In Canada, a group of international highly ranked ski jumpers brought a claim against the Vancouver Organizing Committee for the 2010 Olympic and Paralympic Winter Games (thereafter VANOC), arguing that because VANOC organise the ski jumping events for men, failure to offer an equal event for women violates women's equality rights. However, the court held that VANOC were not subject to equality law, and the IOC selection criteria were not discriminatory.

A key problem for athletes bringing a legal claim of this nature is who to target. Any direct challenge against the IOC would be difficult from a jurisdictional perspective, since they are a Swiss-based organisation who are not bound by the UK or Canadian law (Sagen v VANOC p. 104; Patel, 2010).

In addition, the Canadian court appeared to prioritise sport interests over principles of human rights (Patel, 2010). This places significant power with bodies such as IOC who have the freedom to apply rules in a private and autonomous way, with little regard for international human rights standards (Grell, 2018; Institute for Human Rights and Business, 2017, p. 8). However, for Sam to achieve her primary objective of raising awareness and securing female canoe participation, LOCOG may have been the most pragmatic target.

Although the international ski jumpers lost their legal battle, following continued public pressure and support from Women's Ski Jumping USA (WSJUSA), a non-profit organisation aimed at supporting women's ski jumping and advocates for gender equality in sport, the IOC introduced one female ski-jumping event at the 2014 Winter Olympic Games (Clarke, 2014). Similarly, Sam highlights how her legal case strengthened her fight for female inclusion, with the backing of WomenCAN.

There are risks associated with bringing a legal claim against sport bodies. As we have seen, athletes are reportedly drowned with legal fees or threatened with suspension or exclusion from participation if they access the courts for a remedy (Lenskyj, 2018, p. 29). Where athletes do bring a claim, it can be a lengthy and hostile process. That said, athletes like Sam endanger their careers so that other athletes can benefit from the same fundamental rights and freedoms that all individuals enjoy (Schwab, 2018, p. 182). Former Olympic cyclist Jess Varnish is legally challenging the employment status of athletes in her claim against British Cycling, arguing that she should be recognised and treated as an employee by the law (Varnish v British Cycling Federation, 2019; The Guardian, 2019). Professional footballer Jean-Marc Bosman succeeded in his challenge of the football transfer rules as an infringement of his EU rights. Whilst the case had a landmark impact upon transfer rules and the freedom of players, following the ruling Bosman describes it as a "personal catastrophe" which affected his career, health and relationships (Rumbsy, 2015). The pursuit of a legal claim can, therefore, have a physical, social and emotional impact upon athletes. Conversely, German speed skater Claudia Pechstein who spent several years in a legal battle against a doping ban claims that her fight for justice was a source of motivation (Schalling, 2018).

Instead of pursuing a legal claim, increasingly athletes globally have referred their case to the CAS, possibly in accordance with their contractual agreements with sports bodies, which often bind them to the exclusive authority of arbitration as a means of dispute resolution (Lenskyj, 2018). Arbitration is often considered a preferred method of resolution for parties, since it can be quicker, less expensive, and with experts residing over the matters before them. CAS deals with the validity of rules through application of the doctrine of proportionality. Sports rules must be in the pursuit of a legitimate aim and must not go beyond what is necessary to be valid. However, the ability of an athlete to challenge discriminatory practices before CAS is currently being tested to some extent, in the case involving South African sprinter Caster Semenya (Court of Arbitration for Sport, 2019). She disputed the prohibitive International Association of Athletics Federations (IAAF) Regulations which require a 46 XY DSD athlete with higher than permitted testosterone levels, to take medication to reduce their levels to compete (Morgan, 2019). CAS decided that the Regulations were discriminatory but necessary, reasonable and proportionate for the purpose of maintaining fairness in competition. Semenya explained how the "scrutiny, judgement, speculation and medical intervention" that she endured during her experience has caused her "immense pain and suffering" (Court of Arbitration for Sport, 2019, Para 73).

Prior to Semenya, Indian sprint athlete Dutee Chand successfully challenged her right to compete as a female but described how she faced public speculation, bullying at training camps and hostility from other competitors (Court of Arbitration for Sport, 2019, Para 90; Court of Arbitration for Sport, 2015). Semenya and Chand both received considerable support from the wider community of advocates for equality in sport (BBC Sport, 2019). Semenya has launched an appeal to the Swiss Federal Tribunal (at time of writing). The outcome of the case is likely to have a far-reaching impact on the general approach to sex and gender in sport, and it will also provide useful insights into the way in which an athlete brings a CAS or legal claim and the support they might receive.

Summary: reflecting on supporting athletes through legal action

This chapter has uncovered the largely untold story of an athlete who fought for gender equality in her sport and achieved positive change. Sam's plight demonstrates the isolation that athletes experience when attempting to advocate change and challenge unequal treatment.

Her experience of the legal realm – initially struggling to secure legal representation and then failing to prove that a private sports body should be subject to equality legislation – is reflective of the deeper complex relationship between sport and the law, where sport exceptionalism is often prioritised over athletes' rights. That said, Sam's decision to pursue a legal route, whilst unsuccessful, did bring wider benefits. Whilst the law may have failed her in the court action, the case provided a critical platform to expose the inequality in women's canoe. As a result of Sam's persistence, women's canoe will be included in the 2020 Olympic

Games in Tokyo, signifying a step towards greater equality. Although the international ski jumpers lost their legal case, following continued public pressure, the IOC introduced one female ski-jumping event at the 2014 Winter Olympic Games. The pursuit of a legal claim, therefore, has the potential to draw public attention to key matters. It is equally imperative that the law plays an active role in ensuring the fair and equal treatment of athletes in sport, through a firmer application of legal principles to sport rules and practices.

As with many of the cases discussed in this chapter, the power of the non-profit organisations who advocate for equality in sport clearly emerges throughout the narrative of the athlete. Sam received remarkable aid from WomenCAN and was fortunate to find Pam, whose motivation for gender equality in canoe was aligned with Sam. Sport bodies and the wider sport community need to focus on fostering relationships and connections of this kind to ensure that athletes feel supported and have the information and expertise to navigate the complex interrelationship between legal, media and political strategy. An athlete ombudsman (Centre for Sport and Human Rights, 2019; Anderson & Partington, 2018) or athlete advice bureau may be an appropriate forum for the development of this communication. Indeed, there are now many organisations championing the protection of human rights in sport such as the World Players Association who, amongst other objectives, seek to protect organised players and athletes across professional global sports from human rights breaches through the enactment of the Universal Declaration of Player Rights 2017 (UNI Global Union, 2017).

Since Sam's case, leading sport policymakers have engaged in greater dialogue about how human rights of athletes are guaranteed through the adoption of reformative sport measures. For example, the IOC adopted the Olympic Agenda 2020, a strategic roadmap for the future of the Olympic Movement (International Olympic Committee, 2019). Amongst significant reforms, it seeks to foster gender equality (International Olympic Committee, 2017a). The IOC have also updated the Host City Contract (HCC) 2024, to ensure that any violation of human rights is remedied in a manner consistent with law and with the UN GPs (International Olympic Committee, 2017b, Article 13.2).

Whilst the enforceability of these provisions remains subject to challenge, and whilst gender equality in sport is far from accomplished, this a dynamic and evolving area, with the athlete's voice being increasingly heard. Similar athlete experiences are emerging from the darkness. For example, it has been reported that a request has been made to CAS to include 50K race walking for females into the Olympic programme (Associated Press, 2019; Clarke, 2019). Semenya's case has certainly reinforced a societal change in attitudes towards gender, and we are entering an era where athletes are

> refusing to accept unjustified discriminatory treatment. With that in mind and emphasising Sam's reflections, it would be useful to better educate athletes about their legal rights, the legal process and the nature of arbitration agreements through an independent body. This shifting environment may enable athletes like Sam to receive improved support for a challenge to the rules and structures of sport in the future.

Note

1 The following analysis is provided based on the Statements of Case of each party, which have kindly been provided to the author, with Sam's consent, by Anthony Vaughan of Garden Court Chambers, London, who was instructed in the claim. The English High Court's Crown Office number for the claim is CO/7654/2012 and the case title is R (Samantha Rippington) v London Organising Committee of the Olympic Games.

References

Anderson, J., & Partington, N. (2018). Duty of care in sport: Time for a sports ombudsman? *International Sports Law Review*, 18(1), 3–10.

Associated Press. (2019, June 27). Race walker asks court for Olympic status for women's 50K. *VOA News*. Retrieved from www.voanews.com

BBC News. (2015, October 15). High Court rules bridge is not a sport. *BBC News*. Retrieved from www.bbc.co.uk/news/uk-34537024

BBC Sport. (2019, August 14). Caster Semenya: Double Olympic champion 'never felt supported' by women in sport. *BBC Sport*. Retrieved from www.bbc.co.uk/sport/athletics/49350810

Boyes, S. (2000). The regulation of sport and the impact of the human rights act 1998. *European Public Law*, 6(4), 517–530.

Boyes, S. (2017). Sport in court: Assessing judicial scrutiny of sports governing bodies. *Public Law*, July, 363–381. ISSN 0033–3565

Centre for Sport and Human Rights. (2019). *Mapping accountability and remedy mechanisms for sports-related human rights grievances – background paper for strategic dialogue on remedy, The Hague, 15 October 2018*. Retrieved from www.sporthumanrights.org/en/resources/mapping-accountability-and-remedy-mechanisms-for-sport

Clarke, L. (2014, February 11). Women's ski jumping makes Olympic debut. *The Washington Post*. Retrieved from www.washingtonpost.com/sports/olympics/womens-ski-jumping-makes-olympic-debut/2014/02/11/e14542fe-9365-11e3-83b9-1f024193bb84_story.html

Clarke, L. (2019, November 25). How one high school student fought for women wrestlers everywhere and won. *The Independent*. Retrieved from www.independent.co.uk/news/long_reads/women-wrestling-sports-olympics-high-school-a9204841.html

Court of Arbitration for Sport. (2015). CAS2014/A/3759 Dutee Chand v Athletics Federation of India (AFI) & The International Association of Athletics Federations.

Court of Arbitration for Sport. (2019). CAS 2018/O/5794 Mokgadi Caster Semenya v International Association of Athletics Federations; CAS 2018/O/5798 Athletics South Africa v International Association of Athletics Federations.

Donnelly, P., & Donnelly, M. K. (2013). *The London 2012 Olympics: A gender equality audit*. University of Toronto, Centre for Sport Policy Studies Research Report. Retrieved from https://kpe.utoronto.ca/sites/default/files/donnelly-donnelly–olympic-gender-equality-report.pdf

Dr Renee Richards v United States Tennis Association 93 Misc.2d 713, 400 NYS 2d 267.

Edwards, L., Davis, P., & Forbes, A. (2016). Challenging sex segregation: A philosophical evaluation of the football association's rules on mixed football. *Sport, Ethics and Philosophy*, 9(4), 389–400. https://doi.org/10.1080/17511321.2015.1127995

Ellson, S., & Lohn, M. (2005). Whose Rules are we playing by? *The Entertainment and Sports Law Journal*, 3(2), 5. http://doi.org/10.16997/eslj.115

Gardiner, S., O'Leary, J., Welch, R., Boyes, S., & Naidoo, U. (2012). *Sports law* (4th ed.). London: Routledge.

Grell, T. (2018). The international Olympic committee and human rights reforms: Game changer or mere window dressing? *The International Sports Law Journal*, 17(3), 160–169. https://doi.org/10.1007/s40318-018-0127-x

The Guardian. (2019). Jess Varnish wins right to appeal against verdict in British Cycling case. *The Guardian*. Retrieved from www.theguardian.com/sport/2019/dec/17/jess-varnish-wins-right-to-appeal-verdict-in-case-against-british-cycling

Horne, J., Tomlinson, A., Whannel, G., & Woodward, K. (2012). *Understanding sport: A socio-cultural analysis* (1st ed.). London: Routledge.

Institute for Human Rights and Business. (2017). *Mega sporting events platform for human rights, sporting chance white paper 2.4: Remedy mechanisms for human rights in the sports context*. Retrieved from www.ihrb.org/uploads/reports/MSE_Platform%2C_Remedy_Mechanisms_for_Human_Rights_in_the_Sports_Context%2C_Jan-2017.pdf

International Olympic Committee. (2004). *The Olympic charter 2004*. Retrieved from https://stillmed.olympic.org/media/Document%20Library/OlympicOrg/Olympic-Studies-Centre/List-of-Resources/Official-Publications/Olympic-Charters/EN-2004-Olympic-Charter.pdf

International Olympic Committee. (2017a). *Gender equality review project*. Retrieved from https://stillmed.olympic.org/media/Document%20Library/OlympicOrg/News/2018/03/IOC-Gender-Equality-Report-March-2018.pdf

International Olympic Committee. (2017b). *Host city contract-principles*. Games of the XXXIII Olympiad in 2024. Retrieved from https://stillmed.olympic.org/media/Document%20Library/OlympicOrg/Documents/Host-City-Elections/XXXIII-Olympiad-2024/Host-City-Contract-2024-Principles.pdf

International Olympic Committee. (2019). *The Olympic agenda 2020*. Retrieved from www.olympic.org/olympic-agenda-2020

Lemmon, M. (2019). Evening the playing field: Women's sport as a vehicle for human rights. *International Sports Law Journal*, 19(3), 238–257. https://doi.org/10.1007/s40318-019-00148-5

Lenskyj, H. J. (2018). *Gender, athletes' rights, and the court of arbitration for sport* (1st ed.). Bingley, UK: Emerald Publishing.

Lewis, A., & Taylor, J. (2014). *Sport: Law and practice* (3rd ed.). Haywards Heath, UK: Bloomsbury Professional.

Lewis, A., Taylor, J., De Marco, N., & Segan, J. (2016). *Challenging sports governing bodies* (1st ed.). Haywards Heath, UK: Bloomsbury Professional.

Ministry of Justice. (2019). *Civil procedure rules (CPR)*. Retrieved from www.justice.gov.uk/courts/procedure-rules/civil/rules

Morgan, T. (2019). Caster Semenya testosterone verdict ignites debate about fairness, women's sport and human rights. *The Telegraph*. Retrieved from www.telegraph.co.uk/athletics/2019/05/01/caster-semenya-testosterone-verdict-ignites-debate-fairness/

Patel, S. (2010, July). *Women's ski jumping and Olympic programme inclusion*. World Sports Law Report. Retrieved from https://irep.ntu.ac.uk/id/eprint/25855/1/PubSub2951_Patel.pdf

Patel, S. (2015a). *Inclusion and exclusion in competitive sport: Socio-legal and regulatory perspectives* (1st ed.). London: Routledge.

Patel, S. (2015b, July 22). Women's sport is on the rise but old-fashioned regulators need to catch up. *The Conversation*. Retrieved from https://theconversation.com/womens-sport-is-on-the-rise-but-old-fashioned-regulators-need-to-catch-up-45010

Petty, K., & Pope, S. (2018). A new age for media coverage of women's sport? An analysis of English media coverage of the 2015 FIFA Women's World Cup. *Sociology*, *53*(3), 486–502. https://doi.org/10.1177/0038038518797505

R (Samantha Rippington) v London Organising Committee of the Olympic Games CO/7654/2012.

Roberts, V. L., & Sojo, V. E. (2019). To strive is human, to abuse is malign: Discrimination and non-accidental violence of professional athletes without employee-style statutory protection. *British Journal of Sports Medicine*, *54*(4), 1–2. http://doi.org/10.1136/bjsports-2019-100693

Rumbsy, B. (2015, December 14). Jean-Marc Bosman 20 years on: He paid a heavy price for beating the system, now he wants to end it for good. *The Telegraph*. Retrieved from www.telegraph.co.uk/sport/football/12050567/Jean-Marc-Bosman-20-years-on-He-paid-a-heavy-price-for-beating-the-system-now-he-wants-to-end-it-for-good.html

Sagen v Vancouver Organizing Committee for the 2010 Olympic and Paralympic Winter Games [2009] BCSC 942 (Sup Ct (BC))

Schalling, H. (2018, February 15). Still going strong: German speedskating legend Claudia Pechstein. *Deutsche Welle*. Retrieved from www.dw.com/en/still-going-strong-german-speedskating-legend-claudia-pechstein/a-42481343

Schwab, B. (2018). 'Celebrate humanity': Reconciling sport and human rights through athlete activism. *Journal of Legal Aspects of Sport*, *28*(2), 170–207. https://doi.org/10.18060/22570

UNI Global Union. (2017, December 14). News release: World Players Association launches Universal Declaration of Player Rights. *UNI Global Union*. Retrieved from www.uniglobalunion.org/news/world-players-association-launches-universal-declaration-player-rights

United Nations. (2011). *Guiding principles on business and human rights*. United Nations Human Rights Office of the High Commissioner. Retrieved from www.ohchr.org/Documents/Publications/GuidingPrinciplesBusinessHREN.pdf

Varnish v British Cycling Federation and Anor. (2019). Retrieved from www.matrixlaw.co.uk/wp-content/uploads/2019/01/VARNISH-V-THE-BRITISH-CYCLING-FEDERATION-OTHER-ET.pdf

13
WELLBEING AND WHISTLEBLOWING
What happens?

Pim Verschuuren and Silke Kassner

Introduction

The issue of sexual abuse and harassment illustrates the difficulty of reporting wrongdoings in sport and the impact of omerta on the wellbeing of athletes. Experience demonstrates that reporting abuse, or any wrongdoing, within its own hierarchy presents a difficult and risky choice. It involves potentially conflicting values (loyalty, ethics and morality) and a cognitive dissonance between the rhetoric of the organisation leadership, and the reality faced by individual actors. This chapter presents the actual whistleblowing conditions through the inside view of an experienced sport actor and through examples in one national sporting context (Germany). It will then synthesise the emerging literature and knowledge on the sport specificities which can inhibit reporting behaviour: in particular, the weak power position of athletes, intense organisational loyalties and complex interpersonal and contextual variables. It will then present several steps to ensure that safe, reliable and trustworthy reporting options are provided within the sport system and that whistleblowing is promoted as an individual right for athletes who are witnesses or victims of physical and moral hazards.

PRACTITIONER VOICE

When whistleblowing happens – a surge of abuse cases in the German context

Being both a former athlete and a sport leader in Germany, I witnessed the vulnerability of athletes suffering abusive situations and the hardships of reporting the wrongdoing. It is sickening to observe that recent abuse cases at national level in Germany – in boxing, canoeing and fencing – did not lead to any sanction and that the individual rights and wellbeing of athletes were not respected.

A recent case in German boxing is symptomatic of this situation. A woman reported an abuse case, where the coach was accused of raping a female team member. During travel to a competition, the coach allegedly entered the woman's room and started to grope her in her bed. The woman asked the coach to stop several times; verbally and physically defending herself. However, he did not and subsequently raped her. After the crime was reported, the coach claimed the sexual act was consensual. The case was widespread in the media, with both the national boxing organisation and her local boxing club being aware of the situation and a legal case brought against the coach. Shockingly, the local club and national boxing federation stayed committed to the coach and chose to support him through the ordeal, as opposed to supporting the athlete. The case, which lasted for two years, proved particularly damaging for the athlete and her entire family. They were not provided with any legal support to handle the court proceeding, or provided with any guidance on the media storm that surrounded them. The family had to change their life entirely and relocate to another part of the country. Ultimately, the perpetrator was acquitted due to a lack of evidence.

In the case of fencing, it emerged that a long-standing local club coach was accused of being physically too close to young athletes, and that respectful, decent, physical boundaries were being violated. For the victims, it is often difficult to describe the attacks; as many young athlete were unable to recognise that they were being groomed at the time. As a professional sports coach, strict boundaries should be adhered to in order to respect the intimacy and integrity of young athletes. If the coach crosses such boundaries, it should be considered a physical attack. In all such cases, the difficulty arises as to whether a matter of criminal behaviour, or a matter of disciplinary violation. Furthermore, if the severity of the act can be evidenced, the question is: what sanction should take place? In Germany, sports organisations and clubs usually address such cases in the internal Sport Association Courts, which have less expertise in handling legal or ethical questions related to sexual misdemeanour. Regardless of whether the cases are brought by sport organisations to the disciplinary courts of civil or criminal tribunals, the handling of such cases is not always satisfactory. In the boxing and fencing cases, both stories were widely publicised through the media. However, in both the cases, there was no conviction by a public court, as any proof of crimes could not be evidenced.

The athlete's vulnerability

Every young person participates in sport for fun, solidarity and friendship. Eventually, some develop into professional athletes. Intrinsic motivation to continually practise in their discipline binds them all. However, they join sport with an attitude that can be considered innocent and naïve. Their parents place them, in good faith, in the hands of third agents that theoretically act as a caregiver. In the beginning, the youngsters are unaware of the formal regulations and informal rules, which can only be understood after experiencing the sport ecosystem for many years. Athletes then begin to understand the complex relationships between institutions, individual people and each other's roles and responsibilities. When starting, athletes also are not aware of the various misbehaviours, either alleged or proven, that are rampant in sport, such as match-fixing, sexual abuse or doping.

The hurdle of recognition and evidence

When considering a duty of care, young athletes are often dependent on their individual maturity to recognise a wrongdoing before reporting it to competent and trustworthy persons. Often, they are not aware that what they experienced bears a criminal dimension, for example, that this particular doping practice can be punished under national law, or young girls recognising a sexual assault by a protection officer. Young people first need to develop a sensitivity to such behaviours to understand what might qualify as abuse. When first reporting abuse cases to close persons, young people are often initially discredited. As with the earlier two cases, sporting organisations traditionally trust the reputation of superiors and supervisors, disregarding the athlete's allegation as imagination or fabrication.

An additional challenge is the difficulty for the victim to provide evidence, as most of the cases of abuse (especially sexual or emotional) oppose one statement against another. Here an athlete is often alone, or worse: he or she is still in a dependency relationship with the supervisor/accused. It is not uncommon that while the athlete is focused on their performance and selection, the coach can take advantage of her/his position and threaten non-selection if the athlete reveals wrongdoings. Until a selection is concluded, the under-privileged athletes tend to stand with their "caregivers". In this unequal relationship, only a few athletes might dare to speak up. Moreover, when the allegations become public, the victim enters a long and difficult process where he/she has to explain unpleasant things, with many strangers doubting their credibility. The authoritative and institutionalised position of a coach provides him/her with stronger leverage of the situation, as they are often supported by long-time officeholders in clubs or federations, and the individual escapes punishment for any abuse.

The lack of trustworthy reporting mechanisms and policies

Reporting abuse is not easy. A witness or victim who decides to speak up needs to find a reliable reporting tool. Are they in a position to discuss the event with someone, and if yes, where can they find a trusting ear? Considering the experiences outlined earlier, it is evident that despite enduring the shame of sexual abuse and mustering the courage to report such wrongdoings, further difficulties await. In the often complex sport system of professional responsibilities, financial relations and interdependencies, it is not easy to find a protective person to turn to.

If a witness or athlete wishes to report a crime, policies of how to do so are often neglected. The lack of guidance, coupled with many negative whistleblower experiences, as well as unfit disciplinary procedures, makes it all the more difficult for athletes to feel that they would be trusted as whistleblowers. As soon as they recognise and report these types of wrongdoings, athletes often face the challenge of not being believed, leading to many assuming that they are less able to judge what is right and wrong.

In my experience as an athlete and as former vice-chair of the German Athletes Commission, most of the cases of wrongdoing are not reported (according to personal discussion with the athletes themselves). It seems few sports organisations seem to care about the psychological consequences of wrongdoings to the victims and their families, with little to no aftercare being provided to the victim or their family. The distress sensed and lived by victims in the handling of their case can only convince many victims and observers to stay silent. Unquestionably, it takes immense strength of character to convince oneself to blow the whistle on abuse.

The systemic factor

In Germany, athletes are subject to two different culture/political sport systems. It is interesting to observe that the three main threats to integrity that occur in sports (match-fixing, sexual abuse and doping) can be found in both systems: the liberal, western sport system and the state-sponsored, autocratic system. In their own ways, both systems deter athletes from reporting offences.

In a system characterised as autocratic and state sponsored, sport often serves as a metaphor to demonstrate the grandeur and power of a country. Sport organisations and their managers have the patriotic duty to bring out medals as a parameter of the country's success and world dominance. Perhaps it is no surprise that this context often leads to more doping cases. Indeed many coaches and officials aim to win more medals in this manner in an effort to secure their career. Furthermore, working with successful athletes can often raise the social and economic status of the staff. The system offers no alternative. Considering how all stakeholders – athletes, entourage and coaches – are indoctrinated by this system, there is little motivation to report systematic doping, for example. If an athlete were to speak up, it is highly likely they would be severely punished, cast out and/or need to escape the system. And then what becomes of them? To this day many former athletes of former East Germany testify to such scandals. When considering more liberal societies, the sport system might similarly provide circumstances for possible offences and criminal activities. However, in contrast to autocratic countries, organised crime – such as doping or match-fixing – is generally instigated by an interconnected assemblage and driven by an end purpose of financial benefit. Whilst corruption is evident, the issue is often institutional as opposed to being a national problem.

Throughout the history of organised sport, many athletes suffered personal and performance abuse. Therefore, it is important that the culture of sports organisations changes so that: (1) the breeding ground for such criminal acts and breaches of integrity disappears; (2) the entourage of the athlete and the sport institution act responsibly towards the athletes' wellbeing, health and integrity. To engender such changes, it is fundamentally necessary that investigations, examinations and decisions are undertaken by independent panels and people so that judgements can be made separately from the sport staff and administration, and that cases be investigated fully and without prejudice.

SCHOLAR VOICE

The hardships of whistleblowing: research insights

As underlined by Silke's testimony, reporting wrongdoings conveys many uncertainties, ethical dilemmas and personal risks for an athlete. This also affects non-whistleblowers, since victims of physical and moral harm often lack a listening ear and institutional protection. The Larry Nassar scandal in US gymnastics is a dramatic example of the impact of collective silence on athlete wellbeing. From the 1990s to his conviction in 2017, more than 100 young gymnasts suffered sexual abuse and rape but felt they had nowhere to report the crimes. When turning to the federation, the Olympic committee, the University, the police or even their parents, their reports were not considered, leaving them alone and under the control of a criminal who was empowered by the institutions.

Academic research developed on this subject, driven recently by the unprecedented cases of sexual abuse or doping (e.g. the 2013 confession by Lance Armstrong and the 2014 state sponsored doping scandal in Russia), has explored how whistleblowers played a crucial and painful role. Whitaker, Backhouse, and Long (2014) published results of exploratory interviews with athletes from two different disciplines (rugby league and track and field athletics). Track and field athletes were more prone to speak up than rugby players, potentially implying that organisational cultures bear an influence.

Team sports, where individual responsibilities are diluted and hierarchical forces more prevalent, may be less prone to whistleblowing than individual sports where athletes are more accustomed to stand up to any personal or ethical issue. More recently, Erickson, Backhouse, and Carless (2017) consulted track and field university student-athletes in both the UK and the US and underline the complexity and sensitivities of whistleblowing behaviour. Their primary findings were that athletes would rather confront the doping athlete directly as opposed to becoming a whistleblower, and often they are not aware of the existence of reporting tools in their particular environment. Erickson, Patterson, and Backhouse (2018) went further by presenting a "composite creative non-fiction story" (p. 4), which depicts the real-life experiences of three athletes who have personally acted as whistleblowers. The narratives illuminate the immense difficulties arising along the whole process: before, during and after speaking up. The paper explains how each athlete faced public retaliation and ostracism, psychological and emotional distress, and somehow lost control of the situation, feeling after having reported, they had no power, nor any information on how the information they provided was being processed, and what would happen next. These three papers on whistleblowing in the sport environment are all qualitative and exploratory in nature, yet they echo the personal experiences presented by the practitioner in this chapter; the small probability of the whistleblowing being effective in correcting the original wrongdoing, the lack of whistleblower consideration and protection, and the ultimate fact that most of the bystanders or victims do not report the problem.

Why sport systems produce silent observers

There is a need to dive deep to understand the cultural factors at play. The sport sector might actually be particularly prone to organisational silence (or omerta). A recent literature review synthesised the research on factors leading to whistleblowing behaviour (in companies and public administration) and concluded that these conditions are rarely met in the sport sector (Verschuuren, 2020). As Silke noted, the sport system in itself goes against the act of speaking up. What ethical climate and behavioural values surround athletes in sport organisations? Adler and Adler (1988) studied the performance environment of US college athletics and concluded that its climate is marked by forms of "intense loyalty" (p. 401), conceptualised around five social features: domination, identification, commitment, integration and alignment. Athletes reported being strongly dominated by a head coach, with firm structural authority and personal leadership in place. They identify towards both their organisation and their coach, meaning that loyalty to them becomes equivalent to loyalty towards oneself. The commitment to the team is legally entrenched by the signing of a contract and by the adorning of a number of symbols (such as the colours and logo on the team equipment). Integration refers to the "coalescence of discrete individuals into a cohesive unit" (p. 410) bound together by "unification in opposition" (p. 410), group solidarity and sponsorship (Adler & Adler, 1988). Lastly, the goal alignment factor describes how the athlete's career aims fit with the organisation's winning goal. Adler and Adler (1988) underline that in such "intense loyalty" organisations, subordination is more accepted, to the contrary of dissent and non-conformism. When you have been told since a very young age to strictly obey the rules and the hierarchy, how does an athlete suddenly stand up against an authoritative coach or staff member? Victims or witnesses of wrongdoings might face ethical dilemmas between loyalty and integrity values and those few who take the courageous step to speak up would often be punished, as confirmed by Richardson and McGlynn (2015). Their study analyses the trajectories of whistleblowers in the American collegiate athletics context and argues that the challenges faced by athletes can be identified by two salient sporting features. Firstly, the commercialisation and competitiveness of elite sport raise the sensitivity of sport performances, as the public (mostly through the fans and media) may strongly retaliate against individuals who denounce corruptive behaviours within popular teams or championships. Secondly, the "hypermasculinity" of sport, that is, the fact that femininity is seen as an external and undermining force for traditional sport, leading to even stronger reprisals for women who dare to speak up.

For athletes, this situation can lead to forms of cognitive dissonance ("I have to protect the integrity of my sport" versus "I will be punished if I voice my concern"), and, as a consequence, moral disengagement. Facing strong paradoxes, athletes may choose to reduce the moral dimension of a situation and ignore or deny sensitive issues (Bandura, Barbaranelli, Caprara, & Pastorelli, 1996). These complex psychological mechanisms are strongly related to social contexts, and the performance-focused sport environment has been identified as susceptible to harbouring this moral cognition; for example, on doping practices (Long, Pantaléon, Bruant, & d'Arripe-Longueville, 2006; Boardley & Kavussanu, 2011; Engelberg, Moston, & Skinner, 2015). Other variables such as age (Bredemeier & Shields, 1986), gender (Bredemeier & Shields, 1986) or specific sport disciplines (Lee, Whitehead, & Ntoumanis, 2007) could also amplify moral disengagement within sport contexts.

Weak power positions

Another influential condition against speaking up is the limited power often held by athletes. Notably, this may originate from their contractual precarity, as athletes often rely on short term and unstable contracts and agreements. The power most often lies with the National Governing Body (NGB) of sport; therefore, they do not necessarily benefit from the same protection that workers receive in situations of conflict against their employers (as seen in the Jessica Varnish vs. British Cycling case). As is explicitly discussed by Silke, an athlete's career is often highly dependent on the support of staff and management of the NGB. Literature, especially in the United States, has already studied the unbalanced, if not exploitative, nature of specific agreements administered at many levels in sport, as for example in American college sports, where athletes receive only a minor share of the revenues they produce and have no bargaining power towards authorities (Benford, 2007; Mitten & Davis, 2008). For those athletes who are under professional contracts in team sports, these are systematically short term, with few legal protections; as established by Aubel and Ohl (2015) in the cycling industry. This fragile bargaining power leaves potential dissenters at a higher risk of retaliation and repercussion, especially if NGBs have a quasi-monopoly over their sporting discipline (Smith & Stewart, 2010). As explained by Silke, both the privatised liberal moral of sport and the collectivist systems can produce forms of omerta and disincentives to speak up. The weak unionisation of athletes, the unwillingness of some media outlets and political circles to criticise notorious sport institutions only serve to amplify the vulnerability of the young athlete who might want to denounce forms of wrongdoing. This individual weakness not only contrasts with the depth of the institutional omerta, but it also simultaneously conflicts with the increasingly imposed duty for athletes to report criminal or unethical behaviour such as match manipulation. While athletes might be sanctioned for not reporting fraud, the protection of whistleblowers is largely insufficient – a paradox described by Hanna, Levine, and Moorman (2017) in the context of American college athletics. Adding to this, Edelman and Pacella (2019) expound the lack of protection and whistleblowing incentives in American Gymnastics, perhaps explaining why it took 20 years to unravel the Larry Nassar scandal. The athletes, unaware of the risks, of their rights and of possible support mechanisms available, felt utterly powerless in the hands of a well-established and renowned individual. This network of unbalanced power relationships, also depicted in the German context described earlier, contributes to create what the authors call this "culture of silence" (Edelman & Pacella, 2019, p. 465).

Reconciling whistleblowing with athlete wellbeing

Over the past decade, an increasing number of national and international sport organisations have implemented reporting mechanisms to enable sport actors to signal any type of wrongful behaviour through anonymous hotlines, secured email addresses, confidential web forms or specific mobile and computer applications (Verschuuren, 2020). However, it is critical that the concept of whistleblowing is not interpreted by sport organisations as simply a perfunctory managerial tool to detect and sanction breaches of regulation and impose dangerous responsibilities to sport individuals. Rather, whistleblowing emanates as a freedom of expression and should be promoted as a basic right (beyond duty) for athletes (or other sport persons) who want their training and performance environment to be free of moral and physical malpractice. More importantly, secure reporting protocols are a mechanism for victims of criminal networks, or sexual abuse, to be physically rescued (Edelman & Pacella, 2019). In this regard, providing safe reporting options is a compulsory duty of care action for all sport organisations, especially considering vulnerable populations such as minor athletes. But beyond the mere existence of reporting channels, what are the next steps required to promote and support whistleblowing within sport organisations?

Clarifying the legal and disciplinary framework

The process of whistleblowing remains unclear from a legal vantage, stemming primarily from the heterogeneous legal landscape regarding the practice. Since the US Whistleblower Protection Act of 1989, approximately 30 countries have promulgated specific national legislation regarding whistleblowing processes and protection (Devine, 2016); however, many of these legislations are embryonic, meaning it is not yet clear as to how they apply to both sport and non-sport environments. There are examples where the sport sector is explicitly excluded from public laws on whistleblower protection – such as Romania and Greece, where whistleblowing protection applies to the public sector only. However, there are other examples where the legal protection available is unclear – such as in the UK where whistleblowing legislation applies to all employees across all sectors, but not all athletes are considered "employees" and, therefore, are not protected by such legalities. Coming back to the German context, no specific national law exists in Germany for whistleblower rights, which means that athletes could only be protected on a case-by-case basis. How could they know in advance what their rights and duties are, and most importantly, if they will be supported and protected from reprisals once they step forward? While progress is being made through the creation of a European Union Directive protecting whistleblowers (Council of the European Union, 2019), it remains unclear as to the extent this legislation, when translated into national laws, will apply to all sport instances.

An additional area of complexity to the issue is that private sporting regulations also lack consistency in their approach to whistleblowing. In 2015, the International Olympic Committee (IOC) published the "Olympic Movement Code on the Prevention of the Manipulation of Competitions" (now adopted by most of the international federations of sport), which contains an explicit duty of the individual to report such practices (IOC, 2015). However, for offences such as doping, no such duty explicitly exists, except in sporadic examples such as in the Union Cycliste Internationale (UCI) anti-doping regulations. Of note, the only whistleblowing clause in the World Anti-Doping Agency (WADA) antidoping Code is a "substantial assistance" article (WADA, 2018, p. 65), in which offenders can benefit from a reduced sanction if they provide valuable information to anti-doping authorities. Only a few organisations, such as WADA,[1] recognise whistleblowing as an individual legal right. Conversely, the practice of a sporting organisation introducing legal responsibilities with regard to whistleblowing protection within its own governance is rare. Only a small number of international organisations (e.g. the Asian Football Confederation, WADA, the International Boxing Association) have explicitly declared that their commitment to creating effective reporting mechanisms and protecting whistleblowers (especially with regard to issues on harassment and abuse). However, it should be noted that through the legal due diligence of any sports organisation, there are welfare requirements and ramifications that compel the sport governing bodies to protect athletes from physical and emotional harm, which should include providing access to secure reporting channels, legal support and personal protection (if required).[2] Some national sporting organisations are currently implementing reporting regimes. In Germany, for example, the National Antidoping Agency has a "speak up" policy, allowing anonymous reports on doping-related behaviour. Regarding sexual abuse, German Sport Youth, a private association, has set up a reporting tool, but it relies on the participation of all sport federations and entities to promote it, which may not always be the case.

Supplementing reporting mechanisms with support and protection regimes

In order to both convince victims or witnesses of wrongdoing to speak up, and to protect them after they come forward, organisations need to establish suitable mechanisms with which to advise, guide and support sport actors when it comes to any issues of integrity. We argue that it should be possible for any individual to first ask questions and have an informal exchange before actually blowing the whistle. As Silke discusses at the beginning of the chapter, many potential whistleblowers may question the legitimacy of their concerns and ask themselves multiple questions such as:

- How can I be sure about what I witnessed or was exposed to?
- Is it a violation of the law, or is it a matter of sport disciplinary regulation?
- Am I legally obliged to report it? Can I be sanctioned for not doing so?
- What are my options for reporting the issue, and how should I go about doing it?
- What will happen next? For me? My support team? The potential victim? The potential accused person?

A basic helpdesk should be available to discuss any issue related to integrity, wellbeing and the reporting process. To inspire trust, it should be sufficiently independent of official authorities (Vandekerckhove, 2006; Brown & Olsen, 2008). This service could be operated by an ombudsman or a separate organisation, for example, the Athletes Commission in Germany. It could also be operated by someone inside the sport authorities, if he/she is sufficiently autonomous from the daily administration of the organisation. It could be a safeguarding or welfare officer, dedicated to this task. Whatever approach is adopted, the helpdesk needs to have experience and competence to assist individuals in complex psychological and social situations and should also give guidance to reporting persons with regard to potential confidentiality issues, legal advice or even physical protection if needed. Such a service can be useful to orientate the reporting person to relevant reporting options, on a case-by-case basis. If no reporting option is available or trustworthy within the sporting community, guidance should be provided to report the case to external regulators (e.g. the police, sports ministry or even the media).

We argue that various forms of whistleblowing support should be enforced to ensure the legitimacy of the practice within sports organisations. When considering a duty of care, NGBs should explicitly forbid any form of resistance shown towards an act of whistleblowing and demonstrate severe sanctions for anyone found to be upholding resistance or preventing the required course of action. Furthermore, we consider it is important to reward an individual for speaking up and calling out malpractice, and that their actions should be championed in the public domain (with the agreement of the individual). Also, in many cases, the whistleblower is implicated in the concerned wrongdoing either because he or she knowingly participated to a fixed game, or because he or she accepted the taking of prohibited substances. Avenues of amnesty or plea-bargaining should be allowed for those who come forward. Such mechanisms have long been used by law enforcement to break networks of collective silence. This would also demonstrate that integrity and dissent are rightly defended by the organisation.

Promoting cultural change

A final consideration is that once appropriate reporting mechanisms and whistleblowing procedures are established, strategies that promote communication and raise awareness of such mechanisms should be widely promoted throughout the organisations to ensure all relevant actors, and athletes, in particular, understand and trust the systems. Considering the potential for breakdown of trust within the sport environment, organisations need to nurture a complete value change. The act of ethical reasoning and standing up against harmful behaviours, by any individual within the sport environment, needs to be promoted as an essential dimension of the organisational culture. In order to truly embed a culture of supporting the reporting of wrongdoing within a sports organisation, the whistleblower needs to feel that there is no conflict of interest or moral dilemma linked to their actions, and that their loyalty to the NGB will not be pulled into disrepute. Indeed, taking a stand against moral and physical abuse should fit the organisational values as paramount regardless. However, as is the case with any cultural shift, this might take a long time (Gill, 2002). Until such cultural shifts happen within every sports organisation, available policies on whistleblowing at both national and international levels advise that the individual involved is provided with sufficient capacity and independence to escalate any concerns (doping, corruption, bullying, abuse, safeguarding, etc.) through a support channel that remains as neutral and impartial as possible throughout the process (Miceli, Near, & Dworkin, 2008; UNODC-IOC, 2019).

To be effective and purposeful, NGBs should seek to continuously promote any whistleblowing procedures established and highlight their importance in maintaining safety and integrity in the sporting environment. Furthermore, senior management such as Performance Directors, Head Coaches and Chief Executive Officers should be involved at all stages of procedural planning and communication and be seen to be actively embracing and elevating whistleblowing policies. Furthermore, we suggest that any organisations that provide financial support to sporting bodies (e.g. through government funding or private sponsorship) should also hold organisations liable to providing safe and effective reporting channels and protective schemes for whistleblowers as part of their ongoing financial commitment. The Council of Europe Convention against the manipulation of sports competitions, which came into force in 2019, is one example of such accountability since it allows parties to refrain from subsidising sport organisations that fail to implement integrity measures (Council of Europe, 2014, Article 8). However, much more work is needed to ensure that legal and organisational protection for whistleblowers is consistent across all levels of the sport system and covers all forms of harm and corruption.

> By implementing reporting and support policies, clarifying the disciplinary regulations and promoting cultural change, sport organisations will not only comply with their duty of care and responsibilities to protect athletes from abuse but also encourage ethical reasoning and behaviour as a whole. The current sport system, whether in liberal or collectivist societies, focuses on athletic performance to the detriment of ethical considerations. Because it will allow athletes to raise their position and voice within their environment, the empowerment and invitation to speak up are a key dimension of the athlete's wellbeing.

Conclusion

Our review of the websites of international Olympic federations shows that very few sport organisations have a coherent and trustworthy reporting framework in place. A rare number of national sport organisations, mostly from Western societies, are starting to implement safeguarding policies, especially following the Larry Nassar scandals in the US (and similarly the Harvey Weinstein scandal in Hollywood). However, the lack of protective whistleblower regimes has not prevented a small number of courageous athletes choosing to go public with their whistleblowing by talking to the media, despite this being a potentially precarious action that carries with it a high risk of public retaliation and few guarantees of protection. Perhaps then, this serves to explain why the vast majority of athletes who suffer or witness concerning behaviour feel they have no choice but to disengage and remain silent. The consequence of this collective silence is that serious wrongdoings can sustain over the long term and leave athletes vulnerable as they have no exit options from moral or physical abuse. And so, consequently, without strong individual dissent voices that speak out against wrongdoing, the sport environment continues to nurture a collective omerta where networks of malpractice remain hidden and unchallenged.

More research is needed in the sociology and psychology of sport disciplines to fully understand the determinants of both whistleblowing and remaining silent within various sport contexts. Furthermore, researchers might consider the vantage of sports management in exploring practical solutions that enable sport organisations to foster a climate of care through cultural progresses that inspire trust and confidence in whistleblowing procedures, as well as helping individuals to detect, investigate and sanction any breaches of regulation. However, both athlete testimonies and recent exploratory research agree on a similar conclusion to the problem at hand. Whilst the national and international structures of sport remain pyramidal and the positions of power held between the athlete and the NGB remain unbalanced, the cultural climates of sports organisations have encouraged a legacy of silence and scandal that is detrimental to whistleblowing values and practices and, therefore, most importantly, detrimental to the fundamental aspects of athlete wellbeing.

Notes

1 See Article 6 of the draft Anti-Doping Charter Of Athlete Rights (WADA, 2019). Besides, the WADA Speak Up policy is a good standard for the sector. It allows the whistleblower to sign a legal document listing the full rights and responsibilities for him/herself and WADA. See: WADA (2017).
2 The "Senate Olympics Investigation" report on the Nassar case, published in July 2019 state for example that in the American national framework, "the NGBs were then, and remain now, duty bound by statute to promote amateur athletics and support sports safety" (Senate Olympics Investigation, 2019, p. 6).

References

Adler, P. A., & Adler, P. (1988). Intense loyalty in organizations: A case study of college athletics. *Administrative Science Quarterly*, *33*(3), 401–417. https://doi.org/10.2307/2392716

Aubel, O., & Ohl, F. (2015). From the precariousness of professional bicycle racers to doping practices: The practical economy of the world tour. *Actes de la recherche en sciences sociales*, *209*(4), 28–41.

Bandura, A., Barbaranelli, C., Caprara, G. V., & Pastorelli, C. (1996). Mechanisms of moral disengagement in the exercise of moral agency. *Journal of Personality and Social Psychology*, *71*(2), 364. https://doi.org/10.1037/0022-3514.71.2.364

Benford, R. D. (2007). The college sports reform movement: Reframing the "edutainment" industry. *The Sociological Quarterly*, *48*(1), 1–28. https://doi.org/10.1111/j.1533-8525.2007.00068.x

Boardley, I. D., & Kavussanu, M. (2011). Moral disengagement in sport. *International Review of Sport and Exercise Psychology*, *4*(2), 93–108. https://doi.org/10.1080/1750984X.2011.570361

Bredemeier, B. J., & Shields, D. L. (1986). Moral growth among athletes and nonathletes: A comparative analysis. *The Journal of Genetic Psychology*, *147*(1), 7–18. https://doi.org/10.1080/00221325.1986.9914475

Brown, A., & Olsen, J. (2008). Internal witness support: The unmet challenge. In A. Brown (Ed.), *Whistleblowing in the Australian public sector*. Canberra, AUS: ANU E Press.

Council of Europe. (2014). *Council of Europe convention against manipulation of sports competitions*. Council of Europe. Retrieved from www.coe.int/en/web/conventions/full-list/-/conventions/rms/09000016801cdd7e

Council of the European Union. (2019). *Better protection of whistle-blowers: New EU-wide rules to kick in in 2021* [Press release]. Retrieved from www.consilium.europa.eu/en/press/press-releases/2019/10/07/better-protection-of-whistle-blowers-new-eu-wide-rules-to-kick-in-in-2021/

Devine, T. (2016). International best practices for whistleblower policies. *Government Accountability Project*. Retrieved from www.whistleblower.org/international-best-practices-for-whistleblower-policies/

Edelman, M., & Pacella, J. M. (2019). Vaulted into victims: Preventing further sexual abuse in U.S. Olympic sports through unionization and improved governance. *Forthcoming in Arizona Law Review, Research Paper No. 2018–08–05*. http://doi.org/10.2139/ssrn.3234438

Engelberg, T., Moston, S., & Skinner, J. (2015). The final frontier of anti-doping: A study of athletes who have committed doping violations. *Sport Management Review*, *18*(2), 268–279. https://doi.org/10.1016/j.smr.2014.06.005

Erickson, K., Backhouse, S. H., & Carless, D. (2017). "I don't know if I would report them": Student-athletes' thoughts, feelings and anticipated behaviours on blowing the whistle on doping in sport. *Psychology of Sport and Exercise, 30*(Supplement C), 45–54. https://doi.org/10.1016/j.psychsport.2017.01.005

Erickson, K., Patterson, L. B., & Backhouse, S. H. (2018). "The process isn't a case of report it and stop": Athletes' lived experience of whistleblowing on doping in sport. *Sport Management Review, 22*(5), 724–735. https://doi.org/10.1016/j.smr.2018.12.001

Gill, R. (2002). Change management – Or change leadership? *Journal of Change Management, 3*(4), 307–318. https://doi.org/10.1080/714023845

Hanna, C., Levine, J., & Moorman, A. M. (2017). College athletics whistle-blower protection. *Journal of Legal Aspects of Sport, 27*(2), 209–226. https://doi.org/10.1123/jlas.2017-0001

International Olympic Committee. (2015). *Olympic movement code on the prevention of the manipulation of competitions*. Retrieved from https://stillmed.olympic.org/media/Document%20Library/OlympicOrg/IOC/What-We-Do/Protecting-Clean-Athletes/Competition-manipulation/Code-Prevention-Manipulation-Competitions.pdf

Lee, M. J., Whitehead, J., & Ntoumanis, N. (2007). Development of the attitudes to moral decision-making in youth sport questionnaire (AMDYSQ). *Psychology of Sport and Exercise, 8*(3), 369–392. https://doi.org/10.1016/j.psychsport.2006.12.002

Long, T., Pantaléon, N., Bruant, G., & d'Arripe-Longueville, F. (2006). A qualitative study of moral reasoning of young elite athletes. *The Sport Psychologist, 20*(3), 330–347. https://doi.org/10.1123/tsp.20.3.330

Miceli, M. P., Near, J. P., & Dworkin, T. M. (2008). *Whistle-blowing in organizations*. New York: Routledge.

Mitten, M. J., & Davis, T. (2008). Athlete eligibility requirements and legal protection of sports participation opportunities. *Virginia Sports & Entertainment Law Journal, 8*, 71–146.

Richardson, B. K., & McGlynn, J. (2015). Blowing the whistle off the field of play: An empirical model of whistle-blower experiences in the intercollegiate sport industry. *Communication & Sport, 3*(1), 57–80. https://doi.org/10.1177/2167479513517490

Senate Olympics Investigation. (2019). *The courage of survivors, a call to action*. Offices of Senator Jerry Moran & Senator Richard Blumenthal. Retrieved from www.moran.senate.gov/public/_cache/files/c/2/c232725e-b717-4ec8-913e-845ffe0837e6/FCC5DFDE2005A2EACF5A9A25FF76D538.2019.07.30-the-courage-of-survivors-a-call-to-action-olympics-investigation-report-final.pdf

Smith, A. C. T., & Stewart, B. (2010). The special features of sport: A critical revisit. *Sport Management Review, 13*(1), 1–13. https://doi.org/10.1016/j.smr.2009.07.002

UNODC-IOC. (2019). *Reporting mechanisms in sport*. United Nations Office on Drugs and Crime. Retrieved from www.unodc.org/documents/corruption/Publications/2019/19-09580_Reporting_Mechanisms_in_Sport_ebook.pdf

Vandekerckhove, W. (2006). *Whistleblowing and organizational social responsibility*. Aldershot, UK: Ashgate.

Verschuuren, P. (2020). Whistleblowing determinants and the effectiveness of reporting channels in the international sports sector. *Sport Management Review, 23*(1), 142–154. https://doi.org/10.1016/j.smr.2019.07.002

Whitaker, L., Backhouse, S. H., & Long, J. (2014). Reporting doping in sport: National level athletes' perceptions of their role in doping prevention. *Scandinavian Journal of Medicine & Science in Sports, 24*(6), 515–521. https://doi.org/10.1111/sms.12222

World Anti-Doping Agency. (2017). *WADA whistleblowing program: Policy and procedure for reporting misconduct*. Retrieved from www.wada-ama.org/sites/default/files/whistleblowingprogram_policy_procedure_en.pdf

World Anti-Doping Agency. (2018). *World Anti-doping Code, with 2018 amendments*. Retrieved from www.wada-ama.org/sites/default/files/resources/files/wada_anti-doping_code_2018_english_final.pdf

World Anti-Doping Agency. (2019). *Anti-Doping Charter of Athlete Rights*. Retrieved from www.wada-ama.org/sites/default/files/resources/files/athlete_charter.pdf

14
SUPPORTING ATHLETE CAREERS AND RETIREMENT FROM THE VANTAGE POINT OF SMALLER NATIONAL GOVERNING BODIES

Niels B. Feddersen and Laurence Halsted

Introduction

Laurence Halsted is a retired fencer and two-time Olympian competing at the London 2012 and Rio de Janeiro 2016 Summer Games. He was a part of Team GB (i.e. Great Britain) and competed in the men's foil fencing team on both occasions. The narrative later is a career perspective on his retirement. Laurence describes a career and retirement in a smaller British National Governing Body (NGB), that is, British Fencing (BF). The purpose of the proposed chapter is to provide an original contribution to this topic by examining how British Fencing, a smaller British national governing body of sport (NGB), might be dependent on partnerships, networks, and funding to support athletes during their careers and preparing for retirement. UK Sport is the lead funding organisation for high-performance sport in the United Kingdom. Moving closer to the 2020 Tokyo Olympiad, the 'No Compromise Funding Approach' has resulted in the withdrawal of public funding from a number of British NGB's (e.g. British Fencing and Badminton England). Thus, several athletes enlisted onto these NGB's World Class Performance Programmes could have little choice but to lose support services due to a lack of continued investment. The chapter will, therefore, specifically appraise the networks and partnerships these smaller NGBs create with other institutions like the English Institute of Sport (EIS). The specific focus is on the partnerships formed to provide support services to athletes.

Introducing British Fencing

Fencing is a long-standing Olympic sport, as it has been contested at every Summer Olympic Games since the birth of the modern Olympic movement in

DOI: 10.4324/9780429287923-14

Athens 1896. There are three disciplines in fencing: epee, sabre, and foil. BF is the NGB for the Olympic sport of fencing in the British Isles. And approximately 15,000 members carry out the sport in clubs or with personal coaches.

After London was awarded the 2012 Summer Olympic and Paralympic Games, Britain Fencing received £2,529,335 in UK Sport funding for a World Class programme (WCP). Here, BF represented Team GB with ten fencers and two reserve athletes (one of whom was Laurence Halsted) across all disciplines (BF, 2012; UK Sport, 2012). Two of these fencers qualified through world rankings and European Zonal events, meaning the remaining fencers received host-nation places. For the 2016 Olympic games held in Rio de Janerio, Brazil, BF were to represent one event – the Men's foil team – members were Richard Kruse, Laurence Halsted, James Davis, and Marcus Mepstead (UK Sport, 2016). In preparation for this event, BF received £4,225,261 from UK Sport in January 2013; however, funding for the World Class Programme was terminated in December 2016, just four months after the team finished in sixth place in the 2016 Games. The reason for the funding cut was cited as the expected performance at the 2020 Summer Olympic and Paralympic Games. In 2018, BF (along with other sports outside of the world-class funding programme) received a financial injection of £192,500 as part of a nationwide UK Sport talent programme named the Aspiration Fund.

ATHLETE VOICE

Laurence Halsted and his sporting career in a small UK NGB

Fencing is a small sport globally, and especially in the UK. It is a martial art – it is similar in many ways to other martial arts; and yet, different because of the weapon that we use. There is no money in it. Actually, only the top few fencers in the world might do quite well. But it is been my life. It is a wonderful sport. For me the best sport there is.

I made it to my first world championship when I was 15 and from there it went quite quickly. I won the Junior European Championships when I just started in the junior age group, which is really unusual. Richard, my teammate at the 2012 Olympics, came second. It was our first ever international result, and suddenly we got Great Britain on the fencing map. People were looking at us thinking 'where the hell are these two guys coming from?' Back then, I actually hadn't thought about the option to be a professional fencer. It wasn't really an option in the UK. Instead, I went to university and I was unsure what I was going to be doing afterwards.

My first year at university was my final junior year. I actually combined my freshman year with quite a lot of training and a demanding competition schedule. I was driving back and forth between London and Brighton once or twice a week. Competing loads. Doing the usual World Cup tour. Eventually, I stopped fencing in my second and third years at university. Instead, I played rugby. I was completely out of fencing. But then straight after my graduation, BF received funding for the London 2012 Olympic Games. Because I had trained hard all through my junior years, I was in a position to put my hand up and get taken on immediately as a professional athlete. It actually took me a couple of years to make it to a decent senior level. But then at the end of that first year back, I medalled in the University Games. My next kind of major breakthrough was a silver medal at the 2008 Senior European Championships, which was again kind of a shock result and beating two or three of the absolute best guys in the world and in some style too.

The next major landmark in my career was breaking my fencing wrist in January of the Olympic year. So, I fell over broke a small bone in my wrist. That was a pivotal period for everything that came afterwards. I had two surgeries to put a screw into my wrist and then to take out the wires that were holding it together. After that followed four months from January to May without any fencing. Without holding a weapon. The Olympics was in August. The selection was going to be in June. So, I have gone from being easily a member of the team at the Olympic team to not being sure if I was going to be able to fence at all. That year I also started working with a new psychologist who introduced me to a lot of the ideas that I use to this day. It dealt a lot with how you use values in sport. I spent a good few months working very hard on that approach. Working through my values; figuring out how to not be so bitter about the injury and how to not hold it against my teammates who weren't injured – things like that.

And then I came back! The psychologist helped me with the injury, and I was going to do everything I could to try and get myself back and fit. And with that Olympic carrot at the end, I managed to get back just in time for the selections. But they turned out to be an even bigger disappointment. So, this coach I had been with since my very first club made the decision. To cut me out of the starting line-up. It was a slap in the face. It was just a mind-boggling decision made by my lifetime coach and almost second father. It just felt like a huge betrayal of everything we'd done together. That was almost a darker place than the one I just come back from with the injury. After the selection, the work with the psychologist kind of kicked in again. I spoke with them a lot about that. How to work through the next few months to the Olympics and get out and get as much as I could out of it positively. It paid off and I had a fantastic experience at the Olympics. All in all, it was a huge kind of effort to get a positive experience after that selection. It definitely had the potential to be a crisis. It was a pretty traumatic experience to force me out and just made me fall out of love with the sport. So, after the Olympics, I said: 'screw it, I need a break' and I took two years off. In light of the work I did with the psychologist, it set me up to get a positive experience out of the Olympics and deal with it all in a way that worked out for me. Instead of being depressed, I booked an amazing year travelling the world straight after the 2012 Games. I actually had the best year of my life, which ended with me coming straight back to live in Copenhagen having met my (now) wife. I didn't have the fire in my belly to come back to fencing. So, I was just doing odd jobs, working in an office part time and doing kayak tours around the canals.

I had had two years off from competing when I realised that Team GB had a really strong chance of qualifying as a foil team for the 2016 Games. I went to talk to the NGB, and I spoke to the national coach to tell them that I was interested in coming back – something very few athletes get the chance to do. We negotiated whether I'd be allowed back and if I'd have to move back to the UK and live in London. At the time, BF had a policy that they valiantly attempted to implement; if you wanted to be in the team and receive funding, you had to be based in London. So, we set up a trial and planned three World Cups to see where my performance level was. I paid my own way; however, BF paid for a team event in Paris where we came fifth overall. The best result in two years! All in all, I did pretty well. It was then that I told the coach 'I want to come back to the team, and I think we can qualify for Rio. But I can't come back to London'. It helped that one of my teammates said the same thing. He was living in America at the time; so BF had to acknowledge they needed to flex their policy if they wanted us on the team.

Now that I had settled into a new life in Copenhagen, it wasn't an easy decision for us to make; me to go back to fencing for those two years. I would be going off to training camps and competitions all over the place and be away a lot. It was kind of an agreement we made for a specific time period. My wife was pivotal in making sure that I was prepared for life afterwards as well. I had to be ready with some kind of plan for what would happen after. Which was also a luxury – that I got to quit on my own terms. BF wasn't really involved during this time. It was rather the EIS and my conversations with their Performance-Lifestyle Advisor. BF couldn't really offer that much, I guess there are lots that an NGB could do to prohibit their athletes from having a smooth transition. An NGB could stop you from pursuing other parts of life alongside your sport. Instead, I think that athletes should be researching what they want to do after their career from the beginning, and hats off to BF, they had money available for education separate from everything else.

I retired straight after the Olympics in Rio. I was on a part-time contract as a Performance Director in a Danish club, and I did some volunteer work with sports organisations. Pretty soon after, the Danish Fencing Federation picked me as their Performance Director and I have realised it is an amazing role.

SCHOLAR VOICE

Introduction

This chapter endeavours to view transitions from the vantage point of the sport system in which the athlete is embedded. Doing so involves discussing what makes the support programmes possible instead of looking at the content of the delivery. Most of the research views transitions (e.g. retirement or moving from youth to senior sports) from the vantage point of the athlete (Deason, 2019; Morris, Tod, & Oliver, 2015; Vickers, 2018). Yet athletes' careers and retirements are situated in a broader historical, social, and cultural context (Deason, 2019). They occur in sports-specific cultures and are governed by socio-economic factors, societal values, and policies that all influence this process. And, as Laurence shares, funding was incredibly crucial for enabling his career as a professional athlete and for the support services he received throughout.

Laurence details several essential influences on athlete transitions. His story showcases how internal (e.g. planning skills) and external resources (e.g. social support network) developed over the duration of his career (Stambulova, Alfermann, Statler, & Côté, 2009) and describes how specific relationships and events influenced his unique career and retirement journey. It is, therefore, important to understand how a small NGB, such as BF, manages to support their athletes (Morris et al., 2015). The intention of this chapter is to clarify concepts relating to the context of athletes' transitions and retirement. It will detail the key features of funding and how funding enables inter-organisational partnerships through a context-driven lens (Storm & Larsen, 2020). Using a context-driven lens means that we can consider the importance of inter-organisational structures, funding, and networks of support (Stambulova et al., 2009) and explore how these structures may facilitate or hinder the coping process with transitions (Stambulova et al., 2009).

Widening the lens beyond the athlete

This section widens the lens beyond the athlete. It does so to address the career and retirement from a context-driven perspective (Storm & Larsen, 2020). A context-driven lens argues for considering the system that exists beyond the athlete, and how the components of such systems influence each other in different ways (Schinke & Stambulova, 2017; Storm & Larsen, 2020). In doing so, this chapter considers the influence of the system and environment the athlete is a part of, and how a context-driven perspective allows us to consider the networks and partnerships of athletes. These networks include the linkages and hierarchy between organisations.

The influence of funding

The extent to which athletes in smaller NGBs in the UK enjoy a long-lasting career may be contingent on external funding provided by UK Sport, as such funding creates the conditions for a system of coaches, support services, and competition opportunities among others. Bostock, Crowther, Ridley-Duff, and Breese (2018) detail how NGBs in the UK are constrained by 'extreme funding dependency' (p. 1). In addition, Feddersen, Morris, Abrahamsen, Littlewood, and Richardson (2020) found that most of the NGBs agree that funding bodies (i.e. Sport England and UK Sport) are critical to organisational functioning and delivering support services to athletes and others working in their sport. The significant funding increase in British Olympic and Paralympic sport coincided with (and was a strategic investment in) the rise of Team GB as a global sporting powerhouse. Before detailing the influence of funding on British Fencing and Laurence, it is relevant to trace the rise of Team GB.

The rise of Team GB

The history of Team GB tells us a story of a stratospheric rise to becoming one of the most successful nations at the Summer Olympic and Paralympic Games (UK Sport, 2018). The three most recent summer Olympic Games in 2008 in Beijing, 2012 in London, and 2016 in Rio de Janeiro describe Team GB as a global powerhouse. Indeed, placing fourth, third, and second in the overall medal rankings shows the elite sports system's success of producing medals. The philosophy underpinning this success was developed after three, comparatively poor Olympic Games in Atlanta in 1996 (placing 36th), Sydney 2000 (placing 10th), and in Athens 2004 (placing 10th).

In the wake of the Athens Games, UK Sport issued a press release in November 2004 concerning their new funding approach. It reads: 'It is a tough, no compromise approach that will strengthen the best, support the developing and provoke change in the underperforming' (UK Sport, 2004). And so, Team GB became 'much admired around the world for sporting success and the system that exists beneath it' (Grey-Thompson, 2017, p. 4). The past three Olympic and Paralympic funding cycles marked a more than threefold increase in funding from UK Sport – from £71 million for Beijing in 2008, to £264.1 million for London in 2012, to £274.5 million for Rio de Janeiro in 2016 (UK Sport, 2014). The funding is currently £264 million leading into the 2020 Olympic Games in Tokyo (UK Sport, 2019). The upsurge in funding marked a golden era for high-performance sport catalysed by the decision to award London with the 2012 Summer Olympic/Paralympic Games (Grix & Phillpots, 2011). Even smaller NGBs enjoyed the influx of funding during these cycles (UK Sport, 2014).

British Fencing during the golden era for high-performance sport

The influx of UK Sport funding ahead of the London 2012 Olympic Games and the allocation of 'home-nation opportunities' to BF meant that they reorganised (see Bostock et al., 2018) the elite and talent initiatives. Reorganising the initiatives included setting up a UK Sport World Class Programme and centralising it in London. In Laurence's narrative, he nods to the luxury of being able to simply 'put [his] hand up' to be taken on immediately as a full-time professional athlete, due to the significant increase in funding and support offered to BF. Relating to Laurence's experiences, the increase in funding marked the availability of key support systems such as sport psychology provisions and performance lifestyle support. Grix and Phillpots (2011) explain that funding can both increase and inhibit service delivery of support provisions; however, the majority of sporting NGBs (especially in the UK) are increasingly reliant on a continuous upsurge of public funding to be distributed through quasi-government organisations, such as Sport England (Grix & Phillpots, 2011).

In 2015, BF entered into a partnership with Leon Paul (fencing equipment manufacturer). The partnership established an elite training centre at the Leon Paul Centre in Hendon, London, and a move away from the EIS facility in Lee Valley (BF, 2015). This partnership was considered a performance essential and was achieved through a substantial grant from Sport England; it was viewed as an opportunity to have the best fencers in Great Britain train together in London every day. Yet, as Laurence points out, he and another teammate were pushing for a policy reform whereby athletes had the choice to train outside of the London-based centralised training venue. An agreement was eventually reached but not without significant discussion and pushback from key stakeholders. Afterall, what was the point of such investment in facilities if the top fencers in country were not going to train there?

The new funding policies adopted by UK Sport in 2004 (UK Sport, 2004) to a large extent enabled professionalisation of BF and Olympic sports in the UK. Yet the change in funding policies also marked a narrowing and refocusing of UK Sport's policy goals. Policies turned towards a focus on elite sports and medal outcomes which Grix and Phillpots (2011) explain had a direct impact on how NGBs were funded. The consensus in the 'No Compromise' framework was that medals had to be produced continuously for Olympic and Paralympic sports to maintain their current level of funding (Bostock et al., 2018). However, the increase in financial support also included consolidating funding streams. Whereas NGBs would previously receive funding from multiple agencies, a consolidation meant that all funding was to be distributed from UK Sport and Sport England. In doing so, this new method of funding shifted from a dispersed power system with a plurality of agencies to a concentrated system of two Governing Sports Organisations (GSOs) (Houlihan & Green, 2009). Houlihan and Green (2009) argue that built into the mechanics of the funding framework are functions, which are 'unashamedly about achieving Olympic success' (p. 34). Worryingly, the growing funding dependency reinforces the need to adhere to prescribed structures and to meet immediate physical outputs (i.e. medals) and glorified outcomes (i.e. medal table positions), meaning 'most NGBs are hidebound to their paymasters' (Grix & Phillpots, 2011, p. 9). This reliance on financial hand-outs poses significant economical and moral considerations for smaller NGBs.

Alternative funding streams

Smaller NGBs that are without consistent revenue streams and that do not consistently produce medals are at an increased risk of funding loss – resulting in a termination of support service programmes. Laurence described how fencing was not regarded as a large sport and that it had little mass appeal in the United Kingdom. Berry and Manoli (2018) explain that NGBs outside those with broad commercial and broadcast appeal, such as BF, must cast a wide net in search of consistent revenue streams to remain financially buoyant should the formal funding streams be withdrawn.

Ahead of the 2016 Olympic Games, BF launched crowdfunding campaigns to cover unmet costs of competing, yet a further devastation arose when UK Sport withdrew all funding to BF in December 2016. Therefore, qualifying and attending the Tokyo 2020 Games would require complete self-funding from both athletes and staff. The BF annual report from the 2016 to 2017 season details a successful crowdfunding campaign aiming at sending ten athletes to the world championships. In total, £16,870 was raised to be split between ten athletes to attend the 2017 Senior European Championships (held in Georgia) and the 2017 World Championships (held in Germany). However, a second crowdfunding campaign carried out by BF in 2018 as a push towards the 2020 Olympic Games, yielded only £170 in the first month (Falkingham, 2018). For comparison, it is estimated that the cost of funding one British athlete to compete on the World Cup and Grand Prix circuits, as well as the World and European Championships costs between £10,000 and £15,000 each year (Falkingham, 2018). The outcomes of the two crowdfunding highlight that it can be difficult to sustain elite or talent activities for smaller NGBs without mass appeal. Berry and Manoli (2018) argue that to maintain financial stability, such organisations need to consider tactics such as sponsorships, business and community partnerships, corporate days, philanthropy and donations, facility ownership, event levy and hosting, member registrations, and education programmes and certification. Applying these strategies could be critical to sustaining support for both athletes and staff in the future.

The crippling effect of funding cuts

A unique challenge to smaller NGBs, such as BF, is that this funding accounts for almost all funding allocated for talent development and a WCP. If we extend the scope beyond the 2012 and 2016 cycles, it is evident that many small NGBs experienced dramatic funding reductions or complete withdrawal (UK Sport, 2019). BF did not medal at the London 2012 Olympic Games or the Rio de Janeiro Olympic Games 2016, therefore, fuelling the view of UK that a medal at the Tokyo 2020 Olympic Games was possible, not probable. Collectively, these performance markers resulted in BF losing their WCP funding. However, this predicament is not unique to BF. Table 14.1 is an excerpt of smaller Olympic NGBs and the funding figures for three Olympic cycles (cf. UK Sport, 2014, 2019). These figures evidence the NGBs' financial ability to support athletes.

The reasons for removing funding were in line with the UK Sport contemporary funding policy as it was aimed at 'provoking change in the underperforming sports' (UK Sport, 2004). However, Bostock et al. (2018) detail the potentially crippling influence of removing funding completely on the support services available to, and needed by, elite athletes. Furthermore, Sam (2009) suggests that the knock-on effect of this approach may diminish sports organisations' intended support functions; for example, removing support functions could have an adverse effect on helping athletes develop appropriate coping skills for managing transitions (Park, Lavallee, & Tod, 2013). The over-reliance smaller NGBs experience on unstable sources of funding can, therefore, have an adverse influence on continued service delivery (Bostock et al., 2018). Bostock et al. (2018) explain that the Achilles heel of current high-performance sports management system in the UK is that funding cuts can prompt severe and dramatic retrenchment of an NGB

TABLE 14.1 Funding figures of NGBs that lost 100% of funding after the 2016 Summer Olympic Games

Sport	London 2012	Rio de Janeiro 2016	Tokyo 2020
Archery	£4,408,000	£2,952,237	£600,000*
Badminton	£7,434,900	£5,737,524	£600,000*
Fencing	£2,529,335	£4,225,261	£192,500*
Weightlifting	£1,365,157	£1,709,340	£0

*All funding was initially withdrawn and reintroduced based on performance.

if they do not achieve their targets or are deemed not probable to achieve a performance target in the future.

The role of sports organisations in funding delivery

The performance model adopted by UK Sport is not pioneering. The New Zealand 'performance regime' is often cited as the international leader (Sam, 2012; Sam & Macris, 2014) in developing a system of performance measurement and targeted investments in high-performance sport. Sam (2012) explains that the unintended consequences of this system were that NGBs became less innovative due to increased monitoring and accountability to sports organisations responsible for distributing funding (Sam, 2012). It is, therefore, important to appraise how the different sports organisations in the UK support NGBs.

Laurence explains he experienced a series of challenges including a conflict with a coach, a potentially career-derailing injury, and geographical constraints. He also explained how important the sport psychology provision was during a troublesome period during the 2012 Olympic Games, and the value of receiving performance lifestyle advice whilst preparing for the 2016 Olympic Games. Furthermore, research (Bostock et al., 2018; Feddersen et al., 2020; Grix & Phillpots, 2011) argues that funding is not merely money for a budget; funding also enables a vast set of inter-organisational partnerships. To aide insights to the context and guide readers, it is useful to provide an 'armchair walkthrough' (Morse, 1999) of relevant sports organisations involved in Laurence's narrative. While other publicly funded organisations do exist (e.g. British Athletes Commission, the Talented Athlete Scholarship Scheme), they are omitted as they are not relevant to the current chapter.

The influence of other organisations on support service delivery

Recent research (Feddersen et al., 2020) demonstrates the inter-organisational partnerships between the organisations in Olympic sports (see Table 14.2). Understanding the partnerships, NGBs engage in helps explain the extent to which it is dependent on another organisation to function. As explained, BF's WCP was dependent on funding from UK Sport and Sport England to function. Although one crowdfunding campaign was successful (allowing them to function without UK Sport funding), the example of the second crowdfunding campaign demonstrates how critical the UK Sport and Sport England financial partnerships were.

The dependency between BF and other organisations from Table 14.2 was influenced by the influx of funding from UK Sport prior to the 2012 Summer Olympics. Funding from UK Sport for both the 2012 and 2016 Olympic

TABLE 14.2 Overview of the most salient sports organisations in the United Kingdom

Organisation	Description	Issues to consider
UK Sport	UK's high-performance sports agency funded by the Department for Digital, Culture, Media & Sport and the National Lottery	Critical paymaster for elite sports managing through funding release triggers. Those not able to meet the criteria will have performance funding withheld (Grix & Phillpots, 2011).
Sport England	UK sports agency working with participation and talented youth athletes funded by the Department for Digital, Culture, Media & Sport and the National Lottery	Critical paymaster for youth and grassroots sport. Tasked with ensuring a positive and inclusive culture exists in talent pathways prior to athletes reaching the international level (Sport England, 2018). Enforced co-operation between unequal partners requiring fulfilment of pre-set targets to trigger further funding (Grix & Phillpots, 2011).
The English Institute of Sport (EIS)	Supplies sports science and medical support services	Support services are generally enabled by funding from UK Sport. A lack of funding or sudden withdrawal could remove critical support systems.

Games enabled BF to expand their WCP and acted as a facilitator in enabling the functioning of the delivery of new support services (i.e. performance analysis, nutrition, physiotherapy). Yet Laurence's narrative also illustrates that the inter-organisational partnerships between BF and the EIS meant that BF was less involved in the actual delivery of support, therefore, had less power in sustaining such services. Grix and Phillpots (2011) explain that, in essence, funding enables athletes' access to essential performance and support programmes.

Laurence explains that whilst on the WCP he received access to sport psychology, educational support, and performance lifestyle services, and that all were crucial for navigating the challenges he experienced during his career and for contributing to a positive retirement process. Stambulova and colleagues (2009) detail how the need for supporting athletes through career transitions was recognised in the 1990s. Since then, some discussion has included how to most efficiently implement such services (Stambulova & Ryba, 2014). Yet most of this discussion includes how to design a service programme according to prevailing national culture (Stambulova et al., 2009; Stambulova & Ryba, 2014) and less on the factors that enable such services and access to them. Laurence's narrative supports the consideration that funding enables smaller NGBs to create partnerships with other sports organisations such as the EIS; thus, enabling access to the types of support services discussed. Yet the question entreats whether potentially commercially appealing organisations (such as BF) can access these services without receiving central funding? If not, then surely any NGB would be beholden to those issuing central funding.

What can other NGBs learn from the case of British Fencing?

Moesch, Hauge, Wikman, and Elbe (2013) discuss how there might exist perceived commonalities and/or incompatibilities between sporting bodies and funding organisations. An understanding of commonalities and/or incompatibilities could lead NGBs to assert that what works in one sport does not work for all sports (Skille & Chroni, 2018). Yet the narrative from Laurence reveals that it might also be relevant to put differences aside. The reason for this is that funding for Olympic sports might be tied to the delivery of support services from several public sports organisations. The actual support programmes are delivered not by the NGBs but from the organisations such as the EIS. However, an innovative argument for putting sporting differences aside comes from one of the most successful Winter Olympic and Paralympic systems in the world: Norway. Here, Skille and Chroni (2018) found that several common features existed in different NGBs in a Norwegian setting. One commonality attributed to the success of Norwegian sports federations was organisational closeness (i.e. being close to competencies and expertise of other organisations), allowing sports organisations to share knowledge and competencies (Skille & Chroni, 2018). Smaller NGBs (in any country) could, therefore, enjoy increased success from organisational closeness with NGBs with similar characteristics (e.g. size, funding, organisational structure). In the UK, the apparent perception of incompatibility could, therefore, buffer the adaptation of successful working practices or policies from one sport to the next (Feddersen et al., 2020).

This chapter examined how funding enabled BF to develop operational partnerships with organisations that provided essential performance support services. This partnership was critical to Laurence Halsted, a retired fencer from the UK, and the different wellbeing support services he received throughout his career. Importantly, this chapter has demonstrated how networks of dependency might incite the critical delivery of support service programmes to facilitate athlete wellbeing pre and post retirement from smaller NGBs. Other NGBs can learn from BF by considering how the partnerships – or lack thereof – with other funding organisations enable or limit support for their athletes. The parallels from this case are that smaller NGBs need to consider their reliance on centralised funding and to what extent they can secure continued financial support through other ways of revenue.

References

Berry, R., & Manoli, A. E. (2018). Alternative revenue streams for centrally funded sport governing bodies. *International Journal of Sport Policy and Politics, 10*(3), 429–450. https://doi.org/10.1080/19406940.2017.1387587

Bostock, J., Crowther, P., Ridley-Duff, R., & Breese, R. (2018). No plan B: The achilles heel of high performance sport management. *European Sport Management Quarterly, 18*(1), 25–46. https://doi.org/10.1080/16184742.2017.1364553

British Fencing. (2012). *Three final fencers complete Team GB fencing squad for London 2012*. Retrieved January 28, 2020, from www.britishfencing.com/three-final-fencers-complete-team-gb-fencing-squad-for-london-2012-olympics/

British Fencing. (2015). *New elite training centre for the British World Class Programme*. Retrieved March 20, 2020, from www.britishfencing.com/new-elite-training-centre-for-the-british-fencing-world-class-programme/

Deason, E. (2019). *A theoretical and empirical investigation of the multitude of dual career experiences in sport*. Retrieved from https://repository.lboro.ac.uk/articles/A_theoretical_and_empirical_investigation_of_the_multitude_of_dual_career_experiences_in_sport/9693584/1

Falkingham, K. (2018). *BF: Crowdfunding appeal for Tokyo 2020 raises just £170 in first month*. Retrieved March 20, 2020, from www.bbc.com/sport/fencing/44817910

Feddersen, N. B., Morris, R., Abrahamsen, F. E., Littlewood, M. A., & Richardson, D. J. (2020). The influence of macrocultural change on national governing bodies in British olympic sports. *Sport in Society*, 1–17. https://doi.org/10.1080/17430437.2020.1771306

Grey-Thompson, T. (2017). *Duty of care in sport review*. Retrieved October 26, 2018, from www.gov.uk/government/uploads/system/uploads/attachment_data/file/610130/Duty_of_Care_Review_-_April_2017__2.pdf

Grix, J., & Phillpots, L. (2011). Revisiting the "Governance narrative": "Asymmetrical network governance" and the deviant case of the sports policy sector. *Public Policy and Administration, 26*(1), 3–19. https://doi.org/10.1177/0952076710365423

Houlihan, B., & Green, M. (2009). Modernization and sport: The reform of sport England and UK sport. *Public Administration, 87*(3), 678–698. https://doi.org/10.1111/j.1467-9299.2008.01733.x

Moesch, K., Hauge, M. L. T., Wikman, J. M., & Elbe, A. M. (2013). Making it to the top in team sports: Start later, intensify, and be determined! *Talent Development and Excellence, 5*(2), 85–100.

Morris, R., Tod, D., & Oliver, E. (2015). An analysis of organizational structure and transition outcomes in the youth-to-senior professional soccer transition. *Journal of*

Applied Sport Psychology, 27(2), 216–234. https://doi.org/10.1080/10413200.2014.98 0015

Morse, J. M. (1999). The armchair walkthrough. *Qualitative Health Research, 9*(4), 435–436. https://doi.org/10.1177/104973299129121956

Park, S., Lavallee, D., & Tod, D. (2013). Athletes' career transition out of sport: A systematic review. *International Review of Sport and Exercise Psychology, 6*(1), 22–53. https://doi.org/10.1080/1750984X.2012.687053

Sam, M. P. (2009). The public management of sport. *Public Management Review, 11*(4), 499–514. https://doi.org/10.1080/14719030902989565

Sam, M. P. (2012). Targeted investments in elite sport funding: Wiser, more innovative and strategic? *Managing Leisure, 17*(2–3), 207–220. https://doi.org/10.1080/13606719.2012.674395

Sam, M. P., & Macris, L. I. (2014). Performance regimes in sport policy: Exploring consequences, vulnerabilities and politics. *International Journal of Sport Policy, 6*(3), 513–532. https://doi.org/10.1080/19406940.2013.851103

Schinke, R. J., & Stambulova, N. (2017). Context-driven sport and exercise psychology practice: Widening our lens beyond the athlete. *Journal of Sport Psychology in Action, 8*(2), 71–75. https://doi.org/10.1080/21520704.2017.1299470

Skille, E., & Chroni, S. "Ani" (2018). Norwegian sports federations' organizational culture and national team success. *International Journal of Sport Policy, 10*(2), 321–333. https://doi.org/10.1080/19406940.2018.1425733

Sport England. (2018). *The talent plan: Creating the world's best talent system*. Retrieved from https://sportengland-production-files.s3.eu-west-2.amazonaws.com/s3fs-public/the-talent-plan-for-england.pdf?FMAAxsmgrkyJ0hXIJQl2aB7s9uIpV.uN

Stambulova, N., Alfermann, D., Statler, T., & Côté, J. (2009). ISSP Position stand: Career development and transitions of athletes. *International Journal of Sport and Exercise Psychology, 7*(4), 395–412. https://doi.org/10.1080/1612197X.2009.9671916

Stambulova, N., & Ryba, T. V. (2014). A critical review of career research and assistance through the cultural lens: Towards cultural praxis of athletes' careers. *International Review of Sport and Exercise Psychology, 7*(1), 1–17. https://doi.org/10.1080/1750984X.2013.851727

Storm, L. K., & Larsen, C. H. (2020). Context driven sport psychology: A cultural lens. In D. Hackfort & R. J. Schink (Eds.), *The Routledge international encyclopaedia of sport and exercise psychology: Theoretical and Methodological Concepts*. Abingdon, UK: Routledge.

UK Sport. (2004). *UK Sport statement on funding*. Retrieved May 28, 2019, from www.uksport.gov.uk/news/2004/11/25/uk-sport-statement-on-funding

UK Sport. (2012). *Seven fencing athletes selected to Team GB*. Retrieved January 28, 2020, from www.teamgb.com/news/seven-fencing-athletes-selected-team-gb

UK Sport. (2014). *Historical funding figures*. Retrieved July 1, 2019, from www.uksport.gov.uk/our-work/investing-in-sport/historical-funding-figures

UK Sport. (2016). *Meet the Team GB fencing squad for Rio 2016*. Retrieved January 28, 2020, from www.teamgb.com/news/meet-the-team-gb-fencing-squad-for-rio-2016

UK Sport. (2018). *Public consultation on future funding of high performance sport in the UK*. London: UK Sport.

UK Sport. (2019). *Current funding figures*. Retrieved July 23, 2019, from www.uksport.gov.uk/our-work/investing-in-sport/current-funding-figures

Vickers, E. (2018). *An examination of the dual career pathway and transitions UK student-athletes experience throughout university education* [Doctoral thesis]. Liverpool John Moores University, UK.

15
ATHLETE WELFARE, STAKEHOLDER RESPONSIBILITY, AND ETHICS OF CARE IN ELITE SPORT

An examination of para-sport organisation approaches in France

Geoffery Z. Kohe, Laura G. Purdy, and Arnaud Litou

Introduction

Many professional sport organisations have worked to ensure members are 'appropriately' equipped for their sporting careers and lives beyond. Such entities have educational programmes, mentorship schemes, networking opportunities and support services offering career and professional development opportunities. The range of schemes provides a potentially rich resource for athletes and a degree of comfort and security during their sporting careers. While establishing sector standards and templates, sport organisations' efforts have also been contoured by external forces and cultural shifts that have raised industry expectations regarding how businesses operate for their employees and improve their commitments to their members. To these ends, agendas to equip athletes appear altruistic and morally sensible. In this chapter, we converse with Arnaud Litou, the High Performance Manager within the National Institute of Sport, Expertise, and Performance's (INSEP) Paralympic programme. Arnaud articulates key concerns about the provision of athlete welfare within the French sport system and raises issues that resonate across the wider professional sport sector. To understand the complexity of Arnaud's position, we utilise stakeholder and ethics of care theories. We argue that while notions of social welfare and an ethics of care may characterise welfare initiatives, incongruence with sports workers' social realities may work against their uptake and effectiveness.

DOI: 10.4324/9780429287923-15

Background

Increased global attention to athlete welfare has driven debate and change in organisational practices in the sport sector across and within numerous nations. In response to instances of, and related media exposure about, practices in sport that jeopardise athletes' welfare, and 'cross lines' with regard to what may be deemed as morally and/or legally acceptable (e.g. abuse, bullying, harassment, discrimination), sport organisations are being forced to reflect on and change (where necessary) support structures and mechanisms. In Europe, reports such as the Syndex Report (2013) (that illuminates some working conditions in sport) and, in the UK, The Duty of Care in Sport Review (Grey-Thompson, 2017) (which specifically responds to organisational criticism over athlete wellbeing and safeguarding) have drawn attention to the variable landscapes of welfare provision across regions and sports, enduring inequalities of experience, and demonstrated capacities for change and best practice (Kerr & Kerr, 2020). These discussions have, variously, illustrated that athlete welfare is complex and multifaceted. Moreover, that understanding experiences and consequently provision requires acknowledging the interplay between underlying institutional and structural factors, stakeholder relations, individual social realities and ideological assumptions. In addition, academic debates have highlighted how these issues manifest differently across populations and within individual athletes' lives (Bundon, Ashfield, Smith, & Goosey-Tolfrey, 2018; De Cruz, Spray, & Smith, 2019). In high-performance Para-/disability sport, work has also evidenced how the specificities of disabilities impact athletes' labour, how national governing bodies manage performance and inclusivity imperatives, the roles of coaches and stakeholders in support athlete welfare beyond training and performance spaces, and gender inequalities are exacerbated (Campbell, 2016; Kohe & Peters, 2016; Purdy, Purdy, & Potrac, 2016; Richard, Joncheray, & Dugas, 2017). Such research has exposed areas of concern and has brought about welcome changes in some areas of sport.

Nonetheless, research has stressed that continued examination of the sport sector is needed; particularly, for re-orientating sport organisations' practices and sensibilities towards more ethical, empathetic and democratic ends, and creating new ways of being in sport that better reflect and appreciate the realities of individual worlds and working lives. Furthermore, scope remains to interrogate broader contexts, structures and approaches that inform and produce what welfare 'looks' like in particular local, national or regional settings (Henry, 2013; Purdy, Kohe, & Paulauskas, 2017). This chapter adds to this growing body of scholarship by offering fresh insights on practitioners within a high-performance national sport system. Our investigation also considers how current welfare initiatives are/may be incongruent with sports workers' realities and may work against the meaningfulness of provision. Building on our examinations of European athletes, this chapter focuses on Arnaud Litou, the High Performance Manager within INSEP's (the National Institute of Sport, Expertise, and

Performance) Paralympic programme. Arnaud's experiences draw attention to similar concerns which are manifested in the French system and played out in the welfare resourcing of the nation's Para-sport and disability sport athletes. We conclude the chapter by considering Arnaud's narrative in light of wider theoretical consideration of welfare in sport.

Introducing the practitioner

Arnaud Litou was born, raised and educated in France. His background as an elite cyclist and his experience in the cycling industry led him to a position with the junior national road cycling programme. Based on this work, he was initially contracted by Cycling Canada for the Junior road programme coaching position. Subsequently, Arnaud was asked to assist the Para-cycling team as the High Performance manager. In addition, he served on the Canadian Paralympic High Performance Committee from 2016 to 2018. Following two Paralympic cycles with the Canadian team, Arnaud was looking for a new challenge and saw an opportunity to work with his home nation in the lead up to the Paralympics. So, he returned to France in the position of project manager for 'Paralympic Performance Monitoring' at INSEP. Arnaud was attracted to the role as he could draw upon his experience in Canada to help shape the system in France in relation to the cohesion and efficiency of supports which would, he believed, lead to improved results.

> **PRACTITIONER VOICE**
>
> **Welfare in the French Paralympic high-performance sport system**
>
> When I started working in France, I saw that programmes were in place, the systems were in place, but definitely not running at full speed, and definitely not aligned with their needs. Reading the situation, I then saw my responsibility as one of supporting and assessing the needs of the stakeholders (i.e. athletes, coaches) and the levels of support required as well as making recommendations for funding from the federal government (i.e. Agence Nationale du Sport (ANS)). My role changed in September 2019 when I took up work for the ANS as Paralympic HP expert and adviser; liaising with the sport development stream to optimise alignment, coherence and efficiencies at the National Sport Organisation (NSO) as well as the various government levels. Currently, I see my role as a facilitator, to provide the right information and to make sure the right level of support is invested for the right needs and for the right people.
>
> To execute my role effectively, however, I need to understand the complexities of the French sport system. At the high-performance level,

the [Ministry of Sport] provides regulations, rules of play, targeted social programmes and funding. One specific team in the [Ministry of Sport] is responsible for high-performance management. The second team within the [Ministry of Sport] is INSEP with provision to assess technical aspects of the performance programmes . . . which are basically former High Performance Directors, and former Olympic coaches, and champions at the high-performance level. Recently, there has been amalgamation (or centralising) of resources with the aim of providing parity of access and opportunity for both Olympic and Paralympic athletes. Although this structure provides support for many athletes, there are concerns. One of which is that the level of funding dedicated to Para-athletes is very, very, very shallow. Such funding discrepancies and inequities have had implications on Para-athletes' uptake of welfare programmes. With regards to welfare, there are a range of welfare programmes and funding for athletes provided by the French government via the Ministry of Sport. Firstly, some funding is provided directly to the athletes through the NSO to be used for their sporting needs, for example, equipment and competitions. Secondly, there are programmes that focus on athletes who are working who require time away to compete in their sport. Here, a contract with the employer is needed so some Ministry of Sport funding can be used by the NSO to compensate the employer for athletes' time taken from work. Thirdly, within the suite of welfare support on offer in France, there is a dual-career project. This later project involves looking at the athlete as a whole, having a career, or building a future as a student/worker/professional, looking at specific training courses once they plan to retire and phase out and transition out of the high-performance context.

While the programmes are useful, are morally the 'right thing to do' and are 'on-paper' equitable, there are concerns that there are inherent differences in the demographics of Para- and able-bodied athletes that the system does not acknowledge. Our athletes are usually older and more established in life as professionals, with families, kids, and a different social landscape compared to a lot of able-bodied athletes, or young elite Olympic athletes. Looking at the average age at the games, it is obvious that we are looking at an older group of athletes on the Paralympic side of the business. However, the athletes' needs are much more important on the Para-side. And when you look outside of the athleticism, just on the demographic side of things, disabled athletes in the general population have lower levels of employment. There are more disabled athletes who are on welfare, or struggling financially, and it is important to recognise that this applies to sport . . . the difference between able-bodied and Para is mind-blowing. The level of need is more important generally, so increases in funding have more of an impact, and you can see that difference. Athletes have to feel that there is equity and that they are being recognised, supported and valued, not just being used. The athletes also need to feel confident that when their performance careers are over, their contribution will be recognised and they are going to be taken care of.

The fact of the matter is that the government, through their social programmes, not only for Para-athletes but also for disabled citizens, have equivalent or complementary programmes in places across regions, and in departments. But, currently, we don't have the full perspective, or map, so the field is not fully clear at the moment of what services and programmes are available; at a general level, what services and programmes apply to citizens and in what regions? Therefore, the response to welfare support in Para-sport on the ground is all over the spectrum, from low level to high level understanding and support. And it brings a lot of questions . . . Will [athletes] be well supported and how? Will they be under-supported? Because it's a funding relationship between the organisation and the athlete based on performance, for (what are deemed to be) non-performance related needs . . . But there is not enough, and no transparency as to what athletes have access to at all those different levels. To successfully navigate this, athletes need to know that they have to be proactive, first, to know what programmes exist. What could they be eligible for? Secondly, how successful could they be in funding? And, finally, at the end of the day . . . What does that bring them to? How much funding? How much support? How many programmes do they have access to? It has all exploded, but nothing is centralised. So, from a high-performance agency perspective, there is a lot of grey; a lack of knowledge and information.

In terms of what matters most, from my perspective, is that I need [the provision] to be meaningful to them in a way that better supports them. And . . . that is the jurisdiction of the NSOs. I cannot step in and do their job and definitely don't wish to do that. I work alongside the NSOs to get a proper assessment of what the needs are, what level of support would be needed, and report to my boss what recommendations I make. The FPC (French Paralympic Committee) is working on their front, for example, and in my role, I have more of an inter-institutional relationship with them.

The pressure on sport organisations to provide meaningful programmes has also influenced the wider national context. Generally speaking, I feel that there is a huge sense of 'it is due to me' . . . with this nation. [France] has had a strong social political culture and social programmes . . . over time, and through history, and for decades if not more than that. And, there is a culture that the government is there to provide. But it creates a culture around 'it is due'. Obviously, there are basic needs that one would be blind not to see, not to understand and not to put themselves into someone else's shoes. There is a basic need for empathy, for anyone who is struggling. There are rights, but there is also a duty . . . to provide [athletes] with better conditions. But where does the contract lay? What is asked from them to get a 'return on investment'. I don't see it as a return on investment, I see it as humans taking responsibility on both sides of the fence. It's a good thing having all these programmes in place. But it's one thing to have them, but how much are they used, and how much of a positive impact do they have, and how much do they cover the welfare needs?

What we've come to realise with a new high-performance agency that has recently been created is that government funding at the federal level is one thing. That is what athletes can benefit from through their NSOs. But then, there are other sources and different levels of support that they are eligible for. It could be through their region, their administrative region, very much like a province back in Canada or a district, cities or their departments, which is a subset of the region. I say this from an understanding of what is going on in the international field, and how athletes are supported. There is no perfect system, but there are some good ideas and good programmes put in place in other nations. There is a clear understanding and acknowledgement of Paralympic and Olympic differences, and I think that the level of athletes on the Paralympic side having financial struggles and challenges remains significant. We have seen NSOs working with companies and looking at having a contract for an athlete, supporting great ambassadors for the movement, a great newcomer, or someone with great potential that they strongly believe in. So, they find a partner within the private sector, or with a public service as a sponsor and performance partner to provide a part-time job or a job with time dedicated to training so that they can provide the right social environment as well.

SCHOLAR VOICE

Discussion

Appreciations of, and responsibilities to welfare may vary between sports organisations and sports workers within and across nations. Since arriving at INSEP and more recently working in ANS, Arnaud's primary focus was on reacquainting himself with the sport system in France and understanding the extent and meaningfulness of welfare provision available for athletes in the Para-sport programme. Based on his assessment of this provision, and from working with stakeholders in the system (e.g. The French Paralympic Committee, NSOs, coaches and athletes), Arnaud views himself as 'one link in the chain' which can effect positive changes in the landscape for Para- and disability sport athletes. While this ethos may be echoed by others working in sport in other nations, Arnaud's work is shaped by local factors, and cultural, historical and social conditions. For Arnaud to achieve his aim of delivering a more cohesive, effective and successful performance programme for Para-sport athletes, the challenges are complex and multifactorial. The social realities of athletes with disabilities Arnaud has worked with over the course of his career have highlighted that specific disabilities may inhibit engagement with programmes, individuals may lack awareness of the programmes, may be concentrating on meeting their basic needs, and/or have other priorities.

Regardless of his position or organisational setting, Arnaud has illustrated that an interrogation of welfare concerns within the industry requires acknowledgement of the respective and collective roles and responsibilities each party undertakes (whether explicit and contractual or implicit and moral). As evidenced in Arnaud's narrative, performance demands in elite sport necessitate a focus on ensuring the *in situ* high-performance environment and welfare provision 'works' for all parties. For example, on the part of the athlete, that high performance, developmental, training and participation expectations are achieved, and team philosophies are upheld. On the part of the organisation, that there exists appropriate support, safety and protection provision (Brouwers, Sotiriadou, & De Bosscher, 2015; Friedman, Parent, & Mason, 2004; Purdy et al., 2017). The change in funding structure of high-performance sport in France has invariably been advantageous in creating new resources and opportunities for athlete welfare support. The existence of such programmes, Arnaud noted, was not a guarantee as to their uptake, effectiveness or meaningfulness to athletes. Individual engagement in programmes, for instance, was contingent upon the willingness and desire of athletes, the motivation and encouragements provided by significant others (e.g. coaches, family members and peers), and the priority given to welfare education within the national organisational, regional/local centre and club.

Programmes notwithstanding, Arnaud believes that there is a lack of understanding within organisations related to Para-athlete-specific welfare needs. Relatedly, there is also a fragmented framework of national provision and uptake of welfare support by Para-sport athletes. In addition, there remains a need to have clarity regarding the increasing number of stakeholders and delivery entities involved in welfare support (in and beyond sport). While the ambiguity of provision issues are not specific to Para-sport, the challenges are compounded by the extant conditions Para-sport athletes already face. The observations here also echo those experienced by other practitioners working in high-performance Para- and disability sport (Allan, Smith, Côté, Ginis, & Latimer-Cheung, 2018; Kohe & Peters, 2016). Such work has documented the prevailing funding inequities afforded to the Para-/disability sport sector, the marginalisation or liminal treatment of Para-/disability sport within high-performance funding structures, and specificities of the individuals' welfare being at odds with organisation responses.

Acknowledging disparities, challenges and the idea of mutual responsibilities between the athlete and sport body, for Arnaud, was an important factor ameliorating criticism of organisations' duties of care, athletes' sense of entitlement and contractual obligations of support provision. Essentially, Arnaud's position was that the underpinning principles of the welfare provision should not differentiate between Olympic and Paralympic athletes. Nonetheless, the specificity of athletes' individual lives and the demographics of people with disabilities have an influence on the suitability of welfare provision provided, in this case, by INSEP/ANS and the NSOs. Overall, the issue is one of improving welfare provision to counter inequities, and embedded social realities, within the national sport system. The outcome of which, Arnaud recognises, would fulfil an overarching moral objective to better address the social and economic realities of Para-athletes' and athletes with disabilities' lives for the better.

In understanding Arnaud's experience, we draw upon stakeholder and ethics of care theories to underscore the complex agendas and expectations entangled within sport employment and the politicisation of organisational relations. Stakeholder theory has been well recognised as a means to understand the complexities of relationships with a variety of industry and employment environments (Bridoux & Stoelhorst, 2014; Freeman, 2010; Russo & Perrini, 2010). With a focus on the varied interests parties bring to employment relations, the negotiation of (congruent and conflicting) agendas within business, and institution's intrinsic ethical responsibilities, stakeholder theory provides a useful way to explain individual sport organisations' (and the wider European professional sport sectors) engagement in welfare enterprises in the pursuit of performance success. Moreover, the theory acknowledges that all parties enter relationships for collective and individual interests. Beyond this, however, there is a recognition that while organisations may assume primary decision-making capacity, other stakeholder concerns and interests are legitimate and merit consideration (Donaldson & Preston, 1995; Freeman, 2010; Friedman & Miles, 2002; Miles, 2017). Such a position then makes it possible to argue for sport organisations to appreciate athletes' welfare, and wider career concerns and consider (though not necessarily action) strategies that might be advantageous for their welfare in the immediate and long term. Yet, stakeholder theorists identify, at any one point, organisations will comprise a diverse array of participants whose purposes may or not be congruent (Miles, 2017). As such, there can be difficulty in ascertaining ownership over roles, responsibilities and outcomes (Donaldson & Preston, 1995; Freeman, 2010); a feature Arnaud identifies in French system.

With its intellectual genesis beyond sport, stakeholder theory is also useful in understanding business relations within capitalist economic systems (of which sport is a constituent part) (Freeman, 2010). The theory helps account for how organisations investing in stakeholder relations to concomitantly aid profit maximisation (for elite sport organisations interpreted as fulfilling funding-orientated performance imperatives), and utilise their existing relationships (and investments in those relationships) to add value and demonstrate their wider responsibility. We recall also Arnaud's remarks about the imperatives of INSEP/ANS to deliver on the government funding and performance imperatives, the necessity in his roles to work with key entities to deliver on these objectives and the efforts to improve existing resources and provision across the country. To these ends, while stakeholder network creation is important, adding value to stakeholder relations (and ensuring that all stakeholders are valued within arrangements) is crucial (Jenson, 2010). It may be 'enough' for a sports organisation to provide an amiable environment for athletes and attend to their immediate career needs and welfare. Success and meaningfulness of provision, for Arnaud, derives from the organisation's ability to demonstrate its practical and moral commitment and social responsibility to its 'community' beyond the point of contractual stipulation (Freeman, 2010; Russo & Perrini, 2010). He identifies how attitudes to stakeholder relations are tied, in part, to the social and cultural context in which they are situated. The French context, and more global shifts, have precipitated changes in organisation–athlete interactions and perceptions of expected support. In his experiences in French Parasport, Arnaud acknowledges that these tensions are compounded by an underlying morality and sense of decency among those working in the area.

Arnaud's perspective echoes wider ethos and debate within the sport industry vis-à-vis athlete welfare, duties of care and organisational responsibility (Ronglan, 2015; Tshube & Feltz, 2015). The sport industry in France, for example, is underpinned by strong histories, cultures and narratives within the population regarding the general provision of social support, disability services and public levels of care (Kilcline, 2019). Distinct in Arnaud's position, and congruent with Kohe and Purdy (2020) and Kohe and Purdy (2016), is his recognition of organisational limitations and the sensibilities that need to be shown towards developing national sport networks and approaches to better support athletes (and address funding imperatives to demonstrate greater care). Formal structures notwithstanding, Arnaud recognised a need for practitioners and sport organisations to balance the needs and desires for more holistic welfare provision across the disability sport spectrum with the funding constraints, high-performance priorities, and governing relationship (particularly with NSO) that are directed to particular elite sport imperatives, in this case, towards Paris 2024 and the subsequent Paralympic cycles.

Arnaud's comment regarding tensions between holistic approaches to welfare and contractually defined support highlights the connection between stakeholder theory and ethics of care (Oruc & Sarikaya, 2011; Tronto, 1993). Conceptually, work on the ethics of care has identified that all human (and by extension business) relationships are imbued with moral obligation. More specifically, that while moral obligations may vary between parties, there are inherently individual and collective values, ideals and beliefs that warrant respecting, protection and nurturing (Pettersen, 2011; Tronto, 1993). Fundamental to an ethics of care, theorists argue, is a universal commitment to human flourishing, condemnation of exploitation and hurt and conviction to do no harm (Pettersen, 2011). Arnaud, for example, draws connections between the context of French society and welfare expectations, organisational obligations within sport (that not only include but also go beyond contractual clauses), and the uniqueness of Para-athletes' lives. Here, considering a care ethic within stakeholder relations aids in appreciating the value of Arnaud's position regarding the need for organisations to work together to provide a more holistic and comprehensive account and approach to Para-sport athlete welfare.

Stakeholder care and synergy are evidenced in the work Arnaud is doing in helping map welfare provision across the state, working with other organisations, and learning from others and his experience in sport in various nations. In the pursuit of strengthening stakeholder relations in Para-sport, for example, Arnaud has illustrated the advantages of collaborative work across the sector. Furthermore, in the development of a new performance strategy towards the Paris 2024 Olympics and Paralympics and beyond, there is collective work involving Arnaud, INSEP colleagues, the French Olympic and Paralympic Committees, NGOs and state agencies. The goal of which, invariably, is to work more effectively, efficiently and sustainably within the sports structure.

For Arnaud, effective stakeholder relations are necessary if performance outcomes are to be met (Koggel & Orme, 2010; McEwan & Goodman, 2010). As evidenced in the French system, there appear to be entrenched assumptions within sport organisation – sports worker discourse vis-à-vis moral obligations and duties of organisations and athletes, and social responsibility (observations similar to those noted elsewhere by Freeman (2010) and Greenwood and Van Buren (2010)). From Arnaud's perspective, there is a sense that sport organisations possess an innate duty and responsibility to establish spaces that ensure (Para-)athletes' security, support, development and ultimately their rights are protected and respected. In the same manner, there is a sense that all stakeholders within the system possess an obligation to help support and advance the organisation and, importantly, add value to its mission (i.e. success at the 2024 Paris Olympics and Paralympics).

Building Para-athlete welfare provision that incorporates a more holistic understanding of care is challenging. Organisations already have much to do. Moreover, there are significant variations in the capacities and resources available across sports and France. Yet, given our recognition afforded to stakeholder positions, intentions and relations, we respect that disparity in service and support provision in the sector need not necessarily be considered problematic. In some cases, it may be that universal approaches to athlete welfare cannot be transferred; or, have limited value and uptake once they are localised. As evidenced earlier, it is clear that there are opportunities to improve this provision. Arnaud affirms how shifts in the sport system have brought Para-sport athletes within the high-performance entity (INSEP/ANS). Such change has afforded improved recognition of athletes, and by proxy aided his role, within the French sport system, and further visibility and voice for para-related concerns. Yet, whatever shape and scope initiatives may take, there is a need to consider the extensive, though largely unmapped, landscape of welfare provision for para-athletes across the French state. Furthermore, greater attention is warranted on organisations' perceptions and boundaries of care, what the implications might be for the extent and provision of welfare, and what might matter, be meaningful, of value and of need to all athletes. While the sustainability of, and engagement with, welfare and care initiatives cannot be guaranteed, such conversations may draw attention to ways of appreciating the idiosyncrasies that in this case characterise Para-sport, and how the diversity of athletes might be reflected in future high-performance sport strategies in France and collaborative stakeholder work. Readers may appreciate some similarities to their respective sport sectors and work here and see possibilities for alternate ways of enacting and strengthening welfare provision.

Based on the reflection of Arnaud's experience, and consideration of stakeholder and care theories, we conclude by briefly considering how some of the challenges identified may be addressed. We support Arnaud's mapping of provision at the national level. Within this process, we reiterate the importance he expresses about identifying best practices, opening dialogue across the sector and creating learning opportunities. As Arnaud reiterates, the system is improving, organisational and wider stakeholder support is there, athletes have opportunities available, there is evidence of engagement and some consideration of individual sensitivities. While this may be occurring already, such networking and knowledge transfer cannot be guaranteed, rather it relies on appropriate institutional structures, creation of collegial spaces and the individual goodwill and momentum of constituents. The current concern for Arnaud is that there are disjunctures and unknowns between what is being provided at state level, high performance and national sport organisation level, whether there is engagement, and how meaningful that welfare provision is (related to their specific social realities).

Beyond this, and congruent with arguments put forth by other scholars and practitioners working in Para-/disability sport (Bundon et al., 2018; De Cruz et al., 2019; Kohe & Peters, 2016), we concur with Arnaud's position

> that change begins by first understanding the athlete and the meaningfulness of welfare provision within individuals' lives. Given the extensive stakeholders involved in personal welfare, generally speaking, we agree with Arnaud's assertion that there is a requirement for a multi-sectorial approach. As such, organisations need to do more work together to ensure collective welfare programmes also accommodate and reflect the bespoke, individualised provision Para-sport athletes' need and desire. Such an approach may then be better attuned to the social realities and challenges of individuals with disabilities.

Conclusion

Arnaud's international experience in high-performance sport, and his current role in INSEP, have enabled him to have an impact on the French sport system and the nature of Para-/disability sport participants' lives therein. Arnaud commented how the landscape of French athlete welfare support has improved with regard to opportunities for athletes. In the general sense, there is more programme availability, funding and a wider interest in welfare issues. However, Arnaud has also identified the challenge of divergent stakeholder interests and approaches within the sector which has meant the welfare support is variable and the meaningfulness of the provision remains difficult to discern. Furthermore, while stakeholders have shown an interest in developing programmes for athletes, as a result of funding imperatives, the centralisation of programmes, and generalised approaches to welfare programme development, Arnaud is concerned that they do not best reflect Para-athletes' social realities. To advance, stakeholders within the system need to recognise roles and responsibilities and enter into more frequent, constructive and collaborative dialogue with each other to meet performance objectives and effect more empathetic relations and support. In essence, Arnaud's experience is a reminder for scholars and practitioners to acknowledge that there is a moral dimension of welfare that exists beyond what stakeholders can provision for or contractually provide.

References

Allan, V., Smith, B., Côté, J., Ginis, K. A. M., & Latimer-Cheung, A. E. (2018). Narratives of participation among individuals with physical disabilities: A life-course analysis of athletes' experiences and development in parasport. *Psychology of Sport and Exercise, 37*, 170–178. https://doi.org/10.1016/j.psychsport.2017.10.004

Bridoux, F., & Stoelhorst, J. W. (2014). Microfoundations for stakeholder theory: Managing stakeholders with heterogeneous motives. *Strategic Management Journal, 35*(1), 107–125. https://doi.org/10.1002/smj.2089

Brouwers, J., Sotiriadou, P., & De Bosscher, V. (2015). An examination of the stakeholders and elite athlete development pathways in tennis. *European Sport Management Quarterly, 15*(4), 454–477. https://doi.org/10.1080/16184742.2015.1067239

Bundon, A., Ashfield, A., Smith, B., & Goosey-Tolfrey, V. L. (2018). Struggling to stay and struggling to leave: The experiences of elite para-athletes at the end of their sport careers. *Psychology of Sport and Exercise, 37*, 296–305. https://doi.org/10.1016/j.psychsport.2018.04.007

Campbell, N. (2016). Creating a high performance Para-rowing programme in the USA: From the geography of the land to the generosity of the spirit (and everything in between). In G. Kohe & D. Peters (Eds.), *High performance (dis)ability sports coaching* (pp. 24–44). Abingdon, UK: Routledge.

De Cruz, N. P., Spray, C. M., & Smith, B. (2019). Implicit beliefs of disability and elite sport: The para-athlete experience. *Qualitative Research in Sport, Exercise and Health, 11*(1), 69–91. https://doi.org/10.1080/2159676X.2017.1384753

Donaldson, T., & Preston, L. (1995). The stakeholder theory of the corporation: Concepts, evidence and implications. *Academy of Management Review, 20*(1), 65–91. https://doi.org/10.5465/amr.1995.9503271992

Freeman, R. E. (2010). *Stakeholder theory: The state of the art*. Cambridge: Cambridge University Press.

Friedman, A. L., & Miles, S. (2002). Developing stakeholder theory. *Journal of Management Studies, 39*(1), 1–21. https://doi.org/10.1111/1467-6486.00280

Friedman, M., Parent, M. M., & Mason, D. S. (2004). Building a framework for issues management in sport through stakeholder theory. *European Sport Management Quarterly, 4*(3), 170–190. https://doi.org/10.1080/16184740408737475

Greenwood, M., & Van Buren, H. (2010). Trust and stakeholder theory: Trustworthiness in the organisation-stakeholder relationship. *Journal of Business Ethics, 95*(3), 425–438. https://doi.org/10.1007/s10551-010-0414-4

Grey-Thompson, T. (2017). *Duty of care in sport: Independent report to government*. Retrieved from https://assets.publishing.service.gov.uk/government/uploads/system/u ploads/attachment_data/file/610130/Duty_of_Care_Review_-_April_2017__2.pdf

Henry, I. (2013). Athlete development, athlete rights and athlete welfare: A European Union perspective. *The International Journal of the History of Sport, 30*(4), 356–373. https://doi.org/10.1080/09523367.2013.765721

Jenson, M. C. (2010). Value maximization, stakeholder theory and the corporate objective function. *Journal of Applied Corporate Finance, 22*(1), 32–42. https://doi.org/10.1111/j.1745-6622.2001.tb00434.x

Kerr, R., & Kerr, G. (2020). Promoting athlete welfare: A proposal for an international surveillance system. *Sport Management Review, 23*(1), 95–103. https://doi.org/10.1016/j.smr.2019.05.005.

Kilcline, C. (2019). *Sport and society in global France: Nations, migrations, corporations*. Liverpool, UK: Liverpool University Press.

Koggel, C., & Orme, J. (2010). Care ethics: New theories and applications. *Ethics and Social Welfare, 4*(2), 109–114. https://doi.org/10.1080/17496535.2010.484255

Kohe, G. Z., & Peters, D. (2016). *High performance disability sport coaching*. Abingdon, UK: Routledge.

Kohe, G. Z., & Purdy, L. G. (2016). In protection of whose 'wellbeing'?: Considerations of 'clauses and a/effects' in athlete contracts. *Journal of Sport and Social Issues, 40*(3), 218–236. https://doi.org/10.1177/0193723516633269

Kohe, G. Z., & Purdy, L. G. (2020). Organisational obligations toward athlete transitions: Confronting the bureaucratisation of athlete welfare with an ethics of care. In M. Lang (Ed.), *Routledge handbook of athlete welfare*. Abingdon, UK: Routledge.

McEwan, C., & Goodman, M. K. (2010). Place geography and the ethics of care: Introductory remarks on the geographies of ethics, responsibility and care. *Ethics, Place and Environment, 13*(20), 103–112. https://doi.org/10.1080/13668791003778602

Miles, S. (2017). Stakeholder theory classification: A theoretical and empirical evaluation of definitions. *Journal of Business Ethics, 142*(3), 437–459. https://doi.org/10.1007/s10551-015-2741-y

Oruc, I., & Sarikaya, M. (2011). Normative stakeholder theory in relation to the ethics of care. *Social Responsibility Journal, 7*(3), 381–392.

Pettersen, T. (2011). The ethics of care: Normative structures and empirical implications. *Health Care Analysis, 19*(1), 51–64.

Purdy, L. G., Kohe, G. Z., & Paulauskas, R. (2017). Coaches as sport workers: Professional agency within the employment context of elite European basketball. *Sport, Education and Society, 24*(2), 195–207. https://doi.org/10.1080/13573322.2017.1323201

Purdy, L. G., Purdy, J., & Potrac, P. (2016). Going the distance: A tale of energy, commitment and collaboration. Drew Ferguson, Canada's Para soccer coach. In G. Kohe & D. Peters (Eds.), *High performance (dis)ability sports coaching* (pp. 7–23). Abingdon, UK: Routledge.

Richard, R., Joncheray, H., & Dugas, E. (2017). Disabled sportswomen and gender construction in power football. *International Review for the Sociology of Sport, 52*(1), 61–81. https://doi.org/10.1177/1012690215577398

Ronglan, L. T. (2015). Elite sport in Scandinavian welfare states: Legitimacy under pressure? *International Journal of Sport Policy and Politics, 7*(3), 345–363. https://doi.org/10.1080/19406940.2014.987309

Russo, A., & Perrini, F. (2010). Investigating stakeholder theory and social capital: CSR in large firms and SMEs. *Journal of Business Ethics, 91*(2), 207–221. https://doi.org/10.1007/s10551-009-0079-z

Syndex. (2013). *An analysis of the working conditions of professional sports players financially supported by the European Commission.* Retrieved from www.euathletes.org/wp-content/uploads/2017/06/2013-UNI-An-Analysis-of-Working-Conditions-of-Professional-Sports-Plyers-ilovepdf-compressed-1.pdf

Tronto, J. (1993). *Moral boundaries: A political argument for an ethic of care.* New York: Routledge.

Tshube, T., & Feltz, D. L. (2015). The relationship between dual-career and post-sport career transition among elite athletes in South Africa, Botswana, Namibia and Zimbabwe. *Psychology of Sport and Exercise, 21*, 109–114. https://doi.org/10.1016/j.psychsport.2015.05.005

16
FIGHTING A SYSTEM BUILT TO EXCLUDE QUEER(ING) BODIES

An imperative for athlete wellbeing

Sheree Bekker and Katlego K. Kolanyane-Kesupile

Introduction

Sports organisations are increasingly implementing policies for the regulation of women athletes. These policies, on the surface, appear to be about upholding "fairness" within women's sports. However, when critically interrogated, it has been shown that these policies disempower, disenfranchise, and are ultimately harmful to athlete wellbeing both physically and emotionally. Further, these policies infringe on athletes' human rights. Therefore, it is important to recognise that, whilst organisational policy has the power to be used for good, it does not always have the same outcomes for everyone. In positioning sports organisation policy this way, and comparing and contrasting to the views and experiences of a practitioner in this space, a useful device is created to discuss how the implementation of such policies impact on athlete participation and wellbeing, and what can be done to minimise harm. This chapter thus positions sports organisational policy as a mechanism for (unintentional and intentional) organisational violence, leading to poor outcomes around wellbeing. We discuss the wellbeing implications for athletes themselves and provide, via a human rights framework, practical considerations for those concerned with athlete safety and wellbeing.

PRACTITIONER VOICE

Biological essentialism and the case of Caster Semenya

Some tales seem too dated or warped to write as modern texts, until you live through them. Unfortunately, the Court of Arbitration for Sport (CAS) ruling on the case filed by South African Olympian, Mokgadi Caster Semenya, in favour of the International Association of Athletics Federations (IAAF), didn't shock me. The premise of Semenya having to file a case is nonsensical, as her rights (as an athlete and a human) had been blatantly encroached upon. Yet, you learn something through years of the messy, hands on, and excessively personal work that activists do – you hone your hopeful pessimism.

Upon hearing that Caster was again tackling unfair treatment from the IAAF, my immediate thought was: *here goes another black woman duelling with a system which could have corrected itself ages ago!* While some would prefer to take race out of this conversation, I question what a fitting alternative might be to fill the huge gap left by subcategorising the various discriminations at play. The South African Minister of Sport and Recreation, Tokozile Xasa, rightfully drew parallels between the systematic oppression and segregations of apartheid, and the arbitrary impositions of IAAF on the body, personhood and professional livelihood of an athlete considered to be a national treasure. "Women's bodies, their very identity, their privacy and sense of safety and belonging in the world, are being questioned" observed Xasa, recognising the breadth of matters at hand. Semenya entered professional athletics to compete; only to find a system designed to appreciate bodies like hers if they don't complicate things.

The regulations used against Semenya are not without foundation. Like Eugenics, they are based on the idea that natural biology (not skill) is responsible for athletic greatness, with testosterone centred as the elixir of excellence. However, the scrutiny athletes generally face hasn't been as facetious as that imposed on a black, African woman who sparks questions of femininity – prior to athleticism – in the minds of Western, colonialist custodians. Her "unfeminine" presentation – therefore, lending her to the gaze imposed on the much-afflicted masculine African in the Euro-American universe. Even with the understanding of her sex characteristics being unlike the typical woman, a witch-hunt ensued to try and discredit her abilities to protect the dainty damsels who are gagged as wards of patriarchy.

When protectionists, who believe women exist to be protected by men, and "patriarchy princesses" reared their heads during the furore against the ruling I simply chortled. Some biological essentialists come from unexpected factions. For example, I saw cases where gay men pronounced it obvious that higher testosterone levels should disqualify Caster from competing – not understanding that she is just an androgen-sensitive woman or that her being medicated to compete is violent. While the gay male demographic might seem an easy reference, I do so to show that sometimes people lean on "facts" and ignore the humanity of the situation; the same things used to oppress their predecessors. It was only 40 or so years ago that "facts" qualified male homosexuality as due to producing less testosterone than "real men".

I want to make sure people understand that, in 2019, Caster's case is about more than just whether one of the fastest women living today should be allowed to run; it's about whether athletes should be a science project. The intersecting identities and matters represented by Semenya, in this case, warrant great attention as patriarchy, arbitrary regulation, systemic oppression, and misogyny each plays a role. I have consistently remarked that if we say Caster must regulate her testosterone levels, then there should be complementary arbitrary regulations on male participant levels. *Should* is the operative word here. This will warrant the rejection of males whose natural levels of testosterone are "not sufficient", or those who produce "too much" by these standards. However, with the exponential evolution of knowledge-making can we afford to fixate over arbitrary norms even when we see where progress is leading us?

As a transgender person, I have watched my participation in competitive sport – be it tennis, netball, swimming, dancing or whatever – decrease due to violence from governing institutions and regulations telling people like me that we don't belong. Caster's exclusion strikes at depths I can't quite fully express without trivialisation. However, as of 2018, a young transgender person can join an amateur team aligning with their gender identity; in the 2000s, this barrier stopped me from pursuing national team drafting – understanding the highly binary world of sport. Competing professionally was unfathomable because of its impositions of hyper-performing my gender identity and expression. Caster isn't worried about gender flexing; her issue is a system dictating what makes her woman enough to not be dangerous. This is biological essentialism at its height.

The systemic nature of biological essentialism is difficult to identify unless you're confronted with its blatant oppressions. Were it not for Caster's physique, her internal sex characteristics would not have been brought into question. Were it not for a hate of anything meant to be feminine but isn't soft, there would not have been obsession over Caster's androgen sensitivity. Were it not for holding onto colonial legacies of disciplining black bodies to appear and behave as best pleases the white gaze, Caster's positioning as a strong, fast, black woman wouldn't be seen as double disobedience – since what can be controlled (her skilled body) already disrupts what cannot be tamed (her physiology). It is in this desperate reach for taming her as a person before she is tamed as an athlete, that the institution has resorted to violence against Caster Semenya.

Who is woman, when is she, how is she, what courses through her blood, what do her genes allow and reject – these are all things this ruling against Semenya requires us to talk about. This conversation affects everything within our modern existence if we choose to lean on outdated, unfounded, and violent "biological facts" which don't question institutionally supported stereotypes. Operating within a binary mentality, this scrutiny should be turned on men as well if we are to be equitable. This means that we are still, in 2019, sitting and hypothesising about penises, vaginas, internal testes, and clitorises when we are determining what excellence looks like in an industry we have created. It is almost as if we don't know that we can shift sporting regulations to suit the growth in our collective knowledge.

Institutions should never maintain anything which upholds oppression or self-serving discrimination.

When Nike put its money behind Caster, who is one of their professional ambassadors, to say they support the athlete, it was a sign. The South African government took an official stance on the matter. This begs the question: Is CAS trying to create a biologically moderated and ideal competitive sport industry through this ruling? If so, then I'd like to know when we will address, Olympian, Michael Phelps' mutational advantage situation. From his exceptionally wide arm span, to his short legs, and his body which produces less lactic acid than the average person, thus shortening his recovery time; regulations didn't call for his arms to be shortened or for his body to be injected with extra lactic acid to level the playing field. Phelps achieving the impossible made him inspirational, yet Semenya benefiting from a single hormonal trait makes her abhorrent and in need of regulation?

The problem with accountability is that it's a blanket, not something you fire at a target and forget. If we cover Semenya then we must cover Phelps and everyone else. The lack of sensitivity displayed by IAAF proposing that Semenya run against men if she wants to continue participating in sports at any level, and without restriction, shows how disposable the entity sees people with different sex characteristics to be in the industry and the world. Additionally, it displays the institutionalised racism and misogyny compounded against the bodies and livelihoods of black women in professional sport. Protectionism says to women, and "weak men" (such as the homosexuals): *You'll only be worthy of respect if you can match the prowess of ultimate masculinity.*

The story of Mokgadi Caster Semenya fighting a system built to exclude queer(ing) bodies isn't one I thought would be written in 2019. This is meant to be the stuff of legend, but it seems that biological essentialists refuse to let the world open up and be as marvellous as it is full of diversity. Complexity is what sets the great apart from the good. Running away from this complexity is a sign of laziness; the kind that sets everyone back more than it allows anything to move forward. With such a long history of black women forcing systems to change or implode, Semenya's chapter is loaded and only time will tell how it ends.

SCHOLAR VOICE

The nexus between organisational policy, intentional violence, and athlete wellbeing

Sport is best understood as a complex sociocultural phenomenon consisting of open systems in which people and components interact in different ways (Bekker, 2019; Bekker & Clark, 2016). On this basis, the potential for both positive outcomes (health promotion goals, enjoyment, wellbeing) and negative outcomes (unintentional injury, intentional violence, ill-being) exists. So, whilst sport is often positioned socioculturally as a pedestal for unmitigated (moral) good, sports philosopher Ryall (2016) similarly argues that sport is amoral — it simply presents a multitude of opportunities for people to behave in ways that do good or ways that do bad. In this way, it is important to recognise that, whilst sport has the power to be a force for good, it is not always a space that provides wellbeing outcomes for everyone.

This inherent tension within sport is, usefully and critically, explicated in the preceding narrative by Kolanyane-Kesupile. By following the red thread in what she terms "messy, hands-on and excessively personal" work, we see, in essence, a critical examination of power and how it emerges in sporting policy and practice — ultimately manifesting in negative experiences for some athletes, impacting on both participation rates and wellbeing. Kolanyane-Kesupile rightfully draws parallels between the recognition of the societal importance of "sport as a unification tool" (a force for good) and how this is co-opted into white, western benevolence at the expense of the basic human rights of the disempowered and disenfranchised all in the name of "global development". In this way, we clearly see that whilst sports itself is amoral in essence, the experience thereof can tend towards either polarity, depending on whose point of view is considered. Indeed, the tendency towards framing sport as unmitigated good serves as a powerful tool by which to veil the all too common negative outcomes of sport for some. Teasing out and articulating the experiences of those who have had negative experiences in sport is fundamental to our work in promoting and sustaining athlete wellbeing for all.

This chapter positions sports organisational policy as a mechanism for (unintentional and intentional) organisational violence leading to poor outcomes around wellbeing. The focus will be on discussing the wellbeing implications of certain sports organisation policies for athletes themselves, and providing practical considerations for those concerned with athlete safety and wellbeing in and through interrogating the mechanisms and experiences of organisational policy, procedure, and practice through a human rights framework.

Understanding organisational policy as a potential mechanism for intentional violence

The International Olympic Committee consensus statement on non-accidental violence (harassment and abuse) describes several forms of intentional violence that occur in sport settings (Mountjoy et al., 2016), elsewhere categorised as individual, relational, and organisational forms of harm (Mountjoy,

Rhind, Tiivas, & Leglise, 2015). Whilst individual and relational violence, such as sexual harassment and abuse, have received much research and policy attention in sport settings, *organisational* violence remains comparatively under-acknowledged and under-represented in discussions and actions concerning athlete safety and wellbeing. How is this so? And, importantly, why does this matter so much?

Organisational violence refers to sports settings in which normalised abuse cultures exist, with consequences such as medical mismanagement and systematic doping. For the purposes of this chapter, it is useful to focus on the *organisational policies* that have, in effect, unintentional (and sometimes intentional, as we will come to see) outcomes that may be discriminatory and harmful to athletes, particularly disenfranchised athletes who are specifically disempowered via those policies. In this way, it is important to understand both normative (relating to the culture/ethos) and constitutive (structurally embedded) issues in organisational policy and its outcomes to fully appreciate how organisational violence emerges (Mountjoy et al., 2015, 2016), and how athlete wellbeing is affected.

In much the same way as sport was positioned earlier, understanding sports *organisational policy* as a complex sociocultural phenomenon consisting of open systems in which people and components interact in different ways is useful for our purposes too. On this basis, the potential for both positive (doping control, rules of the game, wellbeing) and negative (corruption, intentional violence, ill-being) outcomes exists.

Nowhere is this more apparent (yet simultaneously hidden and insidious) than in the case of the IAAF eligibility regulation for "women with differences of sex development" (*the Regulation* for the purposes of this chapter). On the 1st of May 2019, the CAS, a private tribunal for the purpose of handling disputes between athletes and sports organisations, handed down its ruling in the case of Caster Semenya and Athletics South Africa versus the IAAF (CAS, 2019). *The ruling* upheld the Regulation, which means that certain women participating in certain IAAF events (of distances from 400 m to 1 mile) must now medically maintain a testosterone level of 5 nanomoles per litre of blood (5 nmol/L) or below to compete.

This matters because, as Kolanyane-Kesupile writes of these organisational policies, these are "arbitrary impositions made by the IAAF on the body, personhood, and professional livelihood of an athlete". Further, these organisational policies infringe on the human rights of athletes, as highlighted in the words of Xasa, per Kolanyane-Kesupile earlier, in that "women's bodies, their very identity, their privacy and sense of safety and belonging in the world are being questioned". Indeed, Semenya herself has stated that these regulations are harmful both mentally and physically (see opening quote).

Wellbeing is conceptualised by the World Health Organization as a human right, requiring complete emotional, social, and physical wellbeing. It then follows that, for athletes who are disempowered for their very being and disenfranchised of their human rights, wellbeing cannot exist. As such, this type of organisational policy "mobilises a version of "fairness" that is a privilege reserved for those with favoured racial, gender, sexual, class or national status" (Karkazis & Jordan-Young, 2018, p. 46). In order for full athlete wellbeing to be achieved for all rather than being reserved for a privileged majority, this type of organisational policy must be examined for its intended and unintended outcomes, and ultimately, I will show, be dismantled if we are to move forward towards sport as a safe space enabling wellbeing for everyone.

The IAAF participation regulation for women with differences of sex development: an overview and why this case matters

Is discrimination ever necessary and justified? When can a woman not compete with other women? How do we define what is "fair" in sport, and for whom? How does sport respond to a wider world that is increasingly recognising and upholding the expression of humanity beyond the (outdated) sex binary? These are questions that athletes, practitioners, and scholars in sport settings are increasingly grappling with (Karkazis & Jordan-Young, 2018; Mitra, 2014; Pielke Jr & Pape, 2019).

These questions are at the core of the contestation of *the Regulation*, which has the intended outcome of regulating the participation only of women who have testosterone levels of over 5 nmol/L, and whose bodies can ostensibly use that testosterone better than other women can (women with differences of sex development, per the IAAF). The IAAF argue that this is necessary because these women have a significant performance advantage. However, this apparent performance advantage is not quite as clear-cut as it may seem on the surface and has been called into question for scientific, medical ethics, and human rights reasons (Tannenbaum & Bekker, 2019).

Firstly, from a scientific standpoint, there is no direct, causal relationship between natural testosterone levels and sports performance (Tannenbaum & Bekker, 2019). Secondly, from a medical ethics perspective, there exists no valid laboratory test to determine the degree of sensitivity to testosterone. This means that current approaches (including under *the Regulation*) make use of "physical, gynaecological, and radiological imaging to determine physical signs (such as an enlarged clitoris) as a proxy for testosterone sensitivity. However, this approach is not reliable, liable to false interpretation and subjectivity, and widely viewed as inappropriate and an invasion of privacy" (Tannenbaum & Bekker, 2019). Indeed, the World Medical Association (WMA, 2019) has called for *the Regulation* to be withdrawn, stating that this policy "constitute(s) a flagrant discrimination based on the genetic variation of female athletes and is contrary to international medical ethics and human rights standards". Thirdly, a number of organisations, including the United Nations Human Rights Council (UNHRC, 2019), have condemned *the Regulation* on human rights grounds. Indeed, despite the final ruling, the CAS panel itself unanimously concluded *the Regulation* to be "prima facie discriminatory since they impose differential treatment based on protected characteristics" (CAS, 2019). Thus, Semenya has appealed her case for the withdrawal of *the Regulation* to the Swiss Federal Supreme Court (the outcome of which is still pending at the time of writing – October 2019).

A final key concern about *the Regulation* is its status as a "living document", meaning that this regulation can evolve, and therefore this CAS ruling does not constitute an accountability measure or precedent against any future update or change. Indeed, this has already happened. During the course of the 2019 CAS hearing, the IAAF shifted the goalposts in changing the wording of the policy to focus exclusively on the outdated term "46XY females" (a medical oversimplification and thus misnomer that was not specified in the 2018 iteration of the policy, likely compounded by issues of medical confidentiality given the small number of athletes who may be part of this group). This places the focus of this regulation on an even smaller group of women with differences in sex development. Further, it is of concern that this shift now potentially sets the scene for what the CAS and IAAF term "necessary discrimination" against women who are transgender and their future regulation in sport. Indeed, this is already the case in the International Olympic participation regulation for transgender women (in which the arbitrary testosterone cut-off point remains at 10 nmol/l).

Yet, when we talk of "necessary discrimination", it is important to ask what this meant to, and feels like, for athletes who are affected by this policy. Here, Kolanyane-Kesupile's account is instructive. She writes, as a transgender person, that "I'd pushed the idea of competing professionally out of my mind due to a full understanding of the complex space of having to perform my gender-identity and gender expression in the highly binary world of sport". In other words, organisational policies such as *the Regulation* are, in effect, actually discouraging participation in sport. Further, for those such as Semenya who continued participation in elite sport despite, and whilst fighting, such discriminatory and harmful policies, details of related practices and procedures affecting mental and physical wellbeing have now emerged (see German broadcaster ARD documentary: www.youtube.com/watch?v=Af4ClrCL3D0).

Policy as a mechanism for potential organisational violence

Mountjoy and colleagues (Mountjoy et al., 2015) state "many actions in sport, while not violent per se, could be construed as violent in many ways and for many reasons" (p. 884). As such, as stated earlier, and as Kolanyane-Kesupile explains in this chapter, it is useful to consider organisational regulations, such as *the Regulation*, as a mechanism that can have violent outcomes that impact disproportionately on disempowered athletes. To best understand this more fully, it is important to note "the cultural context of [intentional violence] is rooted in discrimination based on power differentials across a range of social and personal factors" (Mountjoy et al., 2016, p. 1019).

Through public outcries of gender and race discrimination, the violence inherent in *the Regulation* has been shown to involve reinforcement of stereotypical views of testosterone-driven male hegemony or "T talk" and exposure of fatal flaws in the development and scientific evidence underpinning *the Regulation* itself (Karkazis & Jordan-Young, 2018). And, whilst understanding the scientific, medical ethics, and human rights concerns is vital in this case, there is also a need to move from an individual and interpersonal lens of organisational policy to a sociocultural and structural one. Understanding organisational policy (such as *the Regulation*), including its development and implementation, as value-laden assists in better understanding how it emerges in context. It is important to note that policies, essentially, exist to serve the organisations that they are developed within for purposes of sports governance. Athletes, on the other hand, are positioned by these organisations as commodities and sit at the intersection of sport and human rights (WPA, 2017).

Therefore, the example of *the Regulation* shows that it is imperative to understand – from both a personal and professional stance – not only the intentional but also the unintentional outcomes of policy, including the ways in which regulations may problematically entrench existing power relations (Karkazis & Jordan-Young, 2018), and potentially breach human rights, so that we may best support athletes who may be disproportionally affected by them. The Universal Declaration of Player Rights (WPA, 2017) reminds that an athlete's right to participate in sport cannot be limited by gender (or any other identity-related factor, including sex). So, in this way, it is helpful to consider and understand both this history and unintentional outcomes of policy – including imperial, racial, heteronormative, and gendered power divisions – and are ultimately violent in their disregard for human dignity. Indeed, in line with what Karkazis and Jordan-Young (2018) have shown, Kolanyane-Kesupile correctly identifies that organisational policies such as *the Regulation* "displays the institutionalised racism and misogyny compounded against bodies and livelihoods of black women in professional sport". This basic understanding alone goes a long way to supporting affected athletes and their individual wellbeing because upholding human rights for one is dependent on upholding them for all.

Practitioners should be mindful that just because a policy exists does not mean that it is evidence-based, human rights considered, or even ethically sound. Understanding this – rather than tacitly assuming benevolence on the part of sports organisations – lies at the crux of athlete allyship for practitioners. Herein, an important theory–practice gap emerges in supporting athletes and their wellbeing. We recognise, in that, as Kolanyane-Kesupile writes "institutions should never maintain anything which upholds oppression or self-serving discrimination", particularly as this contributes to athlete ill-being in the sporting context, as shown earlier. Yet, in practice, sports organisations do and are perpetuating oppression and discrimination on a global scale. Better support for individual athlete wellbeing means that we need to not only stand up for the privileged majority, but that we also need to specifically and intentionally dismantle and rebuild the sporting system to be more inclusive for all. Such true inclusivity has been shown to provide better wellbeing outcomes for all.

Insights, considerations, and applied recommendations

Wellbeing in sport settings can only be achieved if the whole is considered as more than the sum of its parts (Bekker, 2019; Bekker & Clark, 2016). Intentional violence via policy in sport settings at the organisational level is a concerning, insidious, and often under-recognised issue, particularly given the powerful systems and structures that underpin it. Thus, the prevention of intentional (organisational) violence, and ultimately the promotion of wellbeing in sport is a complex issue that requires an interdisciplinary approach, and collaboration across and between professional platforms and athletes themselves. This will have much greater impact on athlete wellbeing in terms of recognition that the broader structural issues – including *enhancement* of athlete wellbeing – are essentially and primarily, human rights issues. Therefore, it is useful to turn to human rights literature for best practice when determining effective violence prevention and wellbeing promotion strategies.

The "Children's Rights in the Sports Context" white paper, from Terre des Hommes and UNICEF, with additional input from the Mega Sporting Events Platform (MSE Platform) and endorsed by the Institute for Human Rights and Business (IHRB), states that "since children are more vulnerable than adults and need specific support to guarantee their rights are upheld . . . bodies should adopt an explicit child rights focus" (MSE, 2017, p. 5). Further, it states that the rights accorded in the UN Convention on the Rights of the Child (UN, n.d.) are central to the process of prevention and that these should be incorporated into all policies and procedures (MSE, 2017). This should apply to sport at all levels and is reflected in the World Players Association's new "World Player Rights Policy" that emphasises the needs for explicit recognition that players "sit at the intersection of sport and human rights" (WPA, 2017, p. 1). Championing human rights in the governance of sports bodies thus means that there is a need to not merely "do no harm", but rather that *active* prevention of harm and promotion of wellbeing is key (MSE, 2017).

How is this best achieved? First, an explicit human rights perspective must be embedded into organisational systems, policies, and procedures (MSE, n.d.). This means that, "overall, appropriate structures and policies need to be developed for preventing, reporting, and responding appropriately to violence in . . . sport" (UNICEF, 2010, p. vii). Implementation, in line with best practice and international norms (including the UN Guidance on Business and Human Rights), must consist of four steps: (1) commit and embed, (2) identify risks, (3) take action, and (4) communicate (MSE, n.d.). Similarly, this has elsewhere been conceptualised as: capacity building, implementation, accountability structures, monitoring processes, and enforcement procedures (MSE, 2017). This approach is further mirrored in the new IOC Framework for safeguarding athletes and other participants from harassment and abuse in sport "Games-time Framework" which endorses a similar education, policy, and procedure process (available at www.olympic.org/athlete365/safeguarding/). This, crucially, mirrors much of the above with regards to the minimum standards for violence prevention and wellbeing promotion best practice.

It is thus clear that, at minimum, an *explicit, active focus* on (unintended) organisational violence, rather than ad hoc or responsive measures, is key to prevention and wellbeing response. Further, that this focus must be accountable, supplemented with education and awareness-raising, and monitored for effectiveness. Indeed, "good intentions and written policies mean nothing if they are not translated into action" (UNICEF, 2010, p. 21). Further, good intentions and written policies can have violent effects if human rights are not explicitly embedded into an organisation at every level.

Recommendations for future research, policy, and practice

1. The lack of recognition for, and understanding of, organisational forms of intentional violence in sport settings remains a major gap, which has implications for athlete protection. Develop a literacy of, and the skill to critically appraise, organisational policy, rules, and regulations for both

intended and *unintended* mechanisms and outcomes that may affect, disempower, and/or disenfranchise athletes.

a Evaluate policy and procedure to assess the ways in which these interventions "work" in real-world practice (including problematic and violent mechanisms that may be activated).
b Assess the ways in which policy and procedure are experienced by those who are the subjects thereof, and incorporate their views and voices into the development and implementation of any policy (see Charlton (2000) "nothing about us without us" – lessons from disability rights activists).
c Advocate for more research into the unintentional consequences of policy, including the ways in which safety is gendered and racialised in such a way that it entrenches problematic power relations.
d Move from interpersonal lenses to understanding the cultural and structural mechanisms of intentional violence.
e Understand policy as value-laden (and not necessarily only positive or even neutral) to better understand how it emerges in context – simply because policies and procedures exist, does not mean that they are evidence-based, or even effective (Bekker & Finch, 2016; Bekker, Paliadelis, & Finch, 2017).
f Develop a practitioner and organisational focus on embedding explicit, active human rights, rather than relying solely on passive or assumed basic knowledge.

2 Develop a critical lens that accounts explicitly for characteristics of differentiation, including age, gender, sex, sexuality, race, ethnicity, disability, socio-economic status, country, and region (Mountjoy et al., 2016; UNICEF, 2010) to more effectively understand how organisational policy has different outcomes for different athletes. Taking a human rights lens, it is imperative to uphold and advocate for the rights of minority and disempowered groups.
3 Develop processes for meaningful consultation with athletes and their representatives as key stakeholders, in order to include the athlete voice in all decision-making and policy development and implementation. Support and uphold athlete voice as integral to athlete safety and wellbeing.
4 Follow the lead of key organisations working in this space (World Players Association, United Nations Human Rights Council, World Medical Association, etc.).

Rather than ignoring or writing out complex questions about organisational violence and athlete safety, it is imperative that we look to key examples that help us understand the complexities of sports settings, and how to move forward in and through them, whilst upholding the dignity and human rights of all. Dignity relies on full, enfranchised wellbeing. This, in turn, relies on an explicit, active approach to wellbeing which involves evaluating policy and procedure to better embed and account for education, transparency, accountability, enforcement, redress, and remedy. A human rights-based approach focuses on outcomes and on how outcomes can be achieved, while – importantly – taking into account the reality of athletes' lives.

A rights-based approach should advance the realisation of human rights, respect human rights standards and principles and strengthen the capacities of athletes [rights bearers] and sporting institutions [rights holders] (McConnell & Smith, 2018). It holds that we must look beyond a single organisational policy or the athlete alone, to better understand the systems and structures that enable violence and ill-being – including how best to influence them for better prevention and wellbeing outcomes. A human rights-based approach to research and practice should ensure that the process does no harm.

Sport doesn't happen in a societal vacuum, and this is ultimately about more than sport alone. As Kolanyane-Kesupile writes, this "is about whether athletes should be a science project". As practitioners and academics, we need to take our supportive lead from the athletes themselves in standing up and advocating for their human rights, rather than implicitly standing by whilst athletes are reduced to scientific components. Sport, and this world, will be better for it.

References

Bekker, S. (2019). Shuffle methodological deck chairs or abandon theoretical ship? The complexity turn in injury prevention. *Injury Prevention*, 25(2), 80–82. http://doi.org/10.1136/injuryprev-2018-042905

Bekker, S., & Clark, A. M. (2016). Bringing complexity to sports injury prevention research: From simplification to explanation. *British Journal of Sports Medicine*, 50(24), 1489. http://doi.org/10.1136/bjsports-2016-096457

Bekker, S., & Finch, C. F. (2016). Too much information? A document analysis of sport safety resources from key organisations. *BMJ Open*, 6(5), e010877. http://doi.org/10.1136/bmjopen-2015-010877

Bekker, S., Paliadelis, P., & Finch, C. F. (2017). The translation of sports injury prevention and safety promotion knowledge: Insights from key intermediary organisations. *Health Research Policy and Systems*, 15(1), 25. https://doi.org/10.1186/s12961-017-0189-5

CAS. (2019). *CAS Arbitration: Caster Semenya, Athletics South Africa (ASA) and International Association of Athletics Federations (IAAF): Decision.* Retrieved from www.tas-cas.org/fileadmin/user_upload/Media_Release_Semenya_ASA_IAAF_decision.pdf

Charlton, J. I. (2000). *Nothing about us without us: Disability oppression and empowerment.* Berkley, CA: University of California Press.

Karkazis, K., & Jordan-Young, R. M. (2018). The powers of testosterone: Obscuring race and regional bias in the regulation of women athletes. *Feminist Formations*, 30(2), 1–39. http://doi.org/10.1353/ff.2018.0017.

McConnell, L., & Smith, R. (2018). *Research Methods in Human Rights*. Abingdon, UK: Routledge.

Mitra, P. (2014). The untold stories of female athletes with intersex variations in India. In J. Hargreaves & E. Anderson (Eds.), *The handbook of sport, gender and sexuality* (pp. 384–394). Abingdon, UK: Routledge.

Mountjoy, M., Brackenridge, C., Arrington, M., Blauwet, C., Carska-Sheppard, A., Fasting, K., et al. (2016). International Olympic Committee consensus statement: Harassment and abuse (non-accidental violence) in sport. *British Journal of Sports Medicine, 50*(17), 1019–1029. http://doi.org/10.1136/bjsports-2016-096121

Mountjoy, M., Rhind, D. J. A., Tiivas, A., & Leglise, M. (2015). Safeguarding the child athlete in sport: A review, a framework and recommendations for the IOC youth athlete development model. *British Journal of Sports Medicine, 49*(13), 883–886. http://doi.org/10.1136/bjsports-2015-094619

MSE. (2017). *Children's rights in the sports context*. Mega-Sporting Events Platform for Human Rights. Retrieved from https://sportaide.ca/wp-content/uploads/2019/01/Childrens_Rights_in_the_Sports_Context_Jan._2017.pdf

MSE. (n.d.). *Mega-sporting events platform for human rights*. Mega-Sporting Events. Retrieved from www.uniglobalunion.org/sites/default/files/imce/about_the_mega-sporting_events_platform_for_human_rights.pdf

Pielke Jr., R., & Pape, M. (2019). Science, sport, sex, and the case of Caster Semenya. *Issues in Science and Technology, 36*(1), 56–63.

Ryall, E. (2016). *Philosophy of sport: Key questions*. London: Bloomsbury.

Tannenbaum, C., & Bekker, S. (2019). Sex, gender, and sports. *The BMJ, 364*. http://doi.org/10.1136/bmj.l1120

UN. (n.d.). *UN convention on the rights of the child*. United Nations. Retrieved from https://downloads.unicef.org.uk/wp-content/uploads/2010/05/UNCRC_united_nations_convention_on_the_rights_of_the_child.pdf?_ga=2.234199134.1758838187.1566288625-1410744340.1566288625

UNHRC. (2019). *Promotion and protection of all human rights, civil, political, economic, social and cultural rights, including the right to development: 40/ . . . Elimination of discrimination against women and girls in sport: 40 elimination of discrimination against women and girls in sport*. United Nations Human Rights Council. Retrieved from https://undocs.org/A/HRC/40/L.10/Rev.1

UNICEF. (2010). *Protecting children from violence in sport: A review with a focus on industrialized countries*. UNICEF. Retrieved from www.unicef-irc.org/publications/pdf/violence_in_sport.pdf

WMA. (2019, April 25). *WMA urges physicians not to implement IAAF rules on classifying women athletes*. World Medical Association. Retrieved from www.wma.net/news-post/wma-urges-physicians-not-to-implement-iaaf-rules-on-classifying-women-athletes/

WPA. (2017). *Universal Declaration of Player Rights*. World Players Association. Retrieved from www.uniglobalunion.org/sites/default/files/imce/world_players_udpr_1-page_0.pdf

17
THE ROLE OF ATHLETIC IDENTITY FORECLOSURE IN THE DEVELOPMENT OF POOR ATHLETE MENTAL HEALTH

J. D. DeFreese and Jeni Shannon

Introduction

Within the demanding environment of elite sport, athletes experience a continuum of mental health outcomes ranging from wellbeing to poor mental health. This chapter reviews targeted outcomes of poor athlete mental health including depression, anxiety, and related outcomes, with a critical focus on the relevance of athletic identity to their occurrence. Effective treatment of these outcomes is discussed via a narrative of representative athlete cases of poor athlete mental health based on the experiences of Dr Jeni Shannon, a sport psychologist who works with American collegiate student-athletes. The relevance of athletic identity to the diagnosis, treatment, and prognosis of poor athlete mental health is described with the goal of bridging the gap between theory/research and practice. Relevant theories of athlete identity development and mental health showcase empirical evidence of identity foreclosure as a unique risk factor for poor athlete mental health within the social environment of competitive sport.

PRACTITIONER VOICE

Representing athlete poor mental health treatment case studies

I have been a licenced counselling and sport psychologist for seven years, primarily in the collegiate setting in the United States. I am employed by a Division I University under the Department of Sports Medicine. I have found that identity is deeply connected with wellbeing in cases where injury or performance threatens athlete identity, as well as in cases of transition. I would like to share with the reader two cases in which these specific factors

---

DOI: 10.4324/9780429287923-17

are at play, and how the intersection of identity and sport was significantly related to the athletes' mental health. I have omitted identifying information to protect the confidentiality of these athletes. In sharing these cases, I will describe the presenting concerns and diagnoses along with discussion of the treatment process, interventions, and treatment approaches. Specific therapeutic approaches will be expanded upon in Table 17.1 at the conclusion of the chapter.

The first athlete I will discuss is Cassandra, an 18-year-old Caucasian female, in her first year at the university. She was a scholarship athlete on the swim team from a middle-class intact family from the northeastern United States. She was self-referred to sport psychology after her first semester, noticing an increase in anxiety-related symptoms and struggling with adjustment.

At our first session, Cassandra presented with anxious mood and symptoms including excessive worry, difficulty controlling worry, racing thoughts, rumination, insomnia, and low self-worth. She noted that these symptoms had been present since she was 16-years-old, intensifying since arriving at college. Her anxiety appeared to be generalised but exacerbated by her sport experience. As a result, I diagnosed her with Generalised Anxiety Disorder. In weekly appointments, we explored her experiences as a collegiate athlete. She experienced overwhelming anxiety related to comparisons to other athletes, acknowledging a pressure to be "the best freshman." We identified a strong tendency to base self-worth on performance and feedback from others. As we deepened this exploration, she became emotional recognising how much of her identity was consumed by swimming and contingent on success.

As Cassandra struggled with performance, it became clear how much it threatened her identity. I introduced ways to place less value on outcome and more on the process and values that lead to outcomes. We engaged in values clarification, in line with Acceptance and Commitment Therapy (ACT). She embraced this and focused more on aligning with her values, in contrast to only her identity as an athlete, leading to some improvement in symptoms.

In the following preseason, Cassandra sustained an injury, limiting training significantly. She experienced a notable increase in anxiety as she dealt with the unknown timeline and fears of another disappointing season. I recognised the experience of being injured threatened her athletic identity again. She worried that she would never be the swimmer she once was and would be seen as a failure by others.

We resumed much of the work from the previous year but in greater depth. We explored ways to find value outside of sport, such as volunteering, working in a research lab, and creative endeavours, which expanded her identity in a meaningful way. We engaged in self-worth and compassion work, though a powerful narrative therapy intervention of writing letters to her younger self. I guided her through the narrative therapy process of re-authoring her story allowing her to internalise an empowering version of the story.

I saw significant improvement as Cassandra was able to internalise her values, sense of worth, and expanded identity. Understandably, she struggled at points throughout the season, particularly in missing competitions and not accomplishing her goals. Despite these disappointments, I could see that Cassandra had developed a stronger sense of self, increased compassion, and a decreased reliance on external validation. At the end of the season, Cassandra reflected on being proud of how she handled the challenging season. She still embraced and valued her athletic identity but was able to expand and see worth and value in many ways. By the conclusion of our work together that year, her symptoms were no longer debilitating or consuming. I was encouraged that she continued to value her athletic career but shifted focus to the process, her values, and effort, more so than outcomes. I believe that she will benefit from ongoing counselling to maintain changes, reinforce what is working well, and strengthen her self-worth.

The second athlete I will share is Jerome, a 22-year-old African American male in his fifth year. He was a scholarship athlete on the American football team. He was from an intact family of low socio-economic status in the southeastern United States. Jerome had moderate athletic success, but below his expectations, due to chronic injuries.

Jerome was referred by his team physician after presenting with heightened distress and symptoms of anxiety. When I first sat down with Jerome, he presented with a high level of distress and worry, primarily related to feeling overwhelmed and stating "no one is helping me." He shared a frustration with his football experience, having been injured the entire time he had been at the university. I initially diagnosed him with Generalised Anxiety Disorder.

As we began to meet weekly, clearer depressive symptoms emerged, more prominent than anxiety, and I questioned my initial diagnosis. He described long-standing depressed mood, feeling sad and empty, anhedonia, fatigue and low energy, feelings of worthlessness, difficulty concentrating, and social withdrawal. Based on this information, I changed his diagnosis to Major Depressive Disorder with Anxious Distress. Early on, I introduced the intervention of behavioural activation focusing on identifying rewarding activities, starting with the most manageable, and addressing barriers. This was helpful in coming out of the low energy and low motivation state and a first step in identifying what was meaningful to him.

As we worked together, he reflected on a struggle with self-worth and value related to disappointing football performances and continued injuries. We explored the role of athletic identity, threatened by injury and underperforming. He shared frustration at "only" being seen as a football player, especially by his father. We identified how this connected to feelings of dysphoria and worthlessness.

He recognised that his family's emphasis on sport was adding pressure and stress. The sense that his family valued him for his athletic performance increased his belief that football defined who he was. He recognised that this created distress and feelings of worthlessness when things were not going well. I helped him process the decision to set more boundaries with his family. He was eventually able to communicate how he was feeling and have less of a football focus in their relationship.

After two months, Jerome made the decision to medically retire. He was tearful in expressing how depressed he was at times, recognizing that he didn't realise how sad he was until he felt the relief from the medical retirement. I inquired about what had prevented that awareness for so long, and he reflected on the role of athletic and family culture in not opening up sooner and continuing to "fight past the point that was wise." Jerome reflected on his experience of feeling "weak" and alone in his struggles, fuelled by athletic and masculine culture. I pointed out his tendency to turn to anger and frustration rather than sadness, a common presentation for men who are depressed. He acknowledged the problems this had caused, recognising that emotions were never modelled for him, especially by other men. This led to meaningful exploration related to his identity as an African American man.

At this time, I referred Jerome to the athletic department's support group for athlete medical retirement. This support-based group, facilitated by myself, is open to student-athletes going through medical retirement, addressing themes such as emotional reactions, lifestyle changes, and identity. He benefitted from opening up and connecting with others going through similar struggles. I witnessed the group as a powerful avenue for him to practise openness and vulnerability, as well as connect with emotions. He acknowledged feeling less alone after this experience.

As we continued to meet individually, we processed his retirement and shifted away from athletic identity, engaging in values-focused work from an ACT approach, and meaning-making from an Existential Therapy approach. Jerome was able to connect more deeply with values, explore identity related to his career, and find meaning in helping others. At the conclusion of treatment, I saw significant improvement in Jerome's mood, symptoms, and functioning. When he graduated, he had a stronger sense of self-worth and identity beyond football. He had grieved the loss of sport/athletic identity and found acceptance. He increased his openness and connection with others, leading to more meaningful relationships and support. He recognised the role athletic identity played, with the intersection of being an African American man experiencing mental health issues. He embraced his desire to help others and chose to engage in outreach efforts in the athletic department to share his story. At termination, his depression was in remission, and he was hopeful about the future. I shared with him the importance of remaining attuned to his mental health and recognising if depression symptoms return to seek support early.

SCHOLAR VOICE

Athlete mental health

A recent dialogue has begun in American athletics concerning the mental health experiences of athletes. For example, the recent, well-publicised mental health experience of basketball player Kevin Love has highlighted the experience of anxiety (Love, 2018). While other athletes, such as American collegiate lacrosse athlete Makaela Mason (Mason, 2018), have showcased the important mental health experiences of depression, anxiety, and suicidal ideation. These inspirational stories have shed the light on the important public health issues of athlete mental health, situating clinical mental health concerns within the holistic spectrum of the overall athlete health and wellbeing. Moreover, these high-profile athlete stories have influenced many other athletes to acknowledge their own mental health concerns and seek out support and treatment resources to improve their health, wellbeing, and performance. The overlapping thread on many athlete mental health experiences is the role that athletic identity plays in their occurrence, recognition, and treatment. Identifying strongly as an athlete has the potential to help athletes focus on spending countless hours training their bodies and minds to perform at the highest level and invest thoroughly in the athletic experience. However, this may also come at the expense of other aspects of their identities (as per the case studies; academics, social). That potential for athletic identity to influence athlete mental health is the focus of this chapter. Specifically, we will further explore these issues with a focus on research and theory as well as providing explicit links to how the theory aligns with the earlier case studies of Cassandra and Jerome, both of which illustrate real-life scenarios in which a focus on athletic identity was relevant to the successful treatment of poor athlete mental health.

Within the demanding environment of elite sport, athletes experience a continuum of mental health outcomes from good (adaptive) to poor (maladaptive) mental health. Outcomes of poor athlete mental health may include, but certainly are not limited to, depression and anxiety as well as suicidal ideation (a common presentation of poor mental health). Additionally, other important sub-clinical mental health outcomes such as burnout are also germane to the environment of competitive athletics (Eklund & DeFreese, 2015; Gould & Whitley, 2009). Within high-performance sport, athletes have the opportunity to experience extreme positive outcomes of joy, engagement, and accomplishment. However, the intensive training requirement, mental toil, and social pressure and notoriety of elite sport also represent key stressors that necessitate coping resources so as not to potentially overwhelm the psychological resources of the individual athlete (Balk et al., 2018; Smith, 1986). Factors, like athletic identity, which may impact sport-based stress responses do not cause maladaptive mental health symptoms or experiences but do represent key risk factors germane to the range of athlete mental health experiences on the continuum. Therefore, overidentifying with the athlete role represents an additional risk factor predicting poor athlete mental health outcomes such as the anxiety and depression experienced by Cassandra and Jerome, respectively.

Athlete identity

Though an in-depth discussion of identity development is beyond the scope of this chapter, a brief discussion is important to best explain the rationale for athletic identity as a risk factor for poor athlete mental health development/exacerbation as well as its relevance as a particular area of therapeutic intervention for mental health treatment in athlete populations. Marsh (1990) described identity as part of one's overall self-concept (i.e. self-worth). All individuals, including athletes, gauge perceptions of their self-concept by rating themselves on individual life aspects including academic, social, emotional, and physical among others (Shavelson, Hubner, & Stanton, 1976). Individuals consider these multidimensional aspects of the "self" based on their own perceptions of importance, not needing to rate all areas equally (Marsh, Richards, Johnson, Roche, & Tremayne, 1994). Notably, athletes may be prone to consider aspects of the physical self highly in terms of its impact on their overall self-concept, making constructs such as athlete identity very important to their overall mental health. For example, athletic identity was salient to both the aforementioned cases of Cassandra (a key contributor to her anxiety) and Jerome (a moderator of the impact of injury and performance on his depression) warranting a historical overview of identity in the context of completive sport.

Athletic identity has been defined as "the degree to which an individual identifies with the athlete role" (Brewer, Van Raalte, & Linder, 1993, p. 237). Building on the aforementioned work on the self, research has shown athlete identity to be associated with mental health outcomes including notable research and theory-based examples of depression and burnout (Black & Smith, 2007; Brewer, 1993; Coakley, 1992). Accordingly, the degree to which an athlete identifies with their physical (i.e. athletic) self has direct implications for how poor mental health risk factors, such as stress, training load, social relationships, and non-sport stressors, may influence how an athlete experiences mental health along the mental health continuum of experience (National Collegiate Athletic Association, 2018). This continuum will now be reviewed in more detail prior to further description of how identity is both theoretically/conceptually and empirically supported as a factor salient to athlete mental health.

Mental health continuum

Keyes (2002) describes mental health as a continuum ranging from poor mental health (i.e. marked distress, serious impairment), to emotional problems/concerns (i.e. ranging from moderate distress affecting functioning to mild distress involving temporary impairment), to good mental health (i.e. wellbeing, thriving, resilience). Using depression as an example, poor mental health would involve an experience that is chronic and results in despair, sadness, worthlessness, hopelessness, and/or social isolation with potential suicidal ideation. This experience would also include impairment in functioning in significant areas of the individual's life, for example, school or work, sport, or relationships. As an example, Jerome's depression manifested in sport performance/injury rehabilitation decrements as well as adversely impacting his social relationships beyond sport (i.e. with his father). Emotional problems/concerns would involve a similar constellation of depressive symptoms occurring either more often than not (moderate depressive symptoms of lower intensity/severity) or very generally/minimally in impact (i.e. symptoms causing only mild distress). Finally, good mental health would be exemplified by normal fluctuations in mood as well as potentially positive psychological outcomes such as thriving and/or successfully coping with sport-based stressors or adversities.

This continuum is particularly important in sport where athletes, coaches, and/or parents may have misperceptions about mental health as a potential binary outcome (poor or good mental health only) as well as that poor mental health signifies a lack of "mental toughness". These misconceptions may impact these social actors' abilities not only to recognise poor mental health but also to help an athlete progress towards good mental health, regardless of where they fall on the continuum (Bauman, 2016). To consider this from the vantage of the discipline of positive psychology (Seligman & Csikszentmihalyi, 2000), one does not have to be experiencing a diagnosable poor mental health outcome to benefit from therapeutic or interventional strategies to improve one's psychological wellbeing. For example, both Cassandra and Jerome were advised that they would benefit from continued treatment even after clinical diagnostic symptoms resolved as a means to promote outcomes of good mental health. Ultimately, a more expansive and fluid view of mental health and help-seeking (Gulliver, Griffiths, & Christensen, 2012), combined with a deeper understanding of the potential impact of athletic identity on athlete mental health outcomes, may be particularly useful in sport. Specifically, this view may aid clinicians in their best practice efforts to recognise, diagnose, and treat the poor mental health outcomes of athletes such as Cassandra (anxiety) and Jerome (depression).

Athlete identity foreclosure and poor mental health

The intersection of athlete identity and its potential impact on poor mental health outcomes are linked to the concept of identity foreclosure. Identity foreclosure has been described as an athlete foregoing other facets of identity (i.e. academic, social relationships) to focus almost solely on the athletic experience in terms of evaluating self-complexity (Coakley, 1992). Potential adverse outcomes of identity foreclosure include a potential negative impact on interpersonal relations, performance and/or negative influence on one's self-worth and/or poor mental health outcomes such as burnout and depression, and post-career physical activity levels (Coakley, 1992; Reifsteck, Gill, & Labban, 2016). Accordingly, the potential exists for athletes who identify strongly and potentially singularly (i.e. obtaining a higher percentage of, or one's entire self-worth via sport) to be at higher risk to experience adverse psychological health outcomes in sport. As an example, Cassandra drew a large amount of her self-worth from her athletic performance/accomplishments, which impacted her experiences of anxiety. One exemplary, qualitative study also found evidence of athlete identity to be positively associated with mental and physical outcomes following a serious sport injury (i.e. major sport-based stressor) in a sample of 12 amateur and semi-professional athletes (Podlog & Eklund, 2006). Additionally, the extant theory posits higher levels of athletic identity to be positively associated with other stress-based negative outcomes for athletes (Smith, 1986; Weise-Bjornstal, Smith, Shaffer, & Morrey, 1998). However, results in this area have been mixed suggesting the athletic identity-mental health relationship to be complex (Green & Weinberg, 2001). This overlap between athlete identity foreclosure and athlete experiences along the mental health continuum represents a key conceptual take-home with important implications for clinicians serving athlete mental health needs. As a result, athletic identity may represent a key point of consideration in interventions designed to prevent and treat poor athlete mental health. As such, a theoretical and empirical understanding of athletic identity by sport psychology practitioners, coaches, and parents alike represents an important aspect of promoting athlete physical wellness and mental wellbeing.

Commonly experienced poor athlete mental health outcomes

Research suggests that the three most common presentations of poor athlete mental health are depression, anxiety, and burnout (e.g. Gouttebarge, Frings-Dresen, & Sluiter, 2015). Furthermore, suicidal ideation has potential to manifest in relation to these aforementioned poor mental health outcomes. Because of their prevalence and relevance to the idea of athletic identity foreclosure, we have chosen to review these specific mental health outcomes. Accordingly, depression, anxiety, burnout, and related suicidal ideation will be explained in more detail.

Depression can range along the continuum of mental health, experienced from the presenting of depressed mood and related symptoms to the formal diagnosis of Major Depressive Disorder with situation-specific diagnoses also possible (i.e. Adjustment Disorder). Common manifestations of depression include elongated periods of symptoms (usually longer than four weeks) of sadness, irritability, feelings of emptiness, loneliness, hopelessness, fatigue, changes in appetite or sleep, and social withdrawal (American Psychiatric Association, 2013; Kroenke, Spitzer, & Williams, 2001). In more severe cases, depression can be associated with suicidal ideation (thoughts) or behaviours (American Psychiatric Association, 2013). During 2018–2019, the prevalence of depression was estimated to be 5.3% in American men and 8.7% in American women (National Institute of Mental Health [NIMH], 2019). Broader estimates of depression in athletes can be harder to ascertain; however, the prevalence of depression in American collegiate athletes has been estimated at approximately 25% across various athlete samples (Armstrong, 2007; "NCAA GOALS Study", 2016, Yang et al., 2007). Risk factors for depression in athletes can be multifaceted and often vary across individuals. However, environmental influences such as the stress of training and/or competition, an overemphasis on athletic identity, and/or interactions with key sport-based social agents (e.g. coaches, recruiters, parents, teammates) which promote sport stress and an unhealthy athletic identity merit consideration. Research has also shown depression in athletes to be positively associated with the experience of injury and rehabilitation (Armstrong, Burcin, Bjerke, & Early, 2015; Brewer, 1990; Rees, Mitchell, Evans, & Hardy, 2010).

Anxiety is characterised by excessive and/or unrealistic worry about everyday tasks or events (American Psychiatric Association, 2013) and often manifests in symptoms, such as difficulty concentrating, irritability, restlessness, muscle tension, and sleep issues (National Alliance on Mental Illness, 2019). As with depression, these symptoms can range from non-clinical in nature, to an Adjustment Disorder (based on a specific situation or event), to Generalised Anxiety Disorder (or a variety of other anxiety disorders). The lifetime prevalence of anxiety disorder is estimated to be around 6% (Spitzer, Kroenke, Williams, & Löwe, 2006), while the prevalence of anxiety disorders in the U.S. population in the previous year was estimated to be 14.3% in American men and 23.4% in American women (NIMH, 2019). The prevalence of self-reported anxiety in American collegiate athletes (i.e. unknown whether diagnostic criteria would be met) is on average 40% ("NCAA GOALS Study", 2016). For athletes, anxiety symptoms may impair concentration, social relationships, and in some cases athletic performance. For example,

Cassandra's anxiety impaired her concentration relative to both her sport and academic performance. The stress and/or pressure elite athletes face at the highest levels of competition, a strong athletic identity, and social pressures from sport-based social actors, all represent potential risk factors for athlete anxiety beyond demographic factors, such as sport type, gender, age, and experience (Correia & Rosada, 2019; Rocha & Osório, 2018).

It is not uncommon for depressed or anxious individuals, including athletes, to have thoughts of (or a plan for) wanting to end their lives. It is important to understand that having thoughts of suicidal ideation does not guarantee an individual will act on these thoughts but that death by suicide is a possible outcome for some athletes. For example, British snowboarder Ellie Soutter died by suicide on her 18th birthday after missing a team flight. Her father believed the intense pressure of sport and her history of depression contributed to this outcome (Badshah, 2018). Accordingly, it is critical that those individuals experiencing suicidal ideation are identified and encouraged to seek appropriate professional help. An embedded (i.e. within the sports medicine team) sport psychologist represents an appropriate referral source as athletes can disclose suicidal ideation with confidentiality from those associated primarily with their sport performance (e.g. coaches, teammates). Suicide is often preventable and for many, someone asking about thoughts of suicide is a critical step in getting help. There is a myth that asking about suicidal thoughts will increase their likelihood of acting on them, however, studies suggest that asking does not induce or increase such thoughts or experiences (Dazzi, Gribble, Wessely, & Fear, 2014). Rather, asking someone about suicide may represent an important turning point in the individual seeking treatment for the over-arching poor mental health outcome instigating such thoughts.

The non-clinical mental health outcome of burnout is also salient for athletes. Athlete burnout is a cognitive-affective syndrome characterised by emotional/physical exhaustion, reduced sport accomplishment, and devaluation of sport (Raedeke, 1997). Burnout is negatively associated with athlete motivation and social support (Goodger, Gorely, Lavallee, & Harwood, 2007). Burnout has also been shown to be distinct from, but positively associated with, symptoms of athlete depression and anxiety (Goodger et al., 2007). Athletic identity foreclosure has also been posited to be positively associated with athlete burnout (Coakley, 1992, 2009).

Research- and theory-based recommendations

Based on extant theory and research reviewed herein, a focus on maladaptive forms of athletic identity (i.e. overemphasis/foreclosure) has great potential to aid in interventions or therapeutic treatments of poor athlete mental health. In the realm of clinical mental health, therapeutic treatment (i.e. completed by an appropriately licenced mental health professional) that targets an expansion of the athlete's overall sense of self to include and/ or emphasise other aspects of self beyond athletics may be beneficial. For example, various therapeutic approaches (see Table 17.1) might aim to de-emphasise an individual athlete's singular focus on athletic identity relative to other identity facets (e.g. school, social relationships, non-sport interests). A de-emphasis on athletic identity could certainly involve an individual focus on, for example, academic and non-sport career prospects for dual career athletes. Alternatively, various therapeutic approaches might give an athlete written or active tasks designed to get the athlete to specifically focus on non-sport activities, hobbies, or the overall core values, with the intent to develop a sense of worth in areas beyond sport outcomes. For example, Cassandra participated in ACT therapy to broaden her personal values/sense of self beyond an athletic focused identity.

The use of psychoeducation programmes and non-clinical mental health interventions to promote and encourage the wellbeing of athletes, as well as important sport-based social agents on how their behaviours (or athlete perceptions of their behaviours) could contribute to athletic identify foreclosure (i.e. singular sport focus relative to self-worth) are equally important. For example, a parent asking only (or being perceived to) about their collegiate athlete child's sporting performance, rather than other life aspects, may directly or indirectly influence heightened athletic identity. Moreover, coaches could also have a tendency to ask athletes about their performance-related rest, recovery, and/or nutrition as opposed to other important life aspects such as family, social relationships, or school. In both the cases of Cassandra and Jerome, identity foreclosure could have been mitigated by parents or coaches positively contributing to a more multi-dimensional identity development (beyond sport). Thus, educating parents or coaches on how they could contribute to healthier athlete identity development may reduce this clinical mental health risk factor. Such interventions should be carefully informed by extant research and well as appropriately assessed for safety and effectiveness, as is demonstrated in the two case studies presented. Such work will further add to the athlete identity knowledge base.

As important as research and theory are to successful clinical and non-clinical mental health identity interventions and therapies, there are certainly limits to how these sources should inform the clinical mental healthcare of athletes. More specifically, clinical training and judgement should not be undervalued in approaching each athlete as an individual and in gauging whether identity is relevant to an individual athlete's case. Finally, potential athlete stigmatisation of poor mental health symptom disclosure and help-seeking behaviours (Kroshus, 2017) as well as the cultural competency of the practitioner (American Psychological Association [APA], 2017) should also be emphasised. For example, both Cassandra and Jerome had initial hesitancies to seek treatment and disclose their mental health concerns which were overcome by appropriate therapeutic intervention and the cultural competency of the provider. In conclusion, relevant theories of athlete identity development foreclosure represent a unique consideration relative to athlete mental health. Guided by extant research and theory, healthy athletic identity development has potential to prevent poor athlete mental health and, ultimately, to promote the holistic wellbeing of the individual athlete.

Discrimination

In her account, Katie described a situation where her domestic teammates were prioritised for selection over foreign players. Although there are few accounts of the topic of discrimination in the migrant athlete population, specifically, athletes from different ethnic or religious backgrounds to their host country may be at risk. Empirical evidence provides an inconclusive picture at the elite end of the spectrum of sport, but when professional clubs in host countries are tasked with developing home-grown talent, there is the likelihood that indigenous athletes are given preferential treatment over migrant athletes. Indeed, a 2014 analysis from the National Basketball Association (NBA) in America concluded that wage discrimination existed for foreign players (Hoffer & Freidel, 2014). There is also the likelihood of discrimination on the basis of religion, spirituality, or personal values if this differs significantly from that of the host country – as Katie illustrated when she spoke of the lack of accommodation for vegan athletes in Italy. As expected, discrimination has a powerful negative influence on wellbeing, especially for immigrants (Noh, Beiser, Kaspar, Hou, & Rummens, 1999; Schmitt, Branscombe, Postmes, & Garcia, 2014). It has been reported as the single biggest detriment to life satisfaction and mental health (Berry & Hou, 2017).

Conclusions and recommendations for practitioners

As illustrated in both American collegiate athlete cases along with the theory and research reviewed, identity, specifically athletic identity, has the potential to play a prominent role in the presentation and trajectory of mental health concerns for athletes. Both Cassandra and Jerome were highly identified with the athlete role. Informed by the research and theory reviewed herein, when athletes become "overidentified" this can emerge as a potential risk factor for mental health symptoms and/or poor athlete mental health. Accordingly, it is recommended that practitioners be particularly attuned to situations in which athletic identity is threatened, through injury, medical retirement, or poor performance. For Cassandra, athletic identity impacted the occurrence (and treatment) of her anxiety. Whereas athletic identity was relevant to Jerome via its impact on how his performance, relationships with parents, and manifestation of depression as anger/irritation. While there is no empirical evidence to suggest this over-identification causes mental health issues, it is fair to say that it may exacerbate them. It is also a relevant and important contextual piece in clinical work (i.e. assessments, interventions, and/or treatments) with athletes struggling with mental health issues. As a result, assessing athletic identity should be a part of the intake and initial assessment process whenever clinicians are working with an athlete. It is important for practitioners to consider how to incorporate this focus into their assessment process as was done in both cases. This most often will take the form of information gathered in a clinical interview, but there is also utility in using a psychometric measure, such as the Athletic Identity Measurement Scale (Brewer et al., 1993).

Likewise, when relevant, identity exploration and related interventions should be considered in the treatment of mental health concerns. Identity work becomes even more rich and complex as we consider the intersections of racial identity, gender identity, sexual orientation, and other diverse aspects of identity. For Jerome, his identity as an African American male along with his athletic identity were both central to the recognition, diagnosis, and treatment of his depression. Building on this case example, clinicians working with athletes need to be mindful of their cultural competency related to diverse populations (Brewer et al., 1993), as well as athletic culture. Practitioners should continually be working on their cultural competency and incorporating a cultural lens into all work with athletes.

In sum, all athletes must face their identity being threatened and lost at some point (e.g. loss of playing time, injury, career termination/transition). This was the case with Cassandra and Jerome herein and represents the case for all athletes both during and across seasons and competition levels. If athletic identity is lost or threatened several therapeutic approaches may be helpful, and it is recommended that clinicians be familiar with a number of potentially appropriate interventions (see Table 17.1). Above all, guided by the content of this chapter, helping athletes develop insight around their sense of identity, worth, and values and providing a supportive, empathic space to work through it is paramount to mental health treatment and well-being promotion. We hope this chapter helps in accomplishing this holistic, athlete-focused aim.

TABLE 17.1 Therapeutic approaches for addressing poor mental health via athletic identity

Therapeutic approach	Approach description	Athletic identity focus
Acceptance and Commitment Therapy (Hayes, Strosahl, & Wilson, 2012)	Values refer to what is most important to us and give our lives meaning. They are not goals, but rather like a compass – they help us make choices based on what is most important and the directions in which we want our lives to go. Values guide action and behaviour in an ongoing way. Mindfulness allows one to maintain contact with the present-moment in a non-judgmental manner. It allows an individual to connect with the observing self, rather than the thinking self, and detach from thoughts. Mindfulness skills help individuals better tolerate discomfort and live in ways consistent with their values, while supporting psychological flexibility. Cognitive defusion allows individuals to change how they interact with or relate thoughts in a way that reduces the unhelpful functions.	Helping athletes identify their core values allows them to see that they are more than their accomplishments. When they make choices in their lives that align with their values, they develop a stronger sense of self and can improve self-esteem in a meaningful way. Teaching mindfulness skills allows athletes struggling with mental health issues related to identity to get out of their thoughts, which are often consuming, and being connected to the present-moment to better tolerate anxiety, distress, and feeling overwhelmed. By learning to make space for what they feel, while reconnecting to the present, athletes are better able to work through the challenging emotions that come from identity struggles and find relief. Seeing thoughts as cognitive events and not absolute truths allows clients to separate from them when they are not serving them well. Related to identity, teaching cognitive defusion strategies allows athletes to reduce the believability of thoughts, such as "I am a failure," "people only like me when I have athletic success," "I am nothing without my sport."

Behavioural Activation (Martell, Dimidjian, & Herman-Dunn, 2010)	Behavioural activation is particularly helpful for depressed individuals. It is intended to help the individual increase contact with positive, rewarding activities, recognising that behaviour can influence emotions. In this process, the individual identifies specific goals of engaging in activities that are consistent with the life they want to live and will be rewarding. This is often a gradual process, starting with small steps.	If an athlete is struggling with depression, specifically with symptoms of anhedonia, low energy, low motivation, and withdrawal, behavioural activation can be very helpful. Athletic identity may be very beneficial in this intervention, as it will potentially be a source of small, rewarding activities that hold some meaning. It is important to identify other activities as well, so the athlete is not solely reliant on sport-related activities.
Narrative Therapy (White & Epston, 1990; Madigan, 2011)	Narrative therapy takes the approach that the complexity of life is mediated by our stories, acknowledging a multistoried version of life, in which stories can have many meanings. Narrative therapy is a truly collaborative approach to helping, in which the therapist and client re-author the client's problem story.	Engaging in narrative therapy interventions, such as writing and processing one's story can allow athletes to work through grief or unfinished business related to loss of athletic identity. It can also help them see themselves in a more holistic way and identify growth and strength in their stories. They can re-author the story in a way that is healing and empowering.
Existential Therapy (Yalom, 1980; Frankl, 2006)	Existential therapy posits that all individuals have the capacity for self-awareness and ability to make authentic, self-determined choices. A primary focus is on existence and purpose, helping individuals explore and make meaning in their lives. It also acknowledges anxiety as an unavoidable condition of living and helps individuals learn to tolerate uncertainty and make choices to bring meaning, even in the face of anxiety.	Exploring identity, authenticity, and meaning is at the heart of Existential Therapy and can be a powerful approach for athletes struggling with identity, particularly when that identity is threatened and the athlete may be lacking a sense of purpose. Through a collaborative dialogue, the therapist can help the athlete explore and create meaning in their lives. Many athletes will experience an existential anxiety when their athletic identity is threatened and learning to tolerate this uncertainty is very helpful.

References

American Psychiatric Association. (2013). *Diagnostic and statistical manual of mental disorders* (DSM-5®). Washington, DC: American Psychiatric Association Publishing.

American Psychological Association. (2017). *Multicultural guidelines: An ecological approach to context, identity, and intersectionality.* Retrieved from www.apa.org/about/policy/multicultural-guidelines.pdf

Armstrong, S. N. (2007). Social connectedness, self-esteem, and depression symptomatology among collegiate athletes versus non-collegiate athletes ages 18 to 24: A comparative study. *ProQuest Dissertations and Theses, 57*(5), 120. https://doi.org/10.3200/JACH.57.5.521-526

Armstrong, S. N., Burcin, M. M., Bjerke, W. S., & Early, J. (2015). Depression in student-athletes: A particularly at-risk group?: A systematic review of the literature. *Athletic Insight, 7*(2), 177–193.

Badshah, N. (2018). Ellie Soutter death: Father criticises demands on young athletes. *The Guardian.* Retrieved from www.theguardian.com/uk-news/2018/jul/31/ellie-soutter-death-father-criticises-demands-on-young-athletes

Balk, Y. A., De Jonge, J., Oerlemans, W. G. M., Geurts, S. A. E., Fletcher, D., & Dormann, C. (2018). Balancing demands and resources in sport: Adaptation and validation of the demand-induced strain compensation questionnaire for use in sport. *Journal of Sports Medicine, 17*(2), 237–244.

Bauman, N. J. (2016). The stigma of mental health in athletes: Are mental toughness and mental health seen as contradictory in elite sport? *British Journal of Sports Medicine, 50*(3), 135–136. http://doi.org/10.1136/bjsports-2015-095570

Berry, J.W., & Hou, F. (2017). Acculturation, discrimination and wellbeing among second generation of immigrants in Canada. *International Journal of Intercultural Relations, 61*, 29–39. https://doi.org/10.1016/j.ijintrel.2017.08.003

Black, J. M., & Smith, A. L. (2007). An examination of Coakley's perspective on identity, control, and burnout among adolescent athletes. *International Journal of Sport Psychology, 38*(4), 417–436.

Brewer, B. W. (1990). *Athletic identity as a risk factor for depressive reaction to athletic injury* [Unpublished doctoral dissertation]. Arizona State University, Tempe.

Brewer, B. W. (1993). Self-identity and specific vulnerability to depressed mood. *Journal of Personality, 61*(3), 343–364. https://doi.org/10.1111/j.1467-6494.1993.tb00284.x

Brewer, B. W., Van Raalte, J. L., & Linder, D. E. (1993). Athletic identity: Hercules' muscles or Achilles heel? *International Journal of Sport Psychology, 24*(2), 237–254.

Coakley, J. (1992). Burnout among adolescent athletes: A personal failure or social problem? *Sociology of Sport Journal, 9*(3), 271–285. https://doi.org/10.1123/ssj.9.3.271

Coakley, J. (2009). From the outside in: Burnout as an organizational issue. *Journal of Intercollegiate Sports, 2*(1), 35–41. https://doi.org/10.1123/jis.2.1.35

Correia, M., & Rosada, A. (2019). Anxiety in athletes: Gender and type of sport differences. *International Journal of Psychological Research, 12*(1), 9–17. http://doi.org/10.21500/20112084.3552

Dazzi, T., Gribble, R., Wessely, S., & Fear, N. T. (2014). Does asking about suicide and related behaviours induce suicidal ideation? What is the evidence? *Psychological Evidence, 44*(16), 3361–3363. https://doi.org/10.1017/S0033291714001299

Eklund, R. C., & DeFreese, J. D. (2015). Athlete burnout: What we know, what we could know, and how we can find out more. *International Journal of Applied Sports Science, 27*(2), 63–75. https://doi.org/10.24985/ijass.2015.27.2.63

Frankl, V. E. (2006). *Man's search for meaning.* Boston, MA: Beacon Press.

Goodger, K., Gorely, T., Lavallee, D., & Harwood, C. (2007). Burnout in sport: A systematic review. *The Sport Psychologist, 21*(2), 127–151. https://doi.org/10.1123/tsp.21.2.127

Gould, D., & Whitley, M. A. (2009). Sources and consequences of athletic burnout among college athletes. *Journal of Intercollegiate Sports, 2*(1), 16–30. https://doi.org/10.1123/jis.2.1.16

Gouttebarge, V., Frings-Dresen, M. H. W., & Sluiter, J. K. (2015). Mental and psychosocial health among current and former professional footballers. *Occupational Medicine, 65*(3), 190–196. https://doi.org/10.1093/occmed/kqu202

Green, S. L., & Weinberg, R. S. (2001). Relationships among athletic identity, coping skills, social support, and the psychological impact of injury in recreational participants. *Journal of Applied Sport Psychology, 13*(1), 40–59. https://doi.org/10.1080/10413200109339003

Gulliver, A., Griffiths, K. M., & Christensen, H. (2012). Barriers and facilitators to mental health help-seeking for young elite athletes: A qualitative study. *BioMed Central Psychiatry, 12*, 157. https://doi.org/10.1186/1471-244X-12-157

Hayes, S. C., Strosahl, K. D., & Wilson, K. G. (2012). *Acceptance and commitment therapy: The process and practice of mindful change* (2nd ed.). New York: The Guilford Press.

Hoffer, A. J., & Freidel, R. (2014). Does salary discrimination persist for foreign athletes in the NBA? *Applied Economics Letters, 21*(1), 1–5. https://doi.org/10.1080/13504851.2013.829183

Keyes, C. L. M. (2002). The mental health continuum: From languishing to flourishing in life. *Journal of Health and Social Research, 43*(2), 207–222. https://doi.org/10.2307/3090197

Kroenke, K., Spitzer, R. L., & Williams, J. B. W. (2001). The PHQ-9 – Validity of a brief depression severity measure. *Journal of General Internal Medicine, 16*, 606–613. https://doi.org/10.1046/j.1525-1497.2001.016009606.x

Kroshus, E. (2017). Stigma, coping skills, and psychological help seeking among collegiate athletes. *Athletic Training & Sports Health Care, 9*(6), 254–262. https://doi.org/10.3928/19425864-20171010-02

Love, K. (2018, March 6). *Everyone is going through something*. Retrieved from www.theplayerstribune.com/en-us/articles/kevin-love-everyone-is-going-through-something

Madigan, S. (2011). *Narrative therapy*. Washington, DC: American Psychological Association.

Marsh, H. W. (1990). A multidimensional, hierarchical model of self-concept: Theoretical and empirical justification. *Educational Psychology Review, 2*(2), 77–172.

Marsh, H. W., Richards, G. E., Johnson, S., Roche, L., & Tremayne, P. (1994). Physical self-description questionnaire: Psychometric properties and a multitrait-multimethod analysis of relations to existing instrument. *Journal of Sport & Exercise Psychology, 16*(3), 270–305. https://doi.org/10.1123/jsep.16.3.270

Martell, C. R., Dimidjian, S., & Herman-Dunn, R. (2010). *Behavioral activation for depression: A clinician's guide*. New York: Guilford Press.

Mason, M. (2018, December 8). *Florida lacrosse player Makenzie Mason: 'I have to keep fighting'*. Retrieved from www.espn.com/espnw/sports/article/25419065/florida-gators-lacrosse-player-makenzie-mason-struggles-depression?addata=espn:frontpage

National Alliance of Mental Illness. (2019). *Anxiety disorders*. Retrieved from www.nami.org/Learn-More/Mental-Health-Conditions/Anxiety-Disorders

National Collegiate Athletic Association (NCAA). (2018). *Athletic identity*. Paper presented at 2018 NCAA Inclusion Forum, Indianapolis, IN.

National Institute of Mental Health. (2019). *Major depression.* Retrieved from www.nimh.nih.gov/health/statistics/major-depression.shtml

NCAA GOALS Study of the Student-Athlete Experience: Initial Summary of Findings. (2016). Retrieved from www.ncaa.org/sites/default/files/GOALS_2015_summary_jan2016_final_20160627.pdf

Noh, S., Beiser, M., Kaspar, V., Hou, F., & Rummens, J. (1999). Perceived racial discrimination, depression, and coping: A study of Southeast Asian refugees in Canada. *Journal of Health and Social Behavior, 40*(3), 193–207. https://doi.org/10.2307/2676348

Podlog, L., & Eklund, R. C. (2006). A longitudinal investigation of competitive athletes' return to sport following serious injury. *Journal of Applied Sport Psychology, 18*(1), 44–68. https://doi.org/10.1080/10413200500471319

Raedeke, T. D. (1997). Is athlete burnout more than just stress? A sport commitment perspective. *Journal of Sport & Exercise Psychology, 19*(4), 396–417.

Rees, T., Mitchell, I., Evans, L., & Hardy, L. (2010). Stressors, social support and psychological responses to sport injury in high- and low-performance participants. *Psychology of Sport and Exercise, 11*(6), 505–512. https://doi.org/10.1016/j.psychsport.2010.07.002

Reifsteck, E. J., Gill, D. L., & Labban, J. S. (2016). "Athletes" and "exercisers": Understanding identity, motivation, and physical activity participation in former collegiate athletes. *Sport, Exercise, and Performance Psychology, 5*(1), 25–38. https://doi.org/10.1037/spy0000046

Rocha, V. V. S., & Osório, F. L. (2018). Associations between competitive anxiety, athlete characteristics, and sport context: Evidence from a systematic review and meta-analysis. *Archives of Clinical Psychiatry, 45*(3), 67–74.

Schmitt, M.T., Branscombe, N.R., Postmes, T., & Garcia, A. (2014). The consequences of perceived discrimination for psychological well-being: A meta-analytic review. *Psychological Bulletin, 140*(4), 921–948. https://doi.org/10.1037/a0035754

Seligman. M. E. P., & Csikszentmihalyi, M. (2000). Positive psychology. *American Psychologist, 55,* 5–14.

Shavelson, R. J., Hubner, J. J., & Stanton, G. C. (1976). Validation of construct interpretations. *Review of Educational Research, 46*(3), 407–441. https://doi.org/10.3102/00346543046003407

Smith, R. E. (1986). Toward a cognitive-affective model of athletic burnout. *Journal of Sport Psychology, 8*(1), 36–50. https://doi.org/10.1123/jsp.8.1.36

Spitzer, R. L., Kroenke, K., Williams, J. B. W., & Löwe, B. (2006). A brief measure for assessing generalized anxiety disorder. *Archives of Internal Medicine, 166,* 1092. https://doi.org/10.1001/archinte.166.10.1092

Weise-Bjornstal, D. M., Smith, A. M., Shaffer, S. M., & Morrey, M. A. (1998). An integrated model of response to sport injury: Psychological and sociological dynamics. *Journal of Applied Sport Psychology, 10*(1), 46–69. https://doi.org/10.1080/10413209808406377

White, M., & Epston, D. (1990). *Narrative means to therapeutic ends.* New York: Norton.

Yalom, I. D. (1980). *Existential psychotherapy.* New York: Basic Books.

Yang, J., Peek-asa, C., Corlette, J. D., Cheng, G., Foster, D. T., & Albright, J. (2007). Prevalence of and risk factors associated with symptoms of depression in competitive collegiate student athletes. *Clinical Journal of Sports Medicine, 17*(6), 481–487. https://doi.org/10.1097/JSM.0b013e31815aed6b

18
SUPPORTING ATHLETE WELLBEING DURING A GLOBAL PANDEMIC

The case of COVID-19

Natalie Campbell and Josh Rudd

Introduction

In January 2020, the outbreak of the Corona virus across the globe caused the World Health Organization to issue warnings of an international pandemic on a scale never before seen. The world ground to a halt within a matter of weeks. This chapter explores the reactions, feelings and reflections of the first ten weeks of lockdown in England of Josh – a Performance Lifestyle Advisor for the English Institute of Sport – and the elite swimmers he supports. Salient events from the lockdown period – such as the move to land-based training, the delay of the Tokyo 2020 Olympic Games and the rising of social justice movements – are theorised to explore both the practical and existential challenges that arose from home confinement. The chapter concludes with considerations of how the COVID-19 pandemic might serve as a catalyst to reconceptualise staff and athlete mental health and wellbeing in a design that surpasses prioritising performance and, instead, seeks to prioritise the person first and the athlete second.

PRACTITIONER VOICE

Josh Rudd (performance lifestyle advisor for British Swimming)

It was a Monday afternoon – 16 March 2020 – and I was packing up to leave the training centre for the day when a message was sent to me . . . *It's unlikely we'll be in tomorrow – keep an eye on the news.* Later that night, the country was told to avoid all non-essential travel. And that was that! One day we were training and the next we weren't. Initially, there was a lot of denials – we thought lockdown wouldn't last longer than three weeks. The next day

DOI: 10.4324/9780429287923-18

was a virtual multi-disciplinary team (MDT) meeting. What training were the athletes going to do? How were support services going to be managed? Which services could be delivered remotely? How do we maintain motivation? Being honest, there was no immediate need for me to put Performance Lifestyle (PL) at the front of the agenda – discussions were very performance and training maintenance based at the start. But I needed to gauge the temperature of each individual – *How do you feel about what's happening at the moment?* Some athletes were really happy to chat about how they were feeling, while others were avoiding me like the plague! A priority for me was to make athletes aware that I was here, that PL can be done remotely and that I'd be available for 1:1 support in whatever capacity was needed. It was about keeping calm and riding out the next three weeks.

When the second phase of lockdown was announced, that's when the proverbial sh*t hit the fan. When it was announced that the Tokyo 2020 Olympic and Paralympic Games been delayed to 2021 it was 'OK, so this is serious now!' I think it was the right call. There had been rumours about it being cancelled but no one knew anything, and the relative silence from the IOC was starting to reflect negatively on the athletes' wellbeing. In a matter of days all conditioning was land based. Some had access to endless pools and these were delivered to athletes so they could swim in their gardens. And even though the sport-specific training couldn't possibly be replicated in an endless pool, it was just about being in the water.

By the tenth week of lockdown, the PL conversations became more frequent with more athletes. From early on it was clear which athletes found the fallout of the pandemic a bump in the road and who found it beyond devastating. When the BBC reported that if Tokyo 2020 was pushed back to 2022, it would be scrapped altogether there were some deeper conversations to be had. At first, the focus was immediate practicalities such as athletes needing to defer studies or jobs because they thought they'd be available from September 2020. Then came conversations with athletes planning on retiring – which were definitely challenging at times. Some athletes found a second burst of motivation knowing that they had another 12 months to train, whereas others decided to retire without having that final Games experience – which was heartbreaking. Importantly, what I think is not important! My role is to support the athlete in whatever way they need it; everything is done on their terms. For example, some athlete conversations were along the lines of *I'm done. I'm retiring. Leave me alone. Don't contact me at all* and I had to respect that and say *that's OK – call me whenever you're ready.* They got in touch wanting to discuss life after swimming once they had processed their decision to retire – lockdown had given them time to reflect on why they *didn't* want to swim anymore, as opposed to why they did.

The biggest challenge for PL has been getting athletes to follow through on the plans for personal development. Lockdown has been the perfect opportunity for personal growth, as it has pushed athletes to discover things about themselves outside of swimming – training can sometimes take up so much time that it overshadows their ability to develop away from it. But keeping non-performance-related goals for athletes is tough! The importance of PL was to be cautious, to not push, to do it on their terms – otherwise, it could jeopardise my relationship with athletes if I try to force a goal or an outcome. Let's be real – we're in a global pandemic, the paint from numbers collage task can wait! And when it comes down to it, a lot of athletes have managed themselves as mature human beings. I think that surprised a lot of people – they thought they'd need more direction. I worried at the start because I thought *how will they cope with limited things to do?* but as time went on I realised that for some of them what they needed was to not have a goal – they needed to just 'be'; to be alone, to be with family, to be grateful. To step off the 100 mile an hour hamster wheel that is elite sport and just press pause.

The return to training has begun and the plan is exceptionally robust. It has to be; if one athlete contracts COVID-19 the whole programme has to shut down. There are so many steps that need to happen – enter through this specific door, temperature check, complete monitoring app, allocated changing room spaces, limited swimmers to a lane, no showering, leave immediately. It's not the same environment (obviously), but it's a step in the right direction. When training resumed in phase one of the return, there was this real buzz of excitement to get back into the water again, and athletes were almost desperate to get back to that hard training effort. They'd missed it; they crave it! But two to three weeks later we're now in phase two and some of the athletes are starting to question the point of it all. It's not necessarily about motivation; it's about meaning. "What are we training for?" Lockdown has brought about some pretty rhetorical questions from athletes, and with COVID-19 wiping out the entire swimming competition calendar for pretty much all of this year, it's a difficult question to answer. My worry is that it could go one of two ways. Either, athletes will burn themselves out in the run up to the 2021 Games because they are so fearful of their time out over lockdown, or athletes will become consumed with the background noise of the Games being cancelled altogether and their motivation and focus will suffer. Right now, PL can support the athletes with Olympic preparation, and there is a real need for athletes to understand the silver linings and find the good that has come out of this awful situation. But equally, we are being pragmatic about it all and acknowledging that Tokyo 2021 might not go ahead – we need to keep in mind the "what ifs?", and not forget the athletes who show real potential for Paris 2024, AND not let the athletes get distracted by the scenarios and media speculation. It's a juggling act!

There is no blueprint for this – this is all new to everyone! And we're all doing it differently. Some athletes are living alone, some are homeschooling, some are looking after vulnerable people – we're all just trying our best. Personally, I've had to do a lot of self-care; I found myself working late into the evenings and I could feel burnout starting even just a few weeks into lockdown. Of course my manager checks in to see how I'm doing, but there is no dedicated PL person for staff the same way there is for the athletes. I am now more disciplined. Athletes know I have a life outside of sport, and I try and encourage them to consider that also. I was honest and told them that I needed to look after myself. They've also been really respectful of that view, as individuals in a pandemic, not as athletes. For me, lockdown has meant I've been able to dedicate time to projects that are important but never take priority over performance, for example, the Pride in Water project that I've been leading; a network across British Swimming, aiming to enhance the support, visibility and engagement of the LGBT+ community within the aquatic disciplines. There has been time available to discuss this project with athletes and to open up to them about the how's and why's of it all, which has led to some very philosophical and meaningful conversations with them, free from judgement, centring on "there must be more to life than swimming?". The COVID-19 global pandemic has forced the world to reset; which is not a bad thing, especially if we can learn from the overall lockdown experience. Elite sport is traditionally mapped and predictable, but this has pushed staff and athletes to rethink their approach to adapt, overcome and to explore things differently. We need to reflect on this time to figure out what went well and what could have been done better to support the performance, and the mental health of both staff and athletes during the pandemic – just in case anything like this ever happens again!

SCHOLAR VOICE

Elite sport in times of a global pandemic

On 31 December 2019, the World Health Organization was informed of cases of pneumonia of unknown aetiology detected in Wuhan City, China. One week later, on 7 January 2020, a new strain of virus was identified as Coronavirus (COVID-19 henceforth), sparking an international health pandemic. The velocity and ferocity of the virus were felt across the globe, with the first death in the United Kingdom from COVID-19 being reported on 5 March 2020. On 23 March 2020, the Prime Minister of the United Kingdom, Boris Johnson, announced that the country was to enter a period of enforced "lockdown", periodically reviewed every three weeks, with non-keyworker citizens being permitted to only leave their home for essential food shopping and 1 hour of exercise per day. All public spaces – for example, schools, offices, shops and restaurants – closed with immediate effect, and elite sport in all its forms of training and competition was immediately suspended. Life changed dramatically and instantly. People across the country were left wondering how to continue their daily living in these strange new times, facing challenges, such as homeschooling, financial insecurity and complete social isolation. However, in addition to enduring such challenges, while athletes were coming to terms with rapid and significant changes to their (now home based) training routines, there came news of a historic decision that would meaningfully impact their time in lockdown even more so.

Grieving for the games

The day after the UK entered enforced lockdown, on 24 March 2020, the Japanese Prime Minister Shinzo Abe announced that the Tokyo 2020 Olympic and Paralympic Games were to be postponed until July 2021. Since the opening of the first modern Olympic Games in 1896, the international sports competition has only been cancelled three times: once during World War I (1916) and twice during World War II (1940, 1944). Josh recalls how it was this announcement that underscored the seriousness of the COVID-19 pandemic, perhaps triggering the subsequent tone and direction of his work as a performance lifestyle advisor. Initially, the reaction to the overall situation was one of "denial", and avoidance by most, and that both he and the athletes simply needed to draw upon a contained mindset by keeping "calm" and "riding out the next 3 weeks". The word "denial" takes on a significant role when theorizing the unfolding events in Josh's narrative, perhaps best linked to the Kübler-Ross (1969) model of the five stages of grief: denial, anger, bargaining, depression and acceptance. Josh explains that the "rumours" surrounding the possible cancellation, and subsequent postponement, of the Games had permeated the training environment for some time. Indeed, press statements from the International Olympic Committee (IOC) concerning the go-ahead of the event were continuing to be released throughout February and March 2020, with the president of the IOC urging athletes across the globe to "to continue to prepare for the Olympic Games Tokyo 2020 as best they can" (IOC, 2020). As identified by Josh, these "rumours" perhaps helped to "soften the blow" by reducing the intensity and immediateness of the anger felt by the athletes, especially as a large number of them had voiced their own feelings of anger, anxiety and altruism at the continued push for hosting the Games in 2020. Importantly, Josh highlights how the sustained dubiety regarding the status of the Games began to "reflect negatively on the athlete's wellbeing", which is unsurprising given the brain's insatiable craving for certainty. Extant work in neuropsychology suggests that unpredictability and uncontrollability are central features of stressful experiences (Amat et al., 2005; De Berker et al., 2016; Koolhaas et al., 2011; Miller, 1979; Monat, Averill, & Lazarus,

1972; Pervin, 1963), and that chronic periods of uncertainty can contribute to systemic and brain malfunction (Peters, McEwen, & Friston, 2017). The "negativity" Josh mentions is the resultant cerebral energy required to mitigate and reduce uncertainty about future outcomes; it takes purposeful effort to manage rumination and prevent the perceptual, intangible unknowns from spiralling into the worst case possible scenarios. Indeed, the official information on the postponement of the Games would have come as an affective relief. The Tokyo 2020 Games had officially died, but lock down was still very much alive – which proved challenging for some athletes.

The Kübler-Ross model suggests the third stage of grief to be bargaining; a negotiative process by which individuals attempt to postpone or distance themselves from the reality of the situation. The immediate call for a virtual MDT meeting indicates an attempt to bargain with the lockdown measures during the initial three weeks – how can routine, service and support be maintained (virtually) to conceal the crisis and keep athletes invested in top-level performance. The endless pools, for example, provided some small semblance of normality under very abnormal circumstances. However, once the Games were postponed, the condition of bargaining required morphed into conversations that surpassed the narrative of elite sport and external focus. As "normality" began to recede, athletes found themselves needing to engage in the reality of the situation that decisions – some life changing – needed to be made. Josh candidly admits that for some athletes the postponement was a "bump in the road" while for others it was "beyond devastating". Some athletes remained suspended in the bargaining stage in so far as seeking to negotiate changes in future studies and employment; secondary foci that research argues are supplementary to the successful holistic development of elite performers (Stambulova & Wylleman, 2019). However, for others, the postponement meant a need for Josh to initiate "challenging" conversations regarding retirement. Athletic retirement – voluntary or forced – can be frightening and overwhelming, with literature illuminating experiences of psychological distress (Brown, Kerkhoffs, Lambert, & Gouttebarge, 2017; Mannes et al., 2019), depression and anxiety (Doherty, Hannigan, & Campbell, 2016; Wolanin, 2020), and alcohol and substance misuse and abuse (McDuff et al., 2019). The Kübler-Ross model suggests depression as the fourth stage of grief, and while such symptoms may not have been explicit, Josh has a responsibility to provide appropriate yet boundaried, emotional support to retiring athletes that is – first and foremost – guided by the individual, is purposeful in its intent and serves to engage the athlete in a structured yet reflective transition. This can, in turn, help move the athlete towards the final stage of the model – acceptance.

Finding perspective . . . and the silver linings

For the athletes that remained in training during lockdown, their acceptance of both the postponement of the Games and the overall national situation allowed a metaphysical freedom not often afforded to elite performers. Josh admits that there was an assumed lack of agency at the beginning and was unsure how the athletes would "cope" without having some form of goal to direct their daily routine. Yet, as the reality of the pandemic begins to manifest into the day to day, athletes found themselves acting as independent, "mature human beings". Literature has long incorporated the sociological lens of Foucault to explore the notion that elite athletes lack agency; that high-performance sport systems create docile and directionless automatons (cf. Blackett, Evans, & Piggott, 2019; Denison & Mills, 2014; Lang, 2010). Interestingly, it may be that a global pandemic serves to demonstrate such theorisations further. The juxtaposition of geographical confinement and physical restriction against temporal expansion and mental liberation led to, as Josh describes, "deeper conversations". Unknowingly, time in lockdown might have helped to prevent athlete identity foreclosure (Brewer & Petitpas, 2017) by allowing athletes to "discover things about themselves outside of swimming". Identity foreclosure is linked heavily to athlete burnout (Ronkainen, Kavoura, & Ryba, 2016), however, the imposed circumstances revealed insight that giving athletes increased space to just "be"; forced "pressing pause". And yet relinquishing the relentlessness of high-performance sport allowed the athletes to retreat into alternative explorations and explanations of being. Certainly, lockdown engendered an emotional dissonance in some athletes that would not have been present had life continued status quo, with some attempting to make sense of competing reactions, such as frustration, guilt and appreciation. Josh mentions enhanced feelings of being "grateful" among the athletes – perhaps acknowledging the broader economic and humanitarian cost of the pandemic. Indeed, developing perspective and practicing gratitude is a positive psychology practice that is slowly gathering traction and has been evidenced to enhance athlete mental health, resilience, team cohesion and quality of the coach–athlete relationship (Chen & Wu, 2014; Gabana, Wong, D'Addario, & Chow, 2020; Salim & Wadey, 2019).

As lockdown began to ease and high-performance sports were issued with return to training guidelines, athletes needed to quickly become accustomed to the new COVID-19 secure safety measures. The use of digital data for biomonitoring has continued but perhaps with an implicit shift from individual performance surveillance (Manley, Palmer, & Roderick, 2012) to community altruism tracking. However, Josh explains that the initial "buzz" of returning to training was not enough to quash the (perhaps) newly awakened curiosity of purpose for some athletes. The million-dollar question of "what are we training for" could speak to the literal (in so far as being suspended in the interregnum of the elite sport calendar), or to the existential. Josh explains that motivation was present, but that meaning was lost. Indeed, how can motivation exist *without* meaning? Josh jokes that it is a "difficult question to answer". However, the use of existentialism to inform sport psychology and athlete wellbeing practice is gathering pace. Ronkainen and Nesti (2017) examine in detail the applied use of philosophical underpinnings of existential psychology to guide rhetorical conversations with athletes on topics, such as meaning, authenticity, freedom, identity, loneliness and death. Ryall (2008) hints that the high-performance sport environment is one that strongly serves to enhance the categorical self in athletes. This is the conception of oneself as an object in the environment with regard to appearance (e.g. physicality), traits (e.g. goal orientated), roles (e.g. captain) and abilities (e.g. speed). Thus, the opportunity for an athlete to enhance the existential self – the conception of oneself as an experiencing and acting subject separate from the environment (e.g. individual person) – becomes less frequent the more embedded the athlete becomes in elite sport. The consequence, therefore, is an athlete's sense of self – of purpose, of worth, of value – being increasingly and inextricably linked to their sporting world the longer they stay in it. The pandemic has (temporarily) removed this world, igniting existential considerations of "there must be more to life than swimming?" A small body of literature exists that explores the benefits and drawbacks of different levels of sub-clinical narcissism within elite athletes (cf. Matosic, Ntoumanis, Boardley, Stenling, & Sedikides, 2016; Roberts, Woodman, Hardy, Davis, & Wallace, 2013; Roberts, Woodman, & Sedikides, 2018; Tazegul & Soykan, 2013; Vaughan, Madigan, Carter, & Nicholls, 2019). Wilkowich (2016) suggests that after retirement, some elite athletes experience a psychospiritual transformation in which they work through their narcissism via transpersonal perspective and healing (Almaas, 2001; Wilber, 1986). This transformation encourages the revival of ordinariness and perspective, allowing athletes to separate themselves from their accomplishments and diminish feelings of grandiosity, arrogance and entitlement. It appears that for some athletes, the pandemic has engendered an early transformation. However, Josh admits that the continued uncertainty about the go-head of the Tokyo Games in 2021 has created a situation whereby psychospiritually transformed athletes are training towards a performance goal that might not even materialise. Compellingly, the psychological skills training that must be employed now – as Josh reveals – is to have the athletes *believe* that the Games will happen and derive some form of meaning that circles back to the value of elite sport during a period of such global suffering. And so, to ensure the wellbeing of the athletes is holistically supported throughout these challenging times, Josh has the responsibility of working with the athletes to "understand the silver linings and find the good" from the fallout of the COVID-19 event.

Learning from a global crisis

During the first 12 weeks of the lockdown period in the UK, both narratives of thriving and narratives of surviving were apparent. Uplifting stories of neighbourhood kindness, family togetherness and keyworker appreciation were met with sorrowful tales of financial ruin, domestic abuse and marginalised communities. Some people were thriving, and others merely surviving. Undoubtedly the topic of mental health and wellbeing was catapulted into every stratification of society – schools, businesses, healthcare, government, the arts, sport and more – illuminating the relative lack of understanding, resource and support available. Stressors that might normally affect wellbeing in isolation – for example, loneliness, burnout, anxiety, illness, finance and childcare – seemingly compounded into a singular set of social circumstances that prompted salient conversations on self-care. A small number of research papers exploring the wellbeing effects of working from home (or not) during the COVID-19 pandemic have emerged (Dicu, 2020; Pant & Agarwal, 2020; Zhang, Wang, Rauch, & Wei, 2020), and no doubt more will materialise to demonstrate the benefits and drawbacks of such working practices. Josh admits that his adjustment to working from home quickly escalated into feelings of burnout, which might include feelings of depersonalisation, emotional exhaustion and somatic reactions such as increased irritability and insomnia (Barello, Palamenghi, & Graffigna, 2020). To counter, Josh self-imposed disciplinary strategies to self-manage his emotional and physical wellbeing. Such regulation of the body speaks to neo-liberal considerations of individual responsibility-taking, independent self-steering and self-care – a governance praxis Rose (1996) refers to as "responsibilization". Interestingly, Josh points out the (lack of) measures put in place to navigate, develop and sustain his own fluctuating state of mental wellbeing during lockdown was not given equal attention to that of the athletes – "there is no dedicated PL for staff". Indeed, literature exploring the effects of supporting elite athletes on the mental and physical wellbeing of PL staff and sport psychologists is limited (McCormack, MacIntyre, O'Shea, Campbell, & Igou, 2015), demonstrating that the high-performance sport culture does not necessarily practice on its staff what it preaches to its athletes.

For Josh, time in lockdown has allowed him to dedicate more time to a project that, despite being important to his identity as a practitioner within elite sport, had not previously been given full priority. The development of a pioneering LQBT+ programme within the aquatic disciplines – Pride in Water – has been a catalyst for Josh in his PL conversations with regard to helping athletes make conceptual leaps between self-identity, self-worth, individual purpose and personal wellbeing. Asking his athletes to "open up" about the "how's and why's of it all" has paved the way for much broader sociological observations and discussions of the social injustices that have ensued during lockdown (Pleyers, 2020). Whilst athlete activism (across a number of social spheres) is not unseen, it is perhaps the athletes who have not prioritised examining "life outside sport" that might have benefitted most from PL conversations inviting the exploration of empathy, altruism and concern for the "other". Indeed, the traditional high-performance sport aphorism of performance over people might need to surrender to the significant socio-political-cultural shifts that have manifested during lockdown. Perhaps this speaks to Josh's request for elite sport to "reflect" on the entire experience, both for staff and athletes, to gain a much deeper understanding of what responses to the pandemic supported and encouraged positive wellbeing. The learnings from this global "reset" are vast, yet differentiated, and how such learnings might then translate tangibly into the elite sport environment is yet to be determined. However, NBA basketball star and political activist John Amaechi calls for all industries to consider the pandemic as an opportunity for a "cultural clean slate"; a chance to revaluate and reinvest in both people and purpose. The last decade has shown elite sport to be an environment that can (at times) facilitate emotional abuse (Jacobs, Smits, & Knoppers, 2017; Kavanagh, Brown, & Jones, 2017), sexual abuse (Leahy, 2010; Owton & Sparkes, 2017), bullying (Kerr, 2010; Lebrun, MacNamara, Rodgers, & Collins, 2018) and discrimination (Jones & Edwards, 2013; Roberts & Sojo, 2020) – without question individual and organisational practices that foster experiences of both acute and chronic poor mental health. To what extent, therefore, can the COVID-19 pandemic help to shape the culture of elite sport moving forward? Perhaps at the very least, we should be asking NGBs to reveal their humility and measure their actions with a philosophy of trust, openness, empathy and care for their employees and their athletes. In other words, to put the person first and the athlete second.

Conclusion

Josh's narrative explores the immediate long-term challenges to elite sport and high-performance athletes brought about by the imposed lockdown period in the UK; serving as an example of how services such as performance lifestyle can support athletes through both pragmatic and existential crises. The word "unprecedented" to describe the COVID-19 pandemic has monopolised worldwide discourse – the economic and human cost of the virus is unlike anything witnessed since World War II. However, as Josh observes, there is no "blueprint" to determine how people should merge the commonality of the global crisis with the uniqueness of their personal circumstances. Without question, the toll of the pandemic on the mental health of people across the world is unsurmountable; we are the data for the world's largest wellbeing experiment.

References

Almaas, A. H. (2001). *The point of existence: Transformations of narcissism in selfrealization*. Boston, MA: Shambhala.

Amat, J., Baratta, M. V., Paul, E., Bland, S. T., Watkins, L. R., & Maier, S. F. (2005). Medial prefrontal cortex determines how stressor controllability affects behavior and dorsal raphe nucleus. *Nature Neuroscience*, 8, 365–371. https://doi.org/10.1038/nn1399

Barello, S., Palamenghi, L., & Graffigna, G. (2020). Burnout and somatic symptoms among frontline healthcare professionals at the peak of the Italian COVID-19 pandemic. *Psychiatry Research*, 290, 113–129. https://doi.org/10.1016/j.psychres.2020.113129

Blackett, A. D., Evans, A. B., & Piggott, D. (2019). "They have to toe the line": A Foucauldian analysis of the socialisation of former elite athletes into academy coaching roles. *Sports Coaching Review*, 8(1), 83–102. https://doi.org/10.1080/21640629.2018.1436502

Brewer, B. W., & Petitpas, A. J. (2017). Athletic identity foreclosure. *Current Opinion in Psychology*, 16, 118–122. https://doi.org/10.1016/j.copsyc.2017.05.004

Brown, J. C., Kerkhoffs, G., Lambert, M. I., & Gouttebarge, V. (2017). Forced retirement from professional rugby union is associated with symptoms of distress. *International Journal of Sports Medicine*, 38(08), 582–587. https://doi.org/10.1055/s-0043-103959

Chen, L. H., & Wu, C. H. (2014). Gratitude enhances change in athletes' self-esteem: The moderating role of trust in coach. *Journal of Applied Sport Psychology*, 26(3), 349–362. https://doi.org/10.1080/10413200.2014.889255

De Berker, A. O., Rutledge, R. B., Mathys, C., Marshall, L., Cross, G. F., Dolan, R. J., & Bestmann, S. (2016). Computations of uncertainty mediate acute stress responses in humans. *Nature Communications*, 7, 10996. https://doi.org/10.1038/ncomms10996

Denison, J., & Mills, J. P. (2014). Planning for distance running: Coaching with Foucault. *Sports Coaching Review*, 3(1), 1–16. https://doi.org/10.1080/21640629.2014.953005

Dicu, M. A. (2020). *The impact of working from home on employees' wellbeing during COVID-19* [Masters thesis]. Retrieved from Academia.Edu

Doherty, S., Hannigan, B., & Campbell, M. J. (2016). The experience of depression during the careers of elite male athletes. *Frontiers in Psychology*, 7, 1069. https://doi.org/10.3389/fpsyg.2016.01069

Gabana, N. T., Wong, Y. J., D'Addario, A., & Chow, G. M. (2020). The Athlete Gratitude Group (TAGG): Effects of coach participation in a positive psychology intervention with youth athletes. *Journal of Applied Sport Psychology*, 1–34. https://doi.org/10.1080/10413200.2020.1809551

International Olympic Committee. (2020). *Communications bulletin*. Retrieved from www.olympic.org/news/communique-from-the-international-olympic-committee-ioc-regarding-the-olympic-games-tokyo-2020

Jacobs, F., Smits, F., & Knoppers, A. (2017). 'You don't realize what you see!': The institutional context of emotional abuse in elite youth sport. *Sport in Society*, 20(1), 126–143. https://doi.org/10.1080/17430437.2015.1124567

Jones, C., & Edwards, L. L. (2013). The woman in black: Exposing sexist beliefs about female officials in elite men's football. *Sport, Ethics and Philosophy*, 7(2), 202–216. https://doi.org/10.1080/17511321.2013.777771

Kavanagh, E., Brown, L., & Jones, I. (2017). Elite athletes' experience of coping with emotional abuse in the coach – athlete relationship. *Journal of Applied Sport Psychology*, 29(4), 402–417. https://doi.org/10.1080/10413200.2017.1298165

Kerr, G. (2010). Female coaches' experience of harassment and bullying. In S. Robertson (Ed.), *Taking the lead: Strategies and solutions from female coaches* (pp. 57–72). Alberta: The University of Alberta Press.

Koolhaas, J. M., Bartolomucci, A., Buwalda, B., de Boer, S. F., Flügge, G., Korte, S. M., & Richter-Levin, G. (2011). Stress revisited: A critical evaluation of the stress concept. *Neuroscience & Biobehavioral Reviews*, 35(5), 1291–1301. https://doi.org/10.1016/j.neubiorev.2011.02.003

Kübler-Ross, E. (1969). *On death and dying*. New York: Macmillan.

Lang, M. (2010). Surveillance and conformity in competitive youth swimming. *Sport, Education and Society*, 15(1), 19–37. https://doi.org/10.1080/13573320903461152

Leahy, T. (2010). Working with adult athlete survivors of sexual abuse. In S. J. Hanrahan & M. B. Andersen (Eds.), *Routledge handbook of applied sport psychology: A comprehensive guide for students and practitioners* (pp. 303–312). Abingdon, UK: Routledge.

Lebrun, F., MacNamara, À., Rodgers, S., & Collins, D. (2018). Learning from elite athletes' experience of depression. *Frontiers in Psychology*, 9, 2062. https://doi.org/10.3389/fpsyg.2018.02062

Manley, A., Palmer, C., & Roderick, M. (2012). Disciplinary power, the oligopticon and rhizomatic surveillance in elite sports academies. *Surveillance & Society*, 10(3/4), 303–319.

Mannes, Z. L., Waxenberg, L. B., Cottler, L. B., Perlstein, W. M., Burrell II, L. E., Ferguson, E. G., Edwards, M. E., & Ennis, N. (2019). Prevalence and correlates of psychological distress among retired elite athletes: A systematic review. *International Review of Sport and Exercise Psychology*, 12(1), 265–294. https://doi.org/10.1080/1750984X.2018.1469162

Matosic, D., Ntoumanis, N., Boardley, I. D., Stenling, A., & Sedikides, C. (2016). Linking narcissism, motivation, and doping attitudes in sport: A multilevel investigation involving coaches and athletes. *Journal of Sport and Exercise Psychology*, 38(6), 556–566. https://doi.org/10.1123/jsep.2016-0141

McCormack, H. M., MacIntyre, T. E., O'Shea, D., Campbell, M. J., & Igou, E. R. (2015). Practicing what we preach: Investigating the role of social support in sport psychologists' well-being. *Frontiers in Psychology*, 6, 1854. https://doi.org/10.3389/fpsyg.2015.01854

McDuff, D., Stull, T., Castaldelli-Maia, J. M., Hitchcock, M. E., Hainline, B., & Reardon, C. L. (2019). Recreational and ergogenic substance use and substance use disorders in elite athletes: A narrative review. *British Journal of Sports Medicine*, 53(12), 754–760. http://doi.org/10.1136/bjsports-2019-100669

Miller, S. M. (1979). Controllability and human stress: Method, evidence and theory. *Behaviour Research and Therapy*, 17(4), 287–304. https://doi.org/10.1016/0005-7967(79)90001-9

Monat, A., Averill, J. R., & Lazarus, R. S. (1972). Anticipatory stress and coping reactions under various conditions of uncertainty. *Journal of Personality and Social Psychology*, 24(2), 237–253. https://doi.org/10.1037/h0033297

Owton, H., & Sparkes, A. C. (2017). Sexual abuse and the grooming process in sport: Learning from Bella's story. *Sport, Education and Society*, 22(6), 732–743. https://doi.org/10.1080/13573322.2015.1063484

Pant, S. K., & Agarwal, M. (2020). *A study of the emotional wellbeing of private-sector employees working from home during Covid-19* [PDF]. Retrieved from Academia.Edu

Pervin, L. A. (1963). The need to predict and control under conditions of threat. *Journal of Personality, 31*(4), 570–587. https://doi.org/10.1111/j.1467-6494.1963.tb01320.x

Peters, A., McEwen, B. S., & Friston, K. (2017). Uncertainty and stress: Why it causes diseases and how it is mastered by the brain. *Progress in Neurobiology, 156*, 164–188. https://doi.org/10.1016/j.pneurobio.2017.05.004

Pleyers, G. (2020). The Pandemic is a battlefield. Social movements in the COVID-19 lockdown. *Journal of Civil Society*, 1–18. https://doi.org/10.1080/17448689.2020.1794398

Roberts, R., Woodman, T., Hardy, L., Davis, L., & Wallace, H. M. (2013). Psychological skills do not always help performance: The moderating role of narcissism. *Journal of Applied Sport Psychology, 25*(3), 316–325. https://doi.org/10.1080/10413200.2012.731472

Roberts, R., Woodman, T., & Sedikides, C. (2018). Pass me the ball: Narcissism in performance settings. *International Review of Sport and Exercise Psychology, 11*(1), 190–213. https://doi.org/10.1080/1750984X.2017.1290815

Roberts, V. L., & Sojo, V. E. (2020). To strive is human, to abuse malign: Discrimination and non-accidental violence of professional athletes without employee-style statutory protection. *British Journal of Sports Medicine, 54*(4), 253–254. http://doi.org/10.1136/bjsports-2019-100693

Ronkainen, N. J., Kavoura, A., & Ryba, T. V. (2016). A meta-study of athletic identity research in sport psychology: Current status and future directions. *International Review of Sport and Exercise Psychology, 9*(1), 45–64. https://doi.org/10.1080/1750984X.2015.1096414

Ronkainen, N. J., & Nesti, M. S. (2017). An existential approach to sport psychology: Theory and applied practice. *International Journal of Sport and Exercise Psychology, 15*(1), 12–24.

Rose, N. (1996). Governing 'advanced' liberal democracies. In A. Barry, T. Osbourne, & N. Rose (Eds.), *Foucault and political reason* (pp. 37–64). Chicago, IL: Chicago University Press.

Ryall, E. (2008). Being-on-the-bench: An existential analysis of the substitute in sport. *Sports Ethics and Philosophy, 2*(1), 56–70. https://doi.org/10.1080/17511320801896158

Salim, J., & Wadey, R. (2019). Using gratitude to promote sport injury – Related growth. *Journal of Applied Sport Psychology*, 1–20. https://doi.org/10.1080/10413200.2019.1626515

Stambulova, N. B., & Wylleman, P. (2019). Psychology of athletes' dual careers: A state-of-the-art critical review of the European discourse. *Psychology of Sport and Exercise, 42*, 74–88. https://doi.org/10.1016/j.psychsport.2018.11.013

Tazegul, Ü., & Soykan, A. (2013). The comparison of narcissism levels of the athletes at Individual sports according to their socio-demographic features. *American International Journal of Contemporary Research, 3*(7), 128–133. http://doi.org/10.46827/ejpe.v0i0.403

Vaughan, R., Madigan, D. J., Carter, G. L., & Nicholls, A. R. (2019). The Dark Triad in male and female athletes and non-athletes: Group differences and psychometric properties of the Short Dark Triad (SD3). *Psychology of Sport and Exercise, 43*, 64–72. https://doi.org/10.1016/j.psychsport.2019.01.002

Wilber, K. (1986). The spectrum of development. In K. Wilber, J. Engler, & D. Brown (Eds.), *Transformations of consciousness* (pp. 65–189). Boston, MA: Shambhala.

Wilkowich, M. (2016). *The phenomenological analysis of psychospiritual transformation in athletic retirement and everyday narcissism in former athletes* [Doctoral dissertation]. Lethbridge, Alta.: University of Lethbridge, Faculty of Education.

Wolanin, A. T. (2020). Depression in athletes: Incidence, prevalence, and comparisons with the nonathletic population. In E. Hong & A. L. Rao (Eds.), *Mental health in the athlete modern perspectives and novel challenges for the sports medicine provider* (pp. 25–37). Champaign, IL: Springer.

Zhang, S. X., Wang, Y., Rauch, A., & Wei, F. (2020). Unprecedented disruption of lives and work: Health, distress and life satisfaction of working adults in China one month into the COVID-19 outbreak. *Psychiatry Research, 288*, 112958. https://doi.org/10.1016/j.psychres.2020.112958

POSTSCRIPT

David Lavallee

Imagine the following scenario, with two different responses and outcomes. It involves a number of people operating in a multi-professional context, including an athlete, their coach, the sport's performance director, and the team doctor.

Scenario one

The athlete is presenting a range of symptoms, such as difficulty sleeping, fluctuating moods, and low self-esteem, that is potentially linked to overtraining and has had the view for some time that the training programme is mismatched to their needs. The athlete decides to speak to their coach. The coach's response is to tell them to "toughen-up and get on with it". The athlete subsequently sees the team doctor and presents ill-health indicators. They also disclose to the team doctor that they no longer have a desire to continue competing as a result. The athlete asks the doctor if they could meet with the coach about training practices and the impact it is having on them. The doctor writes to the coach, and the coach avoids a meeting by suggesting they speak to the performance director. So, the doctor approaches the performance director, and the performance director backs the coach and prescribed training programme put in place for this athlete. The doctor's dilemma is that they believe the set of training practices is having negative physical and psychological implications for athletes, but they have no system to go beyond the performance director in this scenario. The end result is the doctor has to resign from their role and is portrayed as not understanding the sport, and the athlete – the participant with the greatest need – retires and is portrayed as brittle and weak. Lots of negative media coverage follows.

DOI: 10.4324/9780429287923-19

Scenario two

In an alternative version of the scenario, following the same initial response from the coach, the athlete discloses their concerns to the team doctor, and the athlete and physician together initiate an immediate support request through an independent wellbeing officer put in place by the sport governing body. The officer's role is not to dwell on questions of rules and violations and consequences. Instead, they gather those affected and collaborate on collectively addressing who has the greatest wellbeing needs, what they need, and whose obligation it is to meet those needs in a way that is respectful to everyone. They hold people accountable by looking forward to what must be done to provide support. The collaboration is conducted and concluded within a week, and the athlete is fully supported regarding their physical and psychological symptoms by modifying the training programme to accommodate a different schedule. The athlete continues to train and compete at the highest level. The doctor also continues to work with the sport, as the system has protected their professional code of conduct. The coach, performance director, and future athletes are also supported, as the collaboration concludes with a debrief of lessons learned fed back into the system. There is no media coverage at all.

Postscript

It has been a privilege to be one of the first to read all the chapters in *Developing and Supporting Athlete Wellbeing: Person First, Athlete Second*. In my opinion, one of the strongest features of the book is the use of case studies by the authors, and the fictitious scenario earlier draws upon many insights from the chapters across this text. The second, alternative response to my scenario earlier also draws upon one of the priority recommendations made by Baroness Tanni Grey-Thompson (2017) in her independent Duty of Care in Sport Review: "For every governing body of sport to have a named board member responsible for duty of care" (p. 6). Although several forward-thinking sports have implemented this recommendation, the way the role is being operationalised is still developing. So, I decided to also go outside of the sport system in the second response to the scenario and drew upon the role of the Data Protection Officer, which is a mandatory role required by European Law for all organisations as part of the General Data Protection Regulation (European Commission, 2020). When checking the details of both responses to the scenario with a lawyer they, interestingly, pointed out how data might actually have more rights than athletes in some countries given data protection laws at present.

I have learned a great deal across all the chapters written by the authors of this book and would like to share three things, in particular. The first, which I appreciate might be construed as controversial given the actual name of this book (!), is related to making a conscious effort to not always using the label 'athlete' given its potential negative impact on identity. The word 'athlete' is used over 3,500 times across the book, including in my own postscript here. What else could one expect in a book on athlete wellbeing? However, some sport wellbeing advisors around the world have stopped using the term 'athlete' wherever possible in response to the loss of identity being a major challenge for many individuals. Jane Lowder who designed and delivered the National Rugby League CareerWise programs in Australia said she recommended such a change because it is counterintuitive to advise people to broaden their identity and sense of who they were while at the same time consistently applying a single label to them. Research evidence weaved throughout the books shows how the use of athletes as a label can have a negative impact by contributing to the misconception that some senior administrators, coaches, and others (still) have about self-development being a distraction and time poorly spent.

The second thing I have learned is that all stakeholders in the sport system have a responsibility to work together and support each other. What has emerged in recent years with regard to wellbeing is important for everyone involved in sport as the current focus is revealing so many hidden and uncovered aspects across the system. Impact is derived from proof, and the system needs to continually generate sufficient proofing with regard to the good work being done. In many ways, it always has been doing this, but the risk now is that the response to the negative press stories is that it goes into a dark hole and does not become an essential feature of a great sporting environment. It needs to be elevated above this and continues to climb the priority stack in sport, including in the minds of leaders in sport. This book has tremendous potential to help progress this significantly.

I have started to develop an integrative model with my colleague Dr Daragh Sheridan outlining how duty of care in sport can be explained and what is important to consider moving forward (see Figure 19.1). A key part of Baroness Grey-Thompson's (2017) report is that duty of care is the responsibility to ensure the safety and wellbeing of others, with others including all participants – athletes, coaches, referees, doctors, volunteers, performance directors, chief executives; in short, everyone. So, responsibility [see #1 in Figure] can be viewed as sitting within a support system made up of people, all with responsibilities – leaders, practitioners, and participants. This support system is the antecedent of duty of care.

In the model, leaders [2] are the custodians in setting a support intention for their participants. Coaches, sports medicine practitioners, sport psychologists, wellbeing advisors, and other practitioners [3] are vital within the support system as they are the catalyst of the support intention [4] of the leader – and have the responsibility to understand and meet the needs of participants. The ultimate validators within the system are the participants [5] who then receive (or do not receive) the support they need [6]. The model then considers what good practice looks like. I believe this is when support is provided to participants when needed. When this occurs, this is how trust [7] is measured and, ultimately, reputation [8] is demonstrated. When trust is validated, the perception of participants of

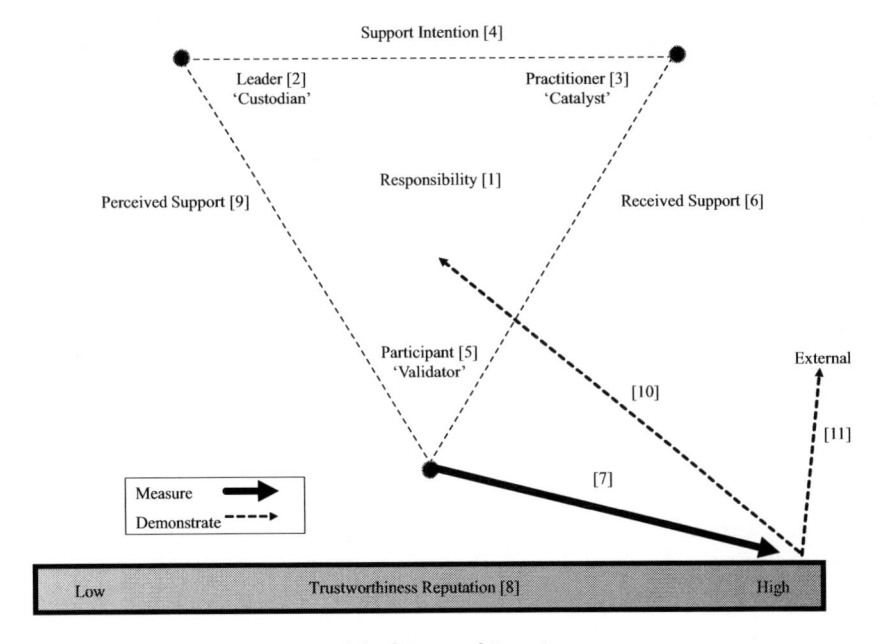

FIGURE 19.1 An integrative model of Duty of Care in sport

whether future support would be provided if needed will be higher. This is what is referred to in the model as perceived support [9]. The demonstration, in this example, is made in two ways – firstly, back into the support system [10] (the leaders, practitioners, and other potential participants, including teammates) and also externally [11] (to, e.g., the media, parents/family, and others).

An important part of the model (which is difficult to demonstrate here, without multiple Figures) is the situation when the practitioner becomes the participant in the system [#5 in the Figure] in need of support, and thus the validator. Support needs to be provided to them, and leaders once again are responsible for setting this support intention.

And then, there also is the situation where the leader becomes the participant and validator [shifted to #5 in the Figure]. This responsibility shifting creates a very different dimension when considering duty of care in sport, and an effective wellbeing system has to be able to accommodate such responsibility shifts.

The final insight I would like to highlight is related to how people in sport are generally phenomenally caring individuals. There is a powerful force that comes from generativity, which is the stage of human development where people transcend their own personal interests and focus on promoting wellbeing to future generations. According to the psychologist Erik Erikson (1982), not everyone reaches this stage of development and some people are naturally generative people or are drawn to generative professions (e.g. teaching). Others develop generative concerns for the future following difficult experiences and suffering (e.g. being bullied). Regardless of how generativity develops, I have learned that a significant number of people want to contribute to the next generation by caring, sharing, and engaging in work that helps pass on their experiences in a positive way to others across sport.

Generative individuals also often have the ability to understand and share the thoughts or feelings of another. This is known as empathy and I have seen a disproportionately high number of individuals in my research who are empathic (please see first thing I learned earlier before labelling these people as empath-letes!) compared to the norm. I firmly believe the world would be a better place with more empathy and hope sport agencies and organisations always recognise the value of these individuals to the system. I have learned that empathy is a choice, and the sport system would be better for everyone overall if organisations also made the choice to be empathic more often. For example, organisations could be more empathic by choosing to treat people in the system as individuals and not numbers. Based on findings from an ongoing big social data project I am conducting, there is a growing number of universities that are treating current and former students (who just happen to be talented at sport) as commodities to be traded through the setting of targets for medals and target numbers of Olympians/Paralympians at the institution.

And finally, I continue to believe the participation and performance gains over the next decade will not come from facilities or technology but from empathy and providing support to individuals when needed – and that these will not be marginal gains; they will be significantly greater. Sport is going through a recalibration period and the wellbeing area is one that can't be solved with a compliance check, tick-box approach. If this is what is adopted by the sport system, there is a significant risk that sport will go into an abyss as people will lose trust in sport and do other things with their valuable time – and not have the opportunity to benefit from all positive impacts highlighted by the chapter authors that sport brings. If a different approach is taken – an approach focused on empathy and providing wellbeing support when needed to everyone in the system – it presents the nothing short of the greatest impact potential in sport, perhaps in its entire history.

References

Erikson, E. H. (1982). *The life cycle completed*. New York: W.W. Norton & Company.
European Commission. (2020). *Data protection in the EU*. Retrieved from https://ec.europa.eu/info/law/law-topic/data-protection/data-protection-eu_en
Grey-Thompson, T. (2017). *Duty of care in sport review*. Retrieved from https://www.gov.uk/government/publications/duty-of-care-in-sport-review

INDEX

Page numbers in **bold** refer to figures, page numbers in *italic* refer to tables.

ableism 122–133; Brown case study 122–125, 133; classification process 123, 126–127; declassification 127; inclusive holistic care 132–133; medical model 126–127; Personal Independent Plans 124–125; psycho-emotional dimensions model 130–132; social model 127–129; social-relational model 129–130; understandings of 125–132
abuse 12, 154; *see also* sexual abuse and harassment
academic support centres 58
Acceptance Commitment Therapy (ACT) 138, 141, 147, 240, *252*
accountability 228, 272
acculturation 84, 87
achievement culture 160
Activity Alliance 129
adaptability 64
addiction 137
Adler, P. 186–187
Adler, P. A. 186–187
agency 3, 64, 68, 98, 100–102, 126–127, 132, 263
AIS High Performance Sport System, Wellbeing Review 4, 6, 13
Aked, J. 7
Algoe, S. B. 29
Amaechi, John 266
anxiety 19, 28, 37–38, 58, 154, 240–241, 246, 247–248, 251

appreciation 23
Armstrong, Lance 185
Ashfield, A. 8
Association of Summer Olympic International Federations 114
athlete activism 266
athlete experience 3
athlete migration, drivers 80–81
athletes: definition 2; demands on 2–6; lived experiences 3; superhuman characterization 3; voice 70
attention 25
Aubel, O. 188
August, R. A. 57
Australia 54
Australian Institute of Sport 4, 6, 96
Australian Sports Commission 96
Australian women's cycling selection camp 104; agency/obedience constituent 100–102; humanisation framework 97–103; individuality/sameness constituent 102–103; non-accidental violence 104; selection, non-selection and deselection 93–96, 96–97; sentient being/technocentric object constituent 99–100
autonomy support 41
awareness mattering *26*

Backhouse, S. 8
Backhouse, S. H. 185, 186

Baker, J. 12
Ball, S. 99–100
Balogun, J. 157
Barnes, C. 127
Barras, M. 96
Bass, B. M. 66–67
Baylis, N. 6
Beamish, R. 4
becoming 27
Behavioural Activation 253
Bekker, S. 231–232
benevolence 114, 234
Berry, R. 204
biological essentialism 225–228, 230, 231–232
biomonitoring 263–264
Biscaia, R. 129
body image 41
Bosman, Jean-Marc 175
Bostock, J. 202, 205–206
Boteler, Pam 166, 167
Boucher, H. 27
Brady, A. 3, 4, 5, 9, 10, 40, 97, 98, 99, 100
brand management 3
Brandstorp, H. 69
Brewer, B. W. 244
Bristol City Women's F.C. 79
British Canoeing 167
British Cycling 175, 188
British Fencing 197–200, 203–204, 204, 205, 207, 208–209
Brittain, I. 129
Brown, Danielle 122–125, 133
Brown, D. J. 9
Brunel Mood Scale 147
bullying 12
Bundon, A. 128
Burdette, T. 115
Burnes, B. 158
burnout 38, 56, 58, 63, 243, 246, 248, 259–260

Canada 54, 174–175; social environment 216
care and caring cultures: boundaries 221; Continual Change Model 158–161, **159**, 162; Emergent Change Modelling 157–158; emergent change theory 161–162; in football culture 150–153, 155–156; funding dependency 206–207; good examples 151; guiding coalition 159–160; Noel case study 150–153, 159; para-sport organisation, France 211–222; and performance 154–155; practice and change model 156–162; relevance 154
career readiness 57
career support 197–209; British Fencing 197–200; context-driven perspective 201; funding 197, 204–205; funding cuts 205–206, 205; funding delivery 205–206; funding dependency 203–204; funding influence 202; Halsted case study 198–200, 201, 203, 204, 206, 208; retirement 200; service delivery 206–208, 207; transitions 199–200, 201, 207–208
caring relationships 154–155, 161; football club culture 83–84
Carless, D. 186
celebrity capital 3
Chand, Dutee 176
change 161–162; continual 158–161, **159**, 162; dialogue 160; Emergent Change Modelling 157–158; football 156–162; guiding coalition 159–160; implementation 156–157, 162; key performance indicators 160–161; management strategies 157; Noel case study 150–153, 159; open–ended process 157–158; resistance to 158
Chelladurai, P. 113
Chen, S. 27
Children's Rights in the Sports Context white paper 234–235
Christoff, K. 4
Chroni, S. 208
coach–athlete relationships 63, 64, 154–155
coach development programmes 64–65, 65
coaches 63–64; adaptability 64; autonomy 43; capacity to influence 11; challenges 63–64, 68, 69–70; and dual careers 50; duties and responsibilities 114; holistic care role 114–116; impacts 65; interactions with parents 34; leadership case study 62–65, 68; leadership role 62–73; personal values and beliefs 65; positive relationships 63, 64, 68; role 63; shared leadership 68–70; spiritual beliefs 118; transformational leadership 66–68
coaching advisory team 70–71
coaching approach, adaptability 64
coaching environments 63, 65
Coach K 112
coded body, the 103
cognitive dissonance 187

collaboration 272
collective identity 112
collective self, the 27
Collins, D. 72–73, 154, 161
commodification, high-performance sport 2
Compassionate Engagement and Action Scale 28
concussion 154
Condello, G. 54
conflict 34
context-based accounts, need for 12
context-driven perspective 201
Continual Change Model 158–161, **159**, 162
continuous learning environments 150–162
conversations-that-matter 18, 29, 30
coping mechanisms 76
Council of Europe Convention against the manipulation of sports competitions 192
Court of Arbitration for Sport 172, 175–176, 177, 225–226, 228, 230, 232
COVID-19 pandemic 257–267; challenges 261, 266; coping mechanisms 263; grieving 261–262; lessons 265–266; lockdowns 257, 257–259, 260–261, 263, 265; performance lifestyle advisors 257–260; and personal development 258–259; return to training 259–260, 263–264; Rudd case study 257–260, 261, 263–265, 265–266; silver linings 263–265
creative analytical practice 95–96
creative non-fiction process 95–96
critical disability studies 125
Cronin, C. 83–84, 155–156, 158, 161
crowdfunding 204
Cruickshank, A. 72–73, 161
cultural capital, wellbeing 1
cultural change 72–73
cultural diversity 112–113
cultural engagement 6
cultural support: Rood case study 77–79, 80–82; women's football 76–88
cultural systems 4
cultural transitions 76–88; accommodation 78, 82–83; challenges 81, 82–88; discrimination 86; food 78, 87; homesickness 81; language barriers 76, 78–79, 81, 85, 88; logistics 85; loneliness 79, 81, 82–83; Rood case study 77–79, 80–82, 82–83, 85, 86; social support 87–88; types 81–82

culture shock 82–83, 84
curiosity 30
Curry, S. 116–117, 117, 118
cycling: Australian women's 92–104; Australian women's cycling selection camp 93–96, 96–97; Sarah case study 93–104
Cycling Australia 96

data protection 272
Data Protection Officers 272
Davis, James 198
decision-making process 70
dehumanisation 3–4, 92, 93–95, 98–99, **98**, 103; technocentric objectification 99–100
de-identification 100–101
Deloitte 18–19
Denison, J. 102
dependency relationships, and sexual abuse and harassment 183
depression 19, 28, 37–38, 137, 144, 154, 241–242, 243, 245, 246, 247, 251
DeSensi, J. T. 113
despair 24
dietary acculturation 87
dignity 116, 118, 237
disability 122–133, 125, 212; Brown case study 122–125, 133; challenges 124, 128; classification process 123, 126–127; complexity 123; declassification 127; inclusive holistic care 132–133; internalised oppression 132; medical model 126–127; micro-traumas 127–128; neglect 122; para-sport organisation, France 211–222; performance demands 217; Personal Independent Payment 128–129; Personal Independent Plans 124–125; psycho-emotional dimensions model 130–132; social model 127–129; social oppression 129; social realities 216–217; social-relational model 129–130; understandings of 124
disciplinary power 100–102
discrimination 86, 108–109, 110, 172, 176, 178, 233; biological essentialism 225–228, 230, 231–232; and mental health 250; necessary 232; organisational policy 228–237, 231–232; women 225–237
diversity 112–113, 116–117
DOCIA 4, 19
doping 185, 190
Dorsch, T. E. 42–43

Dotterer, A. M. 42–43
dual careers 50–59, 214; academic minimums 58; balancing 59; benefits 53–54, 59; burnout 56; career readiness 57; and commitment 50; coping mechanism 58–59; definition 53; Grace case study 50–53, 54, 54–55, 55–56, 56–59; importance 50; post university employment choices 56–59; precarity 55, 59; pressures 52–53, 54, 55, 56; programmes 50, 53, 55; provision 54; stress 51; support 50; threats 59; time constraints 57
Duguay, A. M. 71–72
Dunphy, D. 158
duty of care 13, 147, 182, 191, 212, 217–218, 220, 272; integrative model 273–274, **274**
Duty of Care in Sport Review (Grey-Thompson) 5–6, 13, 212, 272

eating disorders 137, 144
ecological systems approach 5–6, **5**
economic benefits 2
Edelman, M. 188
Edge Hill University 19
education: *see* dual careers
educational programmes 211
eligibility rules 171
Elite Athletes' Rights and Welfare Review, Sport New Zealand 13
elite youth performers: despair 24; holistic wellbeing 18–30; Leggy-Eggy case study 18, 20–26; meaningful relationships 30; mental health 18–19; motivational orientation 24; U MATTER project 19
Elliot, G. 25
Emergent Change Modelling 157–158
emergent change theory 161–162
emotional intelligence 63
emotional labour 156
Emotional Responses of Athletes to Injury Questionnaire 147
emotional support 39, 41
empathy 275
English Institute of Sport 197, *207*, 208
engrossment 155, 161
Enright, K. 83–84, 155–156
EPOCH (engagement, perseverance, optimism, connectedness and happiness) wellbeing model 7
equality 166–169, 177
Equality Act, 2010 166–169, 172
Erickson, K. 186

Erikson, E. 274
ethical considerations 193
ethical obligation 1
ethical reasoning 192
ethics of care 155, 211, 214–215, 218, 219–220
Eugenics 226
European Union Guidelines on Dual Careers of Athletes 13
evidence-base 10
excessive support 39
exclusion 166, 170–171; landscapes of 131
exhaustion 56, 131, 248, 265
existentialism 264
Existential Therapy 242, *253*
expectations: in high performance sport 2, 35, 56, 66–67, 71, 86, 98, 131, 142, 146, 211, 217, 220
exploitation 220

fairness 231; in competition 176; in women's sports 225
faith 107–119; definition 107, 111; and diet 108–109, 117; discrimination 108–109, 110; flexibility 119; and holistic care 114–116, 118; and organisational culture 110, 111–114, 118, 119; problematizing 107–110; relevance 107–110, 111–114; research insights 110–111; and respectful pluralism 116–117, 118
family 9, 24, *26*, 39, 40, 43, 44, 52, 56, 58, 76, 82, 110, 182, 241, 242
faring well 8
fear 129, 144–145; of re-injury 145
Feddersen, N. B. 202, 206, 208
Fink, J. S. 113
Fisher, M. 55
five ways to wellbeing model 7
Fleming, M. 8
Fletcher, D. 5, 66, 69, 72, 86
Flett, G. 23
flourishing 8, 9, 24, 132, 220
food and diet 78, 87, 108–109, 117
football: care and caring cultures in 150–153, 155–156; caring relationships 83–84; Continual Change Model 158–161, **159**; Emergent Change Modelling 157–158; good examples 151, 156; mental health 154; Noel case study 150–153, 155–156, 159, 160; organisational momentum 157; practice and change model 156–162; relevance of care 154; short-term focus 152–153;

support staff 151–152, 162; wellbeing policy 151
Foucault, M. 100–102, 103, 263
France, para-sport organisation approaches 211–222
Fransen, K. 69
Freeman, R. E. 220
funding: alternative streams 204–205; British Fencing 203–204, 204, 205, 207, 208–209; career support 197; cuts 205–206, *205*; delivery 206; dependency 203–204, 206–207; Halsted case study 198–200, 201, 203, 204, 206, 208; influence 202; inter-organisational partnerships 206, *207*; No Compromise Funding Approach 197; para-sport organisation, France 214, 216, 217; performance model 206; Team GB 202; withdrawal of 197, 198

Gaertner, L. 27
Galderisi, S. 8
Galvin, K. T. 3, 97–98
Gaudreau, P. 43
gaze 101
gender discrimination 172
gender equality 166–169, 177
gender flexing 227
gender regime 170
General Data Protection Regulation 272
generative individuals 274–275
generativity 274–275
generosity 30
Gérard, S. 129
German Sport Youth 190
Germany, whistleblowing case study 181–185
Gilbert, P. 28
global development 229
Global Human Rights and Wellbeing 18
global wellbeing 7
goals: well-being 6; group 67; shared 35, 115; organizational 161–162; policy 203; health promotion 229; NCAA GOALS Study 247
Grant, A. M. 25
Grav, S. 38
Green, M. 204
Greenwood, M. 220
Grey-Thompson, T. 146, 202, 212, 272–273
grief 57, 253, 261–262
Grix, J. 203, 207

Hahn, A. 2
Hailey, V. H. 157

Halsted, Laurence 197, 198, 198–200, 201, 203, 204, 206, 208
Hampson, E. 18–19
Hanna, C. 188
happiness 8, 21
Hardy, L. 70–71
Head of Academy Performance 138
Head of Sport Psychology 138
Head Physiotherapist 138, 146
hedonic wellbeing 66, 69, 71
Heil, J. 143
Hicks, D. 116, 118
High5 Nutrition 96
high-performance cultures 10
high performance, definition 2
high-performance expectations 67
high-performance sport: commodification 2; landscape 2–6
Hillyer, S. 115–116
holistic care 114; coaches' role 114–116; inclusive 132–133; key steps 115; faith and spirituality 107, 114, 118, 132
holistic wellbeing: elite youth performers 18–30; Leggy-Eggy case study 18, 20–26; over life course 10–13; U MATTER project 19
Holloway, I. 3, 97–98
homesickness 81
homogenization 102–103
Houlihan, B. 204
human differences, challenging 170
humanisation framework 92, 97–103, **98**; agency/obedience constituent 100–102; individuality/sameness constituent 102–103; sentient being/technocentric object constituent 99–100; sentient being/technocentric object Sentient being/technocentric object 99–100
humanizing behaviours, benefits 3
humanness: denial of 3–4; recognizing 3
human rights 166, 172–173, 175, 177, 225–237; championing strategies 235; organisational policy 228–237; Semenya case study 225–228; wellbeing as 231
Huppert, F. A. 6, 8
Huxhold, O. 39

identity 19, 244; assessing 251; de-emphasis on athletic 249, 272–273; fluid 82; interventions and therapies 248–250, 251, *262–263*; and mental health 239, 239–242, 241, 243–244, 246, 249, 250–251; over lifespan 11
identity foreclosure 239, 246, 249
inclusion 166–169, 170–171

individuality 102, 114
individuation 30
injury: emotional support 41; fear of re-injury 145; mental health problems 143–144; phases of recovery 144–145; psychological struggle 137; psychological support 137–148; psychometric assessment 147; recovery strategies 143; research guidance 143–148; RETURN protocol 137–148, **138**; and selection 199–200
instrumental support 39
integrated models of wellbeing 7
integrative model 273–274, **274**
integrity 190–191
intentional violence 229–231, 233, 234
International Association of Athletics Federations, eligibility regulation 225–226, 230, 231–232, 233
International Canoe Federation 167, 168
International Council on Coaching Excellence 114
International Olympic Committee 144, 167, 170–171, 173, 177, 190, 229–230, 261
International Olympic Committee Consensus Statement on Mental Health in Elite Athletes 13
International Sport Coaching Framework 114
interpersonal skills 34
IOC Olympic Charter 2004 170–171
isolation 39, 58, 59, 83, 85, 93, 103, 145, 176, 245, 261
Italy 78–79

Jackson, P. 114–115
Jacob, A. 18–19
Jordan-Young, R. M. 233
Juventus Women's F.C. 78–79

Kao, S. 25
Kavanagh, E. 3, 97, 98, 99, 100, 266
Kern, M. L. 7
Keverne, E. B. 6
Keyes, C. L. M. 1, 8, 38, 245
Knowles, Z. R. 83–84, 155–156, 158
Kohe, G. Z. 219
Kolanyane-Kesupile, K. K. 229, 230, 233, 234, 237
Koufax, S. 117
Kraus, M. 27
Kruse, Richard 198
Krzyzewski, Mike 112

labour market, transition into 55
language barriers 76, 78–79, 81, 85, 88

languishing 8, 9
Lavallee, D. 3, 11, 41, 44, 53, 82, 205, 248
law and legal action 166–178, 188; court costs 168; gender equality 166–169; Judicial Review 168, 169, 174; outcomes 171; Rippington case study 166, 166–169, 170–171, 173–174, 176–177; and sport 171–176; sport exceptionalism 172; supporting athletes 176–178; targeting 174–175; whistleblowing 189–190
leadership: adaptability 64; athlete training 71–72; coach case study 62–65, 68; coaches 62–73; and faith 119; good 67; high-performance settings 65–66; impacts 62; positive relationships 63, 64, 68; roles 70; shared 65, 68–70, 71–72; theories 66; training 70–71; transformational 65, 66–68, 70, 70–71; trust 63–64; and wellbeing 66
leaveism 19
Lebrun, F. 154
legal obligation 1
Levine, J. 188
Lewes F.C. Women 79
life circumstances 9–10
lifespan approach 10
lifestyle 51, 108
Lincoln Ladies' F.C. 77
Linder, D. E. 244
listening 24
Litou, Arnaud 211, 212–213, 213–216, 216–218, 218–222
lived experiences, athletes 3
London Organising Committee of the Olympic and Paralympic Games 166, 166–169, 170, 173–174
loneliness 79, 81
Long, T. 185
Loughead, T. M. 71–72
Love, Kevin 243
Lowder, Jane 273
Lundqvist, C. 7, 12

McCullough, B. C. 29
Macdougall, H. 7
McKenna, J. 8
M.A.G.I.C. 18, 30
maltreatment 12
Mamatoglu, N. 160
Mandela, Nelson 110–111
Manoli, A. E. 204
Marsh, H. W. 244
Martinkova, I. 114
Mason, M. 243

mattering 18–30; attention 25; awareness 26; conversations 18, 29, 30; forms of 24–26, 26; importance 20, 26; Leggy-Eggy case study 18, 20–26; motivational orientation 24; parental 27; and recognition 23; relational 25; reliance 26; and self-criticism 28; and self-reassurance 28–29; strengthening 30; U MATTER project 19
meaningful relationships 30
measurement developments 7
medical ethics 231–232
medical leadership 65–66, 69
Mega Sporting Events Platform 234–235
mental health 8, 239–253; case studies 239–242; common outcomes 246–248; continuum 239, 243, 245; and discrimination 250; elite youth performers 18–19; experience 243–244; football 154; good 245; and identity 239, 239–242, 241, 243–244, 246, 249, 250–251; and identity foreclosure 239, 246, 249; identity interventions and therapies 248–250, 251, 262–263; and injury 143–144; Leggy-Eggy case study 20–26; misconceptions 245; poor outcomes 239; recommendations 250–251; screening 144; stigmatisation 249–250; stressors 243; treatment 239–242
Mental Health and Advisory Team MHAT-5 67
mental illnesses: initial onset 38; prevalence 37–38
mental toughness 4, 132, 245
mentorship schemes 211
Mepstead, Marcus 198
Merz, E. M. 39
micro-political actions 156
micro-traumas 127–128
military leadership 65–66, 67, 70–71
mind-body connection 77
Minten, S. 72–73
misogyny 233–234
Moesch, K. 208
monitoring: physiological 34; athlete 101; performance 213; organization 206; processes (human rights) 235
Moorman, A. M. 188
Morris, J. 132
Morse, J. M. 206
motivation 181–182, 264
motivational displacement 155, 161
motivational orientation 24
Mountjoy, M. 104

multi-disciplinary team 258, 262
multi-professional context 271–272
Munroe-Chandler, K. J 71–72
mutational advantage 228

narcissism 264
narrative therapy 240, 253
Nassar, Larry 185, 193
National Basketball Association 86, 250
Navarro, K. M. 55
necessary discrimination 232
needs, understanding 156–157
Nesti, M. S. 264
neuropsychology 261–262
New Zealand 77–79
Nike 228
No Compromise Funding Approach 197
Noddings, N. 84, 155, 156, 158, 161
non-accidental violence 104
non-discrimination provisions 172–173
non-maleficence 114
non-normative transitions 80
normative transitions 11, 76, 80
Norway 208
noticing, ways of 27

obedience 100–102
Oberg, K. 84
objectification 4, 99–100, 132
obsessive-compulsive disorder 19
Ohl, F. 188
O'Mara, E. M. 27
organisational analysis 158
organisational culture 72; definition 112; and faith 110, 111–114, 118, 119; and spirituality 111–114
organisational limitations 219
organisational momentum 157
organisational obligations 220
organisational policy 225, 228–237; discrimination 231–232; intentional violence 229–231; and organisational violence 233–234; recommendations 235–237; understanding 230
organisational violence 225; intentional 229–231; and organisational policy 233–234; prevention strategies 234–237
organizational engagement 6
organizations, dehumanizing strategies 4
overtraining syndrome 38, 58
overuse injuries 154

Pacella, J. M. 188
panic disorders 19

paralympic athletes 122–133; Brown case study 122–125, 133; challenges 124, 128; classification process 123, 126–127; declassification 127; inclusive holistic care 132–133; internalised oppression 132; micro-traumas 127–128; neglect 122; Personal Independent Plans 124–125
Paralympic Games 131
Paralympic sports, performance-based practices 125
para-sport organisation, France 211–222; background 212–213; complexities 213–214; ethics of care 211, 214–215, 218, 219–220; funding 214, 216, 217; Litou case study 213–216, 216–218, 218–222; needs 215; organisational limitations 219; performance demands 217; stakeholder responsibility 213, 216, 218, 222; stakeholder theory 218–219, 219–220; welfare support 215, 217–218, 219–222
parental mattering 27
parents 33–37; autonomy 43; benefits 34–35; and broader social network 43–44; celebrating 36; importance 34, 37; inappropriate support 41–42; influence 42–43, 44; interactions 34; investment 36; lack of understanding 36; Leggy-Eggy case study 20–26; negative wellbeing consequences of involvement 35; optimising support 44; parent–child relationship quality 44; parenting style 41; responsiveness 43; supporting 35–36; support strategies 44; types of support 40–41, 44; working with 34–37, 39–44
Parry, J. 114
Pastore, D. L. 113
Patterson, L. B. 186
Pechstein, Claudia 175
pedagogy, questions-based 115
Pederson, D. 115
performance, and care 154–155
performance culture 4
performance demands 217
performance lifestyle advisors 107–110, 200, 257–260
Performance Parents 35
performance production 3
PERMA (positive emotion, engagement, relationships, meaning and achievement) wellbeing model 7
personal development 258–259
Personal Independent Payment 128–129

Personal Independent Plans 124–125
Pettigrew, A. M. 158
Phelps, Michael 228
Phillpots, L. 203, 207
policies and practices 112
Popovich, G. 113
positive psychology 245
post-traumatic stress disorder 19
power dynamics 100–102, 156, 233
power positions 187–188
prayer 117
presenteeism 18
priorities 11
psychoeducation programmes 249
psychological support 141, 143–148; collaboration 141, 147; core principles 138, **138**; holistic approach 146; impacts 142; injury 137–148; managing expectations 142; phases of recovery 144–145; practical implications 147; research guidance 143–148; RETURN protocol 137–148, **138**
psychosocial approaches 5
psychospiritual transformation 264
Purdy, L. G. 219

quality of life 9–10, 126
questions-based pedagogy 115

racism 233–234
reciprocity 155, 158, 161
recognition, and mattering 23
Reeve, D. 130–131, 132
regulation policies: biological essentialism 226, 230, 231–232; organisational policy 228–237; Semenya case study 225–228; women 225–237
rehabilitation 141–142; collaboration 141, 147; core principles 138, **138**; decision to return 146; holistic approach 146; impacts 142; managing expectations 141–142; phases of recovery 144–145; psychometric assessment 147; responsibility 146; RETURN protocol 137–148, **138**
Re-injury Anxiety Inventory 147
re-injury, fear of 145
relationality 27
relational self, the 27
relational sensitivity 27
relational system 18
relationships 25; caring 83–84, 154–155, 161; meaningful 30; positive 63, 64, 68
reliance mattering *26*
religious practices 108–109; *see also* faith

respectful pluralism 116–117, 118
responsibilization 265
responsiveness 43
retirement 56, 127, 145, 197, 201, 207, 242, 262, 264; career programmes 50
RETURN protocol: collaboration 141, 147; core principles 138, **138**; decision to return 145; holistic approach 146; impacts 142; managing expectations 141–142; monitoring 144; practical implications 147; programme 137–143, **138**; psychological support 145; psychologist sessions 146; research guidance 143–148
Rippington, Samantha 166, 166–169, 170–171, 173–174, 176–177
Ritchie, I. 4
Roberts, A. J. B. 69
Ronkainen, N. J. 264
Rood, Katie 77–79
Rooney Rule, the 111
Rosenberg, M. 29
Ross, S. R. 55
Rudd, Josh 257, 257–260, 261, 263–265, 265–266, 266–267
Ryall, E. 229, 264
Ryba, T. V. 54, 80, 82

safeguarding 1, 8, 160, 192, 193, 212, 235
Sagen v VANOC 174–175
sameness 102–103
Sandin, F. 12
Satia-Abouta, J. 87
Schlossberg, N. K. 23
Schneider, R. G. 55
Scott, D. K. 113
Sedikides, C. 27
selection, non-selection and deselection 92–104; agency/obedience constituent 100–102; Australian women's cycling selection camp 93–96, 96–97; creative analytical practice 95–96; dehumanisation 93–95, 98–103, **98**; failure 94–95; humanisation framework 92, 97–103, **98**; individuality/sameness constituent 102–103; and injury 199–200; monitoring 101; non-accidental violence 104; recommendations 104; Sarah case study 93–104; sentient being/technocentric object constituent 99–100
self-assurance 28–29
self-belief 22
self-care 12, 265
self-complexity 246
self-conceptions 27
self-confidence 22
self-criticism 28
Self-Criticism and Self-Reassurance Scale 28
self-esteem 41
self-harm 19, 28
self-knowledge 27
self-perceptions 43
self-worth 19, 240–242, 246
Seligman, M. E. P. 7, 8, 42, 146, 245
Semenya, Caster 176, 177–178, 225–228, 230, 232
Serban, A. 69
sexual abuse and harassment: challenges of reporting 183–184; and dependency relationships 183; German case study 181–185; power positions 187–188; promoting cultural change 192–193; reporting mechanisms 183–184; reporting protocols 188–189, 190; research insights 185–186; silent observers 186–187; support and protection regimes 190–191; support mechanisms 188; systemic factors 184–185; whistleblowing 181–193
Shannon, J. 239, 239–242
shared leadership 65, 68–70, 71–72
Sheridan, D. 273
Shogan, D. 103
siblings 40
Sikhism 108–109
silent observers 186–187
Skille, E. 208
Sluggett, B. 103
Smith, A. L. 42–43
Smith, M. J. 67
social media 3, 12, 25
social network analysis 70
social realities 212
social responsibility 219
social support networks 33, 34, 37–39, 44, 118; benefits 38; impacts 38–39, 39–40; importance 39–40; provision 38; transnational athletes 87–88
social validation 72
So, T. T. 8
Soutter, Ellie 248
spirituality 107, 111; expression 116–117; and holistic care 114, 118; and organisational culture 111–114
sport: inherent tension within 228–229; and the law 171–176; positive outcomes 33; power of 110–111; recalibration 275
Sport and Exercise Psychologists 72

Sport and Physical Activity Workforce Mental Health (SPAWMH) Survey 19
Sport and Recreation Alliance 19
Sport England 203, 206, *207*
sport exceptionalism 172, 176
Sport New Zealand, Elite Athletes' Rights and Welfare Review 13
Stace, D. 158
stakeholder care 220
stakeholder network creation 219
stakeholder relations 212, 218–219, 220
stakeholder responsibility 211, 213, 216, 218, 222
stakeholders 162, 184, 218–219, 222, 273
stakeholder theory 218–219, 219–220
Stambulova, N. 53, 55, 80, 82, 201, 207–208, 262
Stavros, J. 29
Stenling, A. 67, 264
stress 36, 51, 59; lifestyle choices 51; reducing 7
stressors 265
stress responses 243–244
student-athletes: *see* dual careers
suicidal ideation and suicide 144, 247, 248
support services 211; provision 2
Su, R. 8
Syndex Report 212

Tafvelin, S. 67
tailored assistance 151
Tannenbaum, C. 231–232
team culture 72
Team GB, rise of 202
technocentric objectification 99–100
technocentrism 99–100
Tekavc, J. 58
Terre des Hommes 234–235
testosterone levels 225–228, 230, 231–232
Thomas, C. 129
thriving 8, 8–9, 43
Todres, L. 3, 97–98
Tokyo 2020 Olympic Games 257, 258, 261–262, 264
Torres, C. 29
toughness, culture of 38
transformational leadership 65, 66–68, 70, 70–71
transgender 130, 227, 232
transitions 80, 199–200, 201, 207–208; developmental model 11; into labour market 55; out of sport 40
transnational athletes 76–88; career development 82; challenges 81, 82–88; culture shock 83, 84; definition 80; discrimination 86; gender 81; homesickness 81; identity 82; isolation 85; language barriers 76, 78–79, 81, 85, 88; logistics 85–86; loneliness 79, 81, 82–83; motivation 80–81; Rood case study 77–79, 80–82, 82–83, 85, 86; social support 87–88
transnationalism 81–82
trust 63–64, 192

UK Sport 198, 202, 205, 206, 206–207, *207*
UK Sport World Class Programme 197, 198, 203–204
U MATTER 18–30; Leggy-Eggy case study 18, 20–26; multimethod approach 28; project 19–20
UN Convention on the Rights of the Child 235
UNICEF 234–235, 235
Union Cycliste Internationale 190
Union of the Physically Impaired Against Segregation 127
United Kingdom: career support 197–209
United Nations Human Rights Council 231–232
United States of America 54, 58
Universal Declaration of Player Rights 2017 177, 233

Van Buren, H. 220
Van Raalte, J. L. 244
Varnish, Jess 175, 188
violence: intentional 229–231, 233, 234; organisational 225, 229–231, 233–234, 234–237; and organisational policy 233–234; prevention strategies 234–237; unintended 235
vision: leadership 66, 71; organizational care 158–159, 162; U Matter 30
vocabulary of wellbeing 6

Wagstaff, C. R. D. 72, 127
Weinstein, Harvey 193
welfare 8, 30, 92, 151, 190, 211–214, 216–222
wellbeing: benefits 1–2; cultural capital 1; definition 6–7; dialectical nature of 7; ecological systems approach 5–6, **5**; economic benefits 2; global 7; as human right 231; importance 273; integrated models 7; lifespan approach 10–13; measurement developments 7; recognition 13; relevance 6; subjective accounts 9; transdisciplinary concept

5; vocabulary 6–10; *see also* holistic wellbeing
wellbeing contagion effect 11–12
Wellbeing Review, AIS High Performance Sport System 13
Westerbeek, H. 2
Whipp, R. 158
Whistleblower Protection Act, 1989 (US) 189
whistleblowing 181–193; and athlete wellbeing 188–189; challenges 183, 186–188; and dependency relationships 183; ethical considerations 193; German case study 181–185; legal and disciplinary framework 189–190; power positions 187–188; promoting cultural change 192–193; protection 192, 193; reporting mechanisms 183–184; research insights 185–186; role 185–186; support and protection regimes 190–191; support mechanisms 188; systemic factors 184–185; and team commitment 186–187; trajectories 187
Whitaker, L. 185
Whitney, D. 24
Wilson, C. H. 115
Wissing, M. P. 8
women: discrimination 225–237; fairness 225; inclusion 166–169; mental health 247; organisational policy 228–237; power relations 233; regulation policies 225–237; Semenya case study 225–228; sex development 230, 231–232; sporting boundaries 170–171
Women-CAN International 166, 167, 168, 168–169, 177
women's football 76–88, 86; care 83–84; discrimination 86; migration 82; Rood case study 77–79, 80–82; talent pool 76
Wooden, John 115
work 18–19
World Anti-Doping Agency 190
World Health Organization 231, 257, 260
World Medical Association 232
World Player Rights Policy 235
World Players Association 177; World Player Development, Wellbeing, Transition and Retirement Standard 13; World Player Rights Policy 235
worldviews 115–116
worship 117
Wrisberg, C. 4
wrongdoing: difficulty reporting 181; *see also* whistleblowing
Wylleman, P. 11, 40, 44, 53, 58, 82, 262

Xasa, Tokozile 226, 230

Young, Stella 132

Printed in Great Britain
by Amazon